Essentials of Negotiation

Fifth edition

Roy J. Lewicki
The Ohio State University

David M. Saunders
Queen's University

Bruce Barry
Vanderbilt University

McGraw-Hill Irwin

ESSENTIALS OF NEGOTIATION, FIFTH EDITION

Published by McGraw-Hill, a business unit of The McGraw-Hill Companies, Inc., 1221 Avenue of the Americas, New York, NY 10020. Copyright © 2011 by The McGraw-Hill Companies, Inc. All rights reserved. Previous editions © 2007, 2004 and 2001. No part of this publication may be reproduced or distributed in any form or by any means, or stored in a database or retrieval system, without the prior written consent of The McGraw-Hill Companies, Inc., including, but not limited to, in any network or other electronic storage or transmission, or broadcast for distance learning.

Some ancillaries, including electronic and print components, may not be available to customers outside the United States.

This book is printed on acid-free paper.

2 3 4 5 6 7 8 9 0 DOC/DOC 1 0 9 8 7 6 5 4 3 2 1 0

ISBN   978-0-07-353036-9
MHID   0-07-353036-0

Vice President & Editor-in-Chief: *Brent Gordon*
VP EDP/Central Publishing Services: *Kimberly Meriwether David*
Publisher: *Paul Ducham*
Managing Developmental Editor: *Laura Hurst Spell*
Editorial Coordinator: *Jane Beck*
Associate Marketing Manager: *Jaime Halteman*
Project Manager: *Robin A. Reed*
Design Coordinator: *Brenda A. Rolwes*
Cover Designer: *Studio Montage, St. Louis, Missouri*
Cover Image Credit: © *Artville (Photodisk)/PunchStock*
Production Supervisor: *Nicole Baumgartner*
Media Project Manager: *Suresh Babu*
Composition: *S4Carlisle Publishing Services*
Typeface: *10/12 Times Roman*
Printer: *R.R. Donnelley*

Library of Congress Cataloging-in-Publication Data

Lewicki, Roy J.
    Essentials of negotiation / Roy J. Lewicki, Bruce Barry, David M. Saunders.—5th ed.
       p. cm.
    Includes bibliographical references and index.
    ISBN-13: 978-0-07-353036-9 (alk. paper)
    ISBN-10: 0-07-353036-0 (alk. paper)
    1. Negotiation in business. 2. Negotiation. I. Barry, Bruce, 1958– II. Saunders, David M. III. Title.
  HD58.6.L487   2011
  658.4'052—dc22

                                                                        2009048881

All credits appearing on page or at the end of the book are considered to be an extension of the copyright page.

www.mhhe.com

We dedicate this book to all negotiation, mediation, and dispute resolution professionals who try to make the world a more peaceful and prosperous place.

And to John W. Minton (1946–2007): friend, colleague, and co-author.

About the Authors

Roy J. Lewicki   is the Irving Abramowitz Memorial Professor of Business Ethics and Professor of Management and Human Resources at the Max. M. Fisher College of Business, The Ohio State University. He has authored or edited 32 books, as well as numerous research articles. Professor Lewicki has served as the president of the International Association for Conflict Management. He received the Academy of Management's Distinguished Educator Award in 2005 and the David Bradford Outstanding Educator award from the Organizational Behavior Teaching Society for his contributions to the field of teaching in negotiation and dispute resolution.

David M. Saunders   is the dean of Queen's School of Business. Since joining Queen's in 2003 he has led the internationalization of the school, launched two unique MBA programs and a suite of pre-experience Masters programs, and strengthened Queen's international network with the addition of top business school partners in Europe, Asia, and South America. Outside of Queen's, David is the co-author of several articles on negotiation, conflict resolution, employee voice, and organizational justice. He sits on the board of the China Europe International Business School (CEIBS) and the European Foundation for Management Development, an international business school association.

Bruce Barry   is a professor of Management and Sociology at Vanderbilt University. His research on negotiation, influence, ethics, power, and justice has appeared in numerous scholarly journals and volumes. Professor Barry is a past-president of the International Association for Conflict Management and a past chair of the Academy of Management Conflict Management Division.

Welcome to the fifth edition of *Essentials of Negotiation*! Again, this book represents our response to many faculty who wanted a brief version of the longer text, *Negotiation* (Sixth Edition). The objective of this shorter version is to provide the reader with the core concepts of negotiation in a more succinct presentation. Many faculty requested such a book for use in shorter academic course, executive education programs, or as a companion to other resource materials. It is suitable for courses in negotiation, labor relations, conflict management, human resource management, and the like.

Overview of This Book

The organization of this volume generally follows the more complete Sixth Edition of *Negotiation*. The fundamental difference between this and the Sixth Edition text is that this book contains only 12 chapters, while the complete Fifth Edition contains 20 chapters. The first four chapters have only been minimally shortened for this volume, because we believe that the content is essential to any negotiation course. (The shortening process includes editing out some of the more research-oriented references and descriptions, deleting many of the boxes and sidebars, and occasionally some secondary sections.) Similarly, the last chapter is reproduced in full. The other seven chapters from *Negotiation* have been included, but shortened by 25–50 percent each.

For the instructor who was not familiar with *Essentials* (the first four editions) or *Negotiation* (Sixth or earlier editions), a brief overview is in order. The first four chapters introduce the reader to "Negotiation Fundamentals." The first chapter introduces the field of negotiation and conflict management, describes the basic problem of interdependence with other people, and briefly explores the challenges of managing that interdependence. Chapters 2 and 3 then present the two core strategic approaches to negotiation: the basic dynamics of competitive (win-lose) bargaining (Chapter 2) and the basic dynamics of integrative (win-win) negotiation (Chapter 3). Chapter 4 describes the fundamental prework that negotiators must do to get ready for a negotiation: selecting the strategy, framing the issues, defining negotiation objectives, and planning the steps one will pursue to achieve those objectives.

The next five chapters describe the fundamental psychological subprocesses of negotiation: perception, cognition, and emotion; communication; power and influence; and ethical judgment. In Chapter 5, we review the basic processes of perception, cognition, and emotion in negotiation; we specifically examine common cognitive and judgment biases made by negotiators, and how emotion can affect negotiations. In Chapter 6, we examine communication dynamics. We look at the ways that negotiators communicate their interests, positions and goals, and how this information is communicated to the other. Chapter 7 focuses on power. We look at the capabilities negotiators can muster power to pressure the other side, so as to change his or her perspective or give in to our arguments. In Chapter 8, we examine the ethical standards and criteria that surround negotiation. The effective negotiator must recognize when ethical questions are relevant and what factors must be considered to address them effectively.

The next two chapters examine the social contexts in which these negotiations occur, and which also therefore influence how they evolve. In Chapter 9, we examine how the negotiation process changes when the parties have an established relationship with each other, and how the type of relationship affects the negotiation process. We also examine the key roles played by trust, justice and negotiator reputation in shaping negotiations. In Chapter 10, we look at multiparty negotiations, when multiple individuals must work together as a group, team or task force to solve a complex problem or make a decision.

In Chapter 11, we attempt to clarify how international and cross-cultural differences can shape the diverse ways that parties approach negotiations.

Finally, in Chapter 12, we present a new concluding chapter, summarizing the book's content and offering ten "best practices" principles for all negotiators.

Comparison of This Book to the Fourth Edition of *Essentials*

- All of this book has been revised and updated. The authors reviewed every chapter, utilizing extensive feedback from faculty who have used the book in previous editions. The content in some of the chapters has been reorganized to present the material more effectively.

- We have further improved the graphics format and page layout of the book to make it visually more interesting and readable.

- We have added learning objectives to the beginning of each chapter.

- The new structure of this book will be paralleled by a major revision to our readings and classroom activities book, *Negotiation: Readings, Exercises and Cases,* Sixth Edition, edited by Roy Lewicki, Bruce Barry, and David Saunders to appear in 2010. This text and reader can be used together or separately. We encourage instructors to contact their local McGraw-Hill/Irwin representative for an examination copy (or call 800-634-3963, or visit the Web site at www.mhhe.com).

- Instructional resources, including a test bank, chapter outlines, PowerPoint slides, and extensive assistance on ways that new instructors can improve their teaching of negotiation skills, are available to accompany this volume. Instructors should contact their McGraw-Hill/Irwin representative.

Overview of the Chapters in This Book

The book is organized into 12 chapters. The first four chapters address the "fundamentals of negotiation." In addition to this first overview chapter, Chapters 2 and 3 explore the basic strategy and tactics of distributive bargaining and integrative negotiation. Chapter 4 explores how parties can plan and prepare a negotiation strategy and effectively anticipate their encounter with the other negotiator.

The next four chapters explore critical negotiation subprocesses. In Chapter 5, we discuss how a negotiator's perceptions, cognitions, and emotions tend to shape (and often bias) the way the negotiator views and interprets bargaining interaction. Chapter 6 examines the processes by which negotiators effectively communicate their own interests, positions, and goals, and make sense of the other party's communications. Chapter 7 focuses on power in negotiation; the chapter begins by defining the nature of power, and discussing some of the dynamics of using it in negotiation, followed by an exploration of the key sources of power available to most negotiators. Finally, in Chapter 8, we discuss whether there are, or should be, accepted ethical standards to guide negotiations. We identify the major ethical dimensions raised in negotiation, describe the ways negotiators tend to think about these choices, and provide a framework for making informed ethical decisions.

Much of our discussion thus far assumes that the negotiation parties do not have an established long-term relationship. Chapter 9 looks at way that established relationships impact current negotiations, and considers three major concerns: reputations, trust, and fairness—that are particularly critical to effective negotiations within a relationship. In Chapter 10, we examine how negotiations change when there are multiple parties at the table—such as negotiating within groups and teams—who are attempting to achieve a collective agreement or group consensus. In Chapter 11, we examine how different languages and national culture changes the "ground rules" of negotiation. This chapter discusses some of the factors that make international negotiation different, and how national culture affects the rhythm and flow of negotiation.

Finally, in Chapter 12, we reflect on negotiation at a broad level. We look back at the broad perspective we have provided, and suggest 10 "best practices" for those who wish to continue to improve their negotiation skills.

Appreciation

Once again, this book could not have been completed without the assistance of numerous people. We especially thank

- Many of our colleagues in the negotiation and dispute resolution field, whose research efforts have made the growth of this field possible and who have given us helpful feedback about earlier editions to improve the content of this edition.
- The following individuals who reviewed the text and offered their helpful feedback: Nan Stager, Indiana University; Leigh Anne Liu, Georgia State University; J. Keaton Grubbs, Stephen F. Austin State University; Edward Wertheim, Northeastern University; Holly Schroth, University of California–Berkeley; Patrizia Porrini, Long Island University; and Monika Renard, Florida Gulf Coast University.
- The work of John Minton, who helped shape the second, third, and fourth editions of this book and passed away in the Fall of 2007.
- The excellent editorial assistance of Steve Stenner, specifically for his help on copyediting, permissions, and bibliography and for refining the test bank and PowerPoint slides.
- The staff of McGraw-Hill/Irwin, especially our current editor, Laura Spell, and our previous editors Ryan Blankenship, John Weimeister, John Biernat, Kurt Strand, and Karen Johnson; Jane Beck, Allison Cleland, and Trina Hauger, editorial assistants

Contents in Brief

Contents

Chapter 6
Communication 136

Chapter 7
Finding and Using Negotiation Power 151

Chapter 8
Ethics in Negotiation 170

Chapter 12
Best Practices in Negotiations   251

CHAPTER 1

The Nature of Negotiation

Objectives

1. Understand the definition of *negotiation,* the key elements of a negotiation process, and the distinct types of negotiation.

2. Explore how people use negotiation to manage situations of interdependence—that is, that they depend on each other for achieving their goals.

3. Consider how negotiation fits within the broader perspective of processes for managing conflict.

4. Gain an overview of the organization of this book and the content of its chapters.

"That's it! I've had it! This car is dead!" screamed Chang Yang, pounding on the steering wheel and kicking the door shut on his 10-year-old Toysun sedan. The car had refused to start again, and Chang was going to be late for class (again)! Chang wasn't doing well in that management class, and he couldn't afford to miss any more classes. Recognizing that it was finally time to do something about the car, which had been having numerous mechanical problems for the last three months, Chang decided he would trade the Toysun in for another used car, one that would hopefully get him through graduation. After classes that day, he got a ride to the nearby shopping area, where there were several repair garages and used car lots. He knew almost nothing about cars, and didn't think he needed to—all he needed was reliable transportation to get him through the next 18 months.

A major international airline company is close to bankruptcy. The fear of terrorism, a number of new "budget-fare" airlines, and rising costs for fuel have all put the airline under massive economic pressure. The company seeks $800 million in wage and benefit cuts from the pilots' union, the third round of cuts in two years, in order to head off the bankruptcy. Rebuffed by the chief union negotiator for the pilots, the company seeks to go directly to the officers of the Air Line Pilots Association—the international union—to discuss the cuts. If the pilots do not agree to concessions, it is unlikely that other unions—flight attendants, mechanics, and so on—will agree, and bankruptcy will be inevitable.

Janet and Jocelyn are roommates. They share a one-bedroom apartment in a big city where they are both working. Janet, an accountant, has a solid job with a good company, but she has decided that it is time to go back to school to get her MBA. She has enrolled in Big City University's evening MBA program and is now taking classes. Jocelyn works for an advertising company and is on the fast track. Her job not only requires a lot of travel, but also requires a lot of time socializing with clients. The problem is that when Janet is not in evening class, she needs the apartment to read and study and has to have quiet to get her work done. However, when Jocelyn is at the apartment, she talks a lot on the phone, brings friends home for dinner, and is either getting ready to go out for the evening or coming back in very late (and noisily!). Janet has had enough of this disruption and is about to confront Jocelyn.

Thousands of demonstrators opposed to the policies of a nation's government seek to protest a national political convention that will nominate the government's leader to run for reelection. City police forbid protesters from demonstrating near the convention site and authorize a protest location under a crumbling urban expressway, half a mile away from the convention. In response, demonstration organizers request permission to hold a rally in one of the city's major metropolitan parks. The city attempts to ban the demonstration because that park was recently landscaped at a major expense to the city, and it fears the mass of demonstrators will ruin the work. Each side attempts negotiation but also pursues complex legal maneuvers to get the courts on their side.

Ashley Johnson is one of the most qualified recruits this year from a top 25 business school. She is delighted to have secured a second interview with a major consumer goods company, which has invited her to its headquarters city and put her up in a four-star hotel that is world-renowned for its quality facilities and service. After getting in late the night before due to flight delays, she wakes at 7:30 a.m. to get ready for an 8 a.m. breakfast meeting with the senior company recruiter. She steps in the shower, grabs the water control knob to turn it, and the knob falls off in her hand! There is no water in the shower at all; apparently, repairmen started a repair job on it, turned the water off somewhere, and left the job unfinished. Ashley panics at the thought of how she is going to deal with this crisis and look good for her breakfast meeting in 30 minutes.

Do these incidents look and sound familiar? These are all examples of negotiation—negotiations that are about to happen, are in the process of happening, or have happened in the past and created consequences for the present. And they all serve as examples of the problems, issues, and dynamics that we will address throughout this book.

People negotiate all the time. Friends negotiate to decide where to have dinner. Children negotiate to decide which television program to watch. Businesses negotiate to purchase materials and sell their products. Lawyers negotiate to settle legal claims before they go to court. The police negotiate with terrorists to free hostages. Nations negotiate to open their borders to free trade. Negotiation is not a process reserved only for the skilled diplomat, top salesperson, or ardent advocate for an organized lobby; it is something that everyone does, almost daily. Although the stakes are not usually as dramatic as peace accords or large corporate mergers, everyone negotiates; sometimes people negotiate for major things like a new job, other times for relatively minor things like who will wash the dishes.

Negotiations occur for several reasons: (1) to agree on how to share or divide a limited resource, such as land, or property, or time; (2) to create something new that neither party could do on his or her own, or (3) to resolve a problem or dispute between the parties. Sometimes people fail to negotiate because they do not recognize that they are in a negotiation situation. By choosing options other than negotiation, they may fail to achieve their goals, get what they need, or manage their problems as smoothly as they might like to. People may also recognize the need for negotiation but do poorly because they misunderstand the process and do not have good negotiating skills. After reading this book, we hope you will be thoroughly prepared to recognize negotiation situations; understand how negotiation works; know how to plan, implement, and complete successful negotiations; and, most importantly, be able to maximize your results.

A Few Words about Our Style and Approach

Before we begin to dissect the complex social process known as negotiation, we need to say several things about how we will approach this subject. First we will briefly define negotiation. Negotiation is "a form of decision making in which two or more parties talk with one another in an effort to resolve their opposing interests."[1] Moreover, we will be careful about how we use terminology in this book. For most people, *bargaining* and *negotiation* mean the same thing; however, we will be quite distinctive in the way we use the two words. We will use the term *bargaining* to describe the competitive, win–lose situations such as haggling over price that happens at a yard sale, flea market, or used car lot; we will use the term *negotiation* to refer to win–win situations such as those that occur when parties are trying to find a mutually acceptable solution to a complex conflict.

Second, many people assume that the "heart of negotiation" is the give-and-take process used to reach an agreement. While that give-and-take process is extremely important, negotiation is a very complex social process; many of the most important factors that shape a negotiation result do not occur during the negotiation; they occur *before* the parties start to negotiate, or shape the context *around* the negotiation. In the first few chapters of the book, we will examine why people negotiate, the nature of negotiation as a tool for managing conflict, and the primary give-and-take processes by which people try to reach agreement. In the remaining chapters, we examine the many ways that the differences in substantive issues, the people involved, the processes they follow, and the context in which negotiation occurs enrich the complexity of the dynamics of negotiation. We will return to a more complete overview of the book at the end of this chapter.

Third, our insights into negotiation are drawn from three sources. The first is our experience as negotiators ourselves and the rich number of negotiations that occur every day in our own lives and in the lives of people around the world. The second source is the media—television, radio, newspaper, magazine, and Internet—that report on actual negotiations every day. We will use quotes and examples from the media to highlight key points, insights, and applications throughout the book. Finally, the third source is the wealth of social science research that has been conducted on numerous aspects of negotiation. This research has been conducted for more than 50 years in the fields of economics, psychology, political science, communication, labor relations, law, sociology, and anthropology. Each discipline approaches negotiation differently. Like the parable of the blind men who are attempting to describe the elephant by touching and feeling different parts of the animal, each social science discipline has its own theory and methods for studying elements of negotiation, and each tends to emphasize some parts and ignore others. Thus, the same negotiation events and outcome may be examined simultaneously from several different perspectives.[2] When standing alone, each perspective is limited; combined, we begin to understand the rich and complex dynamics of this amazing animal. We draw from all these research traditions in our approach to negotiation. When we need to acknowledge the authors of a major theory or set of research findings, we will use the standard social science research process of citing their work in the text by the author's name and the date of publication of their work; complete references for that work can be found in the bibliography at the end of the book. When we have multiple sources to cite, or anecdotal side comments to make, that information will appear in an endnote at the end of each chapter.

We began this chapter with several examples of negotiations—future, present, and past. To further develop the reader's understanding of the foundations of negotiation, we will develop a story about a husband and wife—Joe and Sue Carter—and a not-so-atypical day in their lives. In this day, they face the challenges of many major and minor negotiations. We will then use that story to highlight three important themes:

1.   The definition of negotiation and the basic characteristics of negotiation situations.

2.   An understanding of *interdependence,* the relationship between people and groups that most often leads them to need to negotiate.

3.   The definition and exploration of the dynamics of conflict and conflict management processes, which will serve as a backdrop for different ways that people approach and manage negotiations.

Joe and Sue Carter

The day started early, as usual. Over breakfast, Sue Carter raised the question of where she and her husband, Joe, would go for their summer vacation. She wanted to sign up for a tour of the Far East being sponsored by her college's alumni association. However, two weeks on a guided tour with a lot of other people he barely knew was not what Joe had in mind. He needed to get away from people, crowds, and schedules, and he wanted to charter a sailboat and cruise the New England coast. The Carters had not argued (yet), but it was clear they had a real problem here. Some of their friends handled problems like this by taking separate vacations. With both of them working full-time, though, Joe and Sue did agree that they would take their vacation together.

Moreover, they were still not sure whether their teenage children—Tracy and Ted—would go with them. Tracy really wanted to go to a gymnastics camp, and Ted wanted to stay home and do yard work in the neighborhood so he could get in shape for the football team and buy a motor scooter with his earnings. Joe and Sue couldn't afford summer camp and a major vacation, let alone deal with the problem of who would keep an eye on the children while they were away.

As Joe drove to work, he thought about the vacation problem. What bothered Joe most was that there did not seem to be a good way to manage the conflict productively. With some family conflicts, they could compromise but, given what each wanted this time, a simple compromise didn't seem obvious. At other times they would flip a coin or take turns—that might work for choosing a restaurant (Joe and Ted like steak houses, Sue and Tracy prefer Chinese), but it seemed unwise in this case because of how much money was involved and how important vacation time was to them. In addition, flipping a coin might make someone feel like a loser, an argument could start, and in the end nobody would really feel satisfied.

Walking through the parking lot, Joe met his company's purchasing manager, Ed Laine. Joe was the head of the engineering design group for MicroWatt, a manufacturer of small electric motors. Ed reminded Joe that they had to settle a problem created by the engineers in Joe's department: the engineers were contacting vendors directly rather than going through MicroWatt's purchasing department. Joe knew that purchasing wanted all contacts with a vendor to go through them, but he also knew that his engineers badly needed technical information for design purposes and that waiting for the information to come through the purchasing department slowed things considerably. Ed Laine was aware of Joe's views about this problem, and Joe thought the two of them could probably find some way to resolve it if they really sat down to work on it. Joe and Ed were also both aware that upper management expected middle managers to settle differences among themselves; if this problem "went upstairs" to senior management, it would make both of them look bad.

Shortly after reaching his desk, Joe received a telephone call from an automobile salesman with whom he had been talking about a new car. The salesman asked whether Sue wanted to test-drive it. Joe wasn't quite sure that Sue would go along with his choice; Joe had picked out a sporty luxury import, and he expected Sue to say it was too expensive and not very fuel efficient. Joe was pleased with the latest offer the salesman had made on the price but thought he might still get a few more concessions out of him, so he introduced Sue's likely reluctance about the purchase, hoping that the resistance would put pressure on the salesman to lower the price and make the deal "unbeatable."

As soon as Joe hung up the phone, it rang again. It was Sue, calling to vent her frustration to Joe over some of the procedures at the local bank where she worked as a senior loan officer. Sue was frustrated working for an old "family-run" bank that was not very automated, heavily bureaucratic, and slow to respond to customer needs. Competitor banks were approving certain types of loans within three hours while Sue's bank still took a week. Sue had just lost landing two big new loans because of the bank's slowness and bureaucratic procedures, and this was becoming a regular occurrence. But whenever she tried to discuss the situation with the bank's senior management, she was met with resistance and a lecture on the importance of the bank's "traditional values."

Most of Joe's afternoon was taken up by the annual MicroWatt budget planning meeting. Joe hated these meetings. The people from the finance department came in and arbitrarily cut everyone's figures by 30 percent, and then all the managers had to argue endlessly to try to get some of their new-project money reinstated. Joe had learned to work with a lot of people, some of whom he did not like very much, but these people from finance were the most arrogant and arbitrary number crunchers imaginable. He could not understand why the top brass did not see how much harm these people were doing to the engineering group's research and development efforts. Joe considered himself a reasonable guy, but the way these people acted made him feel like he had to draw the line and fight it out for as long as it took.

In the evening, Sue and Joe attended a meeting of their town's Conservation Commission, which, among other things, was charged with protecting the town's streams, wetlands, and nature preserves. Sue is a member of the Conservation Commission, and Sue and Joe both strongly believe in sound environmental protection and management. This evening's case involved a request by a real estate development firm to drain a swampy area and move a small creek to build a new regional shopping mall. All projections showed that the new shopping mall would attract jobs and revenue to the area and considerably increase the town's treasury. The new mall would keep more business in the community and discourage people from driving 15 miles to the current mall, but opponents—a coalition of local conservationists and businessmen—were concerned that it would significantly hurt the downtown business district and do major harm to the natural wetland and its wildlife. The debate raged for three hours, and the commission agreed to continue hearings the following week.

As Joe and Sue drove home from the council meeting, they discussed the things they had been involved in that day. Each privately reflected that life is kind of strange—sometimes things go very smoothly and other times things seem much too complicated. As they went to sleep later, they each thought about how they might have approached certain situations differently during the day and were thankful they had a relationship where they could discuss things openly with each other. But they still didn't know what they were going to do about that vacation. . . .

Characteristics of a Negotiation Situation

The Joe and Sue Carter story highlights the variety of situations that can be handled by negotiation. Any of us might encounter one or more of these situations over the course of a few days or weeks. As we defined earlier, *negotiation* is a process by which two or more parties attempt to resolve their opposing interests. Thus, as we will point out later in this chapter, negotiation is one of several mechanisms by which people can resolve conflicts. Negotiation situations have fundamentally the same characteristics, whether they are peace negotiations between countries at war, business negotiations between buyer and seller or labor and management, or an angry guest trying to figure out how to get a hot shower before a critical interview. Those who have written extensively about negotiation argue that there are several characteristics common to all negotiation situations:[3]

1. There are two or more parties—that is, two or more individuals, groups, or organizations. Although people can "negotiate" with themselves—as when someone debates whether to spend a Saturday afternoon studying, playing tennis, or going to the football game—we consider negotiation as a process *between* individuals, within groups, and between groups.[4] In the Carter story, Joe negotiates with his wife, the purchasing manager, and the auto salesman, and Sue negotiates with her husband, the senior management at the bank, and the Conservation Commission, among others. Both still face an upcoming negotiation with the children about the vacation.

2. There is a conflict of needs and desires between two or more parties—that is, what one wants is not necessarily what the other one wants—and the parties must search for a way to resolve the conflict. Joe and Sue face negotiations over vacations, management of their children, budgets, automobiles, company procedures, and community practices for issuing building permits and preserving natural resources, among others.

3. The parties negotiate by *choice*! That is, they negotiate because they think they can get a better deal by negotiating than by simply accepting what the other side will voluntarily give them or let them have. Negotiation is largely a voluntary process. We negotiate because we think we can improve our outcome or result, compared with not negotiating or simply accepting what the other side offers. It is a strategy pursued by choice; seldom are we required to negotiate. There are times to negotiate and times not to negotiate

When You Shouldn't Negotiate

BOX 1.1

There are times when you should avoid negotiating. In these situations, stand your ground and you'll come out ahead.

When you'd lose the farm:

If you're in a situation where you could lose everything, choose other options rather than negotiate.

When you're sold out:

When you're running at capacity, don't deal. Raise your prices instead.

When the demands are unethical:

Don't negotiate if your counterpart asks for something you cannot support because it's illegal, unethical, or morally inappropriate—for example, either paying or accepting a bribe. When your character or your reputation is compromised, you lose in the long run.

When you don't care:

If you have no stake in the outcome, don't negotiate. You have everything to lose and nothing to gain.

When you don't have time:

When you're pressed for time, you may choose not to negotiate. If the time pressure works against you, you'll make mistakes, you give in too quickly, and you may fail to consider the implications of your concessions. When under the gun, you'll settle for less than you could otherwise get.

When they act in bad faith:

Stop the negotiation when your counterpart shows signs of acting in bad faith. If you can't trust their negotiating, you can't trust their agreement. In this case, negotiation is of little or no value. Stick to your guns and cover your position, or discredit them.

When waiting would improve your position:

Perhaps you'll have a new technology available soon. Maybe your financial situation will improve. Another opportunity may present itself. If the odds are good that you'll gain ground with a delay, wait.

When you're not prepared:

If you don't prepare, you'll think of all your best questions, responses, and concessions on the way home. Gathering your reconnaissance and rehearsing the negotiation will pay off handsomely. If you're not ready, just say "no."

Source: J. C. Levinson, M. S. A. Smith, and O. R. Wilson, *Guerrilla Negotiating: Unconventional Weapons and Tactics to Get What You Want* (New York: John Wiley, 1999), pp. 22–23. This material is used by permission of John Wiley & Sons, Inc.

(see Box 1.1 for examples of when we should not negotiate). Our experience is that most individuals in Western culture do not negotiate enough—that is, we assume a price or situation is nonnegotiable and don't even bother to ask or to make a counteroffer!

4. When we negotiate we expect a "give-and-take" process that is fundamental to the definition of negotiation itself. We expect that both sides will modify or move away from their opening statements, requests, or demands. Although both parties may at first argue strenuously for what they want—each pushing the other side to move first— ultimately both sides will modify their opening position in order to reach an agreement. This movement may be toward the "middle" of their positions, called a compromise.

BOX 1.2   Sign in a New York Deli

"For those of you who need to haggle over the price of your sandwich, we will gladly raise the price so we can give you a discount!"

Truly creative negotiations may not require compromise, however; instead the parties may invent a solution that meets the objectives of *all* parties. Of course, if the parties do NOT consider it a negotiation, then they don't necessarily expect to modify their position and engage in this give-and-take (see Box 1.2).

5. The parties prefer to negotiate and search for agreement rather than to fight openly, have one side dominate and the other capitulate, permanently break off contact, or take their dispute to a higher authority to resolve it. Negotiation occurs when the parties prefer to invent their own solution for resolving the conflict, when there is no fixed or established set of rules or procedures for how to resolve the conflict, or when they choose to bypass those rules. Organizations and systems invent policies and procedures for addressing and managing those procedures. Video rental stores have a policy for what they should charge if a rental is kept too long. Normally, people just pay the fine. They might be able to negotiate a fee reduction, however, if they have a good excuse for why the video is being returned late. Similarly, attorneys negotiate or plea-bargain for their clients who would rather be assured of a negotiated settlement than take their chances with a judge and jury in the courtroom. Similarly, the courts may prefer to negotiate as well to clear the case off the docket and assure some punishment. In the Carter story, Joe pursues negotiation rather than letting his wife decide where to spend the vacation; pressures the salesman to reduce the price of the car, rather than paying the quoted price; and argues with the finance group about the impact of the budget cuts, rather than simply accepting them without question. Sue uses negotiation to try to change the bank's loan review procedures, rather than accepting the status quo, and she works to change the shopping mall site plan to make both conservationists and businesses happy, rather than letting others decide it or watch it go to court.

6. Successful negotiation involves the management of *tangibles* (e.g., the price or the terms of agreement) and also the resolution of *intangibles*. Intangible factors are the underlying psychological motivations that may directly or indirectly influence the parties during a negotiation. Some examples of intangibles are (a) the need to "win," beat the other party, or avoid losing to the other party; (b) the need to look "good," "competent," or "tough" to the people you represent; (c) the need to defend an important principle or precedent in a negotiation; and (d) the need to appear "fair," or "honorable" or to protect one's reputation, or (e) the need to maintain a good relationship with the other party after the negotiation is over, primarily by maintaining trust and reducing uncertainty.[5] Intangibles are often rooted in personal values and emotions. Intangible factors can have an enormous influence on negotiation processes and outcomes; it is almost impossible to ignore intangibles because they affect our judgment about what is fair, or right, or appropriate in the resolution of the tangibles. For example, Joe may not want to make Ed Laine angry about the purchasing problem because he needs Ed's support in the upcoming budget negotiations, but Joe also doesn't want

There are times when the urge to win overwhelms logic. Authors Malhotra, Ku, and Murnighan offer the example of a takeover battle between Johnson & Johnson and Boston Scientific to buy Guidant, a medical device maker. Even though Guidant was in the middle of recalling 23,000 pacemakers and telling another 27,000 patients who had pacemakers already implanted to "consult their doctors," the bidding war between the two buyers led to a final price of $27.2 billion, $1.8 billion more than J&J's initial bid. After the recall, Guidant shares went from $23 to $17 a share. *Fortune* magazine later called the acquisition "arguably the second worst ever," only surpassed by AOL's infamous purchase of Time Warner.

What fuels these competitive dynamics that lead to bad decisions? The authors identify several key factors:

- *Rivalry.* When parties are intensely competitive with one another, they are willing to suspend rational decision making.
- *Time pressure.* An artificial deadline, or time pressures such as those in an auction, can push people into quick (and often erroneous) decision making.
- *The spotlight.* If audiences are watching and evaluating the actor, he is more likely to stick to his guns and escalate his investment just to look strong and tough to the audience.
- *The presence of attorneys.* The authors indicate that attorneys, who are more oriented toward "winning" and "losing" in legal battles, may pressure their clients toward winning when options for settlement may clearly be present.

The authors offer several important suggestions to reduce or eliminate the negative impact of these competitive pressures, in order to make more sound and reasoned decisions.

Source: D. H. Malhotra, G. Ku, and J. K. Murnighan, "When Winning is Everything," *Harvard Business Review,* May 2008, pp. 78–86.

to lose face to his engineers, who expect him to support them. Thus, for Joe, the important intangibles are preserving his relationship with Ed Laine and looking strong and "tough" to his engineers.

Intangibles become a major problem in negotiation when negotiators fail to understand how they are affecting decision making or when they dominate negotiations on the tangibles. For example, see Box 1.3 about the problems that the urge to win can create for negotiators.

Interdependence

One of the key characteristics of a negotiation situation is that the parties need each other in order to achieve their preferred objectives or outcomes. That is, either they *must* coordinate with each other to achieve their own objectives, or they *choose* to work together because the possible outcome is better than they can achieve by working on their own. When the parties depend on each other to achieve their own preferred outcome they are *interdependent*.

Most relationships between parties may be characterized in one of three ways: independent, dependent, or interdependent. *Independent* parties are able to meet their own needs without the help and assistance of others; they can be relatively detached, indifferent, and uninvolved with others. *Dependent* parties must rely on others for what they need;

because they need the help, benevolence, or cooperation of the other, the dependent party must accept and accommodate to that provider's whims and idiosyncrasies. For example, if an employee is totally dependent on an employer for a job and salary, the employee will have to either do the job as instructed and accept the pay offered, or go without a job. *Interdependent* parties, however, are characterized by interlocking goals—the parties need each other in order to accomplish their objectives. For instance, in a project management team, no single person could complete a complex project alone; the time limit is usually too short, and no individual has all the skills or knowledge to complete it. For the group to accomplish its goals, each person needs to rely on the other project team members to contribute their time, knowledge, and resources and to synchronize their efforts. Note that having interdependent goals does not mean that everyone wants or needs exactly the same thing. Different project team members may need different things, but they must work together for each to accomplish their goals. This mix of convergent and conflicting goals characterizes many interdependent relationships. (See Box 1.4 for a perspective on interdependence and the importance of intangibles from a famous agent who represents professional athletes.)

Types of Interdependence Affect Outcomes

The interdependence of people's goals, and the *structure* of the situation in which they are going to negotiate, strongly shapes negotiation processes and outcomes. When the goals of two or more people are interconnected so that only one can achieve the goal—such as running a race in which there will be only one winner—this is a competitive situation, also known as a *zero-sum* or *distributive* situation, in which "individuals are so linked together that there is a negative correlation between their goal attainments."[6] Zero-sum or distributive situations are also present when parties are attempting to divide a limited or scarce resource, such as a pot of money, a fixed block of time, and the like. To the degree that one person achieves his or her goal, the other's goal attainment is blocked. In contrast, when parties' goals are linked so that one person's goal achievement helps others to achieve their goals, it is a *mutual-gains* situation, also known as a *non-zero-sum* or *integrative* situation, where there is a positive correlation between the goal attainments of both parties. If one person is a great music composer and the other is a great writer of lyrics, they can create a wonderful Broadway musical hit together. The music and words may be good separately, but fantastic together. To the degree that one person achieves his or her goal, the other's goals are not necessarily blocked, and may in fact be significantly enhanced. The strategy and tactics that accompany each type of situation are discussed further in the upcoming section, Value Claiming and Value Creation, and in Chapters 2 and 3.

Alternatives Shape Interdependence

We noted at the beginning of this section that parties choose to work together because the possible outcome is better than what may occur if they do not work together. Evaluating interdependence therefore also depends heavily on the desirability of *alternatives* to working together. Roger Fisher, William Ury, and Bruce Patton, in their popular book *Getting to Yes: Negotiating Agreement without Giving In,* stress that "whether you should or should not

I have been representing athletes for almost a quarter century, longer than some of them have been alive. During the course of that time, I have developed deep relationships—friendships and partnerships—with many of the executives with whom I do business. We have done dozens of deals with one another over the years. There has been contention and struggle. There have been misunderstandings at times. But in the end, not unlike a marriage, we have stayed together, moved forward, and grown. That kind of shared relationship over time results in a foundation of trust and respect that is immeasurably valuable.

But that kind of trust must be earned. I understood this when I did my first deal 23 years ago. A basic premise of my entire career has been the knowledge that I will be working with the same people again and again. That means that I am always thinking about the deal I am making right now but also about a given player's future deals. It means I see the other party as a potential partner, not as a foe to be vanquished.

If it were not for the team owners, I would not have a profession. If they did not feel that they could operate at a profit, we would not have an industry. I may believe that a player deserves every penny he is paid, but that is only half the equation. The other half depends upon whether the owner believes he can profit by making that payment.

These are not showdowns. In the end they are collaborations. We each have an interest in the success and health of the other. I need and want professional sports to survive and thrive. The various leagues need a steady supply of quality players who are quality people. Each side has something to offer the other. Each side depends on the other.

In any industry in which repeat business is done with the same parties, there is always a balance between pushing the limit on any particular negotiation and making sure the other party—and your relationship with him—survives intact. This is not to suggest that you subordinate your interests to his. But sometimes it is in your best long-term interest to leave something on the table, especially if the other party has made an error that works to your advantage.

No one likes being taken advantage of. We are all human beings. We all have the potential to make a mistake. No matter how much each side stresses preparation, there is no way to consider every factor in a negotiation. There may be times during the process where one party realizes he has made an error in calculation or in interpretation and may ask that that point be revised. There may be times where terms have been agreed to but the other party then sees a mistake and asks you to let him off the hook. You don't have to do it. You could stick him on that point. But you need to ask yourself, Is it worth it? Is what I have to gain here worth what I will lose in terms of this person's willingness to work with me in the future? In most cases, the long-term relationship is much more valuable than the short-term gain. Sometimes the other party may make a mistake and not know it. There are times when the GM or owner I am dealing with makes a major error in his calculations or commits a major oversight, and I can easily take advantage of that and just nail him.

But I don't. He shows me his jugular, and instead of slashing it, I pull back. I might even point out his error. Because if I do crush him, he will eventually realize it. And although I might make a killing on that particular deal, I will also have killed our relationship and, very likely, any possibility of future agreements. Or it might be that the person's mistake costs him his job, in which case someone else might take his place—who is much rougher to deal with and is intent on paying me back for taking his predecessor to the cleaners.

Source: Leigh Steinberg, *Winning with Integrity* (New York: Random House, 1998), pp. 217–18. Used with permission.

agree on something in a negotiation depends entirely upon the attractiveness to you of the best available alternative."[7] They call this alternative a BATNA (an acronym for best alternative to a negotiated agreement) and suggest that negotiators need to understand their own BATNA and the other party's BATNA. The value of a person's BATNA is always relative to the possible settlements available in the current negotiation. A BATNA may offer independence, dependence, or interdependence with someone else. A student who is a month away from graduation and has only one job offer at a salary far lower than he hoped has the choice of accepting that job offer or unemployment; there is little chance that he is going to influence the company to pay him much more than their starting offer. A student who has two offers has a choice between two future interdependent relationships; not only does he have a choice, but he can probably use each job offer to attempt to improve the agreement by playing the employers off against each other (asking employer A to improve his offer over B, etc.). Remember that every possible interdependency has an alternative; negotiators can always say "no" and walk away, although the alternative might not be a very good one. We will further discuss the role and use of BATNAs in Chapters 2, 3, 4, and 7.

Mutual Adjustment

When parties are interdependent, they have to find a way to resolve their differences. Both parties can influence the other's outcomes and decisions, and their own outcomes and decisions can be influenced by the other.[8] This mutual adjustment continues throughout the negotiation as both parties act to influence the other.[9] It is important to recognize that negotiation is a process that transforms over time, and mutual adjustment is one of the key causes of the changes that occur during a negotiation.[10]

Let us return to Sue Carter's job in the small community bank. Rather than continuing to have her loans be approved late, which means she loses the loan and doesn't qualify for bonus pay, Sue is thinking about leaving the small bank and taking a job with Intergalactic Bank in the next city. Her prospective manager, Max, thinks Sue is a desirable candidate for the position and is ready to offer her the job. Max and Sue are now attempting to establish Sue's salary. The job advertisement announced the salary as "competitive." After talking with her husband Joe and looking at statistics on bank loan officers' pay in the state, Sue identified a salary below which she will not work ($50,000) and hopes she might get considerably more. But because Intergalactic Bank has lots of job applicants and is a very desirable employer in the area, Sue has decided not to state her minimally acceptable salary; she suspects that the bank will pay no more than necessary and that her minimum would be accepted quickly. Moreover, she knows that it would be difficult to raise the level if it should turn out that $50,000 was considerably below what Max would pay. Sue has thought of stating her ideal salary ($65,000), but she suspects that Max will view her as either presumptuous or rude for requesting that much. Max might refuse to hire her, or even if they agreed on salary, Max would have formed an impression of Sue as a person with an inflated sense of her own worth and capabilities.

Let's take a closer look at what is happening here. Sue is making her decision about an opening salary request based in part on what bank loan officers are paid in the area, but also very much on how she anticipates Max will react to her actions. Sue recognizes that her actions will affect Max. Sue also recognizes that the way Max acts toward her in the future will be influenced by the way her actions affect him now. As a result, Sue is assessing the indirect impact of her behavior on herself. Further, she also knows that Max is probably alert to this and will look upon any statement by Sue as reflecting a preliminary position on salary rather than a final one. To counter this expected view, Sue will try to find some way to state a proposed salary that is higher than her minimum, but lower than her "dream" salary offer. Sue is choosing among opening requests with a thought not only to how they will affect Max but also to how they will lead Max to act toward Sue. Further, Sue knows that Max believes she will act in this way and makes her decision on the basis of this belief.

The reader may wonder if people really pay attention to all these layers of nuance and complexity or plot in such detail about their negotiation with others. Certainly people don't do this most of the time, or they would likely be frozen into inactivity while they tried to puzzle through all the possibilities. However, this level of thinking can help anticipate the possible ways negotiations might move as the parties move, in some form of mutual adjustment, toward agreement. The effective negotiator needs to understand how people will adjust and readjust, and how the negotiations might twist and turn, based on one's own moves and the others' responses.

It might seem that the best strategy for successful mutual adjustment to the other is grounded in the assumption that the more information one has about the other person, the better. There is the possibility, however, that too much knowledge only confuses.[11] For example, suppose Sue knows the average salary ranges for clerical, supervisory, and managerial positions for banks in her state and region. Does all this information help Sue determine her actions, or does it only confuse things? In fact, even with all of this additional information, Sue may still not have reached a decision about what salary she should be paid, other than a minimum figure below which she will not go. This state of affairs is typical to many negotiations. Both parties have defined their outer limits for an acceptable settlement (how high or low they are willing to go), but within that range, neither has determined what the preferred number should be. The parties need to exchange information, attempt to influence each other, and problem solve. They must work toward a solution that takes into account each person's requirements and, hopefully, optimize the outcomes for both.[12]

Mutual Adjustment and Concession Making

Negotiations often begin with statements of opening positions. Each party states its most preferred settlement proposal, hoping that the other side will simply accept it, but not really believing that a simple "yes" will be forthcoming from the other side (remember our key definitional element of negotiation as the expectation of give-and-take). If the proposal isn't readily accepted by the other, negotiators begin to defend their own initial proposals and critique the others' proposals. Each party's rejoinder usually suggests alterations to the other party's proposal and perhaps also contains changes to his or her own position. When one party agrees to make a change in his or her position, a concession has been made.[13] Concessions restrict the range of options within which a solution or agreement will be reached; when a party makes a concession, the *bargaining range* (the difference between the preferred acceptable settlements) is further constrained. For instance, Sue would like to get a starting salary of $65,000, but she scales her request down to $60,000, thereby eliminating all possible salary options above $60,000. Before making any concessions to a salary below $60,000, Sue probably will want to see some willingness on the part of the bank to improve their salary offer.

Two Dilemmas in Mutual Adjustment

Deciding how to use concessions as signals to the other side and attempting to read the signals in the other's concessions are not easy tasks, especially when there is little trust between negotiators. Two of the dilemmas that all negotiators face, identified by Harold Kelley,[14] help explain why this is the case. The first dilemma, the *dilemma of honesty,* concerns how much of the truth to tell the other party. (The ethical considerations of these dilemmas are discussed in Chapter 8.) On the one hand, telling the other party everything about your situation may give that person the opportunity to take advantage of you. On the other hand, not telling the other person anything about your needs and desires may lead to a stalemate. Just how much of the truth should you tell the other party? If Sue told Max that she would work for as little as $50,000 but would like to start at $60,000, it is quite possible that Max would hire her for $50,000 and allocate the extra money that he might have paid her elsewhere in the budget.[15] If, however, Sue did not tell Max any information about her salary aspirations, then Max would have a difficult time knowing Sue's aspirations and what she would consider an attractive offer. He might make an offer based on the salary of the last person he hired, and wait for her reaction to determine what to say next.

Kelley's second dilemma is the *dilemma of trust:* how much should negotiators believe what the other party tells them? If you believe everything the other party says, then he or she could take advantage of you. If you believe nothing that the other party says, then you will have a great deal of difficulty in reaching an agreement. How much you should trust the other party depends on many factors, including the reputation of the other party, how he or she treated you in the past, and a clear understanding of the pressures on the other in the present circumstances. If Max told Sue that $52,000 was the maximum he was allowed to pay her for the job without seeking approval "from the corporate office," should Sue believe him or not? As you can see, sharing and clarifying information is not as easy as it first appears.

The search for an optimal solution through the processes of giving information and making concessions is greatly aided by trust and a belief that you're being treated honestly and fairly. Two efforts in negotiation help to create such trust and beliefs—one is based on perceptions of outcomes and the other on perceptions of the process. Outcome perceptions can be shaped by managing how the receiver views the proposed result. If Max convinces Sue that a lower salary for the job is relatively unimportant given the high potential for promotion associated with the position, then Sue may feel more comfortable accepting a lower salary. Perceptions of the trustworthiness and credibility of the process can be enhanced by conveying images that signal fairness and reciprocity in proposals and concessions (see Box 1.5). When one party makes several proposals that are rejected by the other party and the other party offers no proposal, the first party may feel improperly treated and may break off negotiations. When people make a concession, they trust the other party and the process far more if a concession is returned. In fact, the belief that concessions will occur in negotiations appears to be almost universal. During training seminars, we have asked negotiators from more than 50 countries if they expect give-and-take to occur during negotiations in their culture; all have said they do. This pattern of give-and-take is not just a characteristic of negotiation; it is also essential to joint problem solving in most interdependent relationships.[16]

Having information about your negotiation partner's perceptions is an important element of negotiation success. When your expectations of a negotiated outcome are based on faulty information, it is likely that the other party will not take you seriously. Take, for example, the following story told to one of the authors:

> At the end of a job interview, the recruiter asked the enthusiastic MBA student, "And what starting salary were you looking for?"
>
> The MBA candidate replied, "I would like to start in the neighborhood of $150,000 per year, depending on your benefits package."
>
> The recruiter said, "Well, what would you say to a package of five weeks' vacation, 14 paid holidays, full medical and dental coverage, company matching retirement fund up to 50 percent of your salary, and a new company car leased for your use every two years . . . say, a red Porsche?"
>
> The MBA sat up straight and said, "Wow! Are you kidding?"
>
> "Of course," said the recruiter. "But you started it."

Satisfaction with negotiation is as much determined by the process through which an agreement is reached as with the actual outcome obtained. To eliminate or even deliberately attempt to reduce this give-and-take—as some legal and labor–management negotiating strategies have attempted[17]—is to short-circuit the process, and it may destroy both the basis for trust and any possibility of achieving a mutually satisfactory result.

Value Claiming and Value Creation

Earlier, we identified two types of interdependent situations—zero-sum and non-zero-sum. Zero-sum or *distributive situations* are ones in which there can be only one winner or where the parties are attempting to get the larger share or piece of a fixed resource, such as an amount of raw material, money, time, and the like. In contrast, non-zero-sum or *integrative or mutual gains situations* are ones in which many people can achieve their goals and objectives.

The structure of the interdependence shapes the strategies and tactics that negotiators employ. In distributive situations negotiators are motivated to win the competition and beat the other party or to gain the largest piece of the fixed resource that they can. To achieve these objectives, negotiators usually employ win–lose strategies and tactics. This approach to negotiation—called *distributive bargaining*—accepts the fact that there can only be one winner given the situation and pursues a course of action to be that winner. The purpose of the negotiation is to *claim value*—that is, to do whatever is necessary to claim the reward, gain the lion's share, or gain the largest piece possible.[18] An example of this type of negotiation is purchasing a used car or buying a used refrigerator at a yard sale. We fully explore the strategy and tactics of distributive bargaining, or processes of claiming value, in Chapter 2, and some of the less ethical tactics that can accompany this process in Chapter 8.

In contrast, in integrative situations the negotiators should employ win–win strategies and tactics. This approach to negotiation—called *integrative negotiation*—attempts to find solutions so both parties can do well and achieve their goals. The purpose of the negotiation is to create value—that is, to find a way for all parties to meet their objectives, either by identifying more resources or finding unique ways to share and coordinate the use of existing resources.

An example of this type of negotiation might be planning a wedding so that the bride, groom, and both families are happy and satisfied, and the guests have a wonderful time. We fully explore the strategy and tactics of integrative, value-creating negotiations in Chapter 3.

It would be simple and elegant if we could classify all negotiation problems into one of these two types and indicate which strategy and tactics are appropriate for each problem. Unfortunately, *most actual negotiations are a combination of claiming and creating value processes*. The implications for this are significant:

1. *Negotiators must be able to recognize situations that require more of one approach than the other:* those that require predominantly distributive strategy and tactics, and those that require integrative strategy and tactics. Generally, distributive bargaining is most appropriate when time and resources are limited, when the other is likely to be competitive, and when there is no likelihood of future interaction with the other party. Every other situation should be approached with an integrative strategy.

2. *Negotiators must be versatile in their comfort and use of both major strategic approaches.* Not only must negotiators be able to recognize which strategy is most appropriate, but they must be able to use both approaches with equal versatility. There is no single "best," "preferred," or "right" way to negotiate; the choice of negotiation strategy requires adaptation to the situation, as we will explain more fully in the next section on conflict. Moreover, if most negotiation issues or problems have components of both claiming and creating values, then negotiators must be able to use both approaches in the same deliberation.

3. *Negotiator perceptions of situations tend to be biased toward seeing problems as more distributive/competitive than they really are.* Accurately perceiving the nature of the interdependence between the parties is critical for successful negotiation. Unfortunately, most negotiators do not accurately perceive these situations. People bring baggage with them to a negotiation: past experience, personality, moods, habits, and beliefs about how to negotiate. These elements dramatically shape how people perceive an interdependent situation, and these perceptions have a strong effect on the subsequent negotiation. Moreover, research has shown that people are prone to several systematic biases in the way they perceive and judge interdependent situations.[19] While we discuss these biases extensively in Chapter 5, the important point here is that the predominant bias is to see interdependent situations as more distributive or competitive than they really are. As a result, there is a tendency to assume a negotiation problem is more zero-sum than it may be and to overuse distributive strategies for solving the problem. As a consequence, negotiators often leave unclaimed value at the end of their negotiations because they failed to recognize opportunities for creating value.

The tendency for negotiators to see the world as more competitive and distributive than it is, and to underuse integrative, creating-value processes, suggests that many negotiations yield suboptimal outcomes. At the most fundamental level, successful coordination of interdependence has the potential to lead to synergy, which is the notion that "the whole is greater than the sum of its parts." There are numerous examples of synergy. In the business world, many research and development joint ventures are designed to bring together experts from different industries, disciplines, or problem orientations to maximize their innovative potential beyond what each company can do individually. Examples abound of new technologies in the areas of medicine, communication, computing, and the like. The fiber-optic cable industry was pioneered by research specialists from the glass industry and specialists in the manufacturing of electrical wire and cable, industry groups that had little previous conversation or contact. A vast amount of new medical instrumentation and technology has been pioneered in partnerships between biologists and engineers. In these situations, interdependence was created between two or more of the parties, and the creators of these enterprises, who successfully applied the negotiation skills discussed throughout this book, enhanced the potential for successful value creation.

Value may be created in numerous ways, and the heart of the process lies in exploiting the differences that exist between the negotiators.[20] The key differences among negotiators include these:

1. *Differences in interests*. Negotiators seldom value all items in a negotiation equally. For instance, in discussing a compensation package, a company may be more willing to concede on a signing bonus than on salary because the bonus occurs only in the first year, while salary is a permanent expense. An advertising company may be quite willing to bend on creative control of a project, but very protective of control over advertising placement. Finding compatibility in different interests is often the key to unlocking the puzzle of value creation.

2. *Differences in judgments about the future*. People differ in their evaluation of what something is worth or the future value of an item. For instance, is that piece of swamp land a good or bad investment of your hard-earned income? Some people can imagine the future house site and swimming pool, whereas others will see it as a bug-infested flood control problem. Real estate developers work hard to identify properties where they see future potential that current owners fail to recognize.

3. *Differences in risk tolerance*. People differ in the amount of risk they are comfortable assuming. A young, single-income family with three children can sustain less risk than a mature, dual-income couple without children. A company with a cash flow problem can assume less risk of expanding its operations than one that is cash rich.

4. *Differences in time preference*. Negotiators frequently differ in how time affects them. One negotiator may want to realize gains now while the other may be happy to defer gains into the future; one needs a quick settlement while the other has no need for any change in the status quo. Differences in time preferences have the potential to create value in a negotiation. For instance, a car salesman may want to close a deal by the end of the week in order to be eligible for a special company bonus, while the potential buyer intends to trade his car in "sometime in the next six months."

In summary, while value is often created by exploiting common interests, differences can also serve as the basis for creating value. The heart of negotiation is exploring both common and different interests to create this value and employing such interests as the foundation for a strong and lasting agreement. Differences can be seen as insurmountable, however, and in that case serve as barriers to reaching agreement. As a result, negotiators must also learn to manage conflict effectively in order to manage their differences while searching for ways to maximize their joint value. Managing conflict is the focus of the next section.

Conflict

A potential consequence of interdependent relationships is conflict. Conflict can result from the strongly divergent needs of the two parties or from misperceptions and misunderstandings. Conflict can occur when the two parties are working toward the same goal and generally want the same outcome or when both parties want very different outcomes. Regardless of the cause of the conflict, negotiation can play an important role in resolving it effectively. In this section, we will define conflict, discuss the different levels of conflict that can occur, review the functions and dysfunctions of conflict, and discuss strategies for managing conflict effectively.

Definitions

Conflict may be defined as a "sharp disagreement or opposition, as of interests, ideas, etc." and includes "the perceived divergence of interest, or a belief that the parties' current aspirations cannot be achieved simultaneously."[21] Conflict results from "the interaction of interdependent people who perceived incompatible goals and interference from each other in achieving those goals."[22]

Levels of Conflict

One way to understand conflict is to distinguish it by level. Four levels of conflict are commonly identified:

1. *Intrapersonal or intrapsychic conflict.* These conflicts occur within an individual. Sources of conflict can include ideas, thoughts, emotions, values, predispositions, or drives that are in conflict with each other. We want an ice cream cone badly, but we know that ice cream is very fattening. We are angry at our boss, but we're afraid to express that anger because the boss might fire us for being insubordinate. The dynamics of intrapsychic conflict are traditionally studied by various subfields of psychology: cognitive psychologists, personality theorists, clinical psychologists, and psychiatrists.[23] Although we will occasionally delve into the internal psychological dynamics of negotiators (e.g., in Chapter 5), this book generally doesn't address intrapersonal conflict.

2. *Interpersonal conflict.* A second major level of conflict is between individuals. Interpersonal conflict occurs between co-workers, spouses, siblings, roommates, or neighbors. Most of the negotiation theory in this book is drawn from studies of interpersonal negotiation and directly addresses the management and resolution of interpersonal conflict.

3. *Intragroup conflict.* A third major level of conflict is within a group—among team and work group members and within families, classes, living units, and tribes. At the intragroup level, we analyze conflict as it affects the ability of the group to make decisions, work productively, resolve its differences, and continue to achieve its goals effectively (see Chapter 10).

4. *Intergroup conflict.* The final level of conflict is intergroup—between organizations, ethnic groups, warring nations, or feuding families or within splintered, fragmented communities. At this level, conflict is quite intricate because of the large number of people involved and the multitudinous ways they can interact with each other. Negotiations at this level are also the most complex.

Functions and Dysfunctions of Conflict

Most people initially believe that conflict is bad or dysfunctional. This belief has two aspects: first, that conflict is an indication that something is wrong, broken or dysfunctional, and, second, that conflict creates largely destructive consequences. Deutsch and others[24] have elaborated on many of the elements that contribute to conflict's destructive image:

1. *Competitive, win–lose goals.* Parties compete against each other because they believe that their interdependence is such that goals are in opposition and both cannot simultaneously achieve their objectives.[25] Competitive goals lead to competitive processes to obtain those goals.

2. *Misperception and bias.* As conflict intensifies, perceptions become distorted. People come to view things consistently with their own perspective of the conflict. Hence, they tend to interpret people and events as being either with them or against them. In addition, thinking tends to become stereotypical and biased—parties endorse people and events that support their position and reject outright those who oppose them.

3. *Emotionality.* Conflicts tend to become emotionally charged as the parties become anxious, irritated, annoyed, angry, or frustrated. Emotions overwhelm clear thinking, and the parties may become increasingly irrational as the conflict escalates.

4. *Decreased communication.* Productive communication declines with conflict. Parties communicate less with those who disagree with them and more with those who agree. The communication that does occur is often an attempt to defeat, demean, or debunk the other's view or to strengthen one's own prior arguments.

5. *Blurred issues.* The central issues in the dispute become blurred and less well defined. Generalizations abound. The conflict becomes a vortex that sucks in unrelated issues and innocent bystanders. The parties become less clear about how the dispute started, what it is "really about," or what it will take to solve it.

6. *Rigid commitments.* The parties become locked into positions. As the other side challenges them, parties become more committed to their points of view and less willing to back down from them for fear of losing face and looking foolish. Thinking processes become rigid, and the parties tend to see issues as simple and "either/or" rather than as complex and multidimensional.

7. *Magnified differences, minimized similarities.* As parties lock into commitments and issues become blurred, they tend to see each other—and each other's positions—as polar opposites. Factors that distinguish and separate them from each other become highlighted and emphasized, while similarities that they share become oversimplified and minimized. This distortion leads the parties to believe they are further apart from each other than they really may be, and hence they may work less hard to find common ground.

8. *Escalation of the conflict.* As the conflict progresses, each side becomes more entrenched in its own view, less tolerant and accepting of the other, more defensive and less communicative, and more emotional. The net result is that both parties attempt to win by increasing their commitment to their position, increasing the resources they are willing to spend to win, and increasing their tenacity in holding their ground under pressure. Both sides believe that by adding more pressure (resources, commitment,

enthusiasm, energy, etc.), they can force the other to capitulate and admit defeat. As most destructive conflicts reveal, however, nothing could be further from the truth! Escalation of the conflict level and commitment to winning can increase so high that the parties will destroy their ability to resolve the conflict or ever be able to deal with each other again.

These are the processes that are commonly associated with escalating, polarized, "intractable" conflict. However, conflict also has many *productive* aspects.[26] Figure 1.1 outlines some of these productive aspects. From this perspective, conflict is not simply destructive or productive; it is both. The objective is not to eliminate conflict but to learn how to manage it to control the destructive elements while enjoying the productive aspects. Negotiation is a strategy for productively managing conflict.

Factors That Make Conflict Easy or Difficult to Manage

Figure 1.2 presents a conflict diagnostic model. This model offers some useful dimensions for analyzing any dispute and determining how easy or difficult it will be to resolve. Conflicts with more of the characteristics in the "difficult to resolve" column will be harder to

FIGURE 1.1 | Functions and Benefits of Conflict

NOLA

- Discussing conflict makes organizational members more aware and able to cope with problems. Knowing that others are frustrated and want change creates incentives to try to solve the underlying problem.
- Conflict promises organizational change and adaptation. Procedures, assignments, budget allocations, and other organizational practices are challenged. Conflict draws attention to those issues that may interfere with and frustrate employees.
- Conflict strengthens relationships and heightens morale. Employees realize that their relationships are strong enough to withstand the test of conflict; they need not avoid frustrations and problems. They can release their tensions through discussion and problem solving.
- Conflict promotes awareness of self and others. Through conflict, people learn what makes them angry, frustrated, and frightened and also what is important to them. Knowing what we are willing to fight for tells us a lot about ourselves. Knowing what makes our colleagues unhappy helps us to understand them.
- Conflict enhances personal development. Managers find out how their style affects their subordinates through conflict. Workers learn what technical and interpersonal skills they need to upgrade themselves.
- Conflict encourages psychological development—it helps people become more accurate and realistic in their self-appraisals. Through conflict, people take others' perspectives and become less egocentric. Conflict helps people believe they are powerful and capable of controlling their own lives. They do not simply need to endure hostility and frustration but can act to improve their lives.
- Conflict can be stimulating and fun. People feel aroused, involved, and alive in conflict, and it can be a welcome break from an easygoing pace. It invites employees to take another look and to appreciate the intricacies of their relationships.

Source: Reprinted with the permission of Lexington Books, an imprint of The Rowman and Littlefield Publishing Group from *Working Together to Get Things Done: Managing for Organizational Productivity* by Dean Tjosvold. Copyright © 1986 by Lexington Books.

FIGURE 1.2 | Conflict Diagnostic Model

Dimension	Viewpoint Continuum	
	Difficult to Resolve	Easy to Resolve
Issue in question	Matter of "principle"—values, ethics, or precedent a key part of the issue	Divisible issue—issue can be easily divided into small parts, pieces, units
Size of stakes—magnitude of what can be won or lost	Large—big consequences	Small—little, insignificant consequences
Interdependence of the parties—degree to which one's outcomes determine the other's outcomes	Zero sum—what one wins, the other loses	Positive sum—both believe that both can do better than simply distributing current outcomes
Continuity of interaction—will they be working together in the future?	Single transaction—no past or future	Long-term relationship—expected interaction in the future
Structure of the parties—how cohesive, organized they are as a group	Disorganized—uncohesive, weak leadership	Organized—cohesive, strong leadership
Involvement of third parties—can others get involved to help resolve the dispute?	No neutral third party available	Trusted, powerful, prestigious third party available
Perceived progress of the conflict—balanced (equal gains and equal harm) or unbalanced (unequal gain, unequal harm)	Unbalanced—one party feels more harm and will want revenge and retribution whereas stronger party wants to maintain control	Balanced—both parties suffer equal harm and equal gain; both may be more willing to call it a "draw"

Source: Reprinted from "Managing Conflict" by L. Greenhalgh, *Sloan Management Review*, Summer 1986, pp. 45–51, by permission of the publisher. Copyright © 1986 by the Sloan Management Review Association. All rights reserved.

settle, while those that have more characteristics in the "easy to resolve" column will be settled quicker.

Effective Conflict Management

Many frameworks for managing conflict have been suggested, and inventories have been constructed to measure negotiator tendencies to use these approaches.[27] Each approach begins with a similar two-dimensional framework and then applies different labels and descriptions to five key points. We will describe these points using the framework proposed by Dean Pruitt, Jeffrey Rubin, and S. H. Kim.[28]

The two-dimensional framework presented in Figure 1.3 is called the *dual concerns model*. The model postulates that people in conflict have two independent types of concern: concern about their own outcomes (shown on the horizontal dimension of the figure) and concern about the other's outcomes (shown on the vertical dimension of the figure). These concerns can be represented at any point from none (representing very low concern) to high (representing very high concern). The vertical dimension is often referred to as the cooperativeness dimension, and the horizontal dimension as the assertiveness dimension. The stronger their concern for their own outcomes, the more likely people will be to pursue strategies located on the right side of the figure, whereas the weaker their concern for their own outcomes, the more likely they will be to pursue strategies located on the left side of the figure. Similarly, the stronger their concern for permitting, encouraging, or even helping the other party achieve his or her outcomes, the more likely people will be to pursue strategies located at the top of the figure. The weaker their concern for the other party's outcomes, the more likely they will be to pursue strategies located at the bottom of the figure.

FIGURE 1.3 | The Dual Concerns Model

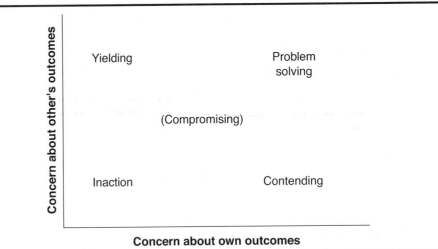

Source: Reprinted from *Social Conflict: Escalation, Stalemate and Settlement* (2nd ed.) by J. Rubin, D. Pruitt, and S. H. Kim by permission of the publisher. Copyright © 1994 by The McGraw-Hill Companies.

Although we can theoretically identify an almost infinite number of points within the two-dimensional space based on the level of concern for pursuing one's own and the other's outcomes, five major strategies for conflict management have been commonly identified in the dual concerns model:

1. *Contending* (also called competing or dominating) is the strategy in the lower right-hand corner. Actors pursuing the contending strategy pursue their own outcomes strongly and show little concern for whether the other party obtains his or her desired outcomes. As Pruitt and Rubin state, "[P]arties who employ this strategy maintain their own aspirations and try to persuade the other party to yield."[29] Threats, punishment, intimidation, and unilateral action are consistent with a contending approach.

2. *Yielding* (also called accommodating or obliging) is the strategy in the upper left-hand corner. Actors pursuing the yielding strategy show little interest or concern in whether they attain their own outcomes, but they are quite interested in whether the other party attains his or her outcomes. Yielding involves lowering one's own aspirations to "let the other win" and gain what he or she wants. Yielding may seem like a strange strategy to some, but it has its definite advantages in some situations.

3. *Inaction* (also called avoiding) is the strategy in the lower left-hand corner. Actors pursuing the inaction strategy show little interest in whether they attain their own outcomes, as well as little concern about whether the other party obtains his or her outcomes. Inaction is often synonymous with withdrawal or passivity; the party prefers to retreat, be silent, or do nothing.

"My concession speech will be brief. You win."

4. *Problem solving* (also called collaborating or integrating) is the strategy in the upper right-hand corner. Actors pursuing the problem-solving strategy show high concern for attaining their own outcomes and high concern for whether the other party attains his or her outcomes. In problem solving, the two parties actively pursue approaches to maximize their joint outcome from the conflict.

5. *Compromising* is the strategy located in the middle of Figure 1.3. As a conflict management strategy, it represents a moderate effort to pursue one's own outcomes and a moderate effort to help the other party achieve his or her outcomes. Pruitt and Rubin do not identify compromising as a viable strategy; they see it "as arising from one of two sources—either lazy problem solving involving a half-hearted attempt to satisfy the two parties' interests, or simple yielding by both parties" (p. 29).[30] However, other scholars who use versions of this model believe that compromising represents a valid strategic approach to conflict; we have inserted it in Rubin, Pruitt, and Kim's framework in Figure 1.3.

Much of the early writing about conflict management strategies—particularly the work in the 1960s and 1970s—had a strong normative value bias against conflict and toward co-operation.[31] Although the models suggested the viability of all five strategic approaches to managing conflict, problem solving was identified as the distinctly preferred approach. These writings stressed the virtues of problem solving, advocated using it, and described how it could be pursued in almost any conflict. However, more recent writing, although still strongly committed to problem solving, has been careful to stress that each conflict management strategy has its advantages and disadvantages and can be more or less appropriate to use given the type of interdependence and conflict context (see Figure 1.4).

Overview of the Chapters in This Book

The book is organized into 12 chapters. The first four chapters address the "fundamentals of negotiation." In addition to this first overview chapter, Chapters 2 and 3 explore the basic strategy and tactics of distributive bargaining and integrative negotiation. Chapter 4 explores how parties can plan and prepare a negotiation strategy and effectively anticipate their encounter with the other negotiator.

The next four chapters explore critical negotiation subprocesses. In Chapter 5, we discuss how a negotiator's perceptions, cognitions, and emotions tend to shape (and often bias) the way the negotiator views and interprets bargaining interaction. Chapter 6 examines the processes by which negotiators effectively communicate their own interests, positions, and goals, and make sense of the other party's communications. Chapter 7 focuses on power in negotiation; the chapter begins by defining the nature of power, and discussing some of the dynamics of using it in negotiation, followed by an exploration of the key sources of power available to most negotiators. Finally, in Chapter 8, we discuss whether there are, or should be, accepted ethical standards to guide negotiations. We identify the major ethical dimensions raised in negotiation, describe the ways negotiators tend to think about these choices, and provide a framework for making informed ethical decisions.

Much of our discussion thus far assumes that the negotiation parties do not have an established long-term relationship. Chapter 9 looks at ways that established relationships

FIGURE 1.4 | Styles of Handling Interpersonal Conflict and Situations Where They Are Appropriate or Inappropriate

Conflict Style	Situations Where Appropriate	Situations Where Inappropriate
Integrating	1. Issues are complex. 2. Synthesis of ideas is needed to come up with better solutions. 3. Commitment is needed from other parties for successful implementation. 4. Time is available for problem solving. 5. One party alone cannot solve the problem. 6. Resources possessed by different parties are needed to solve their common problems.	1. Task or problem is simple. 2. Immediate decision is required. 3. Other parties are unconcerned about outcome. 4. Other parties do not have problem-solving skills.
Obliging	1. You believe you may be wrong. 2. Issue is more important to the other party. 3. You are willing to give up something in exchange for something from the other party in the future. 4. You are dealing from a position of weakness. 5. Preserving relationship is important.	1. Issue is important to you. 2. You believe you are right. 3. The other party is wrong or unethical.
Dominating	1. Issue is trivial. 2. Speedy decision is needed. 3. Unpopular course of action is implemented. 4. Necessary to overcome assertive subordinates. 5. Unfavorable decision by the other party may be costly to you. 6. Subordinates lack expertise to make technical decisions. 7. Issue is important to you.	1. Issue is complex. 2. Issue is not important to you. 3. Both parties are equally powerful. 4. Decision does not have to be made quickly. 5. Subordinates possess high degree of competence.
Avoiding	1. Issue is trivial. 2. Potential dysfunctional effect of confronting the other party outweighs benefits of resolution. 3. Cooling off period is needed.	1. Issue is important to you. 2. It is your responsibility to make decision. 3. Parties are unwilling to defer; issue must be resolved. 4. Prompt attention is needed.
Compromising	1. Goals of parties are mutually exclusive. 2. Parties are equally powerful. 3. Consensus cannot be reached. 4. Integrating or dominating style is not successful. 5. Temporary solution to a complex problem is needed.	1. One party is more powerful. 2. Problem is complex enough to need a problem-solving approach.

Source: Modified and reproduced by special permission of the publisher, Consulting Psychologists Press, Inc., Palo Alto, CA 94303 from *Rahim Organizational Conflict Inventories: Professional Manual* by M. A. Rahim, Copyright © 1990 by Consulting Psychologists Press, Inc. All rights reserved. Further reproduction is prohibited without the publisher's written consent.

impact current negotiations, and considers three major concerns—reputations, trust, and fairness—that are particularly critical to effective negotiations within a relationship. In Chapter 10, we examine how negotiations change when there are multiple parties at the table—such as negotiating within groups and teams—who are attempting to achieve a collective agreement or group consensus. In Chapter 11, we examine how different languages and national culture changes the "ground rules" of negotiation. This chapter discusses some of the factors that make international negotiation different, and how national culture affects the rhythm and flow of negotiation.

Finally, in Chapter 12, we reflect on negotiation at a broad level. We look back at the broad perspective we have provided, and suggest 10 "best practices" for those who wish to continue to improve their negotiation skills.

Endnotes

[1] Pruitt, 1981, p. ix.

[2] For example, Hochberg and Kressel, 1996; Oliver, Balakrishnan, and Barry, 1994; Olekalns, Smith, and Walsh, 1996; Weiss, 1997.

[3] Lewicki, 1992; Rubin and Brown, 1975.

[4] See Bazerman, Tenbrunsel, and Wade-Benzoni, 1998, on the challenge of negotiating with yourself.

[5] Saorin-Iborra, 2006.

[6] Deutsch, 1962, p. 276.

[7] Fisher, Ury, and Patton, 1991.

[8] Goffman, 1969; Pruitt and Rubin, 1986; Raven and Rubin, 1973; Ritov, 1996.

[9] Alexander, Schul, and Babakus, 1991; Donohue and Roberto, 1996; Eyuboglu and Buja, 1993; Pinkley and Northcraft, 1994.

[10] Gray, 1994; Kolb, 1985; Kolb and Putnam, 1997.

[11] Beisecker, Walker, and Bart, 1989; Raven and Rubin, 1973.

[12] Fisher, Ury, and Patton, 1991; Follett, 1940; Nash, 1950; Sebenius, 1992; Sen, 1970; Walton and McKersie, 1965.

[13] Pruitt, 1981.

[14] Kelley, 1966.

[15] We are not suggesting that Max should do this; rather, because the long-term relationship is important in this situation, Max should ensure that both parties' needs are met (see Chapter 3 for an expanded discussion of this point).

[16] Kimmel, Pruitt, Magenau, Konar-Goldband, and Carnevale, 1980; Putnam and Jones, 1982; Weingart, Thompson, Bazerman, and Carroll, 1990.

[17] Raiffa, 1982; Selekman, Fuller, Kennedy, and Baitsel, 1964.

[18] Lax and Sebenius, 1986.

[19] Bazerman, Magliozzi, and Neale, 1985; Neale and Bazerman, 1985; Neale and Northcraft, 1991; Pinkley, 1992; Thompson, 1990a.

[20] Lax and Sebenius, 1986.

[21] Pruitt and Rubin, 1986, p. 4.

[22] Hocker and Wilmot, 1985.

[23] Bazerman, Tenbrunsel, and Wade-Benzoni, 1998.

[24] Deutsch, 1973; Folger, Poole, and Stutman, 1993; Hocker and Wilmot, 1985.

[25] As mentioned earlier, however, the goals may not actually be in opposition and the parties need to compete. Perception is more determinant than reality.

[26] Coser, 1956; Deutsch, 1973.

[27] Filley, 1975; Hall, 1969; Rahim, 1983, 1992; Thomas, 1992; Thomas and Kilmann, 1974.

[28] Rubin, Pruitt, and Kim, 1994.

[29] Pruitt and Rubin, 1986, p. 25.

[30] Ibid., p. 29. Also see Filley, 1975; Hall, 1969; Rahim, 1983, 1992; Thomas, 1992; Thomas and Kilmann, 1974, all of whom believe that compromise is a valid strategic approach to conflict.

[31] Lewicki, Weiss, and Lewin, 1992.

2

Strategy and Tactics of Distributive Bargaining

Objectives

1. Understand the basic elements of a distributive bargaining situation as well as the strategy and tactics of distributive bargaining.

2. Consider the strategic impact of position taken during a negotiation and the role of concessions.

3. Gain the importance of commitment as a communication tactic.

4. Explore options for closing the deal in a distributive situation.

Eighteen months ago Jackson decided to move closer to where he works. Following this decision to move, he put his condo on the market and started to look for a new one—but with no results. Fourteen months later, Jackson finally received an offer to buy his condo and, after a brief negotiation, settled on the selling price. Because he had not yet found a condo to buy, he postponed closing the sale for six months to give himself additional time to look. The buyer, Barbara, was not happy about having to wait that long because of the inconvenience and the difficulty of getting a bank to guarantee an interest rate for a loan so far in advance. Jackson adjusted the price so Barbara would accept this postponement, but it was clear that she would be much happier if he could move the closing date earlier.

There were relatively few condos on the market in the area where Jackson wanted to live, and none of them was satisfactory. He jokingly said that unless something new came on the market, he would be sleeping in a tent on the town common when the leaves turned in the fall. Two months later a condo came on the market that met his requirements. The seller, Sofia, set the asking price at $145,000, which was $10,000 above what Jackson hoped to pay but $5,000 below the most he would be willing to pay. Jackson knew that the more he paid for the condo, the less he would have to make some very desirable alterations, buy draperies and some new furniture, and hire a moving company.

This illustration provides the basic elements of a *distributive bargaining situation*. It is also called competitive, or win–lose, bargaining. In a distributive bargaining situation, the goals of one party are usually in fundamental and direct conflict with the goals of the other party. Resources are fixed and limited, and both parties want to maximize their share. As a result, each party will use a set of strategies to maximize his or her share of the outcomes to be obtained. One important strategy is to guard information carefully—negotiators should only give information to the other party when it provides a strategic advantage. Meanwhile, it is highly desirable to get information from the other party to improve negotiation power. Distributive bargaining is basically a competition over who is going to get the most of a limited resource, which is often money. Whether or not one or both parties achieve their objectives will depend on the strategies and tactics they employ.[1]

For many, the strategies and tactics of distributive bargaining are what negotiation is all about. Images come to mind of smoke-filled rooms packed with men arguing for their points of view. Many people are attracted to this view of negotiation and look forward to learning and sharpening an array of hard-bargaining skills; others are repelled by distributive bargaining and would rather walk away than negotiate this way. They argue that distributive bargaining is old-fashioned, needlessly confrontational, and destructive.

There are three reasons every negotiator should be familiar with distributive bargaining. First, negotiators face some interdependent situations that are distributive, and to do well in them they need to understand how they work. Second, because many people use distributive bargaining strategies and tactics almost exclusively, all negotiators need to understand how to counter their effects. Third, every negotiation situation has the potential to require distributive bargaining skills when at the "claiming-value" stage.[2] Integrative negotiation focuses on ways to create value but also includes a claiming stage, where the value created is distributed. (Integrative negotiation is discussed extensively in Chapter 3.) Understanding distributive strategies and tactics is important and useful, but negotiators need to recognize that these tactics can also be counterproductive, costly, and may not work. Often they cause the negotiating parties to focus so much on their differences that they ignore what they have in common.[3] These negative effects notwithstanding, distributive bargaining strategies and tactics are quite useful when negotiators want to maximize the value obtained in a single deal, when the relationship with the other party is not important, and when they are at the claiming-value stage of negotiations.

Some of the tactics discussed in this chapter will also generate ethical concerns. The topic of ethics and negotiation is discussed in detail in Chapter 8. Do not assume that the other party shares your ethical values when negotiating. While you may not believe that it is ethical to use some of the tactics discussed in this chapter, other negotiators will be quite comfortable using them. Alternatively, you may be comfortable using some tactics that make other negotiators uneasy. Some of the tactics discussed are commonly accepted as ethical when bargaining distributively (portraying your best alternative deal as more positive than it really is, for instance), whereas other tactics are generally considered unacceptable (see the discussion of typical hardball tactics later in this chapter).

The discussion of strategies and tactics in this chapter is intended to help negotiators understand the dynamics of distributive bargaining and thereby obtain a better deal. A thorough understanding of these concepts will also allow negotiators who are by nature not comfortable with distributive bargaining to manage distributive situations proactively. Finally, an understanding of these strategies and tactics will help negotiators at the claiming-value stage of any negotiation.

The Distributive Bargaining Situation

To describe how the distributive bargaining process works, we return to our opening example of Jackson's condo purchase. Several prices were mentioned: (1) Sofia's asking price, (2) the price Jackson would like to pay for a condo, and (3) the price above which Jackson would not buy Sofia's condo. These prices represent key points in the analysis of any distributive bargaining situation. Jackson's preferred price is the *target point,* the point at which a negotiator would like to conclude negotiations—his optimal goal. The target is also sometimes referred to as a negotiator's *aspiration.* The price beyond which Jackson will not go is the *resistance point,* a negotiator's bottom line—the most he will pay as a buyer (for a seller, it's the smallest amount she will settle for). It is also sometimes referred to as a reservation price. Finally, the *asking price* is the initial price set by the seller; Jackson might decide to counter Sofia's asking price with his *initial offer*—the first number he will quote to the seller. Using the condo purchase as an example, we can treat the range of possible prices as a continuum (see Figure 2.1).

How does Jackson decide on his initial offer? There are many ways to answer this question. Fundamentally, however, to make a good initial offer Jackson must understand something about the process of negotiation. In Chapter 1, we discussed how people expect give-and-take when they negotiate, and Jackson needs to factor this into his initial offer. If Jackson opened the negotiation at his target point ($135,000) and then had to make a concession, this first concession would have him moving away from his target point to a price closer to his resistance point. If he really wants to achieve his target, he should make an initial offer that is lower than his target point to create some room for making concessions. At the same time, the starting point cannot be too far from the target point. If Jackson made the first offer too low (e.g., $100,000), Sofia might break off negotiations, believing him to be unreasonable or foolish. Although judgments about how to determine first offers can often be quite complex and can have a dramatic influence on the course of negotiation, let us stay with the simple case for the moment and assume that Jackson decided to offer $133,000 as a reasonable first offer—less than his target point and well below his resistance point. In the meantime, remember that although this illustration concerns only price, all other issues or agenda items for the negotiation have starting, target, and resistance points.

Both parties to a negotiation should establish their starting, target, and resistance points before beginning negotiation. Starting points are often in the opening statements each party makes (i.e., the seller's listing price and the buyer's first offer). The target point is usually learned or inferred as negotiations get under way. People typically give up the margin between their starting points and target points as they make concessions. The resistance point, the point beyond which a person will not go and would rather break off negotiations, is not known to

FIGURE 2.1 | The Buyer's View of the Condo Negotiation

	Jackson's target point		Sofia's asking price	Jackson's resistance point
$130,000	$135,000	$140,000	$145,000	$150,000

DILBERT ©UFS. Reprinted by permission.

the other party and should be kept secret.[4] One party may not learn the other's resistance point even after the end of a successful negotiation, and frequently may underestimate how much the other party would have paid or accepted.[5] After an unsuccessful negotiation, one party may infer that the other's resistance point was near the last offer the other was willing to consider before the negotiation ended.

Negotiators' starting and resistance points are usually arranged in reverse order, with the resistance point being a high price for the buyer and a low price for the seller. Thus, continuing the illustration, Jackson would have been willing to pay up to $150,000 for the condo Sofia listed at $145,000. Jackson can speculate that Sofia may be willing to accept something less than $145,000 and might well regard $140,000 as a desirable figure. What Jackson does not know (but would dearly like to) is the lowest figure that Sofia would accept. Is it $140,000? $135,000? Jackson assumes it is $130,000. Sofia, for her part, initially knows nothing about Jackson's position but soon learns his starting point when he offers $133,000. Sofia may suspect that Jackson's target point is not too far away (in fact it is $135,000, but Sofia doesn't know this) but has no idea of his resistance point ($150,000). This information—what Jackson knows or infers about Sofia's positions—is represented in Figure 2.2.

The spread between the resistance points, called the *bargaining range, settlement range,* or *zone of potential agreement,* is particularly important. In this area the actual bargaining takes place, because anything outside these points will be summarily rejected by one of the two negotiators. When the buyer's resistance point is above the seller's—he is minimally willing to pay more than she is minimally willing to sell for, as is true in the condo example—there is a *positive bargaining range.* When the reverse is true—the seller's resistance point is above

FIGURE 2.2 | The Buyer's View of the Condo Negotiation (Extended)

Sofia's resistance point (inferred)	Jackson's initial offer (public)	Jackson's target point (private)	Sofia's target point (inferred)	Sofia's asking price (public)	Jackson's resistance point (private)
$130,000	$133,000	$135,000	$140,000	$145,000	$150,000

the buyer's, and the buyer won't pay more than the seller will minimally accept—there is a *negative bargaining range*. In the condo example, if Sofia would minimally accept $145,000 and Jackson would maximally pay $140,000, then a negative bargaining range would exist. Negotiations that begin with a negative bargaining range are likely to stalemate. They can be resolved only if one or both parties are persuaded to change their resistance points or if someone else forces a solution upon them that one or both parties dislike. However, because negotiators don't begin their deliberations by talking about their resistance points (they're discussing initial offers and demands instead), it is often difficult to know whether a positive settlement range exists until the negotiators get deep into the process. Both parties may realize that there is no overlap in their resistance points only after protracted negotiations have been exhausted; at that point, they will have to decide whether to end negotiations or reevaluate their resistance points, a process described in more detail later on.

The Role of Alternatives to a Negotiated Agreement

In addition to opening bids, target points, and resistance points, a fourth factor may enter the negotiations: an alternative outcome that can be obtained by completing a deal with someone else. In some negotiations, the parties have only two fundamental choices: (1) reach a deal with the other party or (2) reach no settlement at all. In other negotiations, however, one or both parties may have the possibility of an alternative deal with another party. Thus, in the case of Jackson and Sofia, another condo may come on the market in the neighborhood where Jackson wishes to buy. Similarly, if Sofia waits long enough (or drops the price of the condo far enough), she will presumably find another interested buyer. If Jackson picks a different condo to buy and negotiates the best price that he can with the owner, that price represents his alternative. For the sake of argument, let's assume that Jackson's alternative condo costs $142,000 and that Sofia's alternative buyer will pay $134,000.

An alternative point can be identical to the resistance point, although the two do not have to be the same. If Jackson's alternative is $142,000, then (taking no other factors into account) he should reject any price Sofia asks above that amount. But Jackson's alternative may not be as desirable for reasons other than price—perhaps he likes the neighborhood less, the condo is 10 minutes farther away from where he works, or he likes the way Sofia has upgraded her condo. In any of these situations, Jackson may maintain his resistance point at $150,000; he is therefore willing to pay Sofia up to $8,000 more than his alternative (see Figure 2.3).

FIGURE 2.3 | The Buyer's View of the Condo Negotiation (Extended with Alternatives)

Sofia's resistance point (inferred)	Jackson's initial offer (public)	Sofia's alternative buyer (private)	Jackson's target point (private)	Sofia's target point (inferred)	Jackson's alternative house (private)	Sofia's asking price (public)	Jackson's resistance point (private)
$130,000	$133,000	$134,000	$135,000	$140,000	$142,000	$145,000	$150,000

Alternatives are important because they give negotiators the power to walk away from any negotiation when the emerging deal is not very good. The number of realistic alternatives that negotiators have will vary considerably from one situation to another. For negotiations in which they have many attractive alternatives, they can set their goals higher and make fewer concessions. For negotiations in which they have no attractive alternative, such as when dealing with a sole supplier, they have much less bargaining power. Good distributive bargainers identify their realistic alternatives before starting discussions with the other party so that they can properly gauge how firm to be in the negotiation.[6] Good bargainers also try to improve their alternatives while the negotiation is underway. If Jackson's negotiations with Sofia extend over a period of time, he should keep his eye on the market for other alternatives. He may also continue to negotiate with the owner of the other condo for a better deal. Both courses of action involve efforts by Jackson to maintain and expand his bargaining power by improving the quality of his alternatives. We discuss power and leverage in bargaining in detail in Chapter 7.

Finally, negotiators need to ensure that they have a clear understanding of their *best alternative to a negotiated agreement,* or BATNA.[7] Having a number of alternatives can be useful, but it is really one's *best* alternative that will influence the decision to close a deal or walk away. Understanding the BATNA and making it as strong as possible provides a negotiator with more power in the current negotiation because the BATNA clarifies what he or she will do if an agreement cannot be reached. Negotiators who have a strong BATNA, that is, a very positive alternative to a negotiated agreement, will have more power throughout the negotiation and accordingly should be able to achieve more of their goals (the power of BATNAs is discussed further in Chapter 7).

Settlement Point

The fundamental process of distributive bargaining is to reach a settlement within a positive bargaining range. The objective of both parties is to obtain as much of the bargaining range as possible—that is, to reach an agreement as close to the other party's resistance point as possible.

Both parties in distributive bargaining know that they might have to settle for less than what they would prefer (their target point), but they hope that the agreement will be better than their own resistance point. For agreement to occur, both parties must believe that the settlement, although perhaps less desirable than they would prefer, is the best that they can get. This belief is important, both for reaching agreement and for ensuring support for the agreement after the negotiation concludes. Negotiators who do not think they got the best agreement possible, or who believe that they lost something in the deal, may try to get out of the agreement later or find other ways to recoup their losses. If Jackson thinks he got the short end of the deal, he could make life miserable and expensive for Sofia by making extraneous claims later—claiming that the condo had hidden damages, that the fixtures that were supposed to come with the condo were defective, and so on. Another factor that will affect satisfaction with the agreement is whether the parties will see each other again. If Sofia is moving out of the region, then Jackson may be unable to contact her later for any adjustments and should therefore ensure that he evaluates the current deal very carefully (good advice in any situation, but especially the case here).

Bargaining Mix

In the condo-purchase illustration, as in almost all negotiations, agreement is necessary on several issues: the price, the closing date of the sale, renovations to the condo, and the price of items that could remain in the condo (such as drapes and appliances). The package of issues for negotiation is the *bargaining mix*. Each item in the mix has its own starting, target, and resistance points. Some items are of obvious importance to both parties; others are important only to one party. Negotiators need to understand what is important to them and to the other party, and they need to take these priorities into account during the planning process. See Chapter 4 for a detailed discussion of planning.

For example, in the condo negotiation, a secondary issue important to both parties is the closing date of the sale—the date when the ownership will actually be transferred. The date of sale is part of the bargaining mix. Jackson learned when Sofia's new condo was going to be completed and anticipated that she would want to transfer ownership of her old condo to Jackson shortly after that point. Jackson asked for a closing date very close to when Sofia would probably want to close; thus, the deal looked very attractive to her. As it turned out, Jackson's closing date on his old condo was close to this date as well, thus making the deal attractive for both Jackson and Sofia. If Jackson and Sofia had wanted different closing dates, then that issue would have been a more contentious issue in the bargaining mix (although if Jackson could have moved his closing date earlier, he might have been able to strike a better deal with Barbara, the buyer of his condo). As the bargaining mix gets larger there is more opportunity for trade-offs across issues where negotiator preferences are not identical on each issue. When this occurs, integrative negotiation strategies and tactics may be appropriate; they are discussed in Chapter 3.

Fundamental Strategies

The prime objective in distributive bargaining is to maximize the value of the current deal. In the condo example, the buyer has four fundamental strategies available:

1. To push for a settlement close to the seller's (unknown) resistance point, thereby yielding the largest part of the settlement range for the buyer. The buyer may attempt to influence the seller's view of what settlements are possible by making extreme offers and small concessions.

2. To convince the seller to change her resistance point by influencing the seller's beliefs about the value of the condo (e.g., by telling her that the condo is overpriced), and thereby increasing the bargaining range.

3. If a negative settlement range exists, to convince the seller to reduce her resistance point or to change his own resistance point, to create a positive settlement range. Thus, Sofia could be persuaded to accept a lower price, or Jackson could decide he has to pay more than he wanted to.

4. To convince the seller to believe that this settlement is the best that is possible—rather than having her think that it is all she can get, or that she is incapable of getting more, or that the buyer is winning the negotiation. The distinction between a party believing that an agreement is the best possible (and not the other interpretations) may appear subtle and semantic. However, in getting people to agree it is

important that they feel as though they got the best possible deal. Ego satisfaction is often as important as achieving tangible objectives (recall the discussion of tangibles and intangibles in Chapter 1).

In all these strategies, the buyer is attempting to influence the seller's perceptions of what is possible through the exchange of information and persuasion. Regardless of the general strategy taken, two tasks are important in all distributive bargaining situations: (1) discovering the other party's resistance point and (2) influencing the other party's resistance point.

Discovering the Other Party's Resistance Point

Information is the life force of negotiation. The more you can learn about the other party's target, resistance point, motives, feelings of confidence, and so on, the more able you will be to strike a favorable agreement (see Box 2.1). At the same time, you do not want the other party to have certain information about you. Your resistance point, some of your targets, and confidential information about a weak strategic position or an emotional vulnerability are best concealed.[8] Alternatively, you may want the other party to have certain information—some of it factual and correct, some of it contrived to lead the other party to believe things that are favorable to you. Each side wants to obtain some information and to conceal other information. Each side also knows that the other party wants to obtain and conceal information. As a result of this, communication can become complex. Information is often conveyed in a code that evolves during negotiation. People answer questions with other questions or with incomplete statements to influence the other's perceptions, however, they must establish some points effectively and convincingly.

Influencing the Other Party's Resistance Point

Central to planning the strategy and tactics for distributive bargaining is locating the other party's resistance point and the relationship of that resistance point to your own. The resistance point is established by the value expected from a particular outcome, which in turn is the product of the worth and costs of an outcome. Jackson sets his resistance point based on the amount of money he can afford to pay (in total or in monthly mortgage payments), the estimated market value or worth of the condo, and other factors in his bargaining mix (e.g., closing date). A resistance point will also be influenced by the cost an individual attaches to delay or difficulty in negotiation (an intangible) or in having the negotiations aborted. If Jackson, who had set his resistance point at $150,000, were faced with the choice of paying $151,000 or living on the town common for a month, he might well reevaluate his resistance point. Resistance points should not be changed without considerable thought, however. They play an important role in setting negotiators' limits and unless there is an objective reason to change them they should not be changed.

A significant factor in shaping the other person's understanding of what is possible—and therefore the value he or she places on particular outcomes—is the other's understanding of your own situation. Therefore, when influencing the other's viewpoint, you must also deal with the other party's understanding of your value for a particular outcome, the costs you attach to delay or difficulty in negotiation, and your cost of having the negotiations aborted.

BOX 2.1 | The Piano

When shopping for a used piano, Orvel Ray answered a newspaper ad. The piano was a beautiful upright in a massive walnut cabinet. The seller was asking $1,000, and it would have been a bargain at that price, but Orvel had received a $700 tax refund and had set this windfall as the limit that he could afford to invest. He searched for a negotiating advantage.

He was able to deduce several facts from the surroundings. The piano was in a furnished basement, which also contained a set of drums and an upright acoustic bass. Obviously the seller was a serious musician, who probably played jazz. There had to be a compelling reason for selling such a beautiful instrument.

Orvel asked the first, obvious question, "Are you buying a new piano?"

The seller hesitated. "Well, I don't know yet. See, we're moving to North Carolina, and it would be very expensive to ship this piano clear across the country."

"Did they say how much extra it would cost?" Orvel queried.

"They said an extra $300 or so."

"When do you have to decide?"

"The packers are coming this afternoon."

Now Orvel knew where the seller was vulnerable. He could ship the piano cross-country, or sell it for $700 and still break even. Or he could hold out for his asking price and take his chances. "Here's what I can do: I can give you $700 in cash, right now," Orvel said as he took seven $100 bills out of his pocket and spread them on the keyboard. "And I can have a truck and three of my friends here to move it out of your way by noon today."

The seller hesitated, then picked up the money. "Well, I suppose that would work. I can always buy a new piano when we get settled."

Orvel left before the seller could reconsider. By the time the group returned with the truck, the seller had received three other offers at his asking price, but because he had accepted the cash, he had to tell them that the piano had already been sold.

If the seller had not volunteered the information about the packers coming that afternoon, Orvel might not have been able to negotiate the price.

Source: From J. C. Levinson, M. S. A. Smith, and O. R. Wilson, *Guerrilla Negotiating* (New York: John Wiley, 1999), pp. 15–16.

Tactical Tasks

Within the fundamental strategies of distributive bargaining there are four important tactical tasks concerned with targets, resistance points, and the costs of terminating negotiations for a negotiator in a distributive bargaining situation to consider: (1) assess the other party's target, resistance point, and cost of terminating negotiations; (2) manage the other party's impression of the negotiator's target, resistance point, and cost of terminating negotiation, (3) modify the other party's perception of his or her own target, resistance point, and cost of terminating negotiation, and (4) manipulate the actual costs of delaying or terminating negotiations. Each of these tasks is discussed in more detail below.

Assessing the Other Party's Target, Resistance Point, and Costs of Terminating Negotiations

An important first step for a negotiator is to obtain information about the other party's target and resistance points. The negotiator can pursue two general routes to achieve this task: obtain information indirectly about the background factors behind an issue *(indirect assessment)* or obtain information directly from the other party about their target and resistance points *(direct assessment)*.

Indirect Assessment   An individual sets a resistance point based on many potential factors. For example, how do you decide how much rent or mortgage payment you can afford each month? How do you decide what a condo or used car is really worth? There are lots of ways to go about doing this. Indirect assessment means determining what information an individual likely used to set target and resistance points and how he or she interpreted this information. For example, in labor negotiations, management may infer whether or not a union is willing to strike by how hard the union bargains or by the size of its strike fund. The union decides whether or not the company can afford a strike based on the size of inventories, market conditions for the company's product, and the percentage of workers who are members of the union. In a real estate negotiation, how long a piece of property has been on the market, how many other potential buyers actually exist, how soon a buyer needs the property for business or living, and the financial health of the seller will be important factors. An automobile buyer might view the number of new cars in inventory on the dealer's lot, refer to newspaper articles about automobile sales, read about a particular car's popularity in consumer buying guides (i.e., the more popular the car, the less willing the dealer may be open to bargaining on price), or consult reference guides to find out what a dealer pays wholesale for different cars.

A variety of information sources can be used to assess the other party's resistance point. One can make observations, consult readily available documents and publications, and speak to knowledgeable experts. It is important to note, however, that these are indirect indicators. One person may interpret a given set of data very differently from another person. Having a large inventory of automobiles may make a dealer willing to reduce the price of a car. However, the dealer may expect the market to change soon, may have just started a big promotional campaign of which the buyer is unaware, or may see no real need to reduce prices and instead intends to wait for a market upturn. Indirect measures provide valuable information that *may* reflect a reality the other person will eventually have to face. It is important to remember, however, that the same piece of information may mean different things to different people and therefore may not tell you exactly what you think it does.

Direct Assessment   In bargaining, the other party does not usually reveal accurate and precise information about his or her targets, resistance points, and expectations. Sometimes, however, the other party will provide accurate information. When pushed to the absolute limit and in need of a quick settlement, the other party may explain the facts quite clearly. If company executives believe that a wage settlement above a certain point will drive the company out of business, they may choose to state that absolute limit very clearly and go to considerable lengths to explain how it was determined. Similarly, a condo buyer may tell the seller his absolute maximum price and support it with an explanation of income and other expenses. In these instances, the party revealing the information believes that the proposed agreement is within the settlement range—and that the other party will accept the offered information as true rather than see it as a bargaining ploy. An industrial salesperson may tell the purchaser about product quality and service, alternative customers who want to buy the product, and the time required to manufacture special orders.

intentionally / unintentionally acquired.

Most of the time, however, the other party is not so forthcoming, and the methods of getting direct information are more complex. In international espionage, government agencies may cultivate sources, intercept messages, and break codes. In labor negotiations, companies have been known to recruit informers or bug union meeting rooms, and unions have had their members collect papers from executives' wastebaskets. In real estate negotiations, a seller may entertain a prospective buyer with abundant alcoholic beverages to loosen the buyer's tongue with the hope that he will reveal information.[9] Additional approaches include provoking the other party into an angry outburst or putting the other party under pressure designed to cause him or her to make a slip and reveal valuable information. Negotiators will also simulate exasperation and angrily stalk out of negotiations in the hope that the other, in an effort to avoid a deadlock, will reveal what they really want.

Manage the Other Party's Impressions

An important tactical task for negotiators is to control the information sent to the other party about your target and resistance points, while simultaneously guiding him or her to form a preferred impression of them. Negotiators need to screen information about their positions and to represent them as they would like the other to believe. Generally speaking, screening activities are more important at the beginning of negotiation, and direct action is more useful later on. This sequence also allows time to concentrate on gathering information from the other party, which will be useful in evaluating resistance points, and on determining the best way to provide information to the other party about one's own position.

Screening Activities   The simplest way to screen a position is to say and do as little as possible. Silence is golden when answering questions; words should be invested in asking the other negotiator questions. Reticence reduces the likelihood of making verbal slips or presenting any clues that the other party could use to draw conclusions. A look of disappointment or boredom, fidgeting and restlessness, or probing with interest all can give clues about the importance of the points under discussion. Concealment is the most general screening activity.

Another approach, available when group negotiations are conducted through a representative, is calculated incompetence. With this approach, constituents do not give the negotiating agent all the necessary information, making it impossible for him or her to leak information. Instead, the negotiator is sent with the task of simply gathering facts and bringing them back to the group. This strategy can make negotiations complex and tedious, and it often causes the other party to protest vigorously at the negotiator's inability to divulge important data or to make agreements. Lawyers, real estate agents, and investigators frequently perform this role. Representatives may also be limited, or limit themselves, in their authority to make decisions. For example, a man buying a car may claim that he must consult his wife before making a final decision.

When negotiation is carried out by a team—as is common in diplomacy, labor–management relations, and many business negotiations—channeling all communication through a team spokesperson reduces the chance of inadvertently revealing information. Team negotiations are discussed more extensively in Chapter 10. In addition to reducing the number of people who can actively reveal information, this allows members of the negotiating team to observe and listen carefully to what the other party is saying so they can detect clues and pieces of information about their position. Still another screening activity is to present a great many items for negotiation, only a few of which are truly important to the presenter. In this way, the other party has to gather information about so many different items that it becomes difficult to detect which items are really important. This tactic, called the snow job or kitchen sink, may be considered a hardball tactic (discussed later in this chapter) if carried to an extreme.[10]

Direct Action to Alter Impressions   Negotiators can take many actions to present facts that will directly enhance their position or make it appear stronger to the other party. One of the most obvious methods is *selective presentation,* in which negotiators reveal only the facts necessary to support their case. Negotiators can also use selective presentation to lead the other party to form the desired impression of their resistance point or to create new possibilities for agreement that are more favorable than those that currently exist. Another approach is to explain or interpret known facts to present a logical argument that shows the costs or risks to oneself if the other party's proposals are implemented. An alternative is to say, "If you were in my shoes, here is the way these facts would look in light of the proposal you have presented."

Negotiators should justify their positions and desired outcomes in order to influence the other party's impressions. Power and influence tactics are discussed in more detail in Chapter 7. Negotiators can use industry standards, benchmarks, appeals to fairness, and arguments for the good of the company to draw a compelling picture for the other party to agree to what they want. These arguments are most convincing when the facts have been gathered from a neutral source because then the other party will not see them as biased by your preferred outcome. However, even with facts that you provide, selectivity can be helpful in managing the other party's impression of your preferences and priorities. It is not necessary for the other to agree that this is the way things would look if he or she were you. Nor must the other agree that the facts lead only to the conclusion you have presented. As long as the other party understands how you see things, then his or her thinking is likely to be influenced.

Displaying *emotional reaction* to facts, proposals, and possible outcomes is another form of direct action negotiators can take to provide information about what is important to them. Disappointment or enthusiasm usually suggests that an issue is important, whereas boredom or indifference suggests it is trivial or unimportant. A loud, angry outburst or an eager response suggests the topic is very important and may give it a prominence that will shape what is discussed. Clearly, however, emotional reactions can be real or feigned. We discuss emotions in more detail in Chapter 5. The length of time and amount of detail used in presenting a point or position can also convey importance. Carefully checking through the details the other side has presented about an item, or insisting on clarification and verification, can convey the impression of importance. Casually accepting the other party's arguments as true can convey the impression of disinterest in the topic being discussed.

Taking direct action to alter another's impression raises several potential hazards. It is one thing to select certain facts to present and to emphasize or de-emphasize their importance accurately, but it is a different matter to fabricate and lie. The former is expected and understood in distributive bargaining; the latter, even in hardball negotiations, is resented and often angrily attacked if discovered. Between the two extremes, however, what is said and done as skillful puffery by one may be perceived as dishonest distortion by the other. Ethical considerations are explored in detail in Chapter 8. Other problems can arise when trivial items are introduced as distractions or minor issues are magnified in importance. The purpose is to conceal the truly important and to direct the other's attention away from the significant, but there is a danger: the other person may become aware of this maneuver and, with great fanfare, concede on the minor points, thereby gaining the right to demand equally generous concessions on the central points. In this way the other party can defeat the maneuverer at his or her own game.

Modify the Other Party's Perceptions

A negotiator can alter the other party's impressions of his or her own objectives by making outcomes appear less attractive or by making the cost of obtaining them appear higher. The negotiator may also try to make demands and positions appear more attractive or less unattractive to the other party.

There are several approaches to modifying the other party's perceptions. One approach is to interpret for the other party what the outcomes of his or her proposal will really be. A negotiator can explain logically how an undesirable outcome would result if the other party really did get what he or she requested. This may mean highlighting something that has been overlooked. For example, in union–management negotiations, management may demonstrate that a union request for a six-hour workday would, on the one hand, not increase the number of employees because it would not be worthwhile to hire people for two hours a day to make up for the hours taken from the standard eight-hour day. On the other hand, if the company were to keep production at the present level, it would be necessary to use the present employees on overtime, thereby increasing the total labor cost and, subsequently, the price of the product. This rise in cost would reduce demand for the product and, ultimately, the number of hours worked or the number of workers.

Another approach to modifying the other's perceptions is to conceal information. An industrial seller may not reveal to a purchaser that certain technological changes are going to reduce significantly the cost of producing the products. A seller of real estate may not tell a prospective buyer that in three years a proposed highway will isolate the property being sold from key areas of the city. Concealment strategies may carry with them the ethical hazards mentioned earlier.

Manipulate the Actual Costs of Delay or Termination

Negotiators have deadlines. A contract will expire. Agreement has to be reached before an important meeting occurs. Someone has to catch a plane. Extending negotiations beyond a deadline can be costly, particularly to the person who has the deadline, because that person has to either extend the deadline or go home empty-handed. At the same time, research and practical experience suggest that a large majority of agreements in distributive bargaining are reached when the deadline is near.[11] In addition, time pressure in negotiation appears to reduce negotiatior demands,[12] and when a negotiator represents a constituency, time pressure appears to reduce the likelihood of reaching an agreement.[13] Manipulating a deadline

"Mr. Mosbacher, are you expecting anything via U.P.S.?"

or failing to agree by a particular deadline can be a powerful tool in the hands of the person who does not face deadline pressure. In some ways, the ultimate weapon in negotiation is to threaten to terminate negotiations, denying both parties the possibility of a settlement. One side then will usually feel this pressure more acutely than the other, and so the threat is a potent weapon. There are three ways to manipulate the costs of delay in negotiation: (1) plan disruptive action, (2) form an alliance with outsiders, and (3) manipulate the scheduling of negotiations.

Disruptive Action   One way to encourage settlement is to increase the costs of not reaching a negotiated agreement through disruptive action. In one instance, a group of unionized food-service workers negotiating with a restaurant rounded up supporters, had them enter the restaurant just prior to lunch, and had each person order a cup of coffee and drink it leisurely. When regular customers came to lunch, they found every seat occupied.[14] In another case, people dissatisfied with automobiles they purchased from a certain dealer had their cars painted with large, bright yellow lemons and signs bearing the dealer's name, then drove them around town in an effort to embarrass the dealer into making a settlement. Public picketing of a business, boycotting a product or company, and locking negotiators in a room until they reach agreement are all forms of disruptive action that increase the costs to negotiators for not settling and thereby bring them back to the bargaining table. Such tactics can work, but they may also produce anger and escalate the conflict.

Alliance with Outsiders   Another way to increase the costs of delay or terminate negotiations is to involve other parties who can somehow influence the outcome in the process. In many business transactions, a private party may suggest that if negotiations with a merchant are unsuccessful, he or she will go to the Better Business Bureau and protest the merchant's actions. Individuals who are dissatisfied with the practices and policies of businesses or government agencies form task forces, political action groups, and protest organizations to bring greater collective pressure on the target. For example, individual utility consumers often enhance their negotiation with public service providers on consumer rates and service by citing compliance with public utility commissions' guidelines to substantiate their requests.

Schedule Manipulation   The negotiation scheduling process can often put one party at a considerable disadvantage, and the negotiation schedule can be used to increase time pressure on negotiators. Businesspeople going overseas to negotiate with customers or suppliers often find that negotiations are scheduled to begin immediately after their arrival, when they are still suffering from the fatigue of travel and jet lag. Alternatively, a host party can use delay tactics to squeeze negotiations into the last remaining minutes of a session in order to extract concessions from the visiting party.[15] Automobile dealers likely negotiate differently with a customer half an hour before quitting time on Saturday than at the beginning of the workday on Monday. Industrial buyers have a much more difficult negotiation when they have a short lead time because their plants may have to sit idle if they cannot secure a new contract for raw materials in time.

Positions Taken during Negotiation

Effective distributive bargainers need to understand the process of taking positions during bargaining, including the importance of the opening offer and the opening stance, and the role of making concessions throughout the negotiation process.[16] At the beginning of negotiations, each party takes a position. Typically, one party will then change his or her position in response to information from the other party or in response to the other party's behavior. The other party's position will also typically change during bargaining. Changes in position are usually accompanied by new information concerning the other's intentions, the value of outcomes, and likely zones for settlement. Negotiation is iterative. It provides an opportunity for both sides to communicate information about their positions that may lead to changes in those positions.

Opening Offers

When negotiations begin, the negotiator is faced with a perplexing problem. What should the opening offer be? Will the offer be seen as too low or too high by the other negotiator and be contemptuously rejected? An offer seen as modest by the other party could perhaps have been higher, either to leave more room to maneuver or to achieve a higher eventual settlement. Should the opening offer be somewhat closer to the resistance point, suggesting a more cooperative stance? These questions become less perplexing as the negotiator learns more about the other party's limits and planned strategy. While knowledge about the other party helps negotiators set their opening offers, it does not tell them exactly what to do.

The fundamental question is whether the opening offer should be exaggerated or modest. Studies indicate that negotiators who make exaggerated opening offers get higher settlements than do those who make low or modest opening offers.[17] There are at least two reasons that an exaggerated opening offer is advantageous.[18] First, it gives the negotiator room for movement and therefore allows him or her time to learn about the other party's priorities. Second, an exaggerated opening offer acts as a meta-message and may create, in the other party's mind, the impression that (1) there is a long way to go before a reasonable settlement will be achieved, (2) more concessions than originally intended may have to be made to bridge the difference between the two opening positions, and (3) the other may have incorrectly estimated his or her own resistance point.[19] Two disadvantages of an exaggerated opening offer are that (1) it may be summarily rejected by the other party and halt negotiations prematurely, and (2) it communicates an attitude of toughness that may be harmful to long-term relationships. The more exaggerated the offer, the greater is the likelihood that it will be summarily rejected by the other side. Therefore, negotiators who make exaggerated opening offers should also have viable alternatives they can employ if the opposing negotiator refuses to deal with them.

Opening Stance

A second decision negotiators should make at the outset of distributive bargaining concerns the stance or attitude to adopt during the negotiation. Will you be competitive (fighting to get the best on every point) or moderate (willing to make concessions and compromises)? Some negotiators take a belligerent stance, attacking the positions, offers, and even the character of the other party. In response, the other party may mirror the initial stance, meeting belligerence with belligerence. Even if the other party does not directly mimic a belligerent stance, he or she is unlikely to respond in a warm and open manner. Some negotiators adopt a position of moderation and understanding, seeming to say, "Let's be reasonable people who can solve this problem to our mutual satisfaction." Even if the attitude is not mirrored, the other's response is likely to be constrained by such a moderate opening stance.

It is important for negotiators to think carefully about the message that they wish to signal with their opening stance and subsequent concessions because there is a tendency for negotiators to respond "in kind" to distributive tactics in negotiation.[20] That is, negotiators tend to match distributive tactics from the other party with their own distributive tactics.

To communicate effectively, a negotiator should try to send a consistent message through both the opening offer and stance.[21] A reasonable bargaining position is usually coupled with a friendly stance, and an exaggerated bargaining position is usually coupled with a tougher, more competitive stance. When the messages sent by the opening offer and stance are in conflict, the other party will find them confusing to interpret and answer. Ethical considerations are explored in detail in Chapter 8.

Initial Concessions

An opening offer is usually met with a counteroffer, and these two offers define the initial bargaining range. Sometimes the other party will not counteroffer but will simply state that the first offer (or set of demands) is unacceptable and ask the opener to come back with a more reasonable set of proposals. In any event, after the first round of offers, the next question is, what movement or concessions are to be made? Negotiators can choose to make none, to hold firm and insist on the original position, or to make some concessions. Note that it is not an option to escalate one's opening offer, that is, to set an offer further away from the other party's target point than one's first offer. This would be uniformly met with disapproval from the other negotiator. If concessions are to be made, the next question is, how large should they be? Note that the first concession conveys a message, frequently a symbolic one, to the other party about how you will proceed.

Opening offers, opening stances, and initial concessions are elements at the beginning of a negotiation that parties can use to communicate how they intend to negotiate. An exaggerated opening offer, a determined opening stance, and a very small initial concession signal a position of firmness; a moderate opening offer, a reasonable, cooperative opening stance, and a reasonable initial concession communicate a basic stance of flexibility. By taking a firm position, negotiators attempt to capture most of the bargaining range for themselves so that they maximize their final outcome or preserve maximum maneuvering room for later in the negotiation. Firmness can also create a climate in which the other party may decide that concessions are so meager that he or she might as well capitulate and settle quickly rather than drag things out. Paradoxically, firmness may actually shorten negotiations.[22] There is also the very real possibility, however, that firmness will be reciprocated by the other. One or both parties may become either intransigent or disgusted and withdraw completely.

There are several good reasons for adopting a flexible position.[23] First, when taking different stances throughout a negotiation, one can learn about the other party's targets and perceived possibilities by observing how he or she responds to different proposals. Negotiators may want to establish a cooperative rather than a combative relationship, hoping to get a better agreement. In addition, flexibility keeps the negotiations proceeding; the more flexible one seems, the more the other party will believe that a settlement is possible.

Role of Concessions

Concessions are central to negotiation. Without them, in fact, negotiations would not exist. If one side is not prepared to make concessions, the other side must capitulate or the negotiations will deadlock. People enter negotiations expecting concessions. Negotiators are less satisfied when negotiations conclude with the acceptance of their first offer, likely because they feel they could have done better.[24] Immediate concessions are perceived less valuable than gradual, delayed concessions, which appear to increase the perceived value of the concession.[25] Good distributive bargainers will not begin negotiations with an opening offer too close to their own resistance point, but rather will ensure that there is enough room in the bargaining range to make some concessions. Research suggests that people will generally accept the first or second offer that is better than their target point,[26] so negotiators should try to identify the other party's target point accurately and avoid conceding too quickly to that point.

There is ample data to show that parties feel better about a settlement when the negotiation involved a progression of concessions than when it didn't.[27] Rubin and Brown suggest that bargainers want to believe they are capable of shaping the other's behavior, of causing the other to choose as he or she does.[28] Because concession making indicates an acknowledgment of the other party and a movement toward the other's position, it implies recognition of that position and its legitimacy. The intangible factors of status and recognition may be as important as the tangible issues themselves. Concession making also exposes the concession maker to some risk. If the other party does not reciprocate, the concession maker may appear to be weak. Thus, not reciprocating a concession may send a powerful message about firmness and leaves the concession maker open to feeling that his or her esteem has been damaged or reputation diminished.

A reciprocal concession cannot be haphazard. If one party has made a major concession on a significant point, it is expected that the return offer will be on the same item or one of similar weight and somewhat comparable magnitude. To make an additional concession when none has been received (or when the other party's concession was inadequate) can imply weakness and can squander valuable maneuvering room. After receiving an inadequate concession, negotiators may explicitly state what they expect before offering further concessions: "That is not sufficient; you will have to concede X before I consider offering any further concessions."

To encourage further concessions from the other side, negotiators sometimes link their concessions to a prior concession made by the other. They may say, "Because you have reduced your demand on X, I am willing to concede on Y." A powerful form of concession making involves wrapping a concession in a package. For example, "If you will move on A and B, I will move on C and D." Packaging concessions can lead to better outcomes for negotiators than making concessions singly on individual issues.[29] A particularly effective package is to concede more on lower priority items to gain more on higher priority items. This is an integrative negotiation tactic known as logrolling and is discussed in Chapter 3.

Pattern of Concession Making

The pattern of concessions a negotiator makes contains valuable information, but it is not always easy to interpret. When successive concessions get smaller, the obvious message is that the concession maker's position is getting firmer and that the resistance point is being approached. This generalization needs to be tempered, however, by noting that a concession late in negotiations may also indicate that there is little room left to move. When the opening offer is exaggerated, the negotiator has considerable room available for packaging new offers, making it relatively easy to give fairly substantial concessions. When the offer or counteroffer has moved closer to a negotiator's target point, giving a concession the same size as the initial one may take a negotiator past the resistance point. Suppose a negotiator makes a first offer $100 below the other's target price; an initial concession of $10 would reduce the maneuvering room by 10 percent. When negotiations get to within $10 of the other's target price, a concession of $1 gives up 10 percent of the remaining maneuvering room. A negotiator cannot always communicate such mechanical ratios in giving or interpreting concessions, but this example illustrates how the receiver might construe the meaning of concession size, depending on where it occurs in the negotiating process.

FIGURE 2.4 | Pattern of Concession Making for Two Negotiators

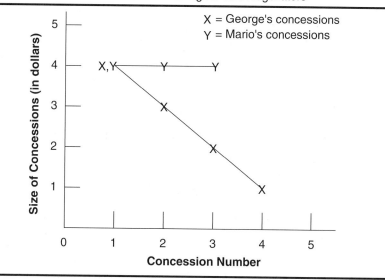

The pattern of concession making is also important. Consider the pattern of concessions made by two negotiators, George and Mario, shown in Figure 2.4. Assume that the negotiators are discussing the unit price of a shipment of computer parts, and that each is dealing with a different client. Mario makes three concessions, each worth $4 per unit, for a total of $12. In contrast, George makes four concessions, worth $4, $3, $2, and $1 per unit, for a total of $10. Both Mario and George tell their counterparts that they have conceded about all that they can. George is more likely to be believed when he makes this assertion because he has signaled through the pattern of his concession making that there is not much left to concede. When Mario claims to have little left to concede, his counterpart is less likely to believe him because the pattern of Mario's concessions (three concessions worth the same amount) suggests that there is plenty left to concede, even though Mario has actually conceded more than George.[30] Note that we have not considered the words spoken by Mario and George as these concessions were made. It is also important to justify concessions to the other party, especially those involving price reductions.[31] Behaviors and words are interpreted by the other party when we negotiate; it is important to signal to the other party with both our actions and our words that the concessions are almost over.

In multi-issue negotiations, skilled negotiators will also suggest different forms of a potential settlement that are worth about the same to them. They recognize that not all issues are worth the same amount to both parties. For example, a negotiator in a purchasing agreement may be interested solely in the total revenue of a package and not care whether it is paid in full within one month without interest or over six months with a financing fee at current interest rates. The length of the repayment period may, however, be critical to the other party who has a cash flow problem; that party may be willing to pay the financing fee for the right to spread the payments over six months. In fact, different combinations of principal, interest rate, and payback period may have the same value for one party but quite a different value for the other.

Final Offers

Eventually a negotiator wants to convey the message that there is no further room for movement—that the present offer is the final one. A good negotiator will say, "This is all I can do" or "This is as far as I can go." Sometimes, however, it is clear that a simple statement will not suffice; an alternative is to use concessions to convey the point. A negotiator might simply let the absence of any further concessions convey the message in spite of urging from the other party. The other party may not recognize at first that the last offer was the final one and might volunteer a further concession to get the other to respond. Finding that no further concession occurs, the other party may feel betrayed and perceive that the pattern of concession–counterconcession was violated. The resulting bitterness may further complicate negotiations.

One way negotiators may convey the message that an offer is the last one is to make the last concession more substantial. This implies that the negotiator is throwing in the remainder of the negotiating range. The final offer has to be large enough to be dramatic yet not so large that it creates the suspicion that the negotiator has been holding back and that there is more available on other issues in the bargaining mix.[32] A concession may also be personalized to the other party ("I went to my boss and got a special deal just for you"), which signals that this is the last concession the negotiator will make.

Commitment

A key concept in creating a bargaining position is that of commitment. One definition of commitment is the taking of a bargaining position with some explicit or implicit pledge regarding the future course of action.[33] An example is a sports agent who says to the general manager of a professional sports team, "If we do not get the salary we want, my player will sit out next year." This act identifies the negotiator's bargaining position and pledges future action if that position is not reached. The purpose of a commitment is to remove ambiguity about the negotiator's intended course of action. By making a commitment, a negotiator signals his or her intention to take this course of action, make this decision, or pursue this objective—the negotiator says, "If you pursue your goals as well, we are likely to come into direct conflict; either one of us will win or neither of us will achieve our goals." Commitments also reduce the other party's options; they are designed to constrain the other party to a reduced portfolio of choices.

A commitment is often interpreted by the other party as a threat—if the other doesn't comply or give in, some set of negative consequences will occur. Some commitments can be threats, but others are simply statements of intended action that leave the responsibility for avoiding mutual disaster in the hands of the other party. A nation that publicly states that it is going to invade another country and that war can be averted only if no other nation tries to stop the action is making a bold and dramatic commitment. Commitments can also involve future promises, such as, "If we get this salary increase, we'll agree to have all other points arbitrated as you request."

Because of their nature, commitments are statements that usually require a follow-through in action. A negotiator who states consequences (e.g., the player will sit out next year), and subsequently fails to get what he or she wanted in the negotiation, is not going to be believed in the future unless he or she acts on the consequences (e.g., the player does not report to training camp). In addition, a person would likely suffer a loss to self-image after not following through on a publicly made commitment. Once a negotiator makes a commitment, therefore, there is strong motivation to hold to it. Because the other party probably will understand this, a commitment, once accepted, will often have a powerful effect on what the other party believes is possible.[34]

Tactical Considerations in Using Commitments

Like many tools, commitments are two-edged. They may be used to gain the advantages described earlier, but they may also fix a negotiator to a particular position or point. Commitments exchange flexibility for certainty of action, but they create difficulties if one wants to move to a new position. For example, suppose that after committing yourself to a course of action, you find additional information indicating that a different position is desirable, such as information showing that your earlier estimate of the other party's resistance point was wrong and that there is actually a negative bargaining range. It may be desirable or even necessary to shift positions after making a commitment. For these reasons, when one makes commitments one should also make contingency plans for a graceful exit should it be needed. For the original commitment to be effective, the contingency plans must be secret. For example, the player's agent might have planned to retire shortly after the expected completion of negotiations. By advancing retirement, the agent can thereby cancel the commitment and leave a new negotiator unencumbered. The purchaser of a condo may be able to back away from a commitment to buy by discovering the hitherto unnoticed cracks in the plaster in the living room or being unable to obtain financing from the bank.

Commitments may be useful to you as a negotiator, but you will find it advantageous to prevent the other party from becoming committed. Further, if the other party should take a committed position, it is to your advantage to keep open one or more ways for him or her to get out of the commitment. The following sections examine these tactical issues in more detail.

Establishing a Commitment

Given that strong, passionate statements—some of which are pure bluff—are made during negotiation, how does a negotiator establish that a statement is to be understood as a commitment? A commitment statement has three properties: a high degree of *finality*, a high degree of *specificity*, and a clear statement of *consequences*.[35] A buyer could say, "We need a volume discount, or there will be trouble." This statement is far less powerful than "We must have a 10 percent volume discount in the next contract, or we will sign with an alternative supplier next month." The latter statement communicates finality (how and when the volume discount must be granted), specificity (how much of a volume discount is expected), and a clear statement of consequences (exactly what will happen if the discount is not given). It is far stronger than the first statement and much more difficult to get released from. Several ways to create a commitment are discussed next.

Public Pronouncement   A commitment statement increases in potency when more people know about it. The sports agent's statement about sitting out the season would have a different impact if made during a television sportscast than if made only at the bargaining table. Some parties in negotiations have called press conferences or placed ads in newspapers or other publications stating what they want and what will or will not happen if they don't get it. In each of these situations, the wider the audience, the less likely the commitment will be changed. The effect of the broader social context on negotiations will be discussed in Chapter 9.

Linking with an Outside Base   Another way to strengthen a commitment is to link with one or more allies. Employees who are dissatisfied with management can form a committee to express their concerns. Industry associations may coalesce to set standards for a product. A variation of this process occurs when negotiators create conditions that make it more difficult for them to break a commitment they have made. For example, by encouraging dedicated colonists to settle on the West Bank near Jerusalem, the Israeli government made it more difficult for Israel to concede this land to the Palestinians, a point the Israelis initially wanted to reinforce.

Increase the Prominence of Demands   Many things can be done to increase the prominence of commitment statements. If most offers and concessions have been made orally, then writing out a statement may draw attention to the commitment. If prior statements have been written, then using a different size typeface or different colored paper will draw attention to the new one. Repetition is one of the most powerful vehicles for making a statement prominent. Using different communication channels to convey a commitment makes the point strongly—for example, telling the other party of a commitment; then handing over a written statement; then reading aloud the statement; then circulating the commitment to others.

Reinforce the Threat or Promise   When making a threat, there is the danger of going too far—stating a point so strongly that you look weak or foolish rather than threatening. Statements like "If I don't get a concession on this point, I'll see that you don't stay in business another day!" are more likely to be greeted with annoyance or dismissal than with concern or compliance. Long, detailed statements that are highly exaggerated undermine credibility. In contrast, simple, direct statements of demands, conditions, and consequences are more effective.

Several things can be done to reinforce the implicit or explicit threat in a commitment. One is to review similar circumstances and their consequences; another is to make obvious preparations to carry out the threat. Facing the prospect of a strike, companies build up their inventories and move cots and food into their factories; unions build strike funds and give advice to their members about how to get by with less income should there be a strike. Another route is to create and carry out minor threats in advance, thereby leading the other party to believe that major threats will be fulfilled. For example, a negotiator could say, "If the progress of these negotiations does not speed up, I am not going to return to the negotiation table after lunch," and then do just that.

Finally, research on threats in negotiation suggests that negotiators who make threats are perceived as more powerful than negotiators who do not.[36] This perception of greater power does not appear to translate into higher negotiation outcomes for threat users, however. In fact, threat users are also perceived as less cooperative, and their outcomes in integrative situations seem to be lower than those of negotiators who do not use threats.[37] Integrative negotiations are discussed in greater detail in Chapter 3.

Preventing the Other Party from Committing Prematurely

All the advantages of a committed position work against a negotiator when the other party becomes committed, so it is important to try to prevent the other negotiator from becoming committed. People often take committed positions when they become angry or feel pushed to the limit; these commitments are often unplanned and can work to the disadvantage of both parties. Consequently, negotiators should pay careful attention to the other party's level of irritation, anger, and impatience.

Good, sound, deliberate commitments take time to establish, for the reasons already discussed. One way to prevent the other party from establishing a committed position is to deny him or her the necessary time. In a real estate deal with an option about to run out, a seller may use up the time by being unavailable or requiring extensive checking of deeds and boundaries, thereby denying time to a potential buyer to make an offer by the deadline and ultimately allowing another buyer who would pay more to enter into negotiation. Another approach to keep the other party from taking a committed position is to ignore or downplay a threat by not acknowledging the other's commitment, or even by making a joke about it. A negotiator might lightheartedly say, "You don't really mean that," or "I know you can't be serious about really going through with that," or simply move negotiations along as though the commitment statement was not heard or understood. If the negotiator can pretend not to hear the other party's statement or not to consider it significant, the statement can be ignored at a later point without incurring the consequences that would have ensued had it been taken seriously. Although the other negotiator can still carry out the threat, the belief that it must be carried out may be reduced.

There are times, however, when it is to a negotiator's advantage for the other party to become committed. When the other party takes a position on an issue relatively early in a negotiation, it may be very much to a negotiator's advantage to solidify that position so it will not be changed as the negotiation on other issues progresses. A negotiator may handle this situation in one of two ways: by identifying the significance of a commitment when it is made or by taking notes and keeping track of the other's statements. An employee might be very upset about the way a particular problem was handled but might also say that she will never get upset enough about it to resign. The manager might focus on this point at the time it is made or refer to it later if the employee has not calmed down. Both actions are designed to keep the employee from making a rash decision out of anger, and may allow a cooling off period before resuming discussions.

Finding Ways to Abandon a Committed Position

Frequently negotiators want to get the other party out of a committed position, and many times that party will also want a way out. How can this be done? We suggest four avenues for escaping commitments.

Plan a Way Out   One method has already been noted: when establishing a commitment, a negotiator should simultaneously plan a private way out. The negotiator may also reword a commitment to indicate that the conditions under which it applied have changed. Sometimes information provided by the other party during negotiations can permit a negotiator to say, "Given what I've learned from you during this discussion, I see I am going to have to rethink my earlier position." The same could be done for the other party. A negotiator, wanting to make it possible for the other to abandon a committed position and yet not lose credibility, might say, "Given what I've told you about the situation [or given this new information], I believe you will see that your earlier position no longer holds." Needless to say, the last thing a negotiator wants to do is to embarrass the other party or make judgmental statements about the shift in position; rather, the other party should be given every opportunity to retreat with dignity and without losing face.

Let It Die Silently   A second way to abandon a commitment is to let the matter die silently. After a lapse of time, a negotiator can make a new proposal in the area of the commitment without mentioning the earlier one. A variation on this process is to make a tentative step in a direction previously excluded by the other's commitment. For example, an employee who has said that he would never accept a certain job assignment may be asked to consider the benefits to his career of a "temporary" placement in that job. In bureaucratic institutions, changes can be introduced as "innovative experiments" to see if they work before they are formally adopted. If the other party, in response to either of these variations, indicates through silence or verbal comment a willingness to let things move in that direction, the negotiation should simply be allowed to progress.

Restate the Commitment   A third route is to restate the commitment in more general terms. The party that wants to abandon a commitment will make a new proposal, changing some of the details to be more in line with his or her current needs, while ostensibly still living with the general principles of the earlier wording. For example, the purchasing agent who demanded a 10 percent volume discount may rephrase this statement later to say simply that a significant volume discount is needed. The other party can then explore what level this "significant" discount could be.

Minimize the Damage   Finally, if the other party backs off from a committed position, it is important to help him or her save face, which means helping minimize any possible damage to the other party's self-esteem or to constituent relationships. One strategy to use in this instance is to make a public attribution about the other party's move to some noble or higher outside cause. Diplomats can withdraw from a committed position because of their deep concern for peace and humankind. A buyer or seller can back off from a point during a real estate transaction to support the economic well-being of the community. Managers can leave a committed position for the good of the company.

A committed position is a powerful tool in negotiation; it is also a rigid tool and must therefore be used with care. As with any other tool, we must be as alert to ways of denying it to the other party as we are to ways we can use it for ourselves. Unfortunately, many commitments are made impulsively out of anger or a desire to stop making concessions, rather than as a result of clearly thought-out tactical planning. In either case, the essential effect of a committed position is to remove an issue from further discussion—to make it no longer negotiable except at serious risk to one or both parties. The committed position has to be believable, and it must appear inevitable—if X happens, Y is inevitable. Convincing the other party that fate is sealed on the matter at hand is a demanding task and requires preparation, time, and skill. Consequently, getting out of a committed position is not easy, but the process is made simpler by planning a means of escape at the time the commitment is being established. Many of the steps a negotiator can use to get out of a commitment can also be used to help the other party get out of a committed position or, even better, to keep him or her from establishing one in the first place.

Closing the Deal

After negotiating for a period of time, and learning about the other party's needs, positions, and perhaps resistance point, the next challenge for a negotiator is to close the agreement. Negotiators can call on several tactics when closing a deal;[38] choosing the best tactic for a given negotiation is as much a matter of art as science.

Provide Alternatives   Rather than making a single final offer, negotiators can provide two or three alternative packages for the other party that are more or less equivalent in value. People like to have choices, and providing a counterpart with alternative packages can be a very effective technique for closing a negotiation. This technique can also be used when a task force cannot decide on which recommendation to make to upper management. If in fact there are two distinct, defensible possible solutions, then the task force can forward both with a description of the costs and benefits of each.

Assume the Close   Salespeople use an assume-the-close technique frequently. After having a general discussion about the needs and positions of the buyer, often the seller will take out a large order form and start to complete it. The seller usually begins by asking for the buyer's name and address before moving on to more serious points (e.g., price, model). When using this technique, negotiators do not ask the other party if he or she would like to make a purchase. Rather, they may say something like "Shall I get the paperwork started?" and act as if the decision to purchase something has already been made.[39]

Split the Difference   Splitting the difference is perhaps the most popular closing tactic. The negotiator using this tactic will typically give a brief summary of the negotiation ("We've both spent a lot of time, made many concessions, etc.") and then suggest that, because things are so close, "why don't we just split the difference?" While this can be an effective closing tactic, it does presume that the parties started with fair opening offers. A negotiator who uses an exaggerated opening offer and then suggests a split-the-difference close is using a hardball tactic (see below).

Exploding Offers   An exploding offer contains an extremely tight deadline in order to pressure the other party to agree quickly and is an extreme version of manipulating negotiating schedules. For example, a person who has interviewed for a job may be offered a very attractive salary and benefits package, but also be told that the offer will expire in 24 hours. The purpose of the exploding offer is to convince the other party to accept the settlement and to stop considering alternatives. This is particularly effective in situations where the party receiving the exploding offer is still in the process of developing alternatives that may or may not turn out to be viable (such as the job candidate who is still interviewing with other firms). People can feel quite uncomfortable about receiving exploding offers, however, because they feel as if they're under unfair pressure. Exploding offers appear to work best for organizations that have the resources to make an exceptionally attractive offer early in a negotiation in order to prevent the other party from continuing to search for a potentially superior offer.

Sweeteners   Another closing tactic is to save a special concession for the close. The other negotiator is told, "I'll give you X if you agree to the deal." For instance, when selling a condo the owner could agree to include the previously excluded curtains, appliances, or light fixtures to close the deal. To use this tactic effectively, however, negotiators need to include the sweetener in their negotiation plans or they may concede too much during the close.

Hardball Tactics

We now turn to a discussion of hardball tactics in negotiation. Many popular books of negotiation discuss using hardball negotiation tactics to beat the other party.[40] Such tactics are designed to pressure negotiators to do things they would not otherwise do, and their presence usually disguises the user's adherence to a decidedly distributive bargaining approach. It is not clear exactly how often or how well these tactics work, but they work best against poorly prepared negotiators. They also can backfire, and there is evidence that very adversarial negotiators are not effective negotiators.[41] Many people find hardball tactics offensive and are motivated for revenge when such tactics are used against them. Many negotiators consider these tactics out-of-bounds for any negotiation situation. (Negotiation ethics are discussed in Chapter 8). We do not recommend the use of any of the following techniques. In fact, it has been our experience that these tactics do more harm than good in negotiations. They are much more difficult to enact than they are to read, and each tactic involves risk for the person using it, including harm to reputation, lost deals, negative publicity, and consequences of the other party's revenge. It is important that negotiators understand hardball tactics and how they work, however, so they can recognize and understand them if hardball tactics are used against them.

Dealing with Typical Hardball Tactics

The negotiator dealing with a party who uses hardball tactics has several choices about how to respond. A good strategic response to these tactics requires that the negotiator identify the tactic quickly and understand what it is and how it works. Most of the tactics are designed either to enhance the appearance of the bargaining position of the person using the tactic or to detract from the appearance of the options available to the other party. How best to respond to a tactic depends on your goals and the broader context of the negotiation (With whom are you negotiating? What are your alternatives?). No one response will work in all situations. We now discuss four main options that negotiators have for responding to typical hardball tactics.[42]

Ignore Them   Although ignoring a hardball tactic may appear to be a weak response, it can in fact be very powerful. It takes a lot of energy to use some of the hardball tactics described here, and while the other side is using energy to play these games, you can be using your energy to work on satisfying your needs. Not responding to a threat is often the best way of dealing with it. Pretend you didn't hear it. Change the subject and get the other party involved in a new topic. Call a break and, upon returning, switch topics. All these options can deflate the effects of a threat and allow you to press on with your agenda while the other party is trying to decide what trick to use next.

Discuss Them   Fisher, Ury, and Patton suggest that a good way to deal with hardball tactics is to discuss them—that is, label the tactic and indicate to the other party that you know what she is doing.[43] Then offer to negotiate the negotiation process itself, such as behavioral expectations of the parties, before continuing on to the substance of the talks. Propose a shift to less aggressive methods of negotiating. Explicitly acknowledge that the other party is a tough negotiator but that you can be tough too. Then suggest that you both change to more productive methods that can allow you both to gain. Fisher, Ury, and Patton suggest that negotiators separate the people from the problem and then be hard on the problem, soft on the people. It doesn't hurt to remind the other negotiator of this from time to time during the negotiation.

Respond in Kind   It is always possible to respond to a hardball tactic with one of your own. Although this response can result in chaos, produce hard feelings, and be counterproductive, it is not an option that should be dismissed. Once the smoke clears, both parties will realize that they are skilled in the use of hardball tactics and may recognize that it is time to try something different. Responding in kind may be most useful when dealing with another party who is testing your resolve or as a response to exaggerated positions taken in negotiations. A participant in a negotiation seminar told one of the authors the following story about bargaining for a carpet in a northern African country:

> I knew that the value of the carpet was about $2,000 because I had been looking at carpets throughout my trip. I found the carpet that I wanted and made sure not to appear too interested. I discussed some other carpets with the vendor before moving on to the carpet that I really wanted. When I asked him the price of this carpet, he replied $9,000. I replied that I would give him *negative* $5,000. We bargained for a while and I bought the carpet for $2,000.

The purchaser in this negotiation clearly responded to a hardball tactic with one of his own. When asked if he felt comfortable with his opening bid, he responded:

> Sure. Why not? The seller knew the value of the carpet was about $2,000. If anything, he seemed to respect me when I bargained this way. If I had opened with a positive number I would have ended up having to pay more than the carpet was worth. And I really wanted the carpet.

Co-Opt the Other Party   Another way to deal with negotiators who are known to use aggressive hardball tactics is to try to befriend them before they use the tactics on you. This approach is built on the theory that it is much more difficult to attack a friend than an enemy. If you can stress what you have in common with the other party and find another element upon which to place the blame (the system, foreign competition), you may then be able to sidetrack the other party and thereby prevent the use of any hardball tactics.

Typical Hardball Tactics

We now discuss some of the more frequently described hardball tactics and their weaknesses.

Good Cop/Bad Cop   The good cop/bad cop tactic is named after a police interrogation technique in which two officers (one kind, the other tough) take turns questioning a suspect; it can frequently be seen in episodes of popular television series such as *Law and Order* and *CSI*. The use of this tactic in negotiations typically goes as follows: the first interrogator (bad cop) presents a tough opening position, punctuated with threats, obnoxious behavior, and intransigence. The interrogator then leaves the room to make an important telephone call or to cool off—frequently at the partner's suggestion. While out of the room, the other interrogator (good cop) tries to reach a quick agreement before the bad cop returns and makes life difficult for everyone. A more subtle form of this tactic is to assign the bad cop the role of speaking only when the negotiations are headed in a direction that the team does not want; as long as things are going well, the good cop does the talking. Although the good cop/bad cop tactic can be somewhat transparent, it often leads to concessions and negotiated agreements.[44]

This tactic has many weaknesses. As mentioned earlier, it is relatively transparent, especially with repeated use. It can be countered by openly stating what the negotiators are doing. A humorously delivered statement like "You two aren't playing the old good cop/bad cop game with me, are you?" will go a long way to deflating this tactic even if both of the other parties deny it self-righteously. The good cop/bad cop tactic is also much more difficult to enact than it is to read; it typically alienates the targeted party and frequently requires negotiators to direct much more energy toward making the tactic work smoothly than toward accomplishing the negotiation goals. Negotiators using this tactic can become so involved with their game playing and acting that they fail to concentrate on obtaining their negotiation goals.

Lowball/Highball   Negotiators using the lowball/highball tactic start with a ridiculously low (or high) opening offer that they know they will never achieve. The theory is that the extreme offer will cause the other party to reevaluate his or her own opening offer and move closer to or beyond their resistance point. For example, one of the authors of this book was in a labor–management negotiation where the union's first offer was to request a 45 percent salary increase over three years. Given that recent settlements in neighboring universities had been 3 to 4 percent, this qualified as a highball offer!

The risk of using this tactic is that the other party will think negotiating is a waste of time and will stop the process. Even if the other party continues to negotiate after receiving a lowball (or highball) offer, however, it takes a very skilled negotiator to be able to justify the extreme opening offer and to finesse the negotiation back to a point where the other side will be willing to make a major concession toward the outrageous bid.

The best way to deal with a lowball/highball tactic is not to make a counteroffer, but to ask for a more reasonable opening offer from the other party (the union in the preceding example responded to this request by tabling an offer for a 6 percent increase, above the industry average but not qualifying as a highball offer). The reason that requesting a reasonable opening offer is important is because this tactic works in the split second between hearing the other party's opening offer and the delivery of your first offer. If you give in to the

GOOD COP, GREAT COP

natural tendency to change your opening offer because it would be embarrassing to start negotiations so far apart, or because the other party's extreme opening makes you rethink where the bargaining zone may lie, then you have fallen victim to this tactic. When this happens, you have been "anchored" by the other party's extreme first offer.

Good preparation for the negotiation is a critical defense against this tactic (see Chapter 4). Proper planning will help you know the general range for the value of the item under discussion and allow you to respond verbally with one of several different strategies: (1) insisting that the other party start with a reasonable opening offer and refusing to negotiate further until he or she does; (2) stating your understanding of the general market value of the item being discussed, supporting it with facts and figures, and, by doing so, demonstrating to the other party that you won't be tricked; (3) threatening to leave the negotiation, either briefly or for good, to demonstrate dissatisfaction with the other party for using this tactic; and (4) responding with an extreme counteroffer to send a clear message you won't be anchored by an extreme offer from the other party.

Bogey Negotiators using the bogey tactic pretend that an issue of little or no importance to them is quite important. Later in the negotiation, this issue can then be traded for major concessions on issues that are actually important to them. This tactic is most effective when negotiators identify an issue that is quite important to the other side but of little value to themselves. For example, a seller may have a product in the warehouse ready for delivery. When negotiating with a purchasing agent, however, the seller may ask for large concessions to process a rush order for the client. The seller can reduce the size of the concession demanded for the rush order in exchange for concessions on other issues, such as the price or the size of the order.

Another example of a bogey is to argue as if you want a particular work assignment or project (when in fact you don't prefer it) and then, in exchange for large concessions from the other party, accept the assignment you actually prefer (but had pretended not to).

This tactic is fundamentally deceptive, and as such it can be a difficult tactic to enact. Typically, the other party will negotiate in good faith and take you seriously when you are trying to make a case for the issue that you want to bogey. This can lead to the very unusual situation of both negotiators arguing against their true wishes—the other party asks for large concessions on other issues to give you the bogey issue (that you really don't want), and you spend time evaluating offers and making arguments for an issue you know you do not want. It can also be very difficult to change gracefully and accept an offer in completely the opposite direction. If this maneuver cannot be done, however, then you may end up accepting a suboptimal deal—the bogey may be something you do not really want, and perhaps the other party doesn't either.

Although the bogey is a difficult tactic to defend against, being well prepared for the negotiation will make you less susceptible to it. When the other party takes a position completely counter to what you expected, you may suspect that a bogey tactic is being used. Probing with questions about why the other party wants a particular outcome may help you reduce the effectiveness of a bogey. Finally, you should be very cautious about sudden reversals in positions taken by the other party, especially late in a negotiation. This may be a sign that the bogey tactic has been in use. Again, questioning the other party carefully about why the reverse position is suddenly acceptable and not conceding too much after the other party completely reverses a position may significantly reduce the effectiveness of the bogey.

The Nibble   Negotiators using the nibble tactic ask for a proportionally small concession (e.g., 1 to 2 percent of the total profit of the deal) on an item that hasn't been discussed previously in order to close the deal. Herb Cohen[45] describes the nibble as follows: after trying many different suits in a clothing store, tell the clerk that you will take a given suit if a tie is included for free. The tie is the nibble. Cohen claims that he usually gets the tie. In a business context, the tactic occurs like this: after a considerable amount of time has been spent in negotiation, when an agreement is close, one party asks to include a clause that hasn't been discussed previously and that will cost the other party a proportionally small amount. This amount is too small to lose the deal over, but large enough to upset the other party. This is the major weakness with the nibble tactic—many people feel that the party using the nibble did not bargain in good faith (as part of a fair negotiation process, all items to be discussed during the negotiation should be placed on the agenda early). Even if the party claims to be very embarrassed about forgetting this item until now, the party who has been nibbled will not feel good about the process and will be motivated to seek revenge in future negotiations.

According to Landon there are two good ways to combat the nibble.[46] First, respond to each nibble with the question "What else do you want?" This should continue until the other party indicates that all issues are in the open; then both parties can discuss all the issues simultaneously. Second, have your own nibbles prepared to offer in exchange. When the other party suggests a nibble on one issue, you can respond with your own nibble on another.

Chicken   The chicken tactic is named after the 1950s challenge, portrayed in the James Dean movie *Rebel without a Cause,* of two people driving cars at each other or toward a cliff until one person swerves to avoid disaster. The person who swerves is labeled a chicken, and the other person is treated like a hero. Negotiators who use this tactic combine a large bluff with a threatened action to force the other party to "chicken out" and give them what they want. In labor–management negotiations, management may tell the union representatives that if they do not agree to the current contract offer the company will close the factory and go out of business (or move to another state or country). Clearly this is a high-stakes gamble. On the one hand, management must be willing to follow through on the threat—if the union calls their bluff and they do not follow through, they will not be believed in the future. On the other hand, how can the union take the risk and call the bluff? If management is telling the truth, the company may actually close the factory and move elsewhere.

The weakness of the chicken tactic is that it turns negotiation into a serious game in which one or both parties find it difficult to distinguish reality from postured negotiation positions. Will the other party really follow through on his or her threats? We frequently cannot know for sure because the circumstances must be grave in order for this tactic to be believable; but it is precisely when circumstances are grave that a negotiator may be most tempted to use this tactic. Compare, for instance, the responses of Presidents Bill Clinton and George W. Bush to Iraq's defiance of the United Nations weapons inspection program. It appears that Iraq felt it could "stare down" President Bush because it had successfully avoided outright conflict during President Clinton's term. The subsequent war in Iraq demonstrated the error of this assessment.

The chicken tactic is very difficult for a negotiator to defend against. To the extent that the commitment can be downplayed, reworded, or ignored, however, it can lose its power. Perhaps the riskiest response is to introduce one's own chicken tactic. At that point neither party may be willing to back down in order not to lose face. Preparation and a thorough understanding of the situations of both parties are absolutely essential for trying to identify where reality ends and the chicken tactic begins. Use of external experts to verify information or to help to reframe the situation is another option.

Intimidation   Many tactics can be gathered under the general label of intimidation. What they have in common is that they all attempt to force the other party to agree by means of an emotional ploy, usually anger or fear. For example, the other party may deliberately use *anger* to indicate the seriousness of a position. One of the authors of this book had the following experience:

> Once while I was negotiating with a car salesman he lost his temper, destroyed his written notes, told me to sit down and listen to him, and went on to explain in a loud voice that this was the best deal in the city and if I did not accept it that evening I should not bother returning to that dealership and wasting his time. I didn't buy the car and I haven't been back, nor I suspect have any of the students in my negotiation classes, to whom I relate this story every year! I suspect that the salesman was trying to intimidate me into agreeing to the deal and realized that if I went elsewhere his deal would not look as good. What he didn't realize was that I had asked the accountant at the dealership for further information about the deal and had found that he had lied about the value of a trade-in; he really lost his cool when I exposed the lie.

Another form of intimidation includes increasing the appearance of _legitimacy_. When legitimacy is high, set policies or procedures in place for resolving disputes. Negotiators who do not have such policies or procedures available may try to invent them and then impose them on the other negotiator while making the process appear legitimate. For example, policies that are written in manuals or preprinted official forms and agreements are less likely to be questioned than those that are delivered verbally;[47] long and detailed loan contracts that banks use for consumer loans are seldom read completely.[48] The greater the appearance of legitimacy, the less likely the other party will be to question the process being followed or the contract terms being proposed.

Finally, _guilt_ can also be used as a form of intimidation. Negotiators can question the other party's integrity or the other's lack of trust in them. The purpose of this tactic is to place the other party on the defensive so that they are dealing with the issues of guilt or trust rather than discussing the substance of the negotiation.

To deal with intimidation tactics, negotiators have several options. Intimidation tactics are designed to make the intimidator feel more powerful than the other party and to lead people to make concessions for emotional rather than objective reasons (e.g., a new fact). When making any concession, it is important for negotiators to understand why they are doing so. If one starts to feel threatened, assumes that the other party is more powerful (when objectively he or she is not), or simply accepts the legitimacy of the other negotiator's "company policy," then it is likely that intimidation is having an effect on the negotiations.

If the other negotiator is intimidating, then discussing the negotiation process with him or her is a good option. You can explain that your policy is to bargain in a fair and respectful manner, and that you expect to be treated the same way in return. Another good option is to ignore the other party's attempts to intimidate you, because intimidation can only influence you if you let it. While this may sound too simplistic, think for a moment about why some people you know are intimidated by authority figures and others are not—the reason often lies in the perceiver, not the authority figure.

Another effective strategy for dealing with intimidation is to use a team to negotiate with the other party. Teams have at least two advantages over individuals in acting against intimidation. First, people are not always intimidated by the same things; while you may be intimidated by one particular negotiator, it is quite possible that other members on your team won't be. In an ongoing negotiation in China when he was younger, one of the authors of this book found that his Chinese counterparts were frequently changing their team members so that older and older members appeared in each subsequent negotiation session. He decided to bring a senior colleague of his own to subsequent meetings in order not to be intimidated by the age and experience of the counterparts on the other negotiating team. The second advantage of using a team is that the team members can discuss the tactics of the other negotiators and provide mutual support if the intimidation starts to become increasingly uncomfortable.

Aggressive Behavior   Similar to tactics described under intimidation, aggressive behavior tactics include various ways of being aggressive to push your position or attack the other person's position. Aggressive tactics include a relentless push for further concessions ("You can do better than that"), asking for the best offer early in negotiations ("Let's not waste any time. What is the most that you will pay?"), and asking the other party to explain and justify his or her proposals item by item or line by line ("What is your cost breakdown for each item?"). The negotiator using these techniques is signaling a hard-nosed, intransigent position and trying to force the other side to make many concessions to reach an agreement.

When faced with another party's aggressive behavior tactics, an excellent response is to halt the negotiations in order to discuss the negotiation process itself. Negotiators can explain that they will reach a decision based on needs and interests, not aggressive behavior. Again, having a team to counter aggressive tactics from the other party can be helpful for the same reasons discussed under intimidation tactics. Good preparation and understanding both one's own and the other party's needs and interests together make responding to aggressive tactics easier because negotiators can highlight the merits to both parties of reaching an agreement.

Snow Job   The snow job tactic occurs when negotiators overwhelm the other party with so much information that he or she has trouble determining which facts are real or important and which are included merely as distractions. Governments use this tactic frequently when releasing information publicly. Rather than answering a question briefly, they release thousands of pages of documents from hearings and transcripts that may or may not contain the information that the other party is seeking. Another example of the snow job is the use of highly technical language to hide a simple answer to a question asked by a nonexpert. Any group of professionals—such as engineers, lawyers, or computer network administrators—can use this tactic to overwhelm ("snow") the other party with information and technical language so that the nonexperts cannot make sense of the answer. Frequently, in order not to be embarrassed by asking "obvious" questions, the recipient of the snow job will simply nod his or her head and passively agree with the other party's analysis or statements.

Negotiators trying to counter a snow job tactic can choose one of several alternative responses. First, they should not be afraid to ask questions until they receive an answer they understand. Second, if the matter under discussion is in fact highly technical, then negotiators may suggest that technical experts get together to discuss the technical issues. Finally, negotiators should listen carefully to the other party and identify consistent and inconsistent information. Probing for further information after identifying a piece of inconsistent information can work to undermine the effectiveness of the snow job. For example, if one piece of incorrect or inconsistent information is discovered in the complete snow job package, the negotiator can question the accuracy of the whole presentation (e.g., "Because point X was incorrect, how can I be sure that the rest is accurate?"). Again, strong preparation is very important for defending effectively against the snow job tactic.

Chapter Summary

In this chapter we examined the basic structure of competitive or distributive bargaining situations and some of the strategies and tactics used in distributive bargaining. Distributive bargaining begins with setting opening, target, and resistance points. One can learn the other party's starting points and his or her target points directly or through inference. Usually one won't know the other party's resistance points (the points beyond which she or he will not go) until late in negotiation—they are often carefully concealed. All points are important, but the resistance points are the most critical. The spread between the parties' resistance points defines the bargaining range. If positive, it defines the area of negotiation within which a settlement is likely to occur, with each party working to obtain as much of the bargaining range as possible. If negative, successful negotiation may be impossible.

It is rare that a negotiation includes only one item; more typically, a set of items, referred to as a bargaining mix, is negotiated. Each item in a bargaining mix can have opening, target, and resistance points. The bargaining mix may provide opportunities for bundling issues together, trading off across issues, or displaying mutually concessionary behavior.

Under the structure of distributive bargaining, a negotiator has many options to achieve a successful resolution, most of which fall within two broad efforts: to influence the other party's belief about what is possible and to learn as much as possible about the other party's position, particularly about their resistance points. The negotiator's basic goal is to reach a final settlement as close to the other party's resistance point as possible. To achieve this goal, negotiators work to gather information about the opposition and its positions; to convince members of the other party to change their minds about their ability to achieve their own goals; and to justify their own objectives as desirable, necessary, or even inevitable.

Distributive bargaining is basically a conflict situation, wherein parties seek their own advantage—sometimes through concealing information, attempting to mislead, or using manipulative actions. All these tactics can easily escalate interaction from calm discussion to bitter hostility. Yet negotiation is the attempt to resolve a conflict without force, without fighting. Further, to be successful, both parties to the negotiation must feel at the end that the outcome was the best they could achieve and that it is worth accepting and supporting. Hence, effective distributive bargaining is a process that requires careful planning, strong execution, and constant monitoring of the other party's reactions. Finally, distributive bargaining skills are important when at the value claiming stage of any negotiation. This is discussed in more detail in the next chapter on integrative negotiation.

Endnotes

[1] Walton and McKersie, 1965.

[2] Lax and Sebenius, 1986.

[3] Thompson and Hrebec, 1996.

[4] Raiffa, 1982.

[5] Larrick and Wu, 2007.

[6] Fisher and Ertel, 1995.

[7] Fisher, Ury, and Patton, 1991.

[8] Stein, 1996.

[9] See Schweitzer and Kerr, 2000.

[10] Karrass, 1974.

[11] See Lim and Murnighan, 1994; Roth, Murnigham, and Schoumaker, 1988; and Walton and McKersie, 1965.

[12] de Dreu, 2003.

[13] Mosterd and Rutte, 2000.

[14] Jacobs, 1951.

[15] Cohen, 1980.

[16] See Tutzauer, 1992.

[17] See Brodt, 1994; Chertkoff and Conley, 1967; Cohen, 2003; Donohue, 1981; Hinton, Hamner, and Pohlan, 1974; Komorita and Brenner, 1968; Liebert, Smith, and Hill, 1968; Pruitt and Syna, 1985; Ritov, 1996; Van Poucke and

Buelens, 2002; and Weingart, Thompson, Bazerman, and Carroll, 1990.

[18] See Pruit, 1981 and Tutzauer, 1991 for further discussion of these points.

[19] Putnam and Jones, 1982; Yukl, 1974.

[20] Weingart, Prietula, Hyder, and Genovese, 1999.

[21] Eyuboglu and Buja, 1993.

[22] See Ghosh, 1996.

[23] Olekalns, Smith, and Walsh, 1996.

[24] Galinsky, Seiden, Kim, and Medvec, 2002.

[25] Kwon and Weingart, 2004.

[26] See Rapoport, Erev, and Zwick, 1995.

[27] See Baranowski and Summers, 1972; Crumbaugh and Evans, 1967; Deutsch, 1958; and Gruder and Duslak, 1973.

[28] Rubin and Brown, 1975.

[29] See Froman and Cohen, 1970; Neale and Bazerman, 1991; and Pruit, 1981.

[30] See Yukl, 1974.

[31] Yama, 2004.

[32] Walton and McKersie, 1965.

[33] Ibid., p. 82.

[34] Pruitt, 1981.

[35] Walton and McKersie, 1965.

[36] See de Dreu, 1995; Shapiro and Bies, 1994.

[37] Shapiro and Bies, 1994.

[38] See Cellich, 1997; Girard, 1989.

[39] See Girard, 1989.

[40] For instance, see Aaronson, 1989; Brooks and Odiorne, 1984; Cohen, 1980; Levinson, Smith, and Wilson, 1999; and Schatzski, 1981.

[41] Schneider, 2002.

[42] See Fisher, Ury, and Patton, 1991; Ury, 1991; and Adler, Rosen, and Silverstein, 1996 for an extended discussion of these points.

[43] Fisher, Ury, and Patton, 1991; Ury, 1991; Weeks, 2001.

[44] Brodt and Tuchinsky, 2000; Hilty and Carnevale, 1993.

[45] Cohen, 1980.

[46] Landon, 1997.

[47] Cohen, 1980.

[48] Hendon and Hendon, 1990.

Strategy and Tactics of Integrative Negotiation

Objectives

1. Understand the basic elements of an integrative negotiation situation.
2. Explore the strategy and tactics of integrative negotiation.
3. Consider the key factors that facilitate successful integrative negotiation.

Introduction

Even well-intentioned negotiators can make the following three mistakes: failing to negotiate when they should, negotiating when they should not, or negotiating when they should but choosing an inappropriate strategy. As suggested by the dual concerns model described in Chapter 1, being committed to the other party's interests as well as to one's own makes problem solving the strategy of choice. In many negotiations there does not need to be winners and losers—all parties can gain. Rather than assume that negotiations are win–lose situations, negotiators can look for win–win solutions—and often they will find them. Integrative negotiation—variously known as cooperative, collaborative, win–win, mutual gains, or problem solving—is the focus of this chapter.

In contrast to distributive negotiating, the goals of the parties in integrative negotiation are not mutually exclusive. If one side achieves its goals, the other is not precluded from achieving its goals as well. One party's gain is not at the other party's expense. The fundamental structure of an integrative negotiation situation is such that it allows both sides to achieve their objectives.[1] Although the situation may initially appear to the parties to be win–lose, discussion and mutual exploration will often suggest alternatives where both parties can gain. A description of the efforts and tactics that negotiators use to discover these alternatives is the major part of this chapter.

What Makes Integrative Negotiation Different?

In Chapter 1 we listed elements common to all negotiations. For a negotiation to be characterized as integrative, negotiators must also:

- Focus on commonalties rather than differences.
- Attempt to address needs and interests, not positions.

BOX 3.1 Characteristics of the Interest-Based Negotiator

A successful interest-based negotiator models the following traits:

Honesty and integrity. Interest-based negotiating requires a certain level of trust between the parties. Actions that demonstrate interest in all players' concerns will help establish a trusting environment.

Abundance mentality. Those with an abundance mentality do not perceive a concession of monies, prestige, control, and so on as something that makes their slice of the pie smaller, but merely as a way to enlarge the pie. A scarcity or zero-sum mentality says, "anything I give to you takes away from me." A negotiator with an abundance mentality knows that making concessions helps build stronger long-term relationships.

Maturity. In his book *Seven Habits of Highly Effective Leaders,* Stephen Covey refers to maturity as having the courage to stand up for your issues and values while being able to recognize that others' issues and values are just as valid.

Systems orientation. Systems thinkers will look at ways in which the entire system can be optimized, rather than focusing on suboptimizing components of the system.

Superior listening skills. Ninety percent of communication is not in one's words but in the whole context of the communication, including mode of expression, body language, and many other cues. Effective listening also requires that one avoid listening only from his or her frame of reference.

Source: Chris Laubach, "Negotiating a Gain-Gain Agreement," *Healthcare Executive,* January/February 1997, p. 14.

- Commit to meeting the needs of all involved parties.
- Exchange information and ideas.
- Invent options for mutual gain.
- Use objective criteria for standards of performance.

These requisite behaviors and perspectives are the main components of the integrative process (see Box 3.1).

An Overview of the Integrative Negotiation Process

Past experience, biased perceptions, and the truly distributive aspects of bargaining make it remarkable that integrative agreements occur at all. But they do, largely because negotiators work hard to overcome inhibiting factors and search assertively for common ground. Those wishing to achieve integrative results find that they must manage both the *context* and the *process* of the negotiation in order to gain the cooperation and commitment of all parties. Key contextual factors include creating a free flow of information, attempting to understand the other negotiator's real needs and objectives, emphasizing commonalities between parties, and searching for solutions that meet the goals and objectives of both parties. Managing integrative negotiations involves creating a process of problem identification, understanding the needs and interests of both parties, generating alternative solutions, and selecting among alternative solutions.

Creating a Free Flow of Information

Effective information exchange promotes the development of good integrative solutions.[2] Research shows that the failure to reach integrative agreements is often linked to the failure to exchange enough information to allow the parties to identify integrative options.[3] For the necessary exchange to occur, negotiators must be willing to reveal their true objectives and to listen to each other carefully. In short, negotiators must create the conditions for a free and open discussion of all related issues and concerns. In contrast, a willingness to share information is not a characteristic of distributive bargaining situations, in which the parties may distrust one another, conceal and manipulate information, and attempt to learn about the other purely for their own competitive advantage.

Creating a free flow of information includes having both parties know and share their alternatives. Pinkley discovered that negotiators who are aware of each other's alternatives to a negotiated agreement were more likely to make their resistance points less extreme, improve negotiating trade-offs, and increase the size of the resource pie compared with situations in which one or both negotiators were not aware of the alternatives.[4] Pinkley concluded that "it is the negotiator with the alternative who is responsible for expanding the pie, but both members of the dyad determine its distribution."[5] Negotiators who did not reveal the availability of a good alternative received some benefits to themselves, but those who did share information about their alternatives received additional benefits.

Attempting to Understand the Other Negotiator's Real Needs and Objectives

Negotiators differ in their values and preferences, as well as their thoughts and behaviors.[6] What one side needs and wants may or may not be the same as what the other party needs and wants. One must understand the other's needs before helping to satisfy them. When negotiators are aware of the possibility that the other's priorities are not the same as their own, this can stimulate the parties to exchange more information, understand the nature of the negotiation better, and achieve higher joint gains.[7] Similarly, integrative agreements are facilitated when parties exchange information about their priorities for particular issues, but not necessarily about their positions on those issues.[8] Throughout the process of sharing information about preferences and priorities, negotiators must make a true effort to understand what the other side really wants to achieve. This is in contrast to distributive bargaining, where negotiators either make no effort to understand the other side's needs and objectives or do so only to challenge, undermine, or even deny the other party the opportunity to have those needs and objectives met. The communicative aspects of information flow and understanding, while critical to integrative negotiation, also require that Kelley's dilemmas of trust and honesty be managed (see Chapter 1).[9] In addition, negotiators may differ in their ability to differentiate needs and interests from positions, such as when one party knows and applies a truly integrative process while the other party is unskilled or naive about negotiations. In such situations, the more experienced party may need to assist the less experienced party in discovering his or her underlying needs and interests.

Emphasizing the Commonalities between the Parties and Minimizing the Differences

To sustain a free flow of information and the effort to understand the other's needs and objectives, negotiators may need a different outlook or frame of reference (see Chapter 5 for a discussion of framing). Individual goals may need to be redefined as best achieved through collaborative efforts directed toward a collective goal. Sometimes the collective goal is clear and obvious. For example, politicians in the same party may recognize that their petty squabbles must be put aside to ensure the party's victory at the polls. Managers who are quarreling over cutbacks in their individual departmental budgets may need to recognize that unless all departments sustain appropriate budget cuts, they will be unable to change an unprofitable firm into a profitable one. At other times, the collective goal is neither so clear nor so easy to keep in sight. For example, one of the authors worked as a consultant to a company that was closing a major manufacturing plant while simultaneously opening several other plants in different parts of the country. The company was perfectly willing to transfer employees to new plants and let them take their seniority up to the time of their move with them; the union agreed to this arrangement. However, conflict developed over the transfer issue. Some employees were able to transfer immediately, whereas others—those who were needed to close and dismantle the old plant—could not. Because workers acquired seniority in the new plants based on the date they arrived, those who stayed to close the old plant would have comparatively less seniority once they arrived at the new plants. The union wanted everyone to go at the same time to avoid this inequity. This was unworkable for management. In the argument that resulted, both parties lost sight of the larger goal—to transfer all willing employees to the new plants with their seniority intact. Only by constantly stressing this larger goal were the parties able to maintain a focus on commonalities that eventually led to a solution; management allowed the workers to select their new jobs in advance and transferred their seniority to those jobs when the choice was made, not when the physical move actually occurred.

Searching for Solutions That Meet the Needs and Objectives of Both Sides

The success of integrative negotiation depends on the search for solutions that meet the needs and objectives of both sides. In this process, negotiators must be firm but flexible—firm about their primary interests and needs, but flexible about how these needs and interests are met.[10] When the parties are used to taking a combative, competitive orientation toward each other, they are generally concerned only with their own objectives. In such a competitive interaction, a low level of concern for the other's objectives may cause two forms of behavior. First, negotiators may work to ensure that what the other obtains does not take away from one's own accomplishments. Second, negotiators may attempt to block the other from obtaining his or her objectives because of a strong desire to win or to defeat the opponent. In contrast, successful integrative negotiation requires both negotiators not only to define and pursue their own goals, but also to be mindful of the other's goals and to search for solutions that satisfy both sides. Outcomes are measured by the degree to which they meet both negotiators' goals. They are not measured by determining whether one party is doing better than the other. If the objective of one party is simply to get more than the other, successful integrative negotiation is very difficult; if both strive to get more than the other, integrative negotiation may be impossible.

In summary, integrative negotiation requires a process fundamentally different than distributive bargaining. Negotiators must attempt to probe below the surface of the other party's position to discover his or her underlying needs. They must create a free and open flow of information and use their desire to satisfy both sides as a guide to structure their dialogue. If negotiators do not have this perspective—if they approach the problem and their "opponent" in win–lose terms—integrative negotiation cannot occur.

Key Steps in the Integrative Negotiation Process

There are four major steps in the integrative negotiation process: (1) identify and define the problem, (2) understand the problem and bring interests and needs to the surface, (3) generate alternative solutions to the problem, and (4) evaluate those alternatives and select among them. The first three steps of the integrative negotiation process are important for *creating value*. To work together to create value, negotiators need to understand the problem, identify the interests and needs of both parties, and generate alternative solutions. The fourth step of the integrative negotiation process, the evaluation and selection of alternatives, involves *claiming value*. Claiming value involves many of the distributive bargaining skills that were discussed in Chapter 2.

The relationship between creating and claiming value is shown graphically in Figure 3.1. The goal of creating value is to push the potential negotiation solutions toward the upper-right-hand side of Figure 3.1. When this is done to the fullest extent possible, the line is called the *Pareto efficient frontier,* and it contains a point where "there is no agreement that would make

FIGURE 3.1 | Creating and Claiming Value and the Pareto Efficient Frontier

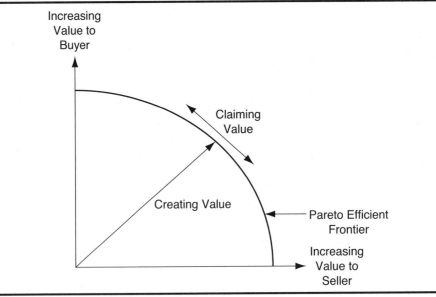

any party better off without decreasing the outcomes to any other party."[11] One way to conceptualize integrative negotiation is that it is the process of identifying Pareto efficient solutions.

The graph shows that there are several possible solutions in a negotiation, in this case between a buyer and a seller. The first three steps to integrative negotiation aim to ensure that negotiators do not agree to solutions that are below the Pareto efficient frontier because these solutions are suboptimal for both negotiators. The fourth step, choosing a solution or claiming value, uses some of the same skills as distributive bargaining. The transition from creating to claiming value in an integrative negotiation must be managed carefully and is discussed in more detail later in this chapter.

It is important that processes to create value precede those to claim value for two reasons: (1) the creating-value process is more effective when it is done collaboratively and without a focus on who gets what and (2) because claiming value involves distributive bargaining processes, it may derail the focus on creating value and may even harm the relationship unless it is introduced effectively.

Identify and Define the Problem

The problem identification step is often the most difficult one, and it is even more challenging when several parties are involved. Consider the following example: a large electronics plant experienced serious difficulty with a product as it moved from the subassembly department to the final assembly department. Various pins and fittings that held part of the product in place were getting bent and distorted. When this happened, the unit would be laid aside as a reject. At the end of the month, the rejects would be returned to the subassembly department to be reworked, often arriving just when workers were under pressure to meet end-of-the-month schedules and were also low on parts. As a result, the reworking effort had to be done in a rush and on overtime. The extra cost of overtime did not fit into the standard cost allocation system. The manager of the subassembly department did not want the costs allocated to his department. The manager of the final assembly department insisted that she should not pay the additional cost; she argued that the subassembly department should bear the cost because its poor work caused the problem. The subassembly department manager countered that the parts were in good condition when they left his area and that it was the poor workmanship in the final assembly area that created the damage. The immediate costs were relatively small. What really concerned both managers was setting a long-term precedent for handling rejects and for paying the costs.

Eventually an integrative solution was reached. During any given month, the subassembly department had some short slack-time periods. The managers arranged for the final assembly department to return damaged products in small batches during those slack periods. It also became clear that many people in the final assembly department did not fully understand the parts they were handling, which may have contributed to some of the damage. These workers were temporarily transferred to the subassembly department during assembly department slack periods to learn more about subassembly and to process some of the rush orders in that department.

Define the Problem in a Way That Is Mutually Acceptable to Both Sides   Ideally, parties should enter the integrative negotiation process with few preconceptions about the solution and with open minds about each other's needs. As a problem is defined jointly, it should accurately reflect both parties' needs and priorities. Unfortunately, this often does not occur. An understandable and widely held concern about integrative negotiation is that during the problem definition process, the other party will manipulate information to state the problem to his or her own advantage. For positive problem solving to occur, both parties must be committed to stating the problem in neutral terms. The problem statement must be acceptable to both sides and not worded so that it lays blame or favors the preferences or priorities of one side over the other. The parties may be required to revise the problem statement several times until they agree on its wording. It is critical to note that problem definition is, and should be, separate from any effort to generate or choose alternatives. Problems must be defined clearly at this stage, if only to accomplish an initial structure within which parties agree to disagree, albeit on a common, distinct issue.

State the Problem with an Eye toward Practicality and Comprehensiveness The major focus of an integrative agreement is to solve the core problem(s). Anything that distracts from this focus should be removed or streamlined to ensure that this objective is achieved. As a result, one might argue that problem statements should be as clear as possible. Yet if the problem is complex and multifaceted, and the statement of the problem does not reflect that complexity, then efforts at problem solving will be incomplete. In fact, if the problem is complex, the parties may not even be able to agree on a statement of the problem. The objective should be to state the problem as succinctly as possible while at the same time ensuring that the most important dimensions and elements are included in the definition. This approach is in stark contrast to the distributive bargaining process (see Chapter 2), in which parties may enhance their positions by bringing in a large number of secondary issues and concerns in order to trade these items off during the hard-bargaining phase. If there are several issues in an integrative negotiation, the parties may want to clearly identify the link among them and decide whether they will be approached as separate problems that may be packaged together later, or as one larger problem.

State the Problem as a Goal and Identify the Obstacles to Attaining This Goal The parties should define the problem as a specific goal to be attained rather than as a solution process. That is, they should concentrate on what they want to achieve rather than how they are going to achieve it. They should then proceed to specify what obstacles must be overcome for the goal to be attained. In the previous example, the goal might have been "to minimize the number of rejects." A clearer and more explicit definition would be "to cut the number of rejects in half." After defining the goal, the parties should specify what they need to know about how the product is made, how defects occur, what must be done to repair the defects, and so on. One key issue is whether the obstacles specified can be changed or corrected by negotiating parties. If the parties cannot address the obstacles effectively, given limited time or other resources, the obstacles then become boundary markers for the overall negotiation. A clear understanding of which obstacles are addressable and which are not can be just as critical to realistic integrative negotiation as an explicit awareness of what is negotiable and what is not.

Depersonalize the Problem When parties are engaged in conflict, they tend to become evaluative and judgmental. They view their own actions, strategies, and preferences in a positive light and the other party's actions, strategies, and preferences in a negative light. Such evaluative judgments can interfere with clear and dispassionate thinking. Telling the other party that "Your point of view is wrong and mine is right" inhibits integrative negoti-ating because you cannot attack the problem without attacking the other negotiator. In con-trast, depersonalizing the definition of the problem—stating, for example, "We have different viewpoints on this problem"—allows both sides to approach the issue as a problem external to the individuals rather than as a problem that belongs to one party only. Another way to say this is "I respect that you have constraints and a way of looking at this problem that may be different than mine. I ask that you recognize that I do as well."

Separate the Problem Definition from the Search for Solutions   Finally, it is important not to jump to solutions until the problem is fully defined. In distributive bargaining, nego-tiators are encouraged to state the problem in terms of their preferred solution and to make concessions based on this statement. In contrast, parties engaged in integrative negotiation should avoid stating solutions that favor one side or the other until they have fully defined the problem and examined as many alternative solutions as possible.

Instead of premature solutions, negotiators should develop standards by which poten-tial solutions will be judged for how well they fit. These standards can be created by asking interested parties questions such as the following:

- How will we know the problem has been solved?
- How will we know that our goal has been attained?
- How would a neutral third party know that our dispute has been settled?
- Is there any legitimate interest or position that remains unaddressed by our outcome?
- Is there any legitimate interest or position that has been disenfranchised by our outcome?

Understand the Problem Fully—Identify Interests and Needs

Many writers on negotiation—most particularly, Roger Fisher, William Ury, and Bruce Patton in their popular book, *Getting to Yes*—have stressed that a key to achieving an integrative agreement is the ability of the parties to understand and satisfy each other's *interests*.[12] Identifying interests is a critical step in the integrative negotiation process. Interests are the underlying concerns, needs, desires, or fears that motivate a negotiator to take a particular position. Fisher, Ury, and Patton explain that while negotiators may have difficulty satisfy-ing each other's specific positions, an understanding of the underlying interests may permit them to invent solutions that meet each other's interests. In this section, we will first define interests more completely and then discuss how understanding them is critical to effective integrative negotiation.

This example reveals the essence of the difference between interests and positions:

Consider the story of two men quarreling in a library. One wants the window open and the other wants it closed. They bicker back and forth about how much to leave it open: a crack, halfway, three-quarters of the way. No solution satisfied them both. Enter the librarian. She asks one why he wants the window open. "To get some fresh air." She asks the other why he wants it closed. "To avoid the draft." After thinking a minute, she opens wide a window in the next room, bringing in fresh air without a draft.[13]

This is a classic example of negotiating over positions and failing to understand underlying interests. The positions are "window open" and "window closed." If they continue to pursue positional bargaining, the set of possible outcomes can include only a victory for the one who wants the window open, a victory for the one who wants it shut, or some compromise in which neither gets what he wants. Note that a compromise here is more a form of lose–lose than win–win for these bargainers because one party believes he won't get enough fresh air with the window partially open and the other believes that any opening is unsatisfactory. The librarian's questions transform the dispute by focusing on *why* each man wants the window open or closed: to get fresh air, to avoid a draft. Understanding these interests enables the librarian to invent a solution that meets the interests of both sides—a solution that was not at all apparent when the two men were arguing over their positions.

In this description, the key word is *why*—why they want what they want. When two parties begin negotiation, they usually expose their position or demands. In distributive bargaining, negotiators trade positions back and forth, attempting to achieve a settlement as close to their targets as possible. However, in integrative negotiation, both negotiators need to pursue the other's thinking and logic to determine the factors that motivated them to arrive at their goals. The presumption is that if both parties understand the motivating factors for the other, they may recognize possible compatibilities in interests that permit them to invent new options that both will endorse.

Types of Interests   Lax and Sebenius have suggested that several types of interests may be at stake in a negotiation and that each type may be intrinsic (the parties value it in and of itself) or instrumental (the parties value it because it helps them derive other outcomes in the future).[14]

Substantive interests are related to focal issues that are under negotiation—economic and financial issues such as price or rate, or the substance of a negotiation such as the division of resources (like the tangible issues discussed in Chapter 1). These interests may be intrinsic or instrumental or both; we may want something because it is intrinsically satisfying to us and/or we may want something because it helps us achieve a long-range goal.

Process interests are related to *how* the negotiation unfolds. One party may pursue distributive bargaining because he enjoys the competitive game of wits that comes from nose-to-nose, hard-line bargaining. Another party may enjoy negotiating because she believes she has not been consulted in the past and wants to have some say in how a key problem is resolved. In the latter case, the negotiator may find the issues under discussion less important than the opportunity to voice her opinions.[15] Process interests can also be both intrinsic and instrumental. Having a voice may be intrinsically important to a group—it allows them to affirm their legitimacy and worth and highlights the key role they play in the organization; it can also be instrumentally important, in that if they are successful in gaining voice in this negotiation, they may be able to demonstrate that they should be invited back to negotiate other related issues in the future.

Relationship interests indicate that one or both parties value their relationship with each other and do not want to take actions that will damage it. Intrinsic relationship interests exist when the parties value the relationship both for its existence and for the pleasure or fulfillment that sustaining it creates. Instrumental relationship interests exist when the parties derive substantive benefits from the relationship and do not wish to endanger future benefits by souring it.

Finally, Lax and Sebenius point out that the parties may have *interests in principle*.[16] Certain principles—concerning what is fair, what is right, what is acceptable, what is ethical, or what has been done in the past and should be done in the future—may be deeply held by the parties and serve as the dominant guides to their action. These principles often involve intangible factors (see Chapter 1). Interests in principles can also be intrinsic (valued because of their inherent worth) or instrumental (valued because they can be applied to a variety of future situations and scenarios).

Bringing interests in principles to the surface will lead negotiators to discuss explicitly the principles at stake and invent solutions consistent with them.

Some Observations on Interests   We have several observations about interests and types of interests in negotiation:

1. *There is almost always more than one type of interest underlying a negotiation.* Parties will often have more than substantive interests about the issues.[17] They can also care deeply about the process, the relationship, or the principles at stake. Note that interests in principles effectively cut across substantive, procedural, and relationship interests as well, so the categories are not exclusive.

2. *Parties can have different types of interests at stake.* One party may care deeply about the specific issues under discussion while the other cares about how the issues are resolved—questions of principle or process. Bringing these different interests to the surface may enable the parties to see that they care about very different things and that there is a need to invent solutions that address the interests of both negotiators.

3. *Interests often stem from deeply rooted human needs or values.* Several authors have suggested that frameworks for understanding basic human needs and values are helpful for understanding interests.[18] According to these frameworks, needs are hierarchical, and satisfaction of the basic or lower order needs will be more important in negotiation than that of higher order needs.

4. *Interests can change.* Like positions on issues, interests can change over time. What was important to the parties last week—or even 20 minutes ago—may not be important now. Interaction between the parties can put some interests to rest, but it may raise others. Negotiators must constantly be attentive to changes in their own interests and the interests of the other side. When one party begins speaking about things in a different way—when the language or emphasis changes—the other party should look for a change in interests.

5. *Surfacing interests.* There are numerous ways to surface interests. Sometimes people are not even sure about their own interests. Negotiators should not only ask themselves "What do I want from this negotiation?" but also "Why do I want that?" "Why is that important to me?" "What will achieving that help me do?" and "What will happen if I don't achieve my objective?" Listening to your own inner voices—fears, aspirations, hopes, desires—is important in order to bring your own interests to the surface.

6. *Surfacing interests is not always easy or to one's best advantage.* Critics of the "interests approach" to negotiation have identified the difficulty of defining interests and taking

them into consideration. Provis suggests that it is often difficult to define interests and that trying to focus on interests alone often oversimplifies or conceals the real dynamics of a conflict.[19] In some cases parties do not pursue their own best objective interests but instead focus on one or more subjective interest(s), which may mislead the other party.[20] Thus, a car buyer may prefer a fast, flashy car (his subjective interest) even though his objective interest is to buy a safe, conservative one.

Generate Alternative Solutions

The search for alternatives is the creative phase of integrative negotiation. Once the parties have agreed on a common definition of the problem and understood each other's interests, they need to generate a variety of alternative solutions. The objective is to create a list of options or possible solutions to the problem; evaluating and selecting from among those options will be their task in the final phase.

Several techniques have been suggested to help negotiators generate alternative solutions. These techniques fall into two general categories. The first requires the negotiators to redefine, recast, or reframe the problem (or problem set) to create win–win alternatives out of what earlier appeared to be a win–lose problem. The second takes the problem as given and creates a long list of options from which the parties can choose. In integrative negotiation over a complex problem, both types of techniques may be used and even intertwined.

Inventing Options: Generating Alternative Solutions by Redefining the Problem or Problem Set   The techniques in this category call for the parties to define their underlying needs and to develop alternatives to meet them.

Peter Carnevale has recently created an Agreement Circumplex that classifies potential agreements into four main types, each with two subtypes (see Figure 3.2). There are four important dimensions underlying this model. Each of these dimensions is discussed here, and the strategies consistent with them are identified. A more complex discussion of the strategies and an extended example to highlight each is in the next section.

1. **Position Accommodation vs. Position Achievement**
   Positions are achieved when each party gets exactly what they wanted in their initial demand. Strategies that achieve positions include expanding the pie and modifying the resource pie. This is in contrast to position accommodation when the parties receive a portion of their initial demand.

2. **Achieve Underlying Interests vs. Substitute Underlying Interests**
   When underlying interests are achieved, the negotiators' interests are completely met. Strategies to meet underlying interests include bridging and cost cutting. Underlying interests may also be substituted, modified, or changed. Nonspecific compensation and superordination are two strategies that change whether or not a negotiator's interests are met or modified in some way.

3. **Simple vs. Complex**
   Some negotiation situations are quite simple in nature, such as a two- or three-item agreement to purchase items from a manufacturer. Other situations can be extremely complex, such as comprehensive lease agreements that cover multiple locations,

FIGURE 3.2 | The Agreement Circumplex

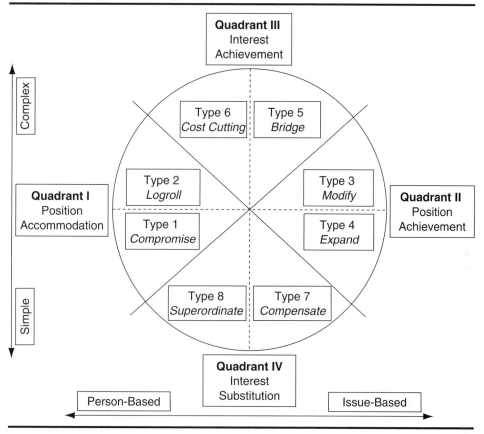

Source: P. J. D. Carnevale, 2006.

sizes, and types of property. The strategies at the bottom of the Agreement Circumplex are more suited to simple situations, while the strategies at the top are more appropriate for more complex situations.

4. **Person-based vs. Issue-based**

    Person-based strategies involve having negotiators making concessions and changing positions such that an agreement is reached through modifying positions on the issues under discussion. Issue-based strategies modify the issues under discussion to fit them to the negotiators needs and desires. Person-based strategies are on the left side of the Agreement Circumplex, while issue-based strategies are on the right side.

Carnevale presents eight different methods for achieving integrative agreements in the Circumplex, which we discuss next.[21] Each method refocuses the issues under discussion and requires progressively more information about the other side's true needs. Solutions move from simpler, distributive agreements to more complex and comprehensive, integrative ones, and there are several paths to finding joint gain.[22]

Each approach will be illustrated by the example of Samantha and Emma, two partners in a successful enterprise called Advanced Management Consulting, that employs eight other nonpartner consultants. The partners are deciding where to locate their new office; half their clients are downtown and half are in the suburbs. There are two possible locations that they are considering leasing. Samantha prefers the downtown location. It has less floor space but is a more prestigious address. While its offices are smaller, its location is equidistant from where both partners live. Emma prefers the location in the suburbs. It has more floor space and larger offices, and it is newer. It is also located closer to Emma's house, but farther from Samantha's.

Compromise (Position Accommodation)   A compromise solution that would not further the interests of either Samantha or Emma would be to stay in their current location and to maintain the status quo. Compromises are not considered to be a good integration strategy except for circumstances where parties are very entrenched and it is unlikely that a more comprehensive agreement is possible.

Logroll (Position Accommodation)   Successful logrolling requires the parties to find more than one issue in conflict and to have different priorities for those issues.[23] The parties then agree to trade off among these issues so that one party achieves a highly preferred outcome on the first issue and the other person achieves a highly preferred outcome on the second issue. If the parties do in fact have different preferences on different issues and each party gets his or her most preferred outcome on a high-priority issue, then each should receive more and the joint outcomes should be higher.[24] For instance, Advanced Management Consulting could lease the downtown location and give Emma the bigger office. Samantha would get her preferred location, which is more important to her, and Emma would receive better working space, which is more important to her.

Logrolling is frequently done by trial and error—as part of the process of experimenting with various packages of offers that will satisfy everyone involved. The parties must first establish which issues are at stake and then decide their individual priorities on these issues. If there are already at least two issues on the table, then any combination of two or more issues may be suitable for logrolling. Research suggests that negotiators reach better agreements as the number of issues being negotiated increases.[25] Negotiator satisfaction may be less when more issues are negotiated, however, because negotiators believe that they could have done better on one or more issues. (Negotiator cognition and satisfaction is discussed in more detail in Chapter 5.) If it appears initially that only one issue is at stake, the parties may need to engage in "unbundling" or "unlinking," which is the process of separating a single issue into two or more issues so that the logrolling may begin.[26] Additional issues of concern may also be generated through the brainstorming processes described later.

Modifying the Resource Pie (Position Achievement)   While expanding the resource pie may be attractive, it does not always work because the environment may not be plentiful enough. For instance, Advanced Management Consulting may not have enough demand for its services to have two offices. A related approach is to modify the resource pie. For instance, Advanced Management Consulting could start a new service and offer information technology (IT) consulting or Web-based marketing consulting in addition to its traditional business consulting. In this case the resource pie is modified in a way to support opening offices both downtown and in the suburbs.

Expand the Pie (Position Achievement)   Many negotiations begin with a shortage of resources, and it is not possible for both sides to satisfy their interests or obtain their objectives under the current conditions. A simple solution is to add resources—expand the pie—in such a way that both sides can achieve their objectives. For instance, Advanced Management Consulting could lease offices both downtown and in the suburbs to serve both sets of its clients. A projected expansion of the business could pay for both leases. In expanding the pie, one party requires no information about the other party except her interests; it is a simple way to solve resource shortage problems. In addition, the approach assumes that simply enlarging the resources will solve the problem. Thus, leasing both locations would be a very satisfactory solution if Samantha and Emma liked both locations and wanted to expand their business. However, expanding the pie would not be a satisfactory solution if their disagreement was based on other grounds—if, for example, they had different visions about the future of the firm—or if the whole firm had to gather for meetings frequently. In addition, to the extent that the negotiation increases the costs of a person or organization not directly involved in the negotiation (e.g., the employees in this example), the solution may be integrative for the negotiators but problematic for other stakeholders.[27]

Find a Bridge Solution (Interest Achievement)   When the parties are able to invent new options that meet all their respective needs they have created a bridge solution. For instance, Advanced Management Consulting could decide to expand the number of partners in the firm and lease a larger space downtown, with new office furniture for everyone and a prestigious street address.

Successful bridging requires a fundamental reformulation of the problem so that the parties are not discussing positions but, rather, they are disclosing sufficient information to discover their interests and needs and then inventing options that will satisfy those needs.[28] Bridging solutions do not always remedy all concerns. Emma may not enjoy the commute and Samantha may not be convinced about growing the firm, but both have agreed that working together is important to them, and they have worked to invent a solution that meets their most important needs. If negotiators fundamentally commit themselves to a win–win negotiation, bridging solutions are likely to be highly satisfactory to both sides.

Cut the Costs for Compliance (Interest Achievement)   Through cost cutting, one party achieves her objectives and the other's costs are minimized if she agrees to go along. For instance, Advanced Management Consulting could decide to lease in the suburbs and provide Samantha with a travel subsidy, a new company car, and a reserved parking space. In this case Emma gets her preferred location, while Samantha's costs for agreeing to the new office location are reduced.

Unlike nonspecific compensation, where the compensated party simply receives something for agreeing, cost cutting is designed to minimize the other party's costs for agreeing to a specific solution. The technique is more sophisticated than logrolling or nonspecific compensation because it requires a more intimate knowledge of the other party's real needs and preferences (the party's interests, what really matters to him, how his needs can be specifically met).

Nonspecific Compensation (Interest Substitution)   Another way to generate alternatives is to allow one person to obtain his objectives and compensate the other person for accommodating his interests. The compensation may be unrelated to the substantive negotiation, but the party who receives it nevertheless views it as adequate for agreeing to the other party's preferences. Such compensation is nonspecific because it is not directly related to the substantive issues being discussed. For instance, Advanced Management Consulting could decide to lease in the suburbs and give Samantha all new office furniture. In this case, Emma gets her preferred location, while Samantha receives new office furniture as nonspecific compensation for agreeing to the new office location.

For nonspecific compensation to work, the person doing the compensating needs to know what is valuable to the other person and how seriously she is inconvenienced (i.e., how much compensation is needed to make her feel satisfied). Emma might need to test several different offers (types and amounts of compensation) to find out how much it will take to satisfy Samantha. This discovery process can turn into a distributive bargaining situation, as Samantha may choose to set very high demands as the price for locating in the suburbs while Emma tries to minimize the compensation she will pay.

Superordination (Interest Substitution)   Superordination solutions occur when "the differences in interest that gave rise to the conflict are superseded or replaced by other interests."[29] For instance, after extensive discussion about the office location Samantha may discover that she would prefer to follow her dream of becoming an artist and become a silent partner in the business. At this point, the office location negotiation stops and Emma chooses how she would like to proceed in the new business model.

The successful pursuit of these eight strategies requires a meaningful exchange of information between the parties. The parties must either volunteer information or ask each other questions that will generate sufficient information to reveal win–win options. We present a series of refocusing questions that may reveal these possibilities in Table 3.1.[30]

Generating Alternative Solutions to the Problem as Given   In addition to the techniques mentioned earlier, there are several other approaches to generating alternative solutions. These approaches can be used by the negotiators themselves or by a number of other parties (constituencies, audiences, bystanders, etc.). Several of these approaches are commonly used in small groups. Groups are frequently better problem solvers than individuals, particularly because groups provide more perspectives and can invent a greater variety of ways to solve a problem. Groups should also adopt procedures for defining the problem, defining interests, and generating options, however, to prevent the group process from degenerating into a win–lose competition or a debating event.

Brainstorming   In brainstorming, small groups of people work to generate as many possible solutions to the problem as they can. Someone records the solutions, without comment, as they are identified. Participants are urged to be spontaneous, even impractical, and

TABLE 3.1 | Refocusing Questions to Reveal Win–Win Options

Expanding or Modifying the Pie

1. How can both parties get what they want?
2. Is there a resource shortage?
3. How can resources be expanded to meet the demands of both sides?

Logrolling

1. What issues are of higher and lower priority to me?
2. What issues are of higher and lower priority to the other negotiator?
3. Are there any issues of high priority to me that are of low priority for the other negotiator, and vice versa?
4. Can I "unbundle" an issue—that is, make one larger issue into two or more smaller ones that can then be logrolled?
5. What are things that would be inexpensive for me to give and valuable for the other negotiator to get that might be used in logrolling?

Nonspecific Compensation

1. What are the other negotiator's goals and values?
2. What could I do that would make the other negotiator happy and simultaneously allow me to get my way on the key issue?
3. What are things that would be inexpensive for me to give and valuable for the other negotiator to get that might be used as nonspecific compensation?

Cost Cutting

1. What risks and costs does my proposal create for the other negotiator?
2. What can I do to minimize the other negotiator's risks and costs so that he or she would be more willing to agree?

Bridging and Superordination

1. What are the other negotiator's real underlying interests and needs?
2. What are my own real underlying interests and needs?
3. What are the higher and lower priorities for each of us in our underlying interests and needs?
4. Can we invent a solution that meets the relative priorities, underlying interests, and needs of both negotiators?

NB: Compromise is not considered a win–win option.

not to censor anyone's ideas (including their own). Moreover, participants are required not to discuss or evaluate any solution when it is proposed so they do not stop the free flow of new ideas. The success of brainstorming depends on the amount of intellectual stimulation that occurs as different ideas are generated. The following rules should be observed:

1. *Avoid judging or evaluating solutions.* Creative solutions often come from ideas that initially seem wild and impractical, and criticism inhibits creative thinking. It is important to avoid judging solutions early, therefore, and no idea should be evaluated or eliminated until the group is finished generating options.

2. *Separate the people from the problem.* Group discussion and brainstorming processes are often constrained because the parties take ownership of preferred solutions and alternatives.[31] Because competitive negotiators assume an offensive posture toward the other party, they are unlikely to see the merits of a suggested alternative that

comes from that party or appears to favor that party's position. It is often not possible to attack the problem without attacking the person who owns it. For effective problem solving to occur, therefore, negotiators must concentrate on depersonalizing the problem and treating all possible solutions as equally viable, regardless of who initiated them.

3. *Be exhaustive in the brainstorming process.* Often the best ideas come after a meeting is over or the problem is solved. Sometimes this happens because the parties were not persistent enough. Research has shown that when brainstormers work at the process for a long time, the best ideas are most likely to surface during the latter part of the activity.

4. *Ask outsiders.* Often people who know nothing about the history of the negotiation, or even about the issues, can suggest options and possibilities that have not been considered. Outsiders can provide additional input to the list of alternatives, or they can help orchestrate the process and keep the parties on track.

Surveys   The disadvantage of brainstorming is that it does not solicit the ideas of those who are not present at the negotiation. A different approach is to distribute a written questionnaire to a large number of people, stating the problem and asking them to list all the possible solutions they can imagine. This process can be conducted in a short time. The liability, however, is that the parties cannot benefit from seeing and hearing each other's ideas, a key advantage of brainstorming.

Electronic Brainstorming   An innovative method for gathering ideas is to engage a professional facilitator and use electronic brainstorming.[32] The facilitator uses a series of questions to guide input from participants who type their responses anonymously into a computer that displays them to the group in aggregate. The facilitator may then ask additional probing questions. Electronic brainstorming may be especially useful for integrative negotiations that involve multiple parties (see Chapter 10) or during preparation for integrative negotiations when there are disparate views within one's team (see Chapter 4 on preparation).

Section Summary

Our discussion of the two basic approaches to generating alternative solutions—generating options to the problem as given and generating options by redefining the problem—may give the impression that if negotiators simply invent enough different options, they will find a solution to solve their problem rather easily. Although identifying options sometimes leads to a solution, solutions are usually attained through hard work and pursuit of several related processes: information exchange, focusing on interests rather than positions, and firm flexibility.[33] Information exchange allows parties to maximize the amount of information available. Focusing on interests allows parties to move beyond opening positions and demands to determine what the parties really want—what needs truly must be satisfied. Finally, firm flexibility allows parties to be firm with regard to what they want to achieve (i.e., interests) while remaining flexible on the means by which they achieve it. Firm flexibility recognizes that negotiators have one or two fundamental interests or principles, although a wide variety of positions, possible solutions, or secondary issues may get drawn into the negotiations.

Thus, among the many viable alternatives that will satisfy a negotiator, the important ones directly address the top priorities. Negotiators need to be able to signal to the other side the positions on which they are firm and the positions on which they are willing to be flexible.

Evaluate and Select Alternatives

The fourth stage in the integrative negotiation process is to evaluate the alternatives generated during the previous phase and to select the best ones to implement. When the challenge is a reasonably simple one, the evaluation and selection steps may be effectively combined into a single step. For those uncomfortable with the integrative process, though, we suggest a close adherence to a series of distinct steps: definitions and standards, alternatives, evaluation, and selection. Following these distinct steps is also a good idea for those managing complex problems or a large number of alternative options. Negotiators will need to weigh or rank-order each option against clear criteria. If no option or set of options appears suitable and acceptable, this is a strong indication that the problem was not clearly defined *(return to definitions),* or that the standards developed earlier are not reasonable, relevant, and/or realistic *(return to standards).* Finally, the parties will need to engage in some form of decision-making process in which they debate the relative merits of each negotiator's preferred options and come to agreement on the best options. The following guidelines should be used in evaluating options and reaching a consensus.[34]

Narrow the Range of Solution Options   Examine the list of options generated and focus on those that one or more negotiators strongly support. This approach is more positive than allowing people to focus on negative, unacceptable criteria and options. Solutions that are not strongly advocated by at least one negotiator should be eliminated at this time.

Evaluate Solutions on the Basis of Quality, Standards, and Acceptability   Solutions should be judged on two major criteria: how good they are and how acceptable they will be to those who have to implement them. To the degree that parties can support their arguments with statements of hard fact, logical deduction, and appeals to rational criteria, their arguments will be more compelling in obtaining the support of others. Fisher, Ury, and Patton suggest that the parties appeal to *objective standards* for making decisions.[35] Thus, the parties should search for precedents, industry standards, arbitration decisions, or other objectively fair outcomes and processes that can be used as benchmarks for legitimizing the fairness of the current settlement. These criteria may be different from what the negotiators judge to be most rational or the best solution. Negotiators have to be prepared to make trade-offs to ensure that the criteria of both quality and acceptability are met.

Agree to the Criteria in Advance of Evaluating Options   Negotiators should agree to the criteria for evaluating potential integrative solutions early in the process.[36] Negotiators can use these criteria when they have to narrow the choice of options to a single alternative— for example, one candidate for a new job—or to select the option most likely to succeed. If the parties first debate criteria and determine which ones are most important, they will be able to decide on criteria independent of the consideration of any particular candidate or option. Then, when they consider the individual candidates or options, they will pick the best one based on these criteria, not on the individual preferences of one side or the other. If the parties agree, they may revise their criteria later to improve their choice, but they should do so only with the agreement of all negotiators. It is a good idea to check criteria periodically and determine whether each negotiator places the same priority on them as before.

Be Willing to Justify Personal Preferences   People often find it hard to explain why they like what they like or dislike what they dislike. When asked "Why do you like that?" the reply is often, "I don't know, I just do." Moreover, negotiators gain little by pressing opponents to justify themselves—doing so usually just makes them angry and defensive; they may feel that a simple statement of preference is not viewed as sufficient. For example, if the topic under negotiation is what to have for dinner, and one party states that she hates clam chowder, no amount of persuasive effort is likely to induce her to eat clam chowder. Yet personal preferences often have a deep-seated rationale—recall our discussion of how interests, values, and needs underlie positions. Inquiries about the other party's preferences may be an effort to probe behind a position and identify underlying interests and needs. If the other party responds defensively to a why question, the negotiator should explain that the intent is to probe for possible underlying interests that might facilitate a collaborative settlement rather than to challenge one's perspective.

Be Alert to the Influence of Intangibles in Selecting Options   One party may favor an option because it helps satisfy an intangible—gaining recognition, looking strong or tough to a constituency, feeling like a winner, and so on. Intangibles or principles can serve as strong interests for a negotiator. Intangibles can lead the negotiator to fight harder to attain a particular solution if that option satisfies both tangible and intangible needs. Some parties may be uncomfortable with discussing intangibles, or even be unaware of their nature and power in the negotiation process. It is useful to help the other party identify those intangibles and make them an open part of the evaluation process. The other party is likely to prefer options that satisfy those intangibles, and to the degree that you can accept them, agreeing to those options may be important concessions.

Use Subgroups to Evaluate Complex Options   Small groups may be particularly helpful when several complex options must be considered or when many people will be affected by the solution. For example, in a recent university collective agreement negotiation a team of management and faculty members formed a subgroup to examine numerous issues around benefits to be included in the next contract. Groups of six to eight people, composed of representatives from each faction, side, or subgroup, are able to work more effectively than large groups.

Take Time Out to Cool Off   Even though the parties may have completed the hardest part of the process—generating a list of viable options—they may become upset if communication breaks down, they feel their preferences are not being acknowledged, or the other side pushes too hard for a particular option. If the parties become angry, they should take a break. They should make their dissatisfaction known and openly discuss the reasons for it. The parties should feel that they are back on an even emotional keel before continuing to evaluate options. Finally, they should work as hard as possible to keep discussions on the specifics of the proposals, not on the people advocating them. The parties should depersonalize the discussion as much as possible so that the options for settlement are not associated with the people who advocated them.

Explore Different Ways to Logroll   Earlier we discussed a variety of ways to invent options. The strategy of logrolling is effective not only in inventing options but also as a mechanism to combine options into negotiated packages. Neale and Bazerman identify a variety of approaches in addition to simply combining several issues into a package.[37] Three of these relate to the matters of outcome, probabilities, and timing—in other words, *what* is to happen, the *likelihood* of it happening, and *when* it happens.

1. *Explore Differences in Risk Preference*   People have different tolerances for risk, and it may be possible to create a package that recognizes differences in risk preferences.[38] For instance, suppose two entrepreneurs are discussing a future business venture. One has little to risk at the moment and everything to gain in the future; the other has a lot on the line now that he does not want to risk losing if the future is bad. If the entrepreneurs simply agree to split profits in the future, the one with a large amount of current risk may feel vulnerable. Logrolling around these interests can create a solution that protects one entrepreneur's current investment first while providing long-term profits for the other entrepreneur as well.

2. *Explore Differences in Expectations*   As with differences in risk, differences in expectations about the likelihood of future events can permit the parties to invent a solution that addresses the needs of both. For example, the entrepreneur with a lot to lose now may also have pessimistic expectations about the future of the joint venture, whereas the entrepreneur with little to lose may be more optimistic about it. The optimist may thus be willing to gamble more on the future profitability and payout, whereas the pessimist may be willing to settle for a smaller but more assured payment. It is also possible to use contingent contracts to manage different expectations about the future.[39] Contingent contracts adjust as circumstances unfold. For instance, one can include changing oil prices into a contract and adjust delivery fees based on quarterly oil prices.

3. *Explore Differences in Time Preferences*   Negotiators may have different time preferences—one may be concerned about meeting short-term needs while the other may be interested in the long-term rewards of their relationship.[40] Parties with short-term interests will need immediate gratification, whereas parties who look for long-term rewards may be willing to make immediate sacrifices to ensure a future payoff. Parties with different time preferences can invent solutions that address both their interests.

Keep Decisions Tentative and Conditional Until All Aspects of the Final Proposal Are Complete   Even though a clear consensus may emerge about the solution option(s) that will be selected, the parties should talk about the solution in conditional terms—a sort of *soft bundling*. Maintaining a tentative tone allows negotiators to suggest changes or revise the final package throughout this stage. Ideally, the integrative negotiation process should be open and flexible. Points agreed upon in earlier discussions are not firm until the entire package is determined. Parties should feel they are able to reopen an earlier option if circumstances in the discussion have changed; nothing should be considered final until everything is final.

Minimize Formality and Record Keeping until Final Agreements Are Closed   Strong integrative negotiators do not want to lock themselves into specific language or written agreements until they are close to an agreement. They want to make sure they will not be firmly held to any comments recorded in notes or transcripts. In general, the fewer the written records during the solution-generating phase, the better. In contrast, when the parties are close to agreement, one side should write down the terms of the agreement. This document may then be used as a single text, to be passed from party to party as often as necessary until all sides agree to the phrasing and wording of their agreement.[41]

We strongly urge groups to avoid the apparent expediency of voting on final agreements, and encourage negotiations to continue until a consensus is reached. While voting closes the discussion, it can also create disenfranchisement of the losing party and make it more likely that "losers" will be less committed than "winners" to the implementation of the negotiated outcome.

Factors That Facilitate Successful Integrative Negotiation

We have stressed that successful integrative negotiation can occur if the parties are predisposed to finding a mutually acceptable joint solution. Many other factors contribute to a predisposition toward problem solving and a willingness to work together to find the best solution. These factors are also the preconditions necessary for more successful integrative negotiations. In this section, we will review in greater detail seven factors: (1) the presence of a common goal, (2) faith in one's own problem-solving ability, (3) a belief in the validity of the other party's position, (4) the motivation and commitment to work together, (5) trust, (6) clear and accurate communication, and (7) an understanding of the dynamics of integrative negotiation.

Some Common Objective or Goal

When the parties believe they are likely to benefit more from working together than from competing or working separately, the situation offers greater potential for successful integrative negotiation. Three types of goals—common, shared, and joint—may facilitate the development of integrative agreements.

A *common goal* is one that all parties share equally, each one benefiting in a way that would not be possible if they did not work together. A town government and an industrial manufacturing plant may debate the amount of taxes the plant owes, but they are more likely to work together if the common goal is to keep the plant open and employ half the town's workforce.

A *shared goal* is one that both parties work toward but that benefits each party differently. For example, partners can work together in a business but not divide the profits equally. One may receive a larger share of the profit because he or she contributed more experience or capital investment. Inherent in the idea of a shared goal is that parties will work together to achieve some output that will be divided among them. The same result can also come from cost cutting, by which the parties can earn the same outcome as before by working together, but with less effort, expense, or risk. This is often described as an "expandable pie" in contrast to a "fixed pie" (see Chapter 5).

A *joint goal* is one that involves individuals with different personal goals agreeing to combine them in a collective effort. For example, people joining a political campaign can have different goals: one wants to satisfy personal ambition to hold public office, another wants to serve the community, and yet another wants to benefit from policies that will be implemented under the new administration. All will unite around the joint goal of helping the new administration get elected.

The key element of an integrative negotiation situation is the belief that all sides can benefit. Whether the sides attain the same outcome or different outcomes, all sides must believe that they will be better off by working in cooperation than by working independently or competing.

Faith in One's Problem-Solving Ability

Parties who believe they can work together are more likely to be able to do so. Those who do not share this belief in themselves and others are less willing to invest the time and energy in the potential payoffs of a collaborative relationship, and they are more likely to assume a contending or accommodating approach to negotiation. If a negotiator has expertise in the focal problem area this strengthens her understanding of the problem's complexity, nuances, and possible solutions. Neale and Northcraft demonstrated in a real estate problem that expert negotiators—corporate real estate executives—achieved significantly better integrative agreements than amateurs did.[42] Expertise increases both the negotiator's knowledge base and his or her self-confidence, both of which are necessary to approach the problem at hand with an open mind. Similarly, direct experience in negotiation increases the negotiator's sophistication in understanding the bargaining process and approaching it more creatively.[43] Finally, there is also evidence that knowledge of integrative tactics leads to an increase in integrative behavior.[44] Taken together, these results suggest that a faith in one's ability to negotiate integratively is positively related to successful integrative negotiations.

A Belief in the Validity of One's
Own Position and the Other's Perspective

In distributive bargaining, negotiators invest time and energy inflating and justifying the value of their own point of view and debunking the value and importance of the other's perspective. In contrast, integrative negotiation requires negotiators to accept both their own and the other's attitudes, interests, and desires as valid.[45] First, one must believe in the validity of your own perspective—that what you believe is worth fighting for and should not be compromised. Kemp and Smith found that negotiators who were firmer about insisting that their own point of view become incorporated into the group solution achieved more integrative agreements than those who were less firm. But one must also accept the validity of the other party's perspective.[46] If one challenges the other party's views, he or she may become angry, defensive, and unproductive in the problem-solving process. The purpose of integrative negotiation is not to question or challenge the other's viewpoint, but to incorporate it into the definition of the problem and to attend to it as the parties search for mutually acceptable alternatives. In addition, the other party's views should be valued no less or more than the negotiator's own position and viewpoint. Kemp and Smith also found that parties who were able to take the perspective of the other appeared to make better agreements than those who were less able to do so. Believing in the validity of the other negotiator's perspective does not mean empathizing with the other party. In fact, there is evidence that negotiators with high empathy for the other party may increase the size of the joint outcomes but receive less of the larger pie than less empathic negotiators.[47]

The Motivation and Commitment to Work Together

For integrative negotiation to succeed, the parties must be motivated to collaborate rather than to compete. They need to be committed to reaching a goal that benefits both of them rather than to pursuing only their own ends. They should adopt interpersonal styles that are more congenial than combative, more open and trusting than evasive and defensive, more flexible (but firm) than stubborn (but yielding). Specifically, they must be willing to make their own needs explicit, to identify similarities, and to recognize and accept differences. They must also tolerate uncertainties and unravel inconsistencies.

Motivation and commitment to problem solving can be enhanced in several ways:

1. Negotiators can learn that they share a common fate. To quote Ben Franklin, "If we do not hang together, we will surely hang separately."

2. Negotiators can demonstrate to each other that there is more to be gained by working together (to increase the payoffs or reduce the costs) than by working separately. The parties can emphasize that they may have to work together after the negotiations are over and will continue to benefit from the relationship they have created. In spite of these efforts, competitive and contentious behavior may persist.

3. Negotiators can engage in commitments to each other before the negotiations begin; such commitments have been called *presettlement settlements*[48] and are distinguished by three major characteristics:

   a. The settlement results in a firm, legally binding written agreement between the parties (it is more than a gentlemen's agreement).

   b. The settlement occurs in advance of the parties undertaking full-scale negotiations, but the parties intend that the agreement will be replaced by a more clearly delineated long-term agreement that is to be negotiated.

   c. The settlement resolves only a subset of the issues on which the parties disagree and may simply establish a framework within which the more comprehensive agreement can be defined and delineated.

4. Negotiators could create an umbrella agreement that provides a framework for future discussions. Stefanos Mouzas suggests that umbrella agreements manage three negotiation challenges:[49]

   a. Umbrella agreements allow flexibility when the negotiating relationship between the parties is evolving.

b. Umbrella agreements provide flexibility for claiming value when the actual future gains are not known at the time of the negotiation.

c. Umbrella agreements can be used when all the issues and contingencies have yet to be identified but the parties know they wish to work together.

Trust

Although there is no guarantee that trust will lead to collaboration, there is plenty of evidence to suggest that mistrust inhibits collaboration. People who are interdependent but do not trust each other will act tentatively or defensively. Defensiveness means that they will not accept information at face value but instead will look for hidden, deceptive meanings. When people are defensive, they withdraw and withhold information. Defensive people also attack the other party's statements and position, seeking to defeat their position rather than to work together. Either of these responses is likely to make the negotiator hesitant, cautious, and distrustful of the other, undermining the negotiation process.[50]

Deepak Malhotra and Mac Bazerman suggest three tactics to elicit information from the other negotiator when he or she mistrusts *you:*[51]

1. *Share information and encourage reciprocity.* One approach is to suggest to the other negotiator that you are willing to describe your needs and interests if he agrees to share his as well. Malhotra and Bazerman caution to ensure there is agreement about the explicit ground rules before proceeding, and to proceed incrementally to be sure.

2. *Negotiate multiple issues simultaneously.* Negotiating several offers simultaneously allows negotiators to identify relative priorities of the other negotiator, as well as obtain some information about his interests. Malhotra and Bazerman suggest watching for issues where the other party is very engaged, emotional, and attempting to control the discussion in order to infer high priority issues.

3. *Make multiple offers at the same time.* A third approach to obtaining information when the other party is distrusting is to make two or three offers at the same time. These offers should be the same value to you. The way that the other negotiator responds to these offers should provide you with information about his relative interests.

In summary, integrative negotiation is easier when the parties trust each other. When there is distrust, negotiating will be more challenging but the three tactics we presented here will help manage this challenge.

Generating trust is a complex, uncertain process; it depends in part on how the parties behave and in part on the parties' personal characteristics. When people trust each other, they are more likely to share information and to communicate accurately their needs, positions, and the facts of the situation.[52] In contrast, when people do not trust each other, they are more likely to engage in positional bargaining, use threats, and commit themselves to tough positions.[53] As with defensiveness, mistrust is likely to be reciprocated and to lead to unproductive negotiations. To develop trust effectively, each negotiator must believe that both she and the other party choose to behave in a cooperative manner; moreover, each must believe that this behavior is a signal of the other's honesty, openness, and a similar mutual commitment to a joint solution.

Clear and Accurate Communication

Another precondition for high-quality integrative negotiation is clear and accurate communication. First, negotiators must be willing to share information about themselves.[54] They must be willing to reveal what they want and, more important, must be willing to state why they want it in specific, concrete terms, avoiding generalities and ambiguities. Second, the other negotiators must understand the communication. At a minimum, they must understand the meaning they each attach to their statements; hopefully, the parties each interpret the basic facts in the same way, but if they don't then they should reconcile them. Other members of the negotiating team can frequently identify ambiguities and breakdowns in communication. If someone on a bargaining team makes a confusing statement, others can address it and try to clarify it. When one person on the other side does not grasp a difficult point, someone else from the same side will often be able to find the words or illustrations to bring out the meaning. Mutual understanding is the responsibility of both sides. The communicator must be willing to test whether the other side has received the message that was intended. Similarly, the listener must engage in active listening, testing to make sure that what he or she received and understood is the message that the sender intended.

Metaphors may also play an important role in communicating during negotiation. Metaphors may be defined as "talking about one thing in terms of another"[55] and are useful when direct communication is difficult or threatening. Thomas Smith suggests that metaphors may play two important roles in negotiation: (1) metaphors help negotiators understand *why* the other party is saying what they said, and (2) metaphors may help identify areas for mutual gain because they provide insight into the other party's needs and motives.[56]

When there are strong negative feelings or when one or more parties are inclined to dominate, negotiators may create formal, structured procedures for communication. Under these circumstances, negotiators should follow a procedure that gives everyone a chance to speak. For example, most rules for debates limit statements to five minutes, and similar rules are often adopted in contentious open meetings or public hearings. In addition, the parties may agree to follow a previously agreed-on agenda so that everyone can be heard and their contributions noted.

An Understanding of the Dynamics of Integrative Negotiation

Negotiators frequently assume that the distributive bargaining process is the only way to approach negotiations. Several studies indicate that training in integrative negotiation enhances the ability of the parties to negotiate integratively. For example, Weingart, Hyder, and Prietula demonstrated that training negotiators in integrative tactics—particularly in how to exchange information about priorities across issues and preferences within issues, and how to set high goals—significantly enhanced the frequency of integrative behaviors and led the parties to achieve higher joint outcomes.[57] This study also found that using distributive tactics, such as strongly trying to persuade the other of the validity of one's own views, was negatively related to joint outcomes. In addition, Lowenstein, Thompson, Gentner, and their colleagues have found that analogical training appears to be an especially powerful way to learn about integrative negotiation.[58] Analogical learning involves the direct comparison of different negotiation examples to identify and understand the underlying principles and structure of the negotiation.

Section Summary

We identified seven fundamental preconditions for successful integrative negotiation: some form of shared or common goals, faith in one's ability to solve problems, a belief in the validity and importance of the other's position, the motivation and commitment to work together, trust in the opposing negotiator, the ability to accurately exchange information in spite of conflict conditions, and an understanding of the dynamics of integrative negotiation. If the parties are not able to meet these preconditions successfully, they will need to resolve challenges in these areas as the integrative negotiation evolves.

Chapter Summary

In this chapter, we have reviewed the strategy and tactics of integrative negotiation. The fundamental structure of integrative negotiation is one within which the parties are able to define goals that allow both sides to achieve their objectives. Integrative negotiation is the process of defining these goals and engaging in a process that permits both parties to maximize their objectives.

The chapter began with an overview of the integrative negotiation process. A high level of concern for both sides achieving their own objectives propels a collaborative, problem-solving approach. Negotiators frequently fail at integrative negotiation because they fail to perceive the integrative potential of the negotiating situation. Successful integrative negotiation requires several processes. First, the parties must create a free flow of information and an open exchange of ideas. Second, they must understand each other's true needs and objectives. Third, they must focus on their similarities, emphasizing their commonalities rather than their differences. Finally, they must engage in a search for solutions that meet the goals of both sides. This is a very different set of processes from those in distributive bargaining, described in Chapter 2. The four key steps in the integrative negotiation process are identifying and defining the problem, identifying interests and needs, generating alternative solutions, and evaluating and selecting alternatives. For each of these steps, we discussed techniques and tactics to make the process successful.

We then discussed various factors that facilitate successful integrative negotiation. First, the process will be greatly facilitated by some form of common goal or objective. This goal may be one that the parties both want to achieve, one they want to share, or one they could not possibly attain unless they worked together. Second, they must have faith in their problem-solving ability. Third, the parties must be willing to believe that the other's needs are valid. Fourth, they must share a motivation and commitment to work together, to make their relationship a productive one. Fifth, they must be able to trust each other and to work hard to establish and maintain that trust. Sixth, there must be clear and accurate communication about what each one wants and an effort to understand the other's needs. Finally, there must be an understanding of the dynamics of integrative negotiations.

In spite of all of these suggestions, integrative negotiation is not easy—especially for parties who are locked in conflict, defensiveness, and a hard-line position. Only by working to create the necessary conditions for integrative negotiation can the process unfold successfully.

Endnotes

[1] Our descriptions draw heavily on the writings of several experts who have studied the integrative process in great detail, and we will note recent research findings that have affirmed the validity of particular strategies and tactics. See Follett, 1940, formalized by Walton and McKersie, 1965; Fisher, Ury, and Patton, 1991; Lax and Sebenius, 1986; Carnevale and Pruitt, 1992; Filley, 1975; and Pruitt, 1981, 1983, among numerous others. We also draw extensively on Pruitt and Carnevale, 1993.

[2] Butler, 1999; Pruit, 1981; Thompson, 1991.

[3] Butler, 1999; Kemp and Smith, 1994.

[4] Pinkley, 1995.

[5] Ibid., p. 409.

[6] Barki and Hartwick, 2004.

[7] Kemp and Smith, 1994.

[8] Olekalns, Smith, and Walsh, 1996.

[9] Kelley, 1966.

[10] Fisher, Ury, and Patton, 1991; Pruitt and Rubin, 1986.

[11] Neale and Bazerman, 1991, p. 23.

[12] Fisher, Ury, and Patton, 1991.

[13] Ibid., p. 40; originally told by Follett, 1940.

[14] Lax and Sebenius, 1986.

[15] See Chapter 5 of Sheppard, Lewicki, and Minton, 1992, for a more complete discussion of the role of "voice" in organizations.

[16] Lax and Sebenius, 1986.

[17] Clyman and Tripp, 2000.

[18] Holaday, 2002; Nierenberg, 1976.

[19] Provis, 1996.

[20] Ibid.

[21] For example, see Neale and Bazerman, 1991; Pruitt, 1981, 1983; Pruitt and Carnevale, 1993; and Pruitt and Lewis, 1975.

[22] Olekalns, 2002.

[23] Tajima and Fraser, 2001.

[24] Moran and Ritov, 2002.

[25] Naquin, 2002.

[26] Lax and Sebenius, 1986; Pruitt, 1981.

[27] Gillespie and Bazerman, 1997.

[28] Butler, 1996.

[29] Carnevale, 2006, p. 426.

[30] Pruitt and Carnevale, 1993; Pruitt and Rubin, 1986.

[31] Filley, 1975; Fisher, Ury, and Patton, 1991; Walton and McKersie, 1965.

[32] Gallupe and Cooper, 1993; Dennis and Reinicke, 2004.

[33] Fisher, Ury, and Patton, 1991; Pruitt, 1983.

[34] For more detailed discussion of this step see Filley, 1975; Pruitt and Carnevale, 1993; Shea, 1983; and Walton and McKersie, 1965.

[35] Fisher, Ury, and Patton, 1991.

[36] Ibid.

[37] Neale and Bazerman, 1991.

[38] Lax and Sebenius, 2002.

[39] Ibid.; Bazerman and Gillespie, 1999.

[40] Lax and Sebenius, 2002.

[41] Fisher, Ury, and Patton, 1991.

[42] Neale and Northcraft, 1986.

[43] Thompson, 1990b.

[44] Weingart, Prietula, Hyder, and Genovese, 1999.

[45] Fisher, Ury, and Patton, 1991.

[46] Kemp and Smith, 1994.

[47] Foo, Elfenbein, Tan, and Aik, 2004; Nelson and Wheeler, 2004.

[48] Gillespie and Bazerman, 1998.

[49] Mouzas, 2006.

[50] Gibb, 1961.

[51] Malhotra and Bazerman, 2007.

[52] Butler, 1999; Tenbrunsel, 1999.

[53] Kimmel, Pruitt, Magenau, Konar-Goldband, and Carnevale, 1980.

[54] Neale and Bazerman, 1991.

[55] Smith, 2005, p. 346.

[56] Ibid.

[57] Weingart, Hyder, and Prietula, 1996.

[58] See Gentner, Loewenstein, and Thompson, 2003; Loewenstein and Thompson, 2000; Loewenstein, Thompson, and Gentner, 1999, 2003; Nadler, Thompson, and Van Boven, 2003; and Thompson, Gentner, and Loewenstein, 2000.

Negotiation: Strategy and Planning

Objectives

1. Understand the importance of setting goals for an upcoming negotiation.
2. Explore the major elements of a negotiation strategy and a process for selecting a strategy.
3. Consider how most negotiations evolve through understandable stages and phases.
4. Gain a comprehensive set of tools for effectively planning for an upcoming negotiation.

In this chapter, we discuss what negotiators should do before opening negotiations. Effective strategy and planning are the most critical precursors for achieving negotiation objectives. With effective planning and target setting, most negotiators can achieve their objectives; without them, results occur more by chance than by negotiator effort.

Our discussion of strategy and planning begins by exploring the broad process of strategy development, starting with defining the negotiator's goals and objectives. We then move to developing a strategy to address the issues and achieve one's goals. Finally, we address the typical stages and phases of an evolving negotiation and how different issues and goals will affect the planning process.

Goals—The Focus That Drives a Negotiation Strategy

The first step in developing and executing a negotiation strategy is to determine one's goals. Negotiators must anticipate what goals they want to achieve in a negotiation and focus on how to achieve those goals. As noted in Chapter 1, negotiators must consider substantive goals (e.g., money or a specific outcome), intangible goals (e.g., winning, beating the other party, or getting a settlement at any cost), and procedural goals (e.g., shaping the agenda or simply having a voice at the table). Effective preparation requires a thorough, thoughtful approach to these goals; negotiators should specify their goals and objectives clearly. This includes listing all goals they wish to achieve in the negotiation, determining the priority among these goals, identifying potential multigoal packages, and evaluating possible trade-offs among multiple goals.

Direct Effects of Goals on Choice of Strategy

Four aspects of how goals affect negotiation are important to understand:

1. Wishes are not goals, especially in negotiation. Wishes may be related to interests or needs that motivate goals (see Chapter 3), but they are not goals themselves. A wish is a fantasy, a hope that something might happen; a goal is a specific, focused target that one can realistically plan to achieve.

2. Goals are often linked to the other party's goals. The linkage between the two parties' goals defines an issue to be settled (see the discussion of issues later in this chapter) and is often the source of conflict. My goal is to get a car cheaply, and the dealer's goal is to sell it at the highest possible price (and profit); thus, the "issue" is the price I will pay for the car. If I could achieve my goal by myself, without the other party, I probably wouldn't need to negotiate.

3. There are boundaries or limits to what goals can be (see the discussion of walkaways and alternatives later in this chapter). If what we want exceeds these limits (i.e., what the other party is capable of or willing to give), we must either change our goals or end the negotiation. Goals must be attainable. If my goal—"to buy this car at a cheap price"—isn't possible because the dealer won't sell the car "cheaply" (notice that "cheaply" is an ambiguous goal at this point), I'm going to either have to change my goal or find another car to buy (perhaps from a different dealer).

4. Effective goals must be concrete, specific, and measurable. The less concrete and measurable our goals are, the harder it is to *(a)* communicate to the other party what we want, *(b)* understand what the other party wants, and *(c)* determine whether an offer on the table satisfies our goals. "To get a car cheaply" or "to agree on a price so that the loan payment does not use all of my paycheck" is not a very clear goal. What do I mean by "use up my paycheck"? Is this every week's paycheck or only one check a month? Do I want the payment to be just under 100 percent of the paycheck, or about 50 percent, or perhaps even 25 percent? Today's paycheck only, or the paychecks expected over the life of the loan? Is this payment the largest amount I think I can possibly pay? Is it the payment that could be paid with little or no inconvenience? Or is it the payment calculated after reading that one shouldn't pay more than 15 percent of one's monthly salary for a car payment? The negotiator has to determine exactly how big a payment can comfortably come out of his or her paycheck at present interest rates and add to that what is available for a down payment in order to be able to negotiate exactly what he or she is willing to pay a month. But as you can see, even this figure is not totally clear.

Goals can also be intangible or procedural. In the car purchase example, intangible goals might include enhancing reputation among one's friends by owning and driving a slick sports car; maintaining an image as a shrewd, pennywise negotiator; or paying any price to ensure convenient, reliable transportation. In other negotiations, intangible goals might include maintaining a reputation as a tough but principled negotiator, establishing a precedent for future negotiations, or conducting the negotiations in a manner that is fair to all sides and assures each party fair treatment. (Refer back to Chapter 1 for further discussion of intangible goals.)

Which of these many criteria should we use? The answer depends on *you:* your specific objectives and your priorities among multiple objectives. Trade-offs will be inevitable and can cloud your perspective while negotiating, so you have to clearly remember what you wanted to achieve when the negotiation started.

Indirect Effects of Goals on Choice of Strategy

Simple and direct goals can often be attained in a single negotiation session and with a simple negotiating strategy. As a result, we often limit our view on the impact of pursuing short-term goals, particularly when the impact is long term. This short-term thinking affects our choice of strategy; in developing and framing our goals, we may ignore the present or future relationship with the other party in favor of a simplistic concern for achieving only the substantive outcome.

Other negotiation goals—particularly ones that are more difficult or require a substantial change in the other party's attitude—may require you to develop a long-range plan for goal attainment. In these cases, progress will be made incrementally, and it may depend on establishing a strong relationship with the other party. Examples here include a substantial increase in one's line of credit with a financial institution or the establishment of a privileged status with an important trading partner. Such relationship-oriented goals should motivate the negotiator toward a strategy choice in which the relationship with the other party is valued as much as (or even more than) the substantive outcome. Thus, relational goals tend to support the choice of a collaborative or integrative strategy (refer back to the dual concerns model described in Chapter 1).

Strategy—The Overall Plan to Achieve One's Goals

After negotiators articulate goals, they move to the second element in the sequence: selecting and developing a strategy. Experts on business strategy define *strategy* as "the pattern or plan that integrates an organization's major targets, policies, and action sequences into a cohesive whole."[1] Applied to negotiations, strategy refers to the overall plan to accomplish one's goals in a negotiation and the action sequences that will lead to the accomplishment of those goals.

Strategy versus Tactics

How are strategy and tactics related? Although the line between strategy and tactics may seem fuzzy, one major difference is that of scale, perspective, or immediacy.[2] Tactics are short-term, adaptive moves designed to enact or pursue broad (or higher-level) strategies, which in turn provide stability, continuity, and direction for tactical behaviors. For example, your negotiation strategy might be integrative, designed to build and maintain a productive relationship with the other party while using a joint problem-solving approach to the issues. In pursuing this strategy, appropriate tactics include describing your interests, using open-ended questions and active listening to understand the others' interests, and inventing options for mutual gain. Tactics are subordinate to strategy; they are structured, directed, and driven by strategic considerations.

Unilateral versus Bilateral Approaches to Strategy

A unilateral choice is one that is made without the active involvement of the other party. Unilaterally pursued strategies are almost completely one-sided and intentionally ignorant of any information about the other negotiator. However, unilateral strategies can be problematic for exactly this reason. Any reasonable strategy should also include processes for gaining information about the other party, and incorporating that information into the choice of a negotiation strategy is always useful. Therefore, while we are going to initially describe strategies as unilateral in nature, they should clearly evolve into ones that fully consider the impact of the other's strategy on one's own.

The Dual Concerns Model as a Vehicle for Describing Negotiation Strategies

In Chapter 1, we used the dual concerns model to describe the basic orientation that people take toward conflict.[3] This model proposes that individuals in conflict have two levels of related concerns: a level of concern for their own outcomes, and a level of concern for the other's outcomes (refer back to Figure 1.3). Savage, Blair, and Sorenson propose a similar model for the choice of a negotiation strategy.[4] According to this model, a negotiator's unilateral choice of strategy is reflected in the answers to two simple questions: (1) How much concern does the actor have for achieving the substantive outcomes at stake in this negotiation (substantive goals)? (2) How much concern does the negotiator have for the current and future quality of the relationship with the other party (relationship goals)? The answers to these questions result in the mix of alternative strategies presented in Figure 4.1.

Alternative Situational Strategies   The power of this model lies in requiring the negotiator to determine the relative importance and priority of the two dimensions in the desired settlement. As Figure 4.1 shows, answers to these two questions suggest at least four types of initial strategies for negotiators: avoidance, accommodation, competition, and collaboration. A strong interest in achieving only substantive outcomes—getting this deal,

FIGURE 4.1 | The Dual Concerns Model

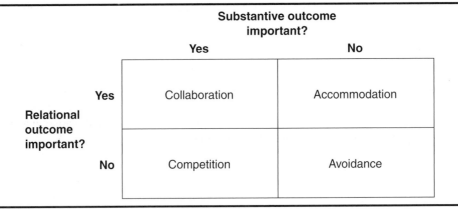

Source: *Academy of Management Executive* by Walter B. Newsom, Copyright 1989 by ACAD OF MGMT. Reproduced with permission of ACAD OF MGMT in the format Textbook via Copyright Clearance Center.

winning this negotiation, with little or no regard for the effect on the relationship or on subsequent exchanges with the other party—tends to support a competitive (distributive) strategy. A strong interest in achieving only the relationship goals—building, preserving, or enhancing a good relationship with the other party—suggests an accommodation strategy. If both substance and relationship are important, the negotiator should pursue a collaborative (integrative) strategy. Finally, if achieving neither substantive outcomes nor an enhanced relationship is important, the party might be best served by avoiding negotiation. Each of these different strategic approaches also has different implications for negotiation planning and preparation.[5] We discuss both nonengagement and engagement strategies next.

The Nonengagement Strategy: Avoidance   Avoidance may serve a number of strategic negotiation purposes. In fact, there are many reasons negotiators might choose not to negotiate (similar to the reasons for conflict avoidance discussed in Chapter 1):

- If one is able to meet one's needs without negotiating at all, it may make sense to use an avoidance strategy.

- It simply may not be worth the time and effort to negotiate (although there are sometimes reasons to negotiate in such situations; see the section on accommodation below).

- The decision to negotiate is closely related to the desirability of available alternatives— the outcomes that can be achieved if negotiations don't work out.

A negotiator with very strong alternatives has considerable power because he or she doesn't need this negotiation to succeed in order to achieve a satisfactory outcome. Having weak alternatives puts negotiators at a disadvantage. The presence of an alternative can influence the decision about whether to avoid negotiation in two ways. First, the negotiator with a strong alternative may wish to avoid negotiation strictly on efficiency grounds—it is simply quicker and easier to take the alternative than to get involved in a negotiation. But having a weak alternative may also suggest avoiding negotiation—once negotiations begin, the pressure of the negotiation process may lead to a poor outcome, which the negotiator may feel obligated to accept because the alternative is also very poor. Alternatively, she or he might gain the desired outcome, but perhaps at a significant cost.

Active-Engagement Strategies: Accommodation, Competition and Collaboration   Competition and collaboration were described extensively in the last two chapters. Competition is described throughout this book as distributive or win–lose bargaining, and collaboration as integrative or win–win negotiation.

Accommodation is as much a win–lose strategy as competition, although it has a decidedly different image—it involves an imbalance of outcomes, but in the opposite direction ("I lose, you win" as opposed to "I win, you lose"). As Figure 4.1 shows, an accommodative strategy may be appropriate when the negotiator considers the relationship outcome more important than the substantive outcome. In other words, the negotiator wants to let the other win, keep the other happy, or not endanger the relationship by pushing hard to achieve some goal on the substantive issues. This strategy is often used when the primary goal of the exchange is to build or strengthen the relationship (or the other party) and the negotiator is willing to sacrifice the outcome. An accommodative strategy may also be necessary if the negotiator expects the relationship to extend past a single negotiation episode. The idea is that if "I lose and you win" this time, over multiple negotiations in the relationship the win–lose accounts will balance. In any long-term social relationship, it is probably healthy for one negotiator or the other to accept a suboptimal outcome in a given negotiation while expecting reciprocal accommodation (tit for tat) from the other negotiator in the future.[6] Such reciprocity has been called the glue that holds social groups together.[7]

How do these three strategies—competition, collaboration, and accommodation—differ? Table 4.1[8] summarizes the three types of strategies (distributive, integrative, and accommodative) and compares and contrasts them across a number of different dimensions.

In addition to their positive characteristics, as described in the table, each of these three negotiation strategies also has certain predictable drawbacks if the strategy is applied blindly, thoughtlessly, or inflexibly:

• Distributive strategies tend to create "we–they" or "superiority–inferiority" patterns and may lead to distortions in judgment regarding the other side's contributions and efforts, as well as to distortions in perceptions of the other side's values, needs, and positions (see the discussion of framing biases in Chapter 5).

• If a negotiator pursues an integrative strategy without regard to the other's strategy, then the other may manipulate and exploit the collaborator and take advantage of the good faith and goodwill being demonstrated. Blind pursuit of an integrative process can also lead negotiators to cease being accountable to their constituencies in favor of pursuit of the negotiation process for its own sake. For example, negotiators who approach the process with an aggressive "we can solve any problem" attitude may produce an agreement that is unacceptable to their constituency (e.g., their companies), which will then be rejected and force the negotiator to resume discussions that others thought were settled.

• Accommodative strategies may generate a pattern of constantly giving in to keep the other happy or to avoid a fight. This pattern establishes a precedent that is hard to break. It could also lead the other to a false sense of well-being due to the satisfaction that comes with the "harmony" of a good relationship, which may completely ignore all the giveaways on substance. Over time, this imbalance is unlikely to perpetuate, but efforts to stop the giving or restore the balance may be met with surprise and resentment.

It is also useful to remember that in presenting these strategies we are describing pure forms that do not capture the mixture of issues and motivations that actually characterize the evolution of most actual negotiation strategies.[9] Just as most conflicts are neither purely competitive nor purely cooperative, most negotiation strategies reflect a variety of goals, intentions, and situational constraints that tend to make any "pure" strategy difficult to follow.

TABLE 4.1 | Characteristics of Different Engagement Strategies

Aspect	Competition (Distributive Bargaining)	Collaboration (Integrative Negotiation)	Accommodative Negotiation
Payoff structure	Usually a fixed amount of resources to be divided	Usually a variable amount of resources to be divided	Usually a fixed amount of resources to be divided
Goal pursuit	Pursuit of own goals at the expense of those of others	Pursuit of goals held jointly with others	Subordination of own goals in favor of those of others
Relationships	Short-term focus; parties do not expect to work together in the future	Long-term focus; parties expect to work together in the future	May be short term (let the other win to keep the peace) or long term (let the other win to encourage reciprocity in the future)
Primary motivation	Maximize own outcome	Maximize joint outcome	Maximize others' outcome or let them gain to enhance relationship
Trust and openness	Secrecy and defensiveness; high trust in self, low trust in others	Trust and openness, active listening, joint exploration of alternatives	One party relatively open, exposing own vulnerabilities to the other
Knowledge of needs	Parties know own needs but conceal or misrepresent them; neither party lets the other know real needs	Parties know and convey real needs while seeking and responding to needs of the other	One party is overresponsive to other's needs so as to repress own needs
Predictability	Parties use unpredictability and surprise to confuse other side	Parties are predictable and flexible when appropriate, trying not to surprise	One party's actions totally predictable, always catering to other side
Aggressiveness	Parties use threats and bluffs, trying to keep the upper hand	Parties share information honestly, treat each other with understanding and respect	One party gives up on own position to mollify the other
Solution search behavior	Parties make effort to appear committed to position, using argumentation and manipulation of the other	Parties make effort to find mutually satisfying solutions, using logic, creativity, and constructiveness	One party makes effort to accommodate the other
Success measures	Success enhanced by creating bad image of the other; increased levels of hostility and strong in-group loyalty	Success demands abandonment of bad images and consideration of ideas on their merit	Success determined by minimizing or avoiding conflict and soothing all hostility; own feelings ignored in favor of harmony
Evidence of unhealthy extreme	Unhealthy extreme reached when one party assumes total zero-sum game; defeating the other becomes a goal in itself	Unhealthy extreme reached when one subsumes all self-interest in the common good, losing self-identity and self-responsibility	Unhealthy extreme reached when one abdication to other is complete, at expense of personal and/or constituent goals
Key attitude	Key attitude is "I win, you lose"	Key attitude is "What's the best way to address the needs of all parties?"	Key attitude is "You win, I lose"
Remedy for breakdown	If impasse occurs, mediator or arbitrator may be needed	If difficulties occur, a group dynamics facilitator may be needed	If behavior becomes chronic, party becomes negotiationally bankrupt

Source: Adapted and expanded from Robert W. Johnston, "Negotiation Strategies: Different Strokes for Different Folks," *Personnel 59* (March–April 1982), pp. 38–39. Used with permission of the author.

Understanding the Flow of Negotiations: Stages and Phases

Before we explore the specific planning processes for negotiation, it is important to understand the typical steps or flow in a negotiation in order to understand how negotiations are likely to evolve and why planning is so important.

Several researchers have studied the flow of negotiations over time—often by classifying the type of communication parties use at various points in the process. This work has confirmed that negotiation, like communication in problem-solving groups and in other forms of ritualistic social interaction, proceeds through distinct phases or stages.[10]

More recently, Greenhalgh has articulated a stage model of negotiation that is particularly relevant for integrative negotiation.[11] Greenhalgh suggests that there are seven key steps to an ideal negotiation process (see Figure 4.2):

Preparation: deciding what is important, defining goals, thinking ahead how to work together with the other party.

Relationship building: getting to know the other party, understanding how you and the other are similar and different, and building commitment toward achieving a mutually beneficial set of outcomes. Greenhalgh argues that this stage is extremely critical to satisfactorily moving the other stages forward.

Information gathering: learning what you need to know about the issues, about the other party and their needs, about the feasibility of possible settlements, and about what might happen if you fail to reach agreement with the other side.

Information using: at this stage, negotiators assemble the case they want to make for their preferred outcomes and settlement, one that will maximize the negotiator's own needs. This presentation is often used to "sell" the negotiator's preferred outcome to the other.

Bidding: the process of making moves from one's initial, ideal position to the actual outcome. Bidding is the process by which each party states their "opening offer" and then makes moves in that offer toward a middle ground. We describe this process extensively in Chapter 2.

Closing the deal: the objective of this stage is to build commitment to the agreement achieved in the previous phase. Both the negotiator and the other party have to assure themselves that they reached a deal they can be happy with, or at least accept.

FIGURE 4.2 | Phases of Negotiation

Phase 1	Phase 2	Phase 3	Phase 4	Phase 5	Phase 6	Phase 7
Preparation →	Relationship building →	Information gathering →	Information using →	Bidding →	Closing the deal →	Implementating the agreement

Source: Reprinted with the permission of The Free Press, an imprint of Simon & Schuster Adult Publishing Group, from *Managing Strategic Relationships: The Key to Business Success* by Leonard Greenhalgh. Copyright © 2001 by Leonard Greenhalgh.

Implementing the agreement: determining who needs to do what once the agreement is reached. Not uncommonly parties discover that the agreement is flawed, key points were missed, or the situation has changed and new questions exist. Flaws in moving through the earlier phases arise here, and the deal may have to be reopened or issues settled by mediators, arbitrators, or the courts.

Greenhalgh argues that this model is largely prescriptive—that is, this is the way people ought to negotiate—and he creates a strong case for why this is so.[12] However, examination of the actual practice of negotiators shows that they frequently deviate from this model and that one can track differences in their practice according to his or her national culture (see Chapter 11). For example, American negotiators typically view the process more in "win–lose" or distributive terms; they don't do much relationship building or planning, and they move directly to bidding, closing, and implementation. In contrast, Asian negotiators spend a great deal of time on relationship building and truncate the steps toward the end of the negotiation process.

Getting Ready to Implement the Strategy: The Planning Process

The foundation for success in negotiation is not in the game playing or the dramatics. The dominant force for success in negotiation is in the planning that takes place prior to the dialogue. Effective planning also requires hard work on the following points:

- Defining the issues.
- Assembling issues and defining the bargaining mix.
- Defining interests.
- Defining resistance points.
- Defining alternatives (BATNA).
- Defining one's own objectives (targets) and opening bids (where to start).
- Assessing constituents and the social context in which the negotiation will occur.
- Analyzing the other party.
- Planning the issue presentation and defense.
- Defining protocol—where and when the negotiation will occur, who will be there, what the agenda will be, and so on.

The remainder of this chapter discusses each of these steps in detail (see also a summary of the planning guide in Table 4.2 that may be used to plan one's own negotiation). The list represents the collective wisdom of several sources,[13] each of which has its own list of key steps, which often vary in order.

1. Defining the Issues

This step itself usually begins with an analysis of what is to be discussed in the negotiation. Some negotiations may only consist of a single issue—for example, the price of an

TABLE 4.2 | Negotiation Planning Guide

1. What are the issues in the upcoming negotiation?
2. Based on a review of *all* the issues, what is the "bargaining mix"? (Which issues do we have to cover? Which issues are connected to other issues?)
3. What are my interests?
4. What is my resistance point—what is my walkaway?
5. What is my alternative?
6. Defining targets and asking prices—where will I start, what is my goal?
7. Who are my constituents and what do they want me to do?
8. Who are the opposing negotiators and what do they want?
9. What overall strategy do I want to select?
10. What protocol needs to be followed in conducting this negotiation?

item, such as the price of a coffee table being purchased at a yard sale or the price of a used car. Other negotiations are more complex. Thus, the purchase of one company by another may include a large number of questions such as price; transfer of inventory; executives and workers who will be retained, transferred, or laid off; new headquarters location; and the like.

The number of issues in a negotiation, together with the relationship between the negotiator and the other party, are often the primary determinant of whether one uses a distributive or integrative strategy. Single-issue negotiations tend to dictate distributive negotiations because the only real negotiation issue is the price or "distribution" of that issue. In contrast, multiple-issue negotiations lend themselves more to integrative negotiations because parties can use processes such as logrolling to create issue "packages" that are mutually beneficial.

While the number of issues affects strategy, it does not preclude the possibility that single-issue negotiations can be made integrative or that multiple-issue negotiations will remain distributive. Single-issue negotiations can often be made integrative by working to *increase* the number of issues. For instance, in buying a house, both parties may begin by believing that price is the only issue but may quickly realize that other issues are equally central: how the purchase will be financed, date of sale, or date of occupancy. They might also identify other issues, such as appliances or patio furniture to be included, repair of a broken fence, or payment for the fuel oil left in the storage tank. During the purchase process, the buyer's lawyer, mortgage financer, or real estate agent might draw up a list of other things to consider: taxes to pay, escrow amounts for undiscovered problems, or a written statement that the seller must leave the house in "broom-clean" condition (as well as the fees to be paid to all these professionals!). Note that it does not take long to generate a fairly detailed list. In any negotiation, a complete list of the issues at stake is best derived from the following sources:

1. An analysis of all the possible issues that need to be decided.
2. Previous experience in similar negotiations.

3. Research conducted to gather information (e.g., study the neighborhood, have the house inspected, or read up on how to buy a house).

4. Consultation with experts in that industry (real estate agents, mortgage lenders, attorneys, accountants, or friends who have bought a house recently).

2. Assembling the Issues and Defining the Bargaining Mix

The next step in planning is to assemble all the issues that have been defined into a comprehensive list. The combination of lists from each side in the negotiation determines the bargaining mix (see Chapter 2). In generating a list of issues, negotiators may feel that they put too much on the table at once or raise too many issues. This may happen if the parties do not talk frequently or if they have lots of business to transact. As we noted in step 1, however, introducing a long list of issues into a negotiation often makes success more, rather than less, likely—provided that all the issues are real. Large bargaining mixes allow many possible components and arrangements for settlement, thus increasing the likelihood that a particular package will meet both parties' needs and therefore lead to a successful settlement.[14] At the same time, large bargaining mixes can lengthen negotiations because they present so many possible combinations of issues to consider, and combining and evaluating all these mixes makes valuing the deal very complex.

After assembling issues on an agenda, the negotiator next must prioritize them. Prioritization includes two steps:

1. *Determine which issues are most important and which are less important.* Once negotiation begins, parties can easily be swept up in the rush of information, arguments, offers, counteroffers, trade-offs, and concessions. For those who are not clear in advance about what they want and what they can do without, it is easy to lose perspective and agree to suboptimal settlements or to get distracted by long debates over points that are relatively unimportant. When negotiators do not have priorities, they may be more likely to yield on those points aggressively argued by the other side rather than to yield based on their own priorities.

    Priorities can be set in a number of ways. One simple way is for the negotiator to rank-order the issues by asking "What is most important?" "What is second most important?" and "What is least important?" An even simpler process is to group issues into categories of high, medium, or low importance. When the negotiator represents a constituency, it is important to involve that group in setting priorities. Priorities can be set for both interests and more specific issues. A third, more precise method is to award a total of 100 points to the total package of issues, and then to divide the points among the issues in proportion to each issue's relative importance. If the negotiator has confidence in the relative weighting of points across the issues, then trading off and "packaging" possible settlements together becomes more systematic.[15]

    It is also important to set priorities (and possibly assign points) for both tangible and intangible issues. Intangible issues are often difficult to discuss and rank-order, yet if they remain subjective and not quantified, negotiators may overemphasize or underemphasize them. It is easy to push such issues aside in favor of concrete, specific, numerical issues—and negotiators must be careful not to let the "hard bargaining" over numbers drive out more ephemeral discussion of intangible issues and interests.

Finally, negotiators may also wish to specify a bargaining range for each issue in the mix. Thus, not only would a "best possible" and "minimally acceptable" package be specified, but also a target and minimally acceptable level would be specified for each issue in the mix.

2. *Determine whether the issues are linked together or separate.* If the issues are separate, they can be easily added or subtracted; if connected, then settlement on one will be linked to settlement on the others and making concessions on one issue will inevitably be tied to some other issue. The negotiator must decide whether the issues are truly connected— for instance, whether the price he will pay for the house is dependent on what the bank will loan him—as opposed to simply being connected in his own mind for the sake of achieving a good settlement.

3. Defining Interests

After defining the issues, the negotiator must proceed to define the underlying interests and needs. As we extensively discussed in Chapters 2 and 3, *positions*—an opening bid or a target point—are what a negotiator wants. *Interests* are why she wants them. A target point of $200,000 for a condo would be a position; this is what the negotiator hopes to pay. The interest would be "to pay a fair market price, and one I can afford, for that two-bedroom condominium." Although defining interests is more important to integrative negotiation than to distributive bargaining, even distributive discussions can benefit from one or both parties identifying the key interests. If issues help us define *what* we want, then understanding interests requires us to ask *why* we want it. Asking "why" questions usually helps critical values, needs, or principles surface that we want to achieve in the negotiation[16] (see Chapter 6). Interests may be

- Substantive, that is, directly related to the focal issues under negotiation.
- Process-based, that is, related to how the negotiators behave as they negotiate.
- Relationship-based, that is, tied to the current or desired future relationship between the parties.

Interests may also be based on the intangibles of negotiation—including principles or standards to which the parties wish to adhere, the informal norms by which they will negotiate, and the benchmarks they will use to guide them toward a settlement—to achieve a fair or reasonable deal or to get the negotiation concluded quickly.

4. Knowing Limits

What will happen if the other party refuses to accept some proposed items for the agenda or states issues in such a way that they are unacceptable? Good preparation requires that you establish two clear points: your *resistance point* and your *alternatives.*

A *resistance point* is the place where you decide that you should absolutely stop the negotiation rather than continue, because any settlement beyond this point is not minimally acceptable. If you are the seller, your resistance point is the least you will take for the item you have for sale; if you are the buyer, your resistance point is the most you will pay for the item.

Setting resistance points as a part of planning is critical. Most of us have been involved in buying situations in which the item we wanted wasn't available, but we allowed ourselves to be talked into a more expensive model. Moreover, some competitive situations generate intense pressures to escalate the price. For example, in an auction, if there is a bidding war with another person, one may pay more than was planned. Gamblers, analogously, may encounter a losing streak and end up losing more money than they had planned. Clear resistance points help keep people from agreeing to deals that they later realize weren't very smart.

5. Knowing Alternatives

On the other hand, *alternatives* are other agreements negotiators could achieve and still meet their needs. Alternatives are very important in both distributive and integrative processes because they define whether the current outcome is better than another possibility. In any situation, the better the alternatives, the more power you have because you can walk away from the current negotiation and still know that your needs and interests can be met (see also Chapters 2 and 7). In the house-purchase example, the more a buyer has researched the real estate market and understands what other comparable houses are available, the more she knows that she can walk away from this negotiation and still have acceptable housing choices.

6. Setting Targets and Asking Prices

After negotiators have defined the issues, assembled a tentative agenda, and consulted others as appropriate and necessary, the next step is to define two other key points: the specific *target point* where one realistically expects to achieve a settlement and the *asking price,* representing the best deal one can hope to achieve.

There are numerous ways to set a target. One can ask, "What is an outcome that I would be pleased with?" "At what point would I be very satisfied?" "What have other people achieved in this situation?" "What would be a fair and reasonable settlement?" Targets may not be as firm and rigid as resistance points or alternatives; one might be able to set a general range or a class of several outcomes that would be equally acceptable.

Similarly, there are numerous ways to set an initial asking price. An opening bid may be the best possible outcome, an ideal solution, something even better than was achieved last time. It is easy to get overly confident, however, and to set an opening that is so unrealistic that the other party immediately laughs, gets angry, or walks away before responding. While openings are usually formulated around a "best possible" settlement, it is also easy to inflate them to the point where they become self-defeating because they are too unrealistic in the eyes of the other negotiator or observers with a more realistic perspective.

There are several principles to keep in mind when setting a *target point:*

1. *Targets should be specific, difficult but achievable, and verifiable.* A lot can be learned about setting a target point from researchers who have studied goal setting as a motivation and performance management tool.[17] First, goals need to be specific. If negotiating a salary, one should set a specific number (e.g., $75,000) rather than a more general goal (e.g., anything better than $60,000 a year). Second, goals should be difficult but achievable. A goal should be set so that it is an improvement over the current situation or circumstances, but not so difficult that it can't be

achieved. Finally, it should be possible to define a goal so that it is clear when it is or is not achieved. This is not a problem if one has set a quantifiable goal like a payment amount or a dollar salary, but it can be a problem if one is setting a more diffuse goal (e.g., get a decent salary that will pay me what I am worth. "Decent" and "what I am worth" are highly subjective targets, and it will be most difficult for the negotiator—and others—to judge when that goal has been truly achieved).

2. *Target setting requires positive thinking about one's* own *objectives.* When approaching a negotiation, it is possible to pay too much attention to the other party—how they behave, what they will probably demand, and what it is like to deal with them. If negotiators focus attention on the other party to the exclusion of themselves, they may set their goals strictly as a reaction to the other's anticipated goals and targets. Reactive strategies are likely to make negotiators feel threatened and defensive and lessen their flexibility and creativity (and perhaps limit the goals they think are achievable). In contrast, being proactive about target setting permits negotiators to be flexible in what they will accept and improves the likelihood of arriving at a mutually satisfactory outcome.

3. *Target setting often requires considering how to package several issues and objectives.* Most negotiators have a mixture of bargaining objectives, so they must consider the best way to achieve satisfaction across multiple issues. To package issues effectively, negotiators need to understand the issues, the relative priorities across the issues, and the bargaining mix. It is possible to define and evaluate some of these packages as "opening bids" and others as "targets" in the same ways as evaluating individual issues. When packages involve intangible issues, or issues for which it is difficult to specify definite targets, it is harder to evaluate and compare the packages explicitly, but efforts should be made to do so.

4. *Target setting requires an understanding of trade-offs and throwaways.* The discussion of packaging raises another possible challenge: What if the other party proposes a package that puts issues A, B, and C as major issues in their opening bid, but only mentions issue D. In the next offer, they never mention issue D—but issue D happens to be something you can easily give them. If you can give easily on issue D, would they be willing to take less on A, B, or C? Negotiators may want to consider giving away "something for nothing" if such an item can be part of the transaction. Even if an issue is unimportant or inconsequential to you, it may be valuable or attractive to the other party. Awareness of the actual or likely value of such concessions in a package can considerably enrich the value of what one offers to the other party at little or no cost to oneself. Using the house example again, the seller may have eight months left on a local parking-lot pass or access to a community recreation facility. Because the money the seller paid for the pass is nonrefundable, the pass will be worthless to the seller once she leaves the area, but the buyer could see the pass as a valuable item.

   To evaluate these packages, negotiators need to have some idea of what each item in the bargaining mix is worth in terms that can be compared or traded-off across issues. As mentioned earlier, it may be desirable to find a common dimension such as dollar value or a scale of utility points to compare issues in the bargaining mix, or to compare tangibles with intangibles, so that one can evaluate all items in the mix on a common dimension. For example, in labor negotiations, each side often tries to value an issue in dollar cost/benefit terms. Even if the fit is not perfect, any guide is better than none. Moreover, if intangibles are a key part of the bargaining mix, negotiators must know the point at which they are willing to abandon the pursuit of an intangible in favor of substantial gains on tangibles.

7. Assessing Constituents and the Social Context of the Negotiation

When people are negotiating for themselves—for example, buying a used racing bicycle or exercise machine—they can determine the bargaining mix on their own. But when people negotiate in a professional context, there may be more than two parties. First, there may be more than two negotiators at the table. Multiple parties at the table often lead to coalitions of negotiators who align with each other in order to win the negotiation.[18] Second, negotiators also have "constituents"—bosses, superiors who make the final decision, or other parties who will evaluate and critique the solution achieved. Moreover, there may be observers of the negotiation who also watch and critique the negotiation. When one has a constituent or observer, other issues arise, such as who conducts the negotiation, who can participate in the negotiation, and who has the ultimate power to ratify negotiated agreements. Finally, negotiation occurs in a context of rules—a social system of laws, customs, common business practices, cultural norms, and political cross-pressures.

One way to assess all the key parties in a negotiation is to complete a "field analysis." Imagine that you are the captain of a soccer team, about to play a game on the field (see Figure 4.3). Assessing constituents is the same as assessing all the parties who are in the soccer stadium:

1. Who is, or should be, on the team on my side of the field? Perhaps it is just the negotiator (a one-on-one game). But perhaps we want other help: an attorney, accountant, or an expert to assist us; someone to coach us, give us moral support, or listen closely to what the other side says; a recorder or note-taker.

2. Who is on the other side of the field? This is discussed in more detail in the next section.

3. Who is on the sidelines and can affect the play of the game? Who are the negotiation equivalents of owners, managers, and strategists? This includes one's direct superior or the person who must approve or authorize the agreement reached. Most importantly, these considerations directly affect how decisions will be made about what is acceptable or unacceptable to those on each side.

4. Who is in the stands? Who is watching the game, is interested in it, but can only indirectly affect what happens? This might include senior managers, shareholders, competitors, financial analysts, the media, or others. When multiple parties enter the negotiation—whether they are parties on the sidelines who are active in the negotiation or "interested parties" who may be affected by the settlement—negotiations will become more complex.

FIGURE 4.3 | A Field Analysis of Negotiation

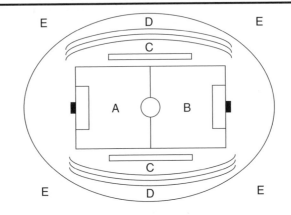

A.   The direct actors (who is on the field on our side?)

B.   The opposition actors (who is on the field on their side?)

C.   Indirect actors (who is on the sidelines?)

D.   Interested observers (who is in the stands?)

E.   Environmental factors (what is going on in the broad environment of the game—outside the stadium, but shaping and defining what happens in the stadium?)

5.   What is going on in the broader environment in which the negotiation takes place? A number of "context" issues can affect negotiation:

- What is the history of the relationship with the other party, and how does it affect the overall expectations they bring to this negotiation (see Chapter 9)?

- What kind of a relationship with the other party is expected or desired for the future, and how do these expectations affect the current negotiation (see Chapter 9)?

- How often do we expect to negotiate in the future—that is, how many rounds of negotiation will there be? Multiround negotiations create issues of managing precedents, planning future agendas, and ensuring that current agreements are enacted and monitored.[19]

- What are the deadlines or time limits? To extend the game metaphor, games have a finite time period that is broken down into periods or segments. Are there similar constraints that bound this negotiation?

- What are the "rules of the game" by which this agreement will be managed? Is there a set of fixed rules, such as a legal structure that will bind and en- force contracts? Is the rule structure itself negotiable so that we can make up our own rules about how certain problems and situations will be handled?

- What is common and acceptable practice in the ethical system in which the deal is being done (see Chapter 8)? How will we decide if one party "cheats"; are there clear rules about what is and is not fair?

Considering these questions is important to the progress of the negotiation process. A negotiator bargaining on behalf of others (a company, union, department, club, family, etc.) must consult with them so that their concerns and priorities are included in the mix. In the house-buying illustration used earlier, let's assume that one member of a couple is doing the negotiating, and the other can't attend the meeting. If that person fails to consider his partner's concerns about the condition in which the house is left, or their children's wish that the move not occur during the school year, then the negotiated resolution may be rejected by the constituents. A negotiator who is representing a constituency is accountable to that constituency and must include their wishes in proposals—subsequently either fulfilling those wishes for them through negotiation or explaining why their desires were not met. When negotiating for a large constituency, such as an entire company or a union or a community, the process of consulting with the constituency can be elaborate and exhaustive. The negotiator may recognize that the constituency's wish list is unrealistic and unobtainable, requiring the negotiator to negotiate with the constituency over what should be included on the agenda and what is realistic to expect. It is also critical to understand what happens when the two parties get close to an agreement. Does the negotiator have authority to reach agreement, or does the approval of the constituents have to be obtained? Constituents control negotiators by limiting how much they can decide on their own, and understanding these limits will keep negotiators in alignment with their constituents.

8. Analyzing the Other Party

Earlier in this section, we discussed the importance of assigning priorities to one's own goals and objectives. Gathering information about the other party is also a critical step in preparing for negotiation. Learning the other's issues, preferences, priorities, interests, alternatives, and constraints is almost as important as determining one's own. If negotiators have not had the opportunity to meet with people from the other side, then they should find a way to start to see the negotiation from the other party's perspective or to gather information to learn about their issues, interests, and priorities. Negotiators might call the other party and speak to them prior to the formal meeting or try to take their perspective and anticipate what they might want. It may also be possible to speak to others who know the other party or to people who have been in their situation before. The goal is to understand how they are approaching the negotiation and what they are likely to want. By comparing this assessment against your own, one can begin to define areas where there may be strong conflict (both parties have a high priority for the same thing), simple trade-offs (both parties want the same group of things but in differing priorities), or no conflict at all (both parties want very different things and both can easily have their objectives and interests met).

What information does one party need about the other party in order to prepare effectively? Several key pieces of background information will be of great importance, including their

- Resources, issues, and bargaining mix.
- Interests and needs.
- Walkaway point and alternative(s).

- Targets and opening bids.
- Constituents, social structure, and authority to make an agreement.
- Reputation and negotiation style.
- Likely strategy and tactics.

In theory, it would be extremely useful to have as much of this information as possible before negotiations occur. In reality, it may not be possible to obtain this information before the negotiation starts. If this is the case, the negotiator should plan to collect as much of this information as possible during the opening stages of the actual deliberations.

The Other Party's Resources, Issues, and Bargaining Mix   The more information one can gather about the other through initial research the better. Which data are most relevant will depend on the issues and likely elements in the bargaining mix. An analysis of the other party's business history or previous negotiations, successful and otherwise, might provide useful clues. Financial data about the other party might be obtained through channels such as Internet searches, financial statements, company records, stock reports, interviews and court documents, or legal judgments. One might investigate the other party's inventories. Sometimes one can learn a great deal simply by visiting the other party or speaking to his or her friends and peers. Another way to learn is to ask questions of people who have done business with the other party. The more the negotiator can get even a general sense of how much the other is capable of addressing and meeting the party's issues or needs, and of what issues they will bring to the bargaining table, the better one can predict how the process is likely to unfold.

The Other Party's Interests and Needs   In addition to learning about the party's major issues and resources, one also needs to get information about his or her current interests and needs (see Chapter 3). This information may be obtained through a variety of routes:

- Conducting a preliminary interview, including a broad discussion of what the other party would like to achieve in the upcoming negotiations (focus on broad interests, not just issues).
- Anticipating the other party's interests (as if you were "in their shoes").
- Asking others who know or have negotiated with the other party.
- Reading how the other party portrays himself or herself in the media.

The importance of the issues or interests, along with the nature of the past relationship with the other party, will influence the depth to which one probes to get information. Although it does take time and effort to get information, the results are usually more than worth the investment because valuable information can often be gathered through a phone call or a visit.

The Other Party's Walkaway Point and Alternatives   We also need to get a sense of the other party's walkaway point and alternatives. How far can they go? What is the maximum they can give us? And what will they do if this negotiation does not succeed? Understanding the other party's limits and alternatives is important because it will give us some information about how far we can "push" them. How good are their alternatives? If the other party has a strong and viable alternative, he or she will probably be confident in negotiation, set high objectives, and be willing to push hard for those objectives. In contrast, if the other party has a weak alternative, then she or he will be more dependent on achieving a satisfactory agreement with you and be less likely to push as hard.

Bear in mind that in a distributive negotiation, the other party may be less likely to disclose this information and/or may misrepresent their limits and alternatives so as to pressure us into a deal that is better for them. In an integrative negotiation, there should be more openness between the parties, which should lead to more accurate disclosure of limits and alternatives.

The Other Party's Targets and Openings   After negotiators have obtained information about the other side's issues, bargaining mix, and interests, they also need to understand his or her goals. People often think stereotypically about the other party's interests and targets; they use their own targets and values as a benchmark and assume (often inappropriately) that others are like themselves and want similar things. A manager who is always after a bigger paycheck may be surprised to learn that some of his subordinates are more interested in having a challenging job, schedule flexibility, or increased leisure time than they are in maximizing their salary.

How can one understand and appraise the other party's targets? Although speculation about another's objectives is seldom sufficient, most people do *not* gather information systematically—but they should. One of the best ways to get this information is directly from the other party. Because information about the other party's targets is so important to the strategy formulation of both parties, professional negotiators will often exchange information about targets or opening proposals days or even weeks before negotiations begin. If this does not occur, then the negotiator should plan to collect as much of this information as possible at the first meeting with the other party.

The Other Party's Constituents, Social Structure, and Authority   As in planning step 7, it is important to understand the broader social context in which the negotiation will occur for the other party. Who will they bring to the table? Who are they accountable to? What rules or procedures are they likely to follow? This analysis can be quite simple for purchasing a used computer but quite complex in a large multinational negotiation.

The most direct impact of the broader social context is on the other negotiator's ability to make binding agreements. When negotiators represent others, their power to make agreements may be restricted in many ways. Sometimes a constituency stipulates that negotiators cannot make any binding agreements; often negotiators can only present proposals from the constituency or collect information and take it back to their superiors.

There are many reasons for limiting a negotiator's authority. Negotiators without decision authority cannot be won over by a persuasive presentation to commit their constituency to something they do not want. They cannot give out sensitive information carelessly. Although these limitations may be helpful to a negotiator, they can also be frustrating. When a negotiator always has to check things out with those he represents, the other party may refuse to continue until someone who has the power to answer questions and make decisions is brought to the table. Negotiating teams should think seriously about sending in a negotiator with limited authority. Although that person will not be able to make unauthorized (and perhaps problematic) agreements, the limited authority may frustrate the other party and create an unproductive tension in the negotiating relationship.

More broadly, the negotiator needs to know how the other party's organization makes decisions to support or ratify an agreement. Is there a senior executive who will dictate the decision? Will people vote? Or is the decision by committee? How decisions are made can have dramatic implications for who needs to be directly influenced on the other side.

The Other Party's Reputation and Negotiation Style   As noted earlier, the other party's past negotiating behavior is a good indication of how he or she will behave in the future. Even if a bargainer has had no previous experience with the other person, speaking to those who have dealt with that person in the past can be very valuable. Has the other party acted distributively or integratively?

This kind of information is an important determinant of how to approach the other party in the negotiation. Whether or not they have a reputation for being cooperative or competitive may affect the strategy pursued in the next negotiation. On the other hand, there is a potential danger in drawing conclusions from this information. Assuming that the other party will act in the future as he or she has been described as acting in the past is just that— an assumption. People can act differently in different circumstances at different times. Although gathering information about the other party's past behavior is a reasonable starting point for making assumptions, keep in mind that people do change over time.

One's impression of the other party's reputation may be based on several factors:

1. How the other party's predecessors have negotiated with you in the past.

2. How the other party has negotiated with you in the past, either in the same or in different contexts.

3. How the other party has negotiated with others in the past.

The Other Party's Strategy and Tactics   Finally, it is also helpful to gain information about the other party's intended strategy and tactics. Although it is unlikely the other party will reveal his or her strategy outright—particularly if he or she is intending to use distributive tactics—one can infer this information from data collected during preparation. Information collected about issues, objectives, reputation, style, alternatives, and authority may indicate a great deal about what strategy the other party intends to pursue. As we have noted before, negotiators will have to gather this information on an emergent basis as the negotiation unfolds; if their expectations have been incorrect, it will be necessary to recalibrate their strategic response.

9. Presenting Issues to the Other Party

One important aspect of negotiations is to present a case clearly and to provide ample supporting facts and arguments; another is to refute the other party's arguments with counterarguments.

Because of the breadth and diversity of issues that can be included in negotiations, it is not possible to specify all the procedures that can be used to assemble information.

There are, however, some good general guides that can be used. A negotiator can ask these questions:

1. What facts support my point of view? How can I validate this information as credible?

2. Whom may I consult or talk with to help me elaborate or clarify the facts? What records, files, or data sources exist that support my arguments? Can I enlist experts to support my arguments?

3. Have these issues been negotiated before by others under similar circumstances? Can I consult those negotiators to determine what major arguments they used, which ones were successful, and which were not?

4. What is the other party's point of view likely to be? What are her or his interests? What arguments is she or he likely to make? How can I respond to those arguments and seek more creative positions that go further in addressing both sides' issues and interests?

5. How can I develop and present the facts so they are most convincing? What visual aids, pictures, charts, graphs, expert testimony, and the like can be helpful or make the best case?

In Chapter 7, we offer extensive advice to the negotiator on how to use power and the power sources that give negotiators the capacity to exert influence.

10. What Protocol Needs to Be Followed in This Negotiation?

A negotiator should consider a number of elements of protocol or process:

*   *What agenda should we follow?* We briefly mentioned this issue in step 7, in assessing the social structure. A negotiator may unilaterally draw up a firm list of issues well before the initial negotiation meeting. This process is valuable because it forces negotiators to think through their positions and decide on objectives. The unilateral list of issues constitutes a preliminary agenda for negotiation. It is what the negotiator wants to discuss, and the *order* or *priority* in which he wants to discuss them (e.g., least versus most important issue first, etc.).

    While the negotiator may propose agendas unilaterally, this approach has a potential risk. If the negotiator's list differs from a preset agenda or the other side's preferred list, the negotiator may bring issues to the table that the other party is unprepared to discuss or may define priorities that cannot be achieved realistically. Negotiators do not welcome surprises or the embarrassment that may come when the other side raises an issue they are completely unprepared to discuss. In this situation, experienced negotiators will ask for a recess to get information and prepare themselves on the new issue, thus creating unanticipated delays. They may even refuse to include the new item on the agenda because they haven't had time to prepare for it. If the other party is also accountable to a constituency, he or she may not want to reopen earlier decisions or take the time to evaluate the new issue. For this reason, many professional negotiators such as labor negotiators and diplomats often exchange and negotiate the agenda in advance. They want to agree on what issues will be discussed on the agenda before engaging in the substantive discussion of those issues.

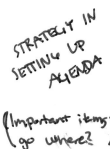

STRATEGY IN SETTING UP AGENDA

(Important items go where?)

- *Where should we negotiate?* Negotiators are more comfortable on their home turf—their own office, building, or city. They know the space, they feel comfortable and relaxed, they have direct access to all the amenities—secretaries, research information, expert advice, computers, and so on. In cross-cultural negotiations (see Chapter 11), language and cultural differences may come into play, and the parties may have to travel across many time zones, stay in unfamiliar locations, eat unfamiliar food, and deal with similar potential problems. If negotiators want to minimize the advantage that comes with home turf, then they need to select neutral territory in which neither party will have an advantage. In addition, negotiators can choose the degree of formality of the environment. Formal deliberations are often held in board or conference rooms or hotel meeting rooms; informal deliberations can be held in restaurants, cocktail lounges, or private airline clubs.

What is the time period of the negotiation? If negotiators expect long, protracted deliberations, they might want to negotiate the time and duration of sessions. When do we start? How long do we meet? When do we need to end? When can we call for coffee breaks or time to caucus with our team?

SETTING BREAKS TO TALK W/ OWN PARTY.

- *What might be done if negotiation fails?* What will happen if we deadlock? Can we "redo" the deal? Will we go to a third-party neutral? Might we try some other techniques?

- *How will we keep track of what is agreed to?* Many negotiators don't consider the importance of recording exactly what was discussed and agreed to. Being a recording secretary may be perceived as a tedious and uninteresting job. Experienced negotiators know that this role is critical, however. First, the person with the best notes often becomes the "memory" of the session, as her or his notes are later consulted to determine what was said and discussed. Second, the person with the best notes may also volunteer to draft the initial agreement; this person may have some latitude in how the agreement is stated and what points are emphasized or deemphasized. Finally, if the agreement is highly technical or complex, one certainly wants to have the agreement reviewed by experts and specialists—attorneys, financial analysts, accountants, engineers, and so on.

  In new bargaining relationships, discussions about these procedural issues should occur *before* the major substantive issues are raised. The ease or difficulty of resolving these procedural issues can be used as litmus tests to determine how the negotiation on the larger substantive issues will proceed. If the negotiator enjoys success in these procedural negotiations, it may be easier to reach agreement later on the substantive issues.

- *How do we know whether we have a good agreement?* Finally, do we have a process in place for ensuring that once the negotiation has concluded, we can systematically evaluate how the deal compares with (1) our initial plan and (2) our sense of the best we can do given the other party and all of the structural and procedural constraints?

Chapter Summary

Planning is a critically important activity in negotiation. Effective planning allows negotiators to design a road map that will guide them to agreement. While this map may frequently need to be modified and updated as discussions with the other side proceed, and as the world around the negotiation changes, working from the map is far more effective than attempting to work without it.

We began this chapter with a basic understanding of the concepts of strategy, and discussed the importance of setting clear goals, based on the key issues at stake. We then presented a model of negotiation strategy choice, returning to the familiar framework of the dual concerns model. A negotiator who carefully plans will make an effort to do the following:

1. Understand the key issues that must be resolved in the upcoming negotiation.

2. Assemble all the issues together and understand the complexity of the bargaining mix.

3. Understand and define the key interests at stake that underlie the issues.

4. Define the limits—the point where we will walk away or stop negotiating.

5. Define the alternatives—other deals we could do if this deal does not work out.

6. Clarify the target points to be achieved and the asking price where we will begin the discussion.

7. Understand my constituents, what they expect of me, and the social context.

8. Understand the other party in the negotiation—their goals, issues, strategies, interests, limits, alternatives, targets, openings, and authority.

9. Plan the process by which I will present and "sell" my ideas to the other party (and perhaps to my own constituency).

10. Define the important points of protocol in the process—the agenda, who will be at the table or observing the negotiation, where and when we will negotiate, and so on.

When negotiators are able to consider and evaluate each of these factors, they will know what they want and will have a clear sense of direction on how to proceed. This sense of direction, and the confidence derived from it, is a very important factor in affecting negotiating outcomes.

Endnotes

[1] Mintzberg and Quinn, 1991.

[2] Quinn, 1991.

[3] Pruitt and Rubin, 1986.

[4] Savage, Blair, and Sorenson, 1989.

[5] See also Johnston, 1982.

[6] Homans, 1961.

[7] For example, Cialdini, 2001.

[8] Adapted from Johnston, 1982.

[9] Lax and Sebenius, 1986.

[10] Douglas, 1962; Greenhalgh, 2001; Morley and Stephenson, 1977.

[11] Greenhalgh, 2001.

[12] Ibid.

[13] See Richardson, 1977; Asherman and Asherman, 1990; Burnstein, 1995; Fisher and Ertel, 1995; Lewicki, Hamm, and Olander, 1996; Lewicki and Hiam, 1999; Greenhalgh, 2001; and Watkins, 2002.

[14] Rubin and Brown, 1975.

[15] See Simons and Tripp, 2002, 2006, for one example.

[16] Ury, 1991.

[17] For example, Locke and Latham, 1984.

[18] Compare Wheeler, 2004.

[19] Ibid.

5

CHAPTER

Perception, Cognition, and Emotion

Objectives

1. Understand the important role played by perceptions, cognitions, and emotions in negotiation.
2. Explore how perceptions can become distorted and lead to biases in negotiation and judgment.
3. Consider the ways that cognitions (information processing) in negotiation can also be affected by biases and framing processes, and how emotions and mood can shape a negotiation.
4. Gain advice on how to manage perception, cognition, and emotions in negotiation situations.

Perception, cognition, and emotion are the basic building blocks of all social encounters, including negotiation, in the sense that our social actions are guided by how we perceive, analyze, and feel about the other party, the situation, and our own interests and positions. A working knowledge of how humans perceive the world around them, process information, and experience emotions is important to understanding why people behave the way they do during negotiations.

We begin the chapter by examining how psychological **perception** is related to the process of negotiation, with particular attention to forms of perceptual distortion that can cause problems of understanding and meaning making for negotiators. We then look at how negotiators use information to make decisions about tactics and strategy—the process of **cognition.** Our discussion here pursues two angles. First, we focus on *framing*—the strategic use of information to define and articulate a negotiating issue or situation. Second, we discuss the various kinds of systematic errors, or *cognitive biases,* in information processing that negotiators are prone to make and that may compromise negotiator performance. This section will also consider how negotiators can manage misperceptions and cognitive biases in order to maximize strategic advantage and minimize their adverse effects.

Social encounters are, however, more than just occasions for perception and cognition. We experience and express **emotion** when we interact with others, and negotiating is certainly no exception. In the final major section of this chapter, we discuss the role of moods and emotions in negotiation—both as causes of behavior and as consequences of negotiated outcomes.

Perception

Perception Defined

Negotiators approach each situation guided by their perceptions of past situations and current attitudes and behaviors. Perception is the process by which individuals connect to their environment. Many things influence how a person understands and assigns meaning to messages and events, including the perceiver's current state of mind, role, and comprehension of earlier communications.[1] In negotiation the goal is to perceive and interpret with accuracy what the other party is saying and meaning. We now examine in more detail how perceptions are created and how they affect what happens in negotiation.

Perception is a "sense-making" process; people interpret their environment so that they can respond appropriately (see Figure 5.1). Environments are typically complex—they present a large number and variety of stimuli, each having different properties such as magnitude, color, shape, texture, and relative novelty. This complexity makes it impossible to process all the available information, so as perceivers we become selective, tuning in on some stimuli while tuning out others. This selective perception occurs through a number of perceptual "shortcuts" that allow us to process information more readily. Unfortunately, the perceptual efficiencies that result may come at the expense of accuracy.

Perceptual Distortion

In any given negotiation, the perceiver's own needs, desires, motivations, and personal experiences may create a predisposition about the other party. This is cause for concern when it leads to biases and errors in perception and subsequent communication. We discuss four major perceptual errors: stereotyping, halo effects, selective perception, and projection. Stereotyping and halo effects are examples of perceptual distortion by generalization: small amounts of information are used to draw large conclusions about individuals. Selective perception and projection are, in contrast, forms of distortion that involve anticipating certain attributes and qualities in another person. The perceiver filters and distorts information to arrive at a predictable and consistent view of the other person.

Stereotyping is a very common distortion of the perceptual process. It occurs when one individual assigns attributes to another solely on the basis of the other's membership in a particular social or demographic category. Stereotypes are formed about a wide variety of different groups; examples include the younger generation, males or females, Italians or Germans, or

FIGURE 5.1 | The Perceptual Process

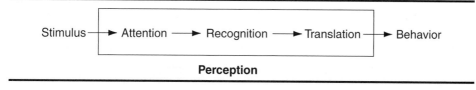

Stimulus → Attention → Recognition → Translation → Behavior

Perception

people of different races, religions, or sexual orientations. In each case, stereotypes tend to be formed in the same way. People assign an individual to a group based on one piece of perceptual information (e.g., the individual is young or old); then they assign a broad range of other characteristics of the group to this individual (e.g., "Old people are conservative; this person is old and therefore is conservative" or "Young people are disrespectful; this person is young and therefore is disrespectful"). There may be no factual basis for the conclusion that this particular older individual is conservative; the conclusion is based on the generalization of qualities that have been attributed—accurately or not—to the larger group. Applying other traits associated with the category to this particular individual may further compound the error.

Once formed, stereotypes can be highly resistant to change. The simple process of using a single criterion—even an arbitrary one—to divide people into groups encourages group members to begin to define themselves as "we" and the other group as "they" and then to make evaluative comparisons between them. Individuals are more likely to resort to stereotyping under certain conditions. Examples include time pressure, cognitive stress, and mood,[2] as well as conflicts involving values, ideologies, and direct competition for resources among groups.[3]

Halo effects in perception are similar to stereotypes. Rather than using a person's group membership as a basis for classification, however, halo effects occur when people generalize about a variety of attributes based on the knowledge of one attribute of an individual.[4] A smiling person is judged to be more honest than a frowning or scowling person, for example, even though there is no consistent relationship between smiling and honesty. Halo effects may be positive or negative. A good attribute may be generalized so that people are seen in a very positive light, whereas a negative attribute has the reverse effect. The more prominent the attribute is in influencing the overall judgment about an individual, the more likely that it will be used to cast further information into a perspective consistent with the initial judgment. Halo effects are most likely to occur in perception (1) when there is very little experience with a person along some dimension (and so the perceiver generalizes about that person from knowledge acquired in other contexts), (2) when the person is well known, and (3) when the qualities have strong moral implications.[5]

Halo effects and stereotypes are common hazards in negotiation. Negotiators are apt to form rapid impressions of each other based on very limited initial information, such as appearance, group membership, or initial statements. Negotiators tend to maintain these judgments as they get to know each other better, fitting each piece of new information into some consistent pattern. Finally, the mere suggestion that the other party can be viewed in moral terms—for example, honest or dishonest, ethical or unethical—is likely to affect the perception of a wide variety of their other attributes.[6]

Selective perception occurs when the perceiver singles out certain information that supports or reinforces a prior belief and filters out information that does not conform to that belief. Selective perception has the effect of perpetuating stereotypes or halo effects: after forming quick judgments about someone on the basis of limited information, people may then filter out further evidence that might disconfirm the judgment. An initial smile from the other party, which leads the negotiator to believe that he or she is honest or cooperative, might also lead the negotiator to downplay any of that party's statements that demonstrate an intention to be crafty or competitive. If the negotiator perceives the same initial smile as a smirk, then the negotiator may downplay the other party's offers to establish an honest and cooperative relationship. In both cases, the negotiator's own biases—the predisposition to view the smile as honest or dishonest—may affect how the other party's behavior is perceived and interpreted.

Projection occurs when people assign to others the characteristics or feelings that they possess themselves. Projection usually arises out of a need to protect one's own self-concept—to see oneself as consistent and good. Negotiators may assume that the other party would respond in the same manner they would if positions were reversed. For instance, if a negotiator is very bothered by delays in negotiations but needs to tell the other party that there will be an unavoidable delay, the negotiator may expect the other party to exhibit frustration at the announcement. While it is possible that the other party will be frustrated, it is also possible that he or she will welcome the delay as an opportunity to complete work on a different project and that any frustration was only a projection from the negotiator's mind. The tendency to project also may lead a negotiator to overestimate how much the other party knows about his or her preferences or desires.[7]

Framing

A key issue in perception and negotiation is framing. A frame is the subjective mechanism through which people evaluate and make sense out of situations, leading them to pursue or avoid subsequent actions.[8] Framing helps explain "how bargainers conceive of ongoing sets of events in light of past experiences"; framing and reframing, along with reevaluation of information and positions, "are tied to information processing, message patterns, linguistic cues, and socially constructed meanings."[9] Framing is about focusing, shaping, and organizing the world around us—making sense of a complex reality and defining it in terms that are meaningful to us. Frames, in short, define a person, event, or process and separate it from the complex world around it.[10]

Framing is a popular concept among social scientists who study cognitive processes, decision making, persuasion, and communication. The importance of framing stems from the fact that two or more people who are involved in the same situation or in a complex problem often see it or define it in different ways.[11] For example, two individuals walk into a room full of people and see different things: one (the extrovert) sees a great party; the other (the introvert) sees a scary and intimidating unfriendly crowd. Because people have different backgrounds, experiences, expectations, and needs, they frame people, events, and processes differently. Moreover, these frames can change depending on perspective, or they can change over time. What starts out as a game of tag between two boys may turn into a fistfight. A football quarterback is a "hero" when he throws a touchdown, but a "loser" when he throws an interception.

Frames are important in negotiation because disputes are often nebulous and open to different interpretations as a result of differences in people's backgrounds, personal histories, prior experiences.[12] A frame is a way of labeling these different individual interpretations of the situation. Early management theorist Mary Parker Follett, who was one of the first to write about integrative negotiation, observed that parties who arrive at a joint agreement achieve unity "not from giving in [compromise] but from 'getting the desires of each side into one field of vision.'"[13] Thus, frames emerge and converge as the parties talk about their preferences and priorities; they allow the parties to begin to develop a shared or common definition of the issues related to a situation and a process for resolving them.

How parties frame and define a negotiating issue or problem is a clear and strong reflection of what they define as critical to negotiating objectives, what their expectations and preferences are for certain possible outcomes, what information they seek and use to argue their case, the procedures they use to try to present their case, and the manner in which they evaluate the outcomes actually achieved.[14] Frames are inevitable; one cannot "avoid" framing. By choosing to define and articulate an aspect of a complex social situation, one has already implicitly "chosen" to use certain frames and to ignore others. This process often occurs without any real intention by the negotiator; one can frame a situation based on deeply buried past experiences, deep-seated attitudes and values, or strong emotions. Frames can also be shaped by the type of information chosen, or the setting and context in which the information is presented.

Understanding framing dynamics helps negotiators consciously elevate the framing process, thereby better controlling it; negotiators who understand how they are framing a problem may understand more completely what they are doing, what the other party is doing, and how to have more control over the negotiation process. Finally, both current theory and a stream of supportive empirical research show that frames may be malleable and, if so, can be shaped or reshaped as a function of information and communication during negotiation. In the next few pages, we will discuss several aspects of frames:

- Different types of frames.
- How frames work in negotiation situations.
- The interests/rights/power approach to negotiation framing.
- How frames change as a negotiation encounter evolves.

Types of Frames

Several researchers have studied different types of frames in different contexts. Drawing on work on framing in environmental disputes,[15] we offer the following examples of frames that parties use in disputes:

1. *Substantive*—what the conflict is about. Parties taking a substantive frame have a particular disposition about the key issue or concern in the conflict.

2. *Outcome*—a party's predisposition to achieving a specific result or outcome from the negotiation. To the degree that a negotiator has a specific, preferred outcome he or she wants to achieve, the dominant frame may be to focus all strategy, tactics, and communication toward getting that outcome. Parties with a strong outcome frame that emphasizes self-interest and downplays concern for the other party are more likely to engage primarily in distributive (win–lose or lose–lose) negotiations than in other types of negotiations.

3. *Aspiration*—a predisposition toward satisfying a broader set of interests or needs in negotiation. Rather than focusing on a specific outcome, the negotiator tries to ensure that his or her basic interests, needs, and concerns are met. Parties who have a strong aspiration frame are more likely to be primarily engaged in integrative (win–win) negotiation than in other types.

4. *Process*—how the parties will go about resolving their dispute. Negotiators who have a strong process frame are less concerned about the specific negotiation issues but more concerned about how the deliberations will proceed, or how the dispute should be managed. When the major concerns are largely procedural rather than substantive, process frames will be strong.

5. *Identity*—how the parties define "who they are." Parties are members of a number of different social groups—gender (male), religion (Roman Catholic), ethnic origin (Italian), place of birth (Brooklyn), current place of residence (London), and the like. These are only a few of the many categories people can use to construct an identity frame that defines themselves and distinguishes themselves from others.

6. *Characterization*—how the parties define the other parties. A characterization frame can clearly be shaped by experience with the other party, by information about the other party's history or reputation, or by the way the other party comes across early in the negotiation experience. In conflict, identity frames (of self) tend to be positive; characterization frames (of others) tend to be negative.

7. *Loss–gain*—how the parties define the risk or reward associated with particular outcomes. For example, a buyer in a sales negotiation can view the transaction in loss terms (the monetary cost of the purchase) or in gain terms (the value of the item). This form of frame is discussed in more detail later in this chapter when we address cognitive biases.

How Frames Work in Negotiation

It is difficult to know what frame a party is using unless that party tells you (you might listen to or read his or her exact words) or unless you make inferences from the party's behavior. Even then, interpretations may be difficult and prone to error. Also, the frames of those who hear or interpret communication may create biases of their own. Nevertheless, research on frames has shed light on how parties define what a negotiation is about, how they use communication to argue for their own frames and try to shape the other's orientation, and how they resolve differences when the two parties are clearly operating from different frames. Here are some insights drawn from studies of framing effects:[16]

1. *Negotiators can use more than one frame.* A land developer discussing a conflict over a proposed golf course that will fill in a wetland can speak about the golf course (the substantive issue), his preferences for how the land should be filled in (an outcome frame), and how much input neighborhood and environmental groups should be able to have in determining what happens to that wetland on his private property (a procedural frame), as well as whether he views these groups favorably or unfavorably (a characterization frame).

2. *Mismatches in frames between parties are sources of conflict.* Two negotiators may be speaking to each other from different frames (e.g., one has an outcome frame and the other has a procedural frame), using different content in the same frame (e.g., they both have a procedural frame but have strong preferences for different procedures), or using different levels of abstraction (e.g., a broad aspiration frame versus a specific outcome frame). Such mismatches cause conflict and ambiguity, which may create misunderstanding, lead to conflict escalation and even stalemate, or lead one or both

parties to "reframe" the conflict into frames that are more compatible and that may lead to resolution. For highly polarized disputes, mutual reframing may not occur without the help of a third party.

3. *Parties negotiate differently depending on the frame.* Frames may evoke certain strategies or cognitive and emotional responses from negotiators. For example, when parties are prompted to frame a negotiation in emotional terms, they tend to be more highly involved and behave competitively, leading to higher impasse rates.[17]

4. *Specific frames may be likely to be used with certain types of issues.* In a negotiation over a job offer, for instance, parties discussing salary may be likely to use outcome frames, while parties discussing relationship issues may be likely to use characterization frames.

5. *Particular types of frames may lead to particular types of agreements.* For example, parties who achieve integrative agreements may be likely to use aspiration frames and to discuss a large number of issues during their deliberations. In contrast, parties who use outcome or negative characterization frames may be likely to hold negative views of the other party and a strong preference for specific outcomes, which may in turn lead to intensified conflict and distributive outcomes (or no agreement at all).

6. *Parties are likely to assume a particular frame because of various factors.* Value differences between the parties, differences in personality, power differences, and differences in the background and social context of the negotiators may lead the parties to adopt different frames. As an example, see Box 5.1.

Another Approach to Frames: Interests, Rights, and Power

Another approach to framing disputes suggests that parties in conflict use one of three frames:[18]

Interests. People are often concerned about what they need, desire, or want. People talk about their "positions," but often what is at stake is their underlying interests. A person says he "needs" a new text messaging cell phone, but what he really wants is a new electronic toy because all his friends have one. Parties who focus on interests in a dispute are often able to find ways to resolve that dispute.

Rights. People may also be concerned about who is "right"—that is, who has legitimacy, who is correct, or what is fair. Disputes about rights are often resolved by helping the parties find a fair way to determine who is "right," or that they can both be "right." This resolution often requires the use of some standard or rule such as "taking turns," "split it down the middle," or "age before beauty" to settle the dispute. Disputes over rights are sometimes referred to formal or informal arbitrators to decide whose standards or rights are more appropriate.

Power. People may elect to frame a negotiation on the basis of power. Negotiations resolved by power are sometimes based on who is physically stronger or is able to coerce the other, but more often, it is about imposing other types of costs—economic pressures, expertise, legitimate authority, and so on. Disputes settled by power usually create clear winners and losers, with all the consequences that come from polarizing the dispute and resolving it in this manner.

Chinese Negotiation Frames BOX 5.1

Although skilled negotiators know that their and their opponents' negotiation frames are shaped through experience and culture, few stop to critically examine the <u>cultural elements</u> that shape others' perceptions about conflict. For example, Catherine Tinsley of Georgetown University has identified the five concepts from Chinese culture that those attempting to negotiate in China should recognize:

- *Social linkage.* The Chinese believe that people should be viewed in the context of their larger social groups rather than as isolated individuals.

- *Harmony.* Because people are inherently imbedded in their social network, peaceful coexistence is highly valued.

- *Roles.* To maintain social harmony, people must understand and abide by the requirements of their role in the relationship network. Roles specify duties, power, and privileges while specifying where in the relational hierarchy an individual falls.

- *Reciprocal obligations.* Each role specifies the obligations that people expect to fulfill and receive within the social network. These obligations persist over time, solidifying the relational network across generations.

- *Face.* The value the Chinese place on saving "face" is central to their perception of social interaction. Face is lost if an individual acts in a manner that is inconsistent with his or her role or fails to fulfill reciprocal obligations. Face is so valued that the threat of losing it is the primary force that ensures fulfillment of obligations and, consequently, continuance of the relational hierarchy.

Negotiators approaching discussions with the Chinese would do well to consider the perspective on conflict that these cultural realities have created. For example, individual negotiators often rely on the power of their personal network to achieve desired ends. This perspective, which Tinsley called the "relational bargaining frame," encourages parties to augment their power by both soliciting the support of powerful people and arguing for the social legitimacy of their position. While those from a more individualistic culture might reject out of hand the argument that a proposed settlement would be unpopular, such an argument would have great power in the more collectivist Chinese culture. Similarly, parties in the relational frame would be more likely to solicit outside opinions. A powerful strategy might be to encourage parties to align their positions to be compatible with the goals of a greater social collective.

Source: C. H. Tinsley, "Understanding Conflict in a Chinese Cultural Context," in R. Bies, R. Lewicki, and B. Sheppard (Eds.), *Research on Negotiation in Organizations,* vol. 6 (Stamford, CT: JAI, 1997), pp. 209–25.

Parties have a choice about how they approach a negotiation in terms of interests, rights, and power; the same negotiation can be framed in different ways and will likely lead to different consequences. For example, consider the situation of a student who has a dispute with a local car repair shop near campus over the cost of fixing an automobile. The student thinks she was dramatically overcharged for the work—the garage did more work than requested, used the most expensive replacement parts, and didn't give her the chance to review the bill before the work was done. The student might "frame" the dispute in one of these three ways:

Interests. The student might argue, "Well, small businesses have a right to charge a fair price for good quality work. I will go in and try to understand the shop owner's system for pricing repair work; we will talk about what is a fair price for the work and I will pay it, and I will probably go back to the shop again."

Rights. The student worked in a garage herself one summer and knows that car repairs are priced on what standard manuals state it will generally cost for the labor (Hours of work $\times$ Payment per hour), plus the cost of the parts. "I will ask to see the manual and the invoice for the parts. I will also go to the garage where I worked myself and ask the owner of that garage if he thinks this bill is inflated. I'll propose to pay for the parts at cost and the labor based on the mechanic's hourly pay rate."

Power. "I'll go in and start yelling at the owner about gouging, and I'll also threaten to tell all my friends not to use this garage. I'll write letters to the student newspaper about how bad this repair shop is. My mom is a lawyer and I'll have her call the owner. I'll teach them a thing or two!"

Note that the different frames are likely to lead to very different discussions between the student and the garage owner. The more the student uses power, the more likely the garage owner is to respond with power of his own (e.g., keep the car until the student pays and not reduce the price at all, and call his own lawyer); the confrontation could become angry and lead the parties into small claims court. In contrast, the more the student uses interests, the more the garage owner may be likely to use interests. The parties will have a discussion about what is fair given the services rendered; while the student may wind up paying more (than if she "won" the power argument), the tone of the discussion is likely to be far different, and the student may be in a much better position to get discounts or consideration in the future.

The Frame of an Issue Changes as the Negotiation Evolves

The definition of issues at stake in a negotiation may change as the discussion evolves. Rather than focus only on the dominant frames that parties hold at the beginning of a negotiation, it is also important to consider patterns of change (transformation) that occur as parties communicate with each other. For example, one classic study of legal disputes suggested that these disputes tend to be transformed through a process of "naming, blaming, and claiming."[19] *Naming* occurs when parties in a dispute label or identify a problem and characterize what it is about. *Blaming* occurs next, as the parties try to determine who or what caused the problem. Finally, *claiming* occurs when the individual who has the problem decides to confront, file charges, or take some other action against the individual or organization that caused the problem.

Frames are shaped by conversations that the parties have with each other about the issues in the bargaining mix. Although both parties may approach the negotiation with initial frames that resemble the categories described earlier, the ongoing interaction between them shapes the discussion as each side attempts to argue from his or her own perspective or counterargue against the other's perspective. Several factors can affect how conversations and frames are shaped:

1. Negotiators tend to argue for *stock issues,* or concerns that are raised every time the parties negotiate. For example, wage issues or working conditions may always be discussed in a labor negotiation; the union always raises them, and management always expects them to be raised and is ready to respond. Negotiations over stock issues can be restructured to include more or fewer issues, increasing the likelihood that a resolution can be found.[20]

2. Seeking to make the *best possible case* for his or her preferred perspective, one party may assemble facts, numbers, testimony, or other evidence to persuade the other party of the validity of his or her argument or perspective. Early in a negotiation, it is not uncommon for the parties to "talk past each other," with each trying to control the conversation with a certain frame or perspective rather than listening to and engaging with the other's case. Eventually, arguments and frames begin to shift as the parties focus on either refuting the other's case or modifying their own arguments on the basis of the other's.[21]

3. Frames may define major *shifts and transitions* in a complex overall negotiation. In diplomatic negotiations, successful bargaining has been described as a two-stage process called "formula/detail."[22] In this process, parties start by developing a broad framework of principles and objectives upon which they can agree. Only after that is accomplished do they work toward detailed points of agreement. The formula-detail model has three stages: *(a) diagnosis,* in which the parties recognize the need for change or improvement, review relevant history, and prepare positions; *(b) formula,* in which the parties attempt to develop a shared perception of the conflict, including common terms, referents, and fairness criteria; and *(c) detail,* in which the parties work out operational details consistent with the basic formula.[23]

4. Finally, *multiple agenda items* operate to shape issue development. Although parties usually have one or two major objectives, priorities, or core issues, there are often a number of lesser or secondary items. When brought into the conversation, these secondary concerns often transform the conversation about the primary issues. Analyzing teacher negotiations in two school districts, one researcher showed how issues became transformed throughout a negotiation.[24] For instance, an issue of scheduling was reframed as an issue of teacher preparation time, and a concern about the cost of personal insurance shifted to an issue about the extent of insurance benefits.

Critical to issue development is the process of *reframing*—changes to the thrust, tone, and focus of a conversation as the parties engage in it. Reframing is a dynamic process that may occur many times in a conversation as parties challenge each other or search for ways to reconcile seemingly incompatible perspectives. Reframing can also occur as one party uses metaphors, analogies, or specific cases to illustrate a point, leading the other to use the

**"Now, when we explain this to Mom and Dad,
let's make sure we give it the right spin."**

metaphor or case as a new way to define the situation. Reframing may be done intentionally by one side or the other, or it may emerge from the conversation as one person's challenges fuel the other's creativity and imagination. In either case, the parties often propose a new way to approach the problem.

Section Summary

Framing is about focusing, shaping, and organizing the world around us—making sense of complex realities and defining them in ways that are meaningful to us. We discussed the different type of frames that exist and their importance for understanding strategic choices in negotiation. We can offer the following prescriptive advice about problem framing for the negotiator:

- *Frames shape what the parties define as the key issues and how they talk about them.* To the extent that the parties have preferences about the issues to be covered, outcomes to be achieved, or processes to be addressed, they should strive to ensure that their own preferred frames are accepted and acknowledged by the others.
- *Both parties have frames.* When the frames match, the parties are more likely to focus on common issues and a common definition of the situation; when they do not match, communication between the parties is likely to be difficult and incomplete.
- *Frames are controllable, at least to some degree.* If negotiators understand what frame they are using and the frame the other party is using, they may be able to shift the conversation toward the frame they would like the other to adopt.
- *Conversations transform frames in ways negotiators may not be able to predict but may be able to manage.* As parties discuss an issue, introduce arguments and evidence, and advocate a course of action, the conversation changes, and the frame may change as well. It is critical for negotiators to track this shift and understand where it might lead.
- *Certain frames are more likely than others to lead to certain types of processes and outcomes.* For example, parties who are competitive are likely to have positive identity frames of themselves, negative characterization frames of each other, and a preference for win–lose approaches to resolving their dispute. Recognizing these tendencies empowers negotiators to reframe their views of themselves, the other, or the dispute resolution mechanism in play in order to pursue a process that will resolve the conflict more productively.

Cognitive Biases in Negotiation

So far we have examined how information is perceived, filtered, distorted, and framed. In this section, we examine how negotiators use information to make decisions during the negotiation. Rather than being perfect processors of information, it is quite clear that negotiators (like all decision makers) have a tendency to make systematic errors when they process information.[25] These errors, collectively labeled cognitive biases, tend to impede negotiator performance; they include (1) the irrational escalation of commitment, (2) the mythical belief that the issues under negotiation are all fixed-pie, (3) the process of anchoring and adjustment in decision making, (4) issue and problem framing, (5) the availability of information, (6) the winner's curse, (7) negotiator overconfidence, (8) the law of small numbers, (9) self-serving biases, (10) the endowment effect, (11) the tendency to ignore others' cognitions, and (12) the process of reactive devaluation. Next, we discuss each of these in more detail.

1. Irrational Escalation of Commitment

Negotiators sometimes maintain commitment to a course of action even when that commitment constitutes irrational behavior on their part. This is an example of a broader psychological phenomenon known as "escalation of commitment," which is the tendency for an individual to make decisions that stick with a failing course of action.[26] Classic examples include a country that continues to pour military resources into an unwinnable armed conflict or an investor who continues to put more money into a declining stock in hopes its fortunes will turn ("throwing good money after bad," as escalation of commitment is sometimes colloquially described). Escalation of commitment is due in part to biases in individual perception and judgment. Once a course of action is decided, negotiators often seek supportive (confirming) evidence for that choice, while ignoring or failing to seek disconfirming evidence. Initial commitments become set in stone (see the later section on anchoring and adjustment), and a desire for consistency prevents negotiators from changing them. This desire for consistency is often exacerbated by a desire to save face and to maintain an impression of expertise or control in front of others. No one likes to admit error or failure, especially when the other party may perceive doing so as a weakness.

What has been done continuously in the past that isn't working?

One way to combat these tendencies is to have an advisor serve as a reality checkpoint—someone who is not consumed by the "heat of the moment" and who can warn negotiators when they inadvertently begin to behave irrationally. Also, research suggests that decision makers are less likely to escalate if they experienced regret following a previous escalation situation.[27]

2. Mythical Fixed-Pie Beliefs

Many negotiators assume that all negotiations involve a fixed pie.[28] Negotiators often approach integrative negotiation opportunities as zero-sum situations or win–lose exchanges. Those who believe in the mythical fixed pie assume there is no possibility for integrative settlements and mutually beneficial trade-offs, and they suppress efforts to search for them.[29] In a salary negotiation, the job applicant who assumes that salary is the only issue may insist on $55,000 when the employer is offering $52,000. Only when the two parties discuss the possibilities further do they discover that moving expenses and starting date can also be negotiated, which may facilitate resolution of the salary issue.

The tendency to see negotiation in fixed-pie terms varies depending on how people view the nature of a given conflict situation.[30] Negotiators focusing on personal interests are most likely to come under the influence of fixed-pie beliefs and approach the situation competitively. Negotiators focusing on values are less likely to see the problem in fixed-pie terms and more inclined to approach the situation cooperatively.

3. Anchoring and Adjustment

Cognitive biases in anchoring and adjustment are related to the effect of the standard (or anchor) against which subsequent adjustments are made during negotiation. A classic example of an anchor in negotiation is hearing the other side's first offer and then thinking, "Gee, that offer was much lower than I expected; perhaps I've misconstrued the value here and should reconsider my goals and tactics." Anchors like this set a potentially hazardous trap for the negotiator on the receiving end because the choice of an anchor (e.g., an initial offer or an intended goal) might well be based on faulty or incomplete information and thus be misleading in and of itself. However, once the anchor is defined, parties tend to treat it as a real, valid benchmark by which to adjust other judgments, such as the value of the thing being negotiated, or the size of one's counteroffer.[31] A study of real estate agents, for example, showed that agents appraising the value of a house were very strongly affected by its asking price.[32] The asking price served as a convenient anchor to use in appraising the value of the house. Goals in negotiation—whether set realistically or carelessly—can also serve as anchors. These anchors may be visible or invisible to the other party (a published market price versus an uncommunicated expectation), and, similarly, the person who holds them may do so consciously or unconsciously (a specific expectation versus an unexamined, unquestioned expectation or norm). Thorough preparation, along with the use of a devil's advocate or reality check, can help prevent errors of anchoring and adjustment.

4. Issue Framing and Risk

As we discussed earlier in this chapter, a frame is a perspective or point of view that people use when they gather information and solve problems. Frames can lead people to seek, avoid, or be neutral about risk in negotiation. The way a negotiation is framed can make negotiators more or less risk averse or risk seeking. For instance, people respond quite differently when they are negotiating to "gain" something rather than to "not lose" something.[33] A basic finding from research that led to the development of what is known as "prospect theory" is that people are more risk-*averse* when a decision problem is framed as a possible *gain,* and risk-*seeking* when it is framed as a *loss.*[34] In other words, negotiators may overreact to a perceived loss when they might react more positively to the same situation if it is framed as a perceived gain. Hence, as a negotiator you must "avoid the pitfalls of being framed while, simultaneously, understanding positively and negatively framing your opponent."[35] When negotiators are risk-averse, they are more likely to accept any viable offer simply because they are afraid of losing. In contrast, when negotiators are risk-seeking, they are apt to wait for a better offer or for future concessions.

This positive/negative framing process is important because the same offer can elicit markedly different courses of action depending on how it is framed in gain–loss terms. Negotiations in which the outcomes are negatively framed tend to produce fewer concessions and reach fewer agreements, and negotiators perceive outcomes as less fair than negotiations in which the outcomes are positively framed.[36] Remedies for the potentially pernicious effects of framing are similar to those we have mentioned for other cognitive biases (e.g., awareness of the bias, sufficient information, thorough analysis, and reality checks) but can be difficult to achieve because frames are often tied to deeply held values and beliefs or to other anchors that are hard to detect.

5. Availability of Information

Negotiators must also be concerned with the potential bias caused by the availability of information or how easy information is to retrieve—that is, how easily it can be recalled and used to inform or evaluate a process or a decision.[37] One way the availability bias operates in negotiation is through presentation of information in vivid, colorful, or attention-getting ways, making it easy to recall, and making it central and critical in evaluating events and options. Information presented through a particularly clear message, diagram, or formula (even one that is oversimplified) will likely be believed more readily than information presented in a confusing or detailed format—regardless of the accuracy of each. The availability of information also affects negotiation through the use of established search patterns. If negotiators have a favorite way of collecting information or looking for key signals, they will use these patterns repeatedly and may overvalue the information that comes from them.

6. The Winner's Curse

The winner's curse refers to the tendency of negotiators, particularly in an auction setting, to settle quickly on an item and then subsequently feel discomfort about a negotiation win that comes too easily.[38] If the other party capitulates too quickly, the negotiator is often left wondering, "Could I have gotten this for less?" or asking "What's wrong with the item/product/option?" The negotiator may suspect that the other party knows too much or has insight into an unseen advantage; thus, either "I could have done better" or "This must be a bad deal."

For example, in an antique store several years ago one of the authors of this book saw a clock that he and his wife fell in love with. After spending the afternoon in the neighborhood deciding on a negotiation strategy (opening offer, bottom line, timing, feigned disinterest, the good guy/bad guy tactic), the author and his wife returned to the store to enact their strategy. The store owner accepted their first offer. Upon arriving home, suffering from the winner's curse, they left the clock in the garage, where it remains collecting dust.

The best remedy for the winner's curse is to prevent it from occurring in the first place by doing the advance work needed to avoid making on offer that is unexpectedly accepted. Thorough investigation and preparation can provide negotiators with independent verification of appropriate settlement values. Negotiators can also try to secure performance or quality guarantees from the other party to make sure the outcome is not faulty or defective.

7. Overconfidence

Overconfidence is the tendency of negotiators to believe that their ability to be correct or accurate is greater than is actually true. Overconfidence has a double-edged effect: (1) it can solidify the degree to which negotiators support positions or options that are incorrect or inappropriate, and (2) it can lead negotiators to discount the worth or validity of the judgments of others, in effect shutting down other parties as sources of information, interests, and options necessary for a successful integrative negotiation. One study found that negotiators who were not trained to be aware of the overconfidence heuristic tended to overestimate their probability of being successful, and were significantly less likely to compromise or reach agreements than trained negotiators.[39] In another study, overconfident individuals were more persistent and were more concerned about their own outcomes than were the realistically confident negotiators.[40] This does not mean, however, that negotiators should always seek to suppress confidence or optimism. Research on distributive bargaining found that negotiators biased toward optimism achieved more profitable settlements compared with negotiators with accurate perceptions or with a bias toward pessimism.[41] Clearly, more research is needed on the interplay of optimism, overconfidence, and negotiation outcomes.

8. The Law of Small Numbers

In decision theory, the law of small numbers refers to the tendency of people to draw conclusions from small sample sizes. In negotiation, the law of small numbers applies to the way negotiators learn and extrapolate from their own experience. If that experience is limited in time or in scope (e.g., if all of one's prior negotiations have been hard-fought and distributive), the tendency is to extrapolate prior experience onto future negotiations (e.g., all negotiations are distributive). This tendency will often lead to a self-fulfilling prophecy, as follows: people who expect to be treated in a distributive manner will (1) be more likely to perceive the other party's behavior as distributive and (2) treat the other party in a more distributive manner. The other party will then likely interpret the negotiator's behavior as evidence of a distributive tendency and will therefore respond in kind. The smaller the prior sample (i.e., the more limited the negotiation experience), the greater the possibility that past lessons will be erroneously used to infer what will happen in the future. Styles and strategies that worked in the past may not work in the future, and they certainly will not work if future negotiations differ significantly from past experiences.

9. Self-Serving Biases

People often explain another person's behavior by making attributions, either to the person (i.e., the behaviors were caused by internal factors such as ability, mood, or effort) or to the situation (i.e., the behaviors were caused by external factors such as the task, other people, or fate).[42] In "explaining" another person's behavior, the tendency is to overestimate the causal role of personal or internal factors and underestimate the causal role of situational or external factors. For example, consider the student who arrives late for a morning class. Perhaps she is lazy (an internal, dispositional explanation), or perhaps she had a flat tire driving to campus (an external, situational explanation). Absent other information, the professor tends to be biased toward the internal explanation (she's lazy). Perceptual biases are often exacerbated by the actor–observer effect, in which people tend to attribute their own behavior to situational factors, but attribute others' behaviors to personal factors saying in effect, "If I mess up, it's bad luck (the situation, someone else's fault, etc.); if you mess up, it's your fault!"[43]

Research has documented the effects of self-serving biases on the negotiation process. For instance, one study found that negotiators in different school districts chose comparison school districts in a self-serving way; that is, the districts they chose as comparison standards for their own district's activities were those that made their districts look most favorable.[44]

Another study found that negotiators believed that they used more constructive tactics than their counterparts and that the strength of this self-serving bias increased with the strength of the conflict between the parties.[45]

Perceptual error may also be expressed in the form of biases or distortions in the evaluation of information. For instance, the false-consensus effect is a tendency to overestimate the degree of support and consensus that exists for one's own position, opinions, or behaviors.[46] We also have a tendency to assume that our personal beliefs or opinions are based on credible information, while opposing beliefs are based on misinformation.[47] Any of these biases can seriously damage a negotiation effort—negotiators subject to them would make faulty judgments regarding tactics or outcome probabilities.

10. Endowment Effect

The endowment effect is the tendency to overvalue something you own or believe you possess. The existence of the endowment effect was shown rather dramatically in a series of experiments involving coffee mugs.[48] In one experiment, some participants were asked whether they would prefer a sum of money or the mug at various possible dollar levels. Based on their responses, it could be determined that they assigned an average value of just over $3.00 to the mug. Other participants were asked to value the mug as a potential buyer; the average value they assigned to the mug was just under $3.00. Members of a third group were actually given the mug and then asked if they would sell the mug for various amounts. Their answers indicated that they placed a value of more than $7.00 on the mug!

In negotiation, the endowment effect can lead to inflated estimations of value that interfere with reaching a good deal. Discussing endowment effects in the context of negotiations over environmental issues, Max Bazerman and his colleagues argued that the status quo serves as a "potentially dysfunctional anchor point, making mutually beneficial trades more difficult."[49] A similar process occurs upon accepting an offer in a negotiation. One study demonstrated that once accepted, a proposal was liked more by negotiators than other proposals that they themselves had offered during the negotiation process.[50]

11. Ignoring Others' Cognitions

Negotiators often don't ask about the other party's perceptions and thoughts, which leaves them to work with incomplete information, and thus produces faulty results. Failure to consider others' cognitions allows negotiators to simplify their thinking about otherwise complex processes; this usually leads to a more distributive strategy and causes a failure to recognize the contingent nature of both sides' behaviors and responses. Although this "failure to consider" might be attributed to some basic, underlying bias against the other party, research suggests that it is more often a way to make the complex task of decision making under conditions of risk and uncertainty more manageable.[51] Research also suggests that training and awareness of this trap reduces its effects only modestly.[52] The drive to ignore others' cognitions is very deep-seated, and it can be avoided only if negotiators explicitly focus on putting in the effort needed to form an accurate understanding of the other party's interests, goals, and perspectives.

12. Reactive Devaluation

Reactive devaluation is the process of devaluing the other party's concessions simply because the other party made them.[53] Such devaluation may be based in emotionality ("I just don't like him") or on distrust fostered by past experience. Reactive devaluation leads negotiators to minimize the magnitude of a concession made by a disliked other, to reduce their willingness to respond with a concession of equal size, or to seek even more from the other party once a concession has been made.[54] Reactive devaluation may be minimized by maintaining an objective view of the process, by assigning a colleague to do this task, by clarifying each side's preferences on options and concessions before any are made,[55] or by using a third party to mediate or filter concession-making processes.

Managing Misperceptions and Cognitive Biases in Negotiation

Misperceptions and cognitive biases typically arise out of conscious awareness as negotiators gather and process information. The question of how best to manage perceptual and cognitive bias is a difficult one. Certainly the first level of managing such distortions is to be aware that they can occur. However, awareness by itself may not be enough; research evidence shows that simply telling people about misconceptions and cognitive biases does little to counteract their effects.[56] For example, researchers in one study tried to teach students to avoid the winner's curse in a series of auction simulations. They told students about the results of 128 auctions over a four-week period but found that the training had little impact on reducing the winner's curse.[57]

"Careful—it might be a trap!"

More research is needed to provide negotiators with advice about how to overcome the negative effects of misperception and cognitive biases in negotiation. Until then, the best advice that negotiators can follow is simply to be aware of the negative aspects of these effects and to discuss them in a structured manner within their team and with their counterparts.

Mood, Emotion, and Negotiation

Research on negotiation has been dominated by views that have favored rational, cognitive, economic analyses of the negotiation process. These approaches have tended to analyze the rationality of negotiation, examine how negotiators make judgment errors that deviate from rationality, or assess how negotiators can optimize their outcomes. Negotiators are portrayed as rational beings who seem calculating, calm, and in control. But, this overlooks the role played by emotion in negotiation.

The role of mood and emotion in negotiation has been the subject of an increasing body of recent theory and research during the last decade.[58] The distinction between mood and emotion is based on three characteristics: specificity, intensity, and duration. Mood states are more diffuse, less intense, and more enduring than emotion states, which tend to be more intense and directed at more specific targets.[59] Emotions play important roles at various stages of negotiation interaction.[60] There are many new and exciting developments in the study of mood, emotion, and negotiation, and we can present only a limited overview here. The following are some selected findings.

Negotiations Create Both Positive and Negative Emotions   Positive emotions can result from being attracted to the other party, feeling good about the development of the negotiation process and the progress that the parties are making, or liking the results that the negotiations have produced.[61] Conversely, negative emotions can result from being turned off by the other party, feeling bad about the development of the negotiation process and the progress being made, or disliking the results. Positive emotions tend to be classified under the single term *happiness,* but we tend to discriminate more precisely among negative emotions.[62] Some negative emotions may tend to be based in dejection while others are based in agitation. Dejection-related emotions result from feeling disappointed, frustrated, or dissatisfied, while agitation-related emotions result from feeling anxious, fearful, or threatened.[63] Dejection-related emotions may lead negotiators to act aggressively, while agitation-related emotions may lead negotiators to try to retaliate or to get out of the situation.[64]

Positive Emotions Generally Have Positive Consequences for Negotiations   Positive emotions can lead to these consequences:

- *Positive feelings are more likely to lead the parties toward more integrative processes.* Researchers have shown that negotiators who feel positive emotions toward each other are more likely to strive for integrative agreements and are more likely to be flexible in how they arrive at a solution to a problem.[65]

- *Positive feelings create a positive attitude toward the other side.* When negotiators like the other party, they tend to be more flexible in the negotiations. Having a positive attitude toward the other increases concession making, lessens hostile behaviors, and builds trust among the parties.[66]

- *Positive feelings promote persistence.* If negotiators feel positively attracted, they are more likely to feel confident and, as a result, to persist in trying to get their concerns and issues addressed in the negotiation and to achieve better outcomes.[67]

Aspects of the Negotiation Process Can Lead to Positive Emotions   Researchers have begun to explore the emotional consequences of negotiation. Here are two findings regarding how the negotiation process shapes emotion-related outcomes:

- *Positive feelings result from fair procedures during negotiation.* Researchers have explored how emotional responses are related to the experience of fairness during the negotiation process. Findings indicate that negotiators who see the process as fair experience more positive feelings and are less inclined to express negative emotions following the encounter.[68]

- *Positive feelings result from favorable social comparisons.* Evidence shows that individual satisfaction after a negotiation is higher when the individual negotiator's outcomes compare favorably with others in similar situations.[69] Interestingly, however, this finding for so-called *external* social comparisons (comparing your outcome to others outside the negotiation that just took place) do not hold for *internal* social comparisons (comparing your outcome to the counterpart with whom you just negotiated). This may occur because comparisons with an opponent—even favorable ones—focus the negotiator's attention on missed opportunities to claim additional value in this negotiation.

Negative Emotions Generally Have Negative Consequences for Negotiations   As we noted earlier, negative feelings may be based either in dejection or in agitation, one or both parties may feel the emotions, and the behavior of one may prompt the emotional reaction in the other. Some specific research findings follow. (See Box 5.2 for some advice on how to deal with an opponent who brings negative emotion to the table.)

- *Negative emotions may lead parties to define the situation as competitive or distributive.* A negative mood increases the likelihood that the actor will increase belligerent behavior toward the other.[70] In a negotiation situation, this negative behavior is most likely to take the shape of a more distributive posture on the issues.

- *Negative emotions may undermine a negotiator's ability to analyze the situation accurately, which adversely affects individual outcomes.* Research indicates that angry negotiators are less accurate at judging the other party's interests and at recalling their own interests, compared with negotiators with neutral emotion.[71] It is noteworthy that the experimental manipulation of anger in this study was unrelated to the negotiation itself—anger was aroused during what subjects believed was a separate experiment preceding the negotiation experiment. This carryover effect of anger highlights the power of negative emotion to divert one's attention and focus from the negotiation problem at hand.

- *Negative emotions may lead parties to escalate the conflict.* When the mood is negative—more specifically, when both parties are dejected, frustrated, and blame

Emotions are inevitable in negotiations, and it isn't realistic to try to avoid them or eradicate them from the encounter. Negotiation scholar Barbara Gray argues that effective negotiators figure out how to handle emotional outbursts from others who may be simply trying to "push our hot buttons." She offers these suggestions for dealing with an opponent who has expressed his or her feelings in a volatile or even hurtful way:

1. *Separate the emotion from its expression.* Perhaps the emotion is really a way for the other person to signal an important interest. Why is the other person acting this way? What interest is important enough to justify it?

2. *Turn the table.* Put yourself in the other person's position, and ask yourself, "Why would I behave that way?" This may help you identify a circumstance in which this sort of emotional outburst would be legitimate. The idea is not to accept the other person's (unacceptable) behavior, but to view it as a reflection of some identifiable need or interest to be addressed in the negotiation.

3. *Reflect the emotion being expressed back to the other party.* Sometimes strong feelings are an indication that the other party simply wants to be heard. Confirm that you are listening and that the concern that triggered the emotion is understood. This need not signal that you are agreeing with the concern or conceding anything; you are simply acknowledging that the other party is human and has feelings. This may be all the other party needs.

4. *Ask questions to uncover the issue or interest behind the emotion.* Knowing what the underlying concern is makes it possible for you to move on from emotion to substance, and to treat that concern (once you know what it is) as an issue on the table for negotiation.

Source: Adapted from B. Gray, "Negotiating with Your Nemesis," *Negotiation Journal* 19 (2003a), pp. 299–310.

the other—conflict is likely to become personal, the number of issues in the conflict may expand, and other parties may be drawn into the dispute.[72] Expressions of anger by one party may trigger anger from the other party, reducing the chances for a successful settlement of the dispute.[73]

- *Negative emotions may lead parties to retaliate and may thwart integrative outcomes.* When the parties are angry with each other, and when their previous interaction has already led one party to seek to punish the other, the other may choose to retaliate.[74] Negative emotions may also lead to less effective outcomes. The more a negotiator holds the other responsible for destructive behavior in a previous interaction, the more anger and less compassion he or she feels for the other party. This in turn leads to less concern for the other's interests and a lower likelihood of discovering mutually beneficial negotiated solutions.[75]

- *Not all negative emotions have the same effect.* Anger may tend to escalate conflict and foster retaliation, but what about less "hot" negative emotions, such as worry, disappointment, guilt, and regret? Research shows that negotiators make smaller demands of worried or disappointed opponents, presumably feeling sorry for their situation, but make fewer concessions to guilty or regretful opponents. Negotiators do, however, report more favorable impressions of regretful opponents, viewing them as more interpersonally sensitive than opponents experiencing worry or disappointment.[76]

Aspects of the Negotiation Process Can Lead to Negative Emotions   As with positive emotion, research exploring the negative emotional consequences of negotiation is recent and limited. Here are two findings:

- *Negative emotions may result from a competitive mind-set.* Negotiators with a fixed-pie perception of the situation tend to be less satisfied with negotiated outcomes than those with an integrative orientation. This may stem from the perception that when a negotiation is viewed as zero-sum, the other party's gains mean an equivalent loss for self.[77]

- *Negative emotions may result from impasse.* When a negotiation ends in impasse, negotiators are more likely to experience negative emotions such as anger and frustration compared with negotiators who successfully reach agreement.[78] However, people with more confidence in their negotiating ability may be less likely to experience negative emotion in the wake of impasse. This is important because impasse is not always a bad thing—the goal is achieving a good outcome, not merely reaching an agreement.

- *Negative emotions may result merely from the prospect of beginning a negotiation.* We might assume that inexperienced negotiators are most apt to be nervous about an upcoming bargaining session, but even experienced negotiators may feel anxiety going in to the encounter. Anxiety isn't all bad, however; it may spark creativity that can help produce constructive outcomes.[79]

The Effects of Positive and Negative Emotion in Negotiation   It is possible for positive emotion to generate negative outcomes and for negative feelings to elicit beneficial outcomes, as we explain here:

- *Positive feelings may have negative consequences.* First, negotiators in a positive mood may be less likely to examine closely the other party's arguments. As a result, they may be more susceptible to a competitive opponent's deceptive tactics.[80] In addition, because negotiators with positive feelings are less focused on the arguments of the other party, they may achieve less-than-optimal outcomes.[81] Finally, if positive feelings create strong positive expectations, parties who are not able to find an integrative agreement are likely to experience the defeat more strongly and perhaps treat the other party more harshly.[82]

- *Negative feelings may create positive outcomes.* Just as positive emotions can create negative outcomes, it is clear that negative emotions can create positive consequences for negotiation. First, negative emotion has information value. It alerts the parties that the situation is problematic and needs attention, which may motivate them to either leave the situation or resolve the problem.[83] There is also recent evidence that when a negotiator uses words that trigger negative emotions, others become more optimistic that the negotiation will be successfully resolved.[84] In short, anger and other negative emotions can serve as a danger signal that motivates both parties to confront the problem directly and search for a resolution.[85]

Anger, of course, may also signal that a negotiator is tough or ambitious, and researchers have found negotiators concede more often to an angry opponent than to a happy or unemotional partner.[86] But even if it sometimes pays to be angry in competitive negotiations (as a signal of toughness or reluctance to compromise), research also tells us when anger can backfire. Anger is less likely to elicit concessions when the party on the receiving end of anger either (1) has the opportunity to respond with deception (e.g., misrepresent his own interests) or (2) has little at stake, meaning little to fear from having the angry opponent say no to an offer.[87]

Emotions Can Be Used Strategically as Negotiation Gambits   Finally, we have been discussing emotions as though they were genuine. Given the power that emotions may have in swaying the other side toward one's own point of view, emotions may also be used strategically and manipulatively as influence tactics within negotiation. For example, negotiators may intentionally manipulate emotion in order to get the other side to adopt certain beliefs or take certain actions.[88]

In one study, negotiators who were coached to implement a positive emotional tone were more likely to reach agreements that incorporated a future business relationship between the parties compared to those implementing a negative or neutral emotional strategy. Negotiators exhibiting positive emotionality were more likely to induce compliance with ultimatum offers.[89]

Beyond the strategic expression of one's own (genuine or fabricated) emotions, negotiators may also engage in the regulation or management of the emotions of the other party. Effective negotiators are able to adjust their messages to adapt to what they perceive as the other party's emotional state.[90] Some psychologists regard the ability to perceive and regulate emotions as a stable individual difference that has come to be known as emotional intelligence.[91]

In summary, emotions are critical features of negotiation encounters that supplement the classical view that negotiation is primarily a rational process of decision making under risk and uncertainty. In the traditional view, we understand negotiation by looking at how negotiators weigh information and make judgments that optimize their outcomes. Negotiators, as we said at the outset of this chapter, are seen as rational actors who are calculating, calm, and in control. But as researchers have come to realize, negotiations involve humans who not only deviate from rational judgments, but who inevitably experience and express emotions in circumstances where much is at stake.

Chapter Summary

In this chapter we have taken a multifaceted look at the role of perception, cognition, and emotion in negotiation. The first portion of the chapter presented a brief overview of the perceptual process and discussed four types of perceptual distortions: stereotyping, halo effects, selective perception, and projection. We then turned to a discussion of how framing influences perceptions in negotiation and how reframing and issue development both change negotiator perceptions during negotiations.

The chapter then discussed one of the most important recent areas of inquiry in negotiation, that of cognitive biases in negotiation. This was followed by consideration of ways to manage misperception and cognitive biases in negotiation. In a final section we considered mood and emotion in negotiation, which provides an important alternative to cognitive and perceptual processes for understanding negotiation behavior.

Endnotes

[1] Babcock, Wang, and Loewenstein, 1996; de Dreu and van Lange, 1995; Thompson, 1995; Thompson and Hastie, 1990a.

[2] de Dreu, 2003; Devine, 1989; Forgas and Fiedler, 1996.

[3] Sherif, Harvey, White, Hood, and Sherif, 1988.

[4] Cooper, 1981.

[5] Bruner and Tagiuri, 1954.

[6] Ibid.

[7] Van Boven, Gilovich, and Medvec, 2003.

[8] Bateson, 1972; Goffman, 1974.

[9] Putnam and Holmer, 1992, p. 129.

[10] Buechler, 2000.

[11] Thompson, 1998.

[12] Roth and Sheppard, 1995.

[13] Follett, 1942, quoted in Putnam and Holmer, 1992.

[14] Note that frames themselves cannot be "seen." They are abstractions, perceptions, and thoughts that people use to define a situation, organize information, determine what is important, what is not, and so on. We can infer other people's frames by asking them directly about their frames, by listening to their communication, and by watching their behavior. Similarly, we can try to understand our own frames by thinking about what aspects of a situation we should pay attention to, emphasize, focus on, or ignore—and by observing our own words and actions. One cannot see or directly measure a frame, however.

[15] Gray, 1997; Gray and Donnellon, 1989; Lewicki, Gray, and Elliott, 2003.

[16] Gray, 1991, 1997; Lewicki, Gray, and Elliott, 2003.

[17] Conlon and Hunt, 2002; Hunt and Kernan, 2005.

[18] Ury, Brett, and Goldberg, 1988.

[19] Felstiner, Abel, and Sarat, 1980–81.

[20] Jensen, 1995.

[21] Putnam and Wilson, 1989; Putnam, Wilson, and Turner, 1990.

[22] Ikle, 1964.

[23] Zartman, 1977; Zartman and Berman, 1982.

[24] Putnam, 1994.

[25] For extensive reviews of research on cognitive biases in negotiation, see Bazerman and Carroll, 1987; Neale and Bazerman, 1992a; and Thompson and Hastie, 1990b. Whether negotiators misperceive information or misprocess information remains a technical debate in the communication and negotiation literature that is beyond the scope of this book.

[26] Brockner, 1992; Staw, 1981.

[27] Ku, 2008.

[28] Thompson, 1990a.

[29] Pinkley, Griffith, and Northcraft, 1995; Thompson and Hastie, 1990a, 1990b.

[30] Harinck, de Dreu, and Van Vianen, 2000.

[31] Kristensen and Garling, 1997. See also Diekmann, Tenbrunsel, Shah, Schroth, and Bazerman, 1996; Ritov, 1996.

[32] Northcraft and Neale, 1987.

[33] Schurr, 1987. See also Bazerman, Magliozzi, and Neale, 1985; de Dreu, Carnevale, Emans, and van de Vliert; 1994; Neale, Huber, and Northcraft, 1987.

[34] Kahneman and Tversky, 1979.

[35] Neale and Bazerman, 1992b, p. 50.

[36] Bazerman and Neale, 1992.

[37] Tversky and Kahneman, 1982.

[38] Bazerman and Samuelson, 1983. See also Ball, Bazerman, and Carroll, 1991; Foreman and Murnighan, 1996.

[39] Neale and Bazerman, 1983.

[40] Lim, 1997.

[41] Bottom and Paese, 1999.

[42] Heider, 1958.

[43] Jones and Nisbett, 1976.

[44] Babcock, Wang, and Loewenstein, 1996.

[45] de Dreu, Nauta, and van de Vliert, 1995.

[46] Ross, Greene, and House, 1977.

[47] Fragale and Heath, 2004.

[48] Kahneman, Knetsch, and Thaler, 1990.

[49] Bazerman, Moore, and Gillespie, 1999, p. 1288.

[50] Curhan, Neale, and Ross, 2004.

[51] Carroll, Bazerman, and Maury, 1988.

[52] Carroll, Delquie, Halpern, and Bazerman, 1990.

[53] Stillenger, Epelbaum, Keltner, and Ross, 1990.

[54] Neale and Bazerman, 1992a.

[55] Stillenger et al., 1990.

[56] Babcock and Loewenstein, 1997; Thompson and Hastie, 1990a.

[57] Foreman and Murnighan, 1996.

[58] For reviews of research literature on emotion in negotiation, see Allred, Mallozzi, Matsui, and Raia, 1997; Barry, Fulmer, and Goates, 2006; Barry, Fulmer, and Van Kleef, 2004; Kumar, 1997.

[59] Forgas, 1992; Parrott, 2001.

[60] Barry and Oliver, 1996.

[61] Carver and Scheir, 1990.

[62] Kumar, 1997.

[63] Higgins, 1987.

[64] Berkowitz, 1989.

[65] Carnevale and Isen, 1986; Isen and Baron, 1991.

[66] Baron, 1990; Druckman and Broome, 1991; Pruitt and Carnevale, 1993.

[67] Kramer, Pommerenke, and Newton, 1993.

[68] Hegtvedt and Killian, 1999.

[69] Novemsky and Schweitzer, 2004.

[70] Veitch and Griffith, 1976.

[71] Gonzalez, Lerner, Moore, and Babcock, 2004.

[72] Kumar, 1997.

[73] Friedman, Anderson, Brett, Olekalns, Goates, and Lisco, 2004.

[74] Allred, 1999; Bies and Tripp, 1998.

[75] Allred, Mallozzi, Matsui, and Raia, 1997.

[76] Van Kleef, de Dreu, and Manstead, 2006.

[77] Thompson and DeHarpport, 1994.

[78] O'Connor and Arnold, 2001.

[79] Wheeler, 2004.

[80] Bless, Bohner, Schwartz, and Strack, 1988.

[81] Kumar, 1997.

[82] Parrott, 1994.

[83] van de Vliert, 1985.

[84] Schroth, Bain-Chekal, and Caldwell, 2005.

[85] Daly, 1991.

[86] Sinaceur and Tiedens, 2006; Van Kleef, de Dreu, and Manstead, 2004.

[87] van Dijk, Van Kleef, Steinel, and van Beest, 2008.

[88] Barry, 1999.

[89] Kopelman, Rosette, and Thompson, 2006.

[90] Thompson, Nadler, and Kim, 1999.

[91] Mayer, Salovey, and Caruso, 2000.

6

CHAPTER

Communication

Objectives

1. Explore what is communicated in a negotiation and how people communicate.
2. Consider the ways that communication might be improved in negotiation.
3. Gain practical tools for how to improve communication processes in any negotiation.

Reduced to its essence, negotiation is a form of interpersonal communication. Communication processes, both verbal and nonverbal, are critical to achieving negotiation goals and to resolving conflicts. In this chapter we examine the process by which negotiators communicate their own interests, positions, and goals—and in turn make sense of those of the other party and of the negotiation as a whole. The chapter opens with a discussion of *what* is communicated in a negotiation, followed by an exploration of *how* people communicate in negotiation. The chapter concludes with discussions of how to improve communication in negotiation and of special communication considerations at the close of negotiations.

What Is Communicated during Negotiation?

One of the fundamental questions that researchers in communication and negotiation have examined is, What is communicated during negotiation? This work has taken several different forms but generally involves audio taping or videotaping negotiation role-plays and analyzing the patterns of communication that occur in them. In one study, researchers videotaped executives who participated in a 60-minute, three-person negotiation involving two oil companies.[1] The researchers found that more than 70 percent of the verbal tactics that buyers and sellers used during the negotiation were integrative. In addition, buyers and sellers tended to behave reciprocally—when one party used an integrative tactic, the other tended to respond with an integrative tactic.

Most of the communication during negotiation is not about negotiator preferences.[2] Although the blend of integrative versus distributive content varies as a function of the issues being discussed, it is also clear that the content of communication is only partly responsible for negotiation outcomes.[3] For example, one party may choose not to communicate certain things (e.g., the reason she chose a different supplier), so her counterpart (e.g., the supplier not chosen) may be unaware why some outcomes occur. In the following sections, we discuss five different categories of communication that take place during negotiations and then consider the question of whether more communication is always better than less communication.

1. Offers, Counteroffers, and Motives

Among the most important communications in negotiation are those that convey offers and counteroffers.[4] Bargainers have definite preferences and exhibit rational behavior by acting in accordance with those preferences. A negotiator's preferences reflect in good measure his or her underlying motivations, which are also communicated during a negotiation, and they can have a powerful influence on the actions of the other party and on negotiation outcomes. A communicative framework for negotiation is based on the assumptions that (1) the communication of offers is a dynamic process (the offers change or shift over time), (2) the offer process is interactive (bargainers influence each other), and (3) various internal and external factors (e.g., time limitations, reciprocity norms, alternatives, constituency pressures) drive the interaction.[5] In other words, the offer–counteroffer process is dynamic and interactive, and subject to situational and environmental constraints. This process constantly revises the parameters of the negotiation, eventually narrowing the bargaining range and guiding the discussion toward a settlement point.

2. Information about Alternatives

Communication in negotiation is not limited to the exchange of offers and counteroffers, however. Another important aspect that has been studied is how sharing information with the other party influences the negotiation process. For instance, is simply having a best alternative to a negotiated agreement (BATNA) sufficient to give a negotiator an advantage over the other party? Should one's BATNA be communicated to the other person? Research suggests that the existence of a BATNA changes several things in a negotiation: (1) compared to negotiators without attractive BATNAs, negotiators with attractive BATNAs set higher reservation prices for themselves than their counterparts did; (2) negotiators whose counterparts have attractive BATNAs set lower reservation points for themselves; and (3) when both parties are aware of the attractive BATNA that one of the negotiators has, that negotiator receives a more positive negotiation outcome.[6] Thus, negotiators with an attractive BATNA should tell the other party about it if they expect to receive its full benefits. We hasten to add that the style and tone used to convey information about an attractive BATNA matters. Politely (even subtly) making the other party aware of one's good alternative can provide leverage without alienating the other party. On the other hand, waving a good BATNA in the other party's face in an imposing or condescending manner may be construed as aggressive and threatening.

3. Information about Outcomes

Researcher Leigh Thompson and her colleagues examined the effects of sharing information on negotiators' evaluations of their own success.[7] The study focused on how winners and losers evaluated their negotiation outcomes (winners were defined as negotiators who received more points in the negotiation simulation). Thompson and her colleagues found that winners and losers evaluated their own outcomes equally when they did not know how

well the other party had done, but if they found out that the other negotiator had done better, or was simply pleased with his or her outcome, then negotiators felt less positive about their own outcome. Another study suggests that even when negotiators learn that the other party did relatively poorly, they are less satisfied with the outcome than when they have no comparison information.[8] Taken together, these findings suggest that negotiators should be cautious about sharing their outcomes or even their positive reactions to outcomes with the other party, especially if they are going to negotiate with that party again in the future.

4. Social Accounts

Another type of communication that occurs during negotiation consists of the "social accounts" that negotiators use to explain things to the other party, especially when negotiators need to justify bad news.[9] Three types of explanations are important: (1) explanations of mitigating circumstances, where negotiators suggest that they had no choice in taking the positions they did; (2) explanations of exonerating circumstances, where negotiators explain their positions from a broader perspective, suggesting that while their current position may appear negative, it derives from positive motives (e.g., an honest mistake); and (3) reframing explanations, where outcomes can be explained by changing the context (e.g., short-term pain for long-term gain).[10] Negotiators who use multiple explanations are more likely to have better outcomes, and the negative effects of poor outcomes can be alleviated by communicating explanations for them.[11]

5. Communication about Process

Lastly, some communication is about the negotiation process itself—how well it is going or what procedures might be adopted to improve the situation. Some of this communication takes the form of seemingly trivial "small talk" that breaks the ice or builds rapport between negotiators. Clearly, though, some communication about process is not just helpful, but critical, as when conflict intensifies and negotiators run the risk of letting hostilities overtake progress. One strategy involves calling attention to the other party's contentious actions and explicitly labeling the process as counterproductive.[12] Negotiators seeking to break out of a conflict spiral should resist the natural urge to reciprocate contentious communication from the other party. Negotiators, like other busy humans, may be tempted to forge ahead with offers and counteroffers in pursuit of an outcome rather than pause and "waste" time to discuss a process gone sour. Sometimes that break in the substantive conversation and attention to process is precisely what's needed.

We conclude this section on *what* is communication in negotiation with three key questions.

Are Negotiators Consistent or Adaptive?

Effective negotiators are able to adapt their strategy and style to particular bargaining situations. But while this may be good advice, research indicates that when it comes to communication patterns, negotiators are more likely to be consistent in their strategies than to vary their approach.[13] Negotiators react to only a small proportion of the available cues communicated by their partner and use only a small proportion of possible response. Moreover, this proportion becomes smaller as the negotiation proceeds, meaning there is less variation in forms of communication the longer a negotiation goes on.[14] It appears that when it comes to making choices about communication, many negotiators prefer sticking with the familiar rather than venturing into improvisation.

Does It Matter What Is Said Early in the Negotiation?

A relatively small amount of communication in a negotiation encounter can have large effects on the outcomes that result. Researchers find that "thin slices" of negotiation—communication patterns during the first five minutes—have a large effect on the negotiated agreements that the parties eventually reach.[15] The tone of the conversation during those first few minutes matters: the more negotiators speak with emphasis, varying vocal pitch and volume, the worse they do and the better the other party does.[16] In other words, controlling "the floor" early in the negotiation helps, but not dominating it with emotional or hyperbolic communication.

Controlling the conversation early on may help an individual negotiator do better, but does it help the pair achieve integrative outcomes? There is evidence that joint gains are influenced by what happens early on. One study found greater joint gains when negotiators move beyond posturing to exchanging information about issues and priorities before the negotiation is too far along.[17]

Is More Information Always Better?

Some research has suggested that receiving too much information during negotiation may actually be detrimental to negotiators; this is sometimes called the information-is-weakness effect.[18] Negotiators who know the complete preferences of both parties may have more difficulty determining fair outcomes than negotiators who do not have this information.

There is evidence that having more information does not automatically translate into better negotiation outcomes. One study found that the amount of information exchanged did not improve the overall accuracy of the parties' perceptions of each other's preferences.[19] The influence of the exchange of accurate information on negotiation outcomes is not as direct as people might expect—that is, simply exchanging information does not automatically lead to better understanding of the other party's preferences or to better negotiation outcomes.

How People Communicate in Negotiation

While it may seem obvious that how negotiators communicate is as important as what they have to say, research has examined different aspects of how people communicate in negotiation. We address three aspects related to the "how" of communication: the characteristics of language that communicators use, the use of nonverbal communication in negotiation, and the selection of a communication channel for sending and receiving messages.

Characteristics of Language

In negotiation, language operates at two levels: the *logical* level (for proposals or offers) and the *pragmatic* level (semantics, syntax, and style). The meaning conveyed by a

BOX 6.1   Are All Threats Created Equal?

Is a threat simply a statement about bad things that will happen to the others if they resist? Or is there more to it? Gibbons, Bradac, and Busch (1992) identify five linguistic dimensions of making threats:

1. The use of *polarized language,* in which negotiators use positive words when speaking of their own positions (e.g., generous, reasonable, or even-handed) and negative words when referring to the other party's position (e.g., tight-fisted, unreasonable, or heavy-handed).

2. The conveyance of *verbal immediacy* (a measure of intended immediacy, urgency, or relative psychological distance), either high and intended to engage or compel the other party ("OK, here is the deal" or "I take great care to . . . ") or low and intended to create a sense of distance or aloofness ("Well, there it is" or "One should take great care to . . . ").

3. The degree of *language intensity:* high intensity conveys strong feelings to the recipient (as with statements of affirmation or the frequent use of profanity) and low intensity conveys weak feelings.

4. The degree of *lexical diversity* (i.e., the command of a broad, rich vocabulary), where high levels of lexical diversity denote comfort and competence with language and low levels denote discomfort, anxiety, or inexperience.

5. The extent of a *high-power language style,* with low power denoted by the use of verbal hedges, hesitations, or politeness to the point of deference and subordination and high power denoted by verbal dominance, clarity and firmness of expression, and self-assurance.

According to Gibbons, Bradac, and Busch, threats are more credible if they incorporate negatively polarized descriptions of the other party and his or her position, high immediacy, high intensity, high lexical diversity, and a distinctively high-power style.

Source: Adapted from P. Gibbons, J. J. Bradac, and J. D. Busch. "The Role of Language in Negotiations: Threats and Promises," in L. Putnam and M. Roloff (Eds.), *Communication and Negotiation* (Newbury Park, CA: Sage, 1992), pp. 156–75.

proposition or statement is a combination of one logical surface message and several pragmatic (i.e., hinted or inferred) messages. In other words, it is not only what is said and how it is said that matters but also what additional, veiled, or subsurface information is intended, conveyed, or perceived in reception. By way of illustration, consider threats. We often react not only to the substance of a threatening statement but also (and frequently more strongly) to its unspoken messages that might imply something about the likelihood that the threat will be carried out or about our relationship or our prospects for working together in the future. Box 6.1 illustrates how threats, which on the surface seem straightforward enough as negotiation gambits intended to compel the other party to make a concession, are actually complex and nuanced when analyzed in terms of the specific elements of language used within them.

Whether the intent is to command and compel, sell, persuade, or gain commitment, how parties communicate in negotiation would seem to depend on the ability of the speaker to encode thoughts properly, as well as on the ability of the listener to understand and decode the intended message(s). In addition, negotiators' use of idioms or colloquialisms is often problematic, especially in cross-cultural negotiations. The meaning conveyed might be clear to the speaker but confusing to the listener (e.g., "I'm willing to stay until the last dog is hung"—a statement of positive commitment on the part of some regional Americans, but confusing at best to those with different cultural backgrounds, even within the United States). Even if the meaning is clear, the choice of a word or metaphor may convey a lack of sensitivity or create a sense of exclusion, as is often done when men relate strategic business concerns by using sports metaphors ("Well, it's fourth down and goal to go; this is no time to drop the ball"). Because people generally aren't aware of the potential for such miscommunication with someone from their own culture, they are less well prepared to deal with such miscommunication than they would be if the person were from a different culture.

Finally, a negotiator's choice of words may not only signal a position but also shape and predict the conversation that ensues. Researcher Tony Simons examined linguistic patterns of communication in negotiation; two of his findings are relevant here:[20]

1. Parties whose statements communicated interests in both the substance of the negotiation (things) and the relationship with the other party achieved better, more integrative solutions than parties whose statements were concerned solely with either substance or relationship.

2. Linguistic patterns early in the negotiation help define issues in ways that may help the parties discover integrative possibilities later on.

Use of Nonverbal Communication

Much of what people communicate to one another is transmitted with nonverbal communication. Examples include facial expressions, body language, head movements, and tone of voice, to name just a few. Some nonverbal acts, called *attending behaviors,* are particularly important in connecting with another person during a coordinated interaction like negotiation; they let the other know that you are listening and prepare the other party to receive your message. We discuss three important attending behaviors: eye contact, body position, and encouraging.

Make Eye Contact   Dishonest people and cowards are not supposed to be able to look people in the eye. Poets claim that the eye is the lens that permits us to look into a person's soul. These and other bits of conventional wisdom illustrate how important people believe eye contact to be. In general, making eye contact is one way to show others you are paying attention and listening and that you consider them important. Of course, it is possible to listen very well even when not looking at the other person; in fact, it may be easier to look away because you can focus on the spoken words and not be confused by visual information. But the point is that by not making eye contact, you are not providing the other person with an important cue that you are engaged and listening.

When persuading someone, it is important to make eye contact when delivering the most important part of the message.[21] Having the verbal and nonverbal systems in parallel at this point emphasizes the importance of the message that is being sent. Also, one should maintain eye contact not only when speaking but when receiving communication as well.[22] It is important to recognize, however, that the patterns described here are characteristic of Western society. In other parts of the world, different patterns prevail. In some Asian societies, for example, keeping one's eyes down while the other is speaking is a sign of respect.[23]

Adjust Body Position   Parents frequently advise their children about how to stand and sit, particularly when they are in formal settings such as school, church, or dinner parties. The command "Sit up!" is often accompanied by "And pay attention!" Here the parent is teaching the child another widely held belief—one's body position indicates whether or not one is paying attention to the other party. To ensure that others know you are attentive to them, hold your body erect, lean slightly forward, and face the other person directly.[24] If you accept and endorse the others' message, care needs to be taken not to show disrespect with body position by slouching, turning away, or placing feet on the table.[25] In contrast, crossing arms, bowing the head, furrowing the brow, and squeezing eyebrows together all can signal strong rejection or disapproval of the message.[26]

Nonverbally Encourage or Discourage What the Other Says   One can indicate attention and interest in what another is saying through a variety of simple behaviors. A head nod, a simple hand gesture to go on, or a murmured "unh hunh" to indicate understanding all tell the other person to continue, that you are listening. In fact, you can encourage someone to continue to speak about many subjects by simply nodding your head as he or she is speaking. Brief eye contact or a smile and a nod of the head will both provide encouraging cues. Similarly, a frown, a scowl, a shake of the head, or a grab of one's chest in mock pain will signal disapproval of the other's message.

Nonverbal communication—done well—may help negotiators achieve better outcomes through mutual coordination. One study compared the development of rapport between negotiators who did or did not have visual access to each other while negotiating. The researchers defined rapport as "a state of mutual positivity and interest that arises through the convergence of nonverbal expressive behavior in an interaction."[27] They found that face-to-face interaction stimulated rapport through nonverbal communication, which in turn enhanced coordination and led to higher joint gains. Of course, these benefits will presumably arise only to the extent that parties are able to interpret nonverbal communication accurately.

Selection of a Communication Channel

Communication is experienced differently when it occurs through different channels. We may think of negotiation as typically occurring face to face—an assumption reinforced by the common metaphor of the "negotiation table." But the reality is that people negotiate through a variety of communication media: over the telephone, in writing, and increasingly through electronic channels such as e-mail, teleconferencing, instant messaging, and even text messaging. The use of network-mediated information technologies in negotiation is sometimes referred to as *virtual negotiation* (also at times "e-negotiation"). The use of a particular channel shapes both perceptions of the communication task at hand and norms regarding appropriate behavior; accordingly, channel variations have potentially important effects on negotiation processes and outcomes.[28]

The key variation that distinguishes one communication channel from another is *social bandwidth*—the ability of a channel to carry and convey subtle social and relational cues from sender to receiver that go beyond the literal text of the message itself.[29] For example, as an alternative to face-to-face interaction, the telephone preserves one's ability to transmit social cues through inflection or tone of voice but forfeits the ability to communicate through facial expressions or physical gestures. In written communication, there are only the words and symbols on paper, although one's choice of words and the way they are arranged can certainly convey tone, (in)formality, and emotion.

E-mail, as a ubiquitous mode of personal and organizational communication, can be viewed as simply another form of written communication that happens to involve electronic transmission. There are, however, important distinctions between e-mail and other forms of written communication. Many people, treating e-mail as a highly informal medium, are comfortable sending messages that are stylistically or grammatically unpolished in situations (such as on the job) where they would never send a carelessly written communication on paper. Some people incorporate text-based *emoticons* to convey emotional social cues in their messages (the notorious smiley face [:-)] is the best known emoticon). Early research on interpersonal and small-group communication through computers indicated that the lack of social cues lowers communicator inhibition and leads to more aggressive communication behavior.[30] However, much of that early research into computer-mediated communication focused on anonymous interaction. It is not clear that reduced social cues have the same effect in a communication context, such as negotiation, where the parties are known to each other, and in fact may know each other quite well.[31]

Researchers have been examining the effects of channels in general, and e-mail in particular, on negotiation processes and outcomes during much of the past decade. Unfortunately, there are few consistent findings that point to clear effects. We do know that interacting parties can more easily develop personal rapport in face-to-face communication compared with other channels,[32] and that face-to-face negotiators are more inclined to disclose information truthfully, increasing their ability to attain mutual gain.[33] Research has found that negotiation through written channels is more likely to end in impasse than negotiation that occurs face to face or by phone.[34]

There is also evidence that e-mail negotiators reach agreements that are more equal (a balanced division of resources) than face-to-face negotiators.[35] This may occur to the extent that electronic communication "levels the playing field" between strong and weak negotiators. By giving the individual a chance to ponder at length the other party's message, and to review and revise one's own communication, e-mail may indeed help less interpersonally skilled parties improve their performance, especially when the alternative is negotiating spontaneously (face to face or by phone) with a more accomplished other party.

A growing body of evidence points to the conclusion that negotiators using e-mail need to work harder at building personal rapport with the other party if they are to overcome limitations of the channel that would otherwise inhibit optimal agreements or fuel impasse. What e-mail negotiations lack is *schmoozing*—off-task or relationship-focused conversations that are often present in face-to-face negotiations.[36] Schmoozing is an important avenue for building rapport and establishing trust in the negotiation relationship. In one study, negotiators who schmoozed on the phone prior to e-mail negotiations reached more negotiated agreements, and achieved better outcomes, increased cooperation, and greater trust and optimism regarding future working relationships with the other party.[37]

With so much attention to e-mail, it is important to keep in mind that other online mechanisms exist for virtual negotiations. One study compared negotiations over e-mail with those conducted and via instant messaging (IM). The important difference between these two channels is speed of turn-taking: e-mail is a "slow-tempo" medium, while IM is "fast-tempo" medium that more closely approximates oral communication. In a simulated

BOX 6.2

Top 10 Rules for Virtual Negotiation

1. Take steps to create a face-to-face relationship before negotiation, or early on, so that there is a face or voice behind the e-mail.

2. Be explicit about the normative process to be followed during the negotiation.

3. If others are present in a virtual negotiation (on either your side or theirs) make sure everyone knows who is there and why.

4. Pick the channel (face to face, videoconference, voice, e-mail, etc.) that is most effective at getting all the information and detail on the table so that it can be fully considered by both sides.

5. Avoid "flaming"; when you must express emotion, label the emotion explicitly so the other knows what it is and what's behind it.

6. Formal turn-taking is not strictly necessary, but try to synchronize offers and counteroffers. Speak up if it is not clear "whose turn it is."

7. Check out assumptions you are making about the other's interests, offers, proposals, or conduct. Less face-to-face contact means less information about the other party and a greater chance that inferences will get you in trouble, so ask questions.

8. In many virtual negotiations (e.g., e-mail) everything is communicated in writing, so be careful not to make unwise commitments that can be used against you. Neither should you take undue advantage of the other party in this way; discuss and clarify until all agree.

9. It may be easier to use unethical tactics in virtual negotiation because facts are harder to verify. But resist the temptation: the consequences are just as severe, and perhaps more so, given the incriminating evidence available when virtual negotiations are automatically archived.

10. Not all styles work equally well in all settings. Work to develop a personal negotiation style (collaboration, competition, etc.) that is a good fit with the communication channel you are using.

Source: Adapted from R. J. Lewicki and B. R. Dineen, "Negotiating in Virtual Organizations," in R. L. Heneman and D. B. Greenberger (Eds.), *Human Resource Management in the Virtual Organization* (New York: John Wiley and Sons, 2003).

buyer–seller negotiation, some sellers were provided with intricate arguments to use in support of their position; others were provided with simple arguments. The researchers predicted and found that sellers did better with complex arguments in the "quick" medium (IM) but not in the "slow" medium (e-mail).[38] This occurred, their results suggest, because sellers armed with intricate arguments were more able to dominate the conversation in the rapid turn-taking environment of IM, and in so doing extract concessions from the other party.

In summary, negotiations via e-mail and other network-mediated technologies create opportunities but also pose crucial challenges that negotiators would do well to understand before selecting a particular medium for an important occasion. See Box 6.2 for a list of additional ways to maximize effectiveness when negotiations occur in virtual environments.

How to Improve Communication in Negotiation

Given the many ways that communication can be disrupted and distorted, we can only marvel at the extent to which negotiators can actually understand each other. Failures and distortions in perception, cognition, and communication are the paramount contributors to breakdowns and failures in negotiation. Research consistently demonstrates that even those parties whose goals are compatible or integrative may fail to reach agreement or reach suboptimal agreements because of the misperceptions of the other party or because of breakdowns in the communication process.

Three main techniques are available for improving communication in negotiation: the use of questions, listening, and role reversal.

The Use of Questions

Questions are essential elements in negotiations for securing information; asking good questions enables negotiators to secure a great deal of information about the other party's position, supporting arguments, and needs.

Questions can be divided into two basic categories: those that are manageable and those that are unmanageable and cause difficulty (see Table 6.1).[39] Manageable questions cause attention or prepare the other person's thinking for further questions ("May I ask you a question?"), get information ("How much will this cost?"), and generate thoughts ("Do you have any suggestions for improving this?"). Unmanageable questions cause difficulty, give information ("Didn't you know that we couldn't afford this?"), and bring the discussion to a false conclusion ("Don't you think we've talked about this enough?"). Unmanageable questions are more likely to produce defensiveness and anger in the other party. Although these questions may yield information, they are likely to make the other party feel uncomfortable and less willing to provide information in the future.

Negotiators can also use questions to manage difficult or stalled negotiations. Aside from their typical uses for collecting and diagnosing information or assisting the other party in addressing and expressing needs and interests, questions can also be used tactically to pry or lever a negotiation out of a breakdown or an apparent dead end. Table 6.2 identifies a number of such situations and suggest specific questions for dealing with them.[40] The value of such questions seems to be in their power to assist or force the other party to confront the effects or consequences of his or her behavior, intended and anticipated or not.

Listening

"Active listening" and "reflecting" are terms commonly used in the helping professions such as counseling and therapy.[41] Counselors recognize that communications are frequently loaded with multiple meanings and that the counselor must try to identify these different meanings without making the communicator angry or defensive. There are three major forms of listening:

1. **Passive listening** involves receiving the message while providing no feedback to the sender about the accuracy or completeness of reception. Sometimes passive listening is itself enough to keep a communicator sending information. A negotiator whose counterpart is talkative may find that the best strategy is to sit and listen while the other party eventually works into, or out of, a position on his or her own.

2. **Acknowledgment** is the second form of listening, slightly more active than passive listening. When acknowledging, receivers occasionally nod their heads, maintain eye contact, or interject responses like "I see," "mm-hmm," "interesting," "really," "sure," "go on," and the like. These responses are sufficient to keep communicators sending

TABLE 6.1 | Questions in Negotiation

Manageable Questions	Examples
Open-ended questions—ones that cannot be answered with a simple yes or no. *Who, what, when, where,* and *why* questions.	"Why do you take that position in these deliberations?"
Open questions—invite the other's thinking.	"What do you think of our proposal?"
Leading questions—point toward an answer.	"Don't you think our proposal is a fair and reasonable offer?"
Cool questions—low emotionality.	"What is the additional rate that we will have to pay if you make the improvements on the property?"
Planned questions—part of an overall logical sequence of questions developed in advance.	"After you make the improvements to the property, when can we expect to take occupancy?"
Treat questions—flatter the opponent at the same time as you ask for information.	"Can you provide us with some of your excellent insight on this problem?"
Window questions—aid in looking into the other person's mind.	"Can you tell us how you came to that conclusion?"
Directive questions—focus on a specific point.	"How much is the rental rate per square foot with these improvements?"
Gauging questions—ascertain how the other person feels.	"How do you feel about our proposal?"

Unmanageable Questions	Examples
Close-out questions—force the other party into seeing things your way.	"You wouldn't try to take advantage of us here, would you?"
Loaded questions—put the other party on the spot regardless of the answer.	"Do you mean to tell me that these are the only terms that you will accept?"
Heated questions—high emotionality, trigger emotional responses.	"Don't you think we've spent enough time discussing this ridiculous proposal of yours?"
Impulse questions—occur "on the spur of the moment," without planning, and tend to get conversation off the track.	"As long as we're discussing this, what do you think we ought to tell other groups who have made similar demands on us?"
Trick questions—appear to require a frank answer, but really are "loaded" in their meaning.	"What are you going to do—give in to our demands, or take this to arbitration?"
Reflective trick questions—reflects the other into agreeing with your point of view.	"Here's how I see the situation—don't you agree?"

Source: From Gerard Nierenberg, *Fundamentals of Negotiating* (New York: Hawthorn Books, 1973), pp. 125–26. Used with permission of the author.

TABLE 6.2 | Questions for Tough Situations

The Situation	Possible Questions
"Take it or leave it" ultimatums	"If we can come up with a more attractive alternative than that, would you still want me to 'take or leave' your offer?" "Do I have to decide now, or do I have some time to think about it?" "Are you feeling pressure to bring the negotiation to a close?"
Pressure to respond to an unreasonable deadline	"Why can't we negotiate about this deadline?" "If you're under pressure to meet this deadline, what can I do to help remove some of that pressure?" "What's magical about this afternoon? What about first thing in the morning?"
Highball or lowball tactics	"What's your reasoning behind this position?" "What would *you* think I see as a fair offer?" "What standards do you think the final resolution should meet?"
An impasse	"What else can either of us do to close the gap between our positions?" "Specifically what concession do you need from me to bring this to a close right now?" "If it were already six weeks from now and we were looking back at this negotiation, what might we wish we had brought to the table?"
Indecision between accepting and rejecting a proposal	"What's your best alternative to accepting my offer right now?" "If you reject this offer, what will take its place that's better than what you know you'll receive from me?" "How can you be sure that you will get a better deal elsewhere?"
A question about whether the offer you just made is the same as that offered to others	"What do you see as a fair offer, and given that, what do you think of my current offer to you?" "Do you believe that I think it's in my best interest to be unfair to you?" "Do you believe that people can be treated differently, but still all be treated fairly?"
Attempts to pressure, control, or manipulate	"Shouldn't we both walk away from this negotiation feeling satisfied?" "How would you feel if our roles were reversed, and you were feeling the pressure I'm feeling right now?" "Are you experiencing outside pressures to conclude these negotiations?"

Source: Adapted from Sam Deep and Lyle Sussman, *What to Ask When You Don't Know What to Say* (1993). Used by permission of the publisher, Prentice Hall/A Division of Simon & Schuster, Englewood Cliffs, NJ.

messages, but a sender may misinterpret them as the receiver's agreement with his or her position, rather than as simple acknowledgments of receipt of the message.

3. **Active listening** is the third form. When receivers are actively listening, they restate or paraphrase the sender's message in their own language. Here are a few examples of active listening:[42]

SENDER: I don't know how I am going to untangle this messy problem.

RECEIVER: You're really stumped on how to solve this one.

SENDER: Please, don't ask me about that now.

RECEIVER: Sounds like you're awfully busy right now.

SENDER: I thought the meeting today accomplished nothing.

RECEIVER: You were very disappointed with our session.

In negotiation, it may appear initially that active listening is unsuitable because, unlike a counselor, the receiver normally has a set position and may feel strongly about the issues. By recommending active listening we are not suggesting that receivers should automatically agree with the other party's position and abandon their own. Rather, we regard active listening as a skill that encourages others to speak more fully about their feelings, priorities, frames of reference, and, by extension, the positions they are taking. When the other party does so, negotiators will better understand the other's positions; the factors and information that support it; and the ways the position can be compromised, reconciled, or negotiated in accordance with their own preferences and priorities.

Role Reversal

Continually arguing for one particular position in debate leads to a "blindness of involvement," or a self-reinforcing cycle of argumentation that prohibits negotiators from recognizing the possible compatibility between their own position and that of the other party.[43] While discussing active listening, we suggested that one objective was to gain an understanding of the other party's perspective or frame of reference. Active listening is, however, still a somewhat passive process. Role-reversal techniques allow negotiators to understand more completely the other party's positions by actively arguing these positions until the other party is convinced that he or she is understood. For example, someone can ask you how you would respond to the situation that he or she is in. In doing so, you can come to understand that person's position, perhaps accept its validity, and discover how to modify both of your positions to make them more compatible.

Research suggests that role reversal is a useful tool for improving communication and the accurate understanding and appreciation of the other party's position in negotiation.[44] This may be most useful during the preparation stage of negotiation or during a team caucus when things are not going well. However, increasing understanding does not necessarily lead to easy resolution of the conflict, particularly when accurate communication reveals a fundamental incompatibility in the positions of the two sides.

Special Communication Considerations at the Close of Negotiations

As negotiations move toward a close with agreement in sight, negotiators must attend to two key aspects of communication and negotiation simultaneously: the avoidance of fatal mistakes and the achievement of satisfactory closure in a constructive manner.

Avoiding Fatal Mistakes

Achieving closure in negotiation generally involves making decisions to accept offers, to compromise priorities, to trade off across issues with the other party, or to take some combination of these steps. Such decision-making processes can be divided into four key elements: framing, gathering intelligence, coming to conclusions, and learning from feedback.[45] The first three of these elements we have discussed elsewhere; the fourth element, that of learning (or failing to learn) from feedback, is largely a communication issue, which involves "keeping track of what you expected would happen, systematically guarding against self-serving expectations, and making sure you review the lessons your feedback has provided the next time a similar decision comes along."[46] In Chapter 5, we discussed the decision traps that may result from perceptual and cognitive biases that negotiators will inevitably encounter. Although some of these traps may occur in earlier stages of the negotiation, we suspect that several of them are likely to arise at the end of a negotiation, when parties are in a hurry to wrap up loose ends and cement a deal.

Achieving Closure

Gary Karrass, focusing on sales negotiations in particular, has specific advice about communication near the end of a negotiation.[47] Karrass enjoins negotiators to "know when to shut up," to avoid surrendering important information needlessly, and to refrain from making "dumb remarks" that push a wavering counterpart away from the agreement he or she is almost ready to endorse. The other side of this is to recognize the other party's faux pas and dumb remarks for what they are and refuse to respond to or be distracted by them. Karrass also reminds negotiators of the need to watch out for last-minute problems, such as nitpicking or second-guessing by parties who didn't participate in the bargaining process but who have the right or responsibility to review it. Karrass advises negotiators to expect such challenges and to be prepared to manage them with aplomb. Finally, Karrass notes the importance of reducing the agreement to written form, recognizing that the party who writes the contract is in a position to achieve clarity of purpose and conduct for the deal.

Chapter Summary

In this chapter we have considered elements of the art and science of communication that are relevant to understanding negotiations.

We first addressed *what* is communicated during negotiation. Rather than simply being an exchange of preferences about solutions, negotiation covers a wide-ranging number of topics in an environment where each party is trying to influence the other. This was followed by an exploration of three issues related to *how* people communicate in negotiation: the characteristics of language, nonverbal communication, and the selection of a communication channel. We discussed at some length how the decision to negotiate in online environments (e.g., e-mail) alters negotiator behavior and outcomes.

In the closing sections of the chapter we considered ways to improve communication in negotiation, including improvement of listening skills and the use of questions, and special communication considerations at the close of negotiation.

Endnotes

[1] Alexander, Schul, and Babakus, 1991.

[2] Carnevale, Pruitt, and Seilheimer, 1981.

[3] Weingart, Hyder, and Prietula, 1996; Olekalns, Smith, and Walsh, 1996.

[4] Tutzauer, 1992.

[5] Ibid.

[6] Pinkley, 1995; Pinkley, Neale, and Bennett, 1994.

[7] Thompson, Valley, and Kramer, 1995.

[8] Novemsky and Schweitzer, 2004.

[9] Bies and Shapiro, 1987; Shapiro, 1991.

[10] Sitkin and Bies, 1993.

[11] Ibid.

[12] Brett, Shapiro, and Lytle, 1998.

[13] Taylor and Donald, 2003.

[14] Ibid.

[15] Curhan and Pentland, 2007.

[16] Ibid.

[17] Adair and Brett, 2005.

[18] See Roth and Malouf, 1979; Schelling, 1960; Siegel and Fouraker, 1960.

[19] O'Connor, 1997.

[20] Simons, 1993.

[21] Beebe, 1980; Burgoon, Coker, and Coker, 1986; Kleinke, 1986.

[22] Kellerman, Lewis, and Laird, 1989.

[23] Ivey and Simek-Downing, 1980.

[24] Ibid.

[25] Stacks and Burgoon, 1981.

[26] Nierenberg and Calero, 1971.

[27] Drolet and Morris, 2000, p. 27.

[28] Bazerman, Curhan, Moore, and Valley, 2000; Lewicki and Dineen, 2002.

[29] Barry and Fulmer, 2004. See also Short, Williams, and Christie, 1976, who used the term "social presence."

[30] Sproull and Kiesler, 1986.

[31] Barry and Fulmer, 2004.

[32] Drolet and Morris, 2000.

[33] Valley, Moag, and Bazerman, 1998.

[34] Ibid.

[35] Croson, 1999.

[36] Morris, Nadler, Kurtzberg, and Thompson, 2000.

[37] Ibid.

[38] Loewenstein, Morris, Chakravarti, Thompson, and Kopelman, 2005.

[39] Nierenberg, 1976.

[40] Deep and Sussman, 1993.

[41] Rogers, 1957, 1961.

[42] These examples are from Gordon, 1977.

[43] Rapoport, 1964.

[44] Johnson, 1971; Walcott, Hopmann, and King, 1977.

[45] Russo and Schoemaker, 1989.

[46] Ibid., p. 3.

[47] Karrass, 1985.

Finding and Using Negotiation Power

Objectives

1. Understand different approaches to understanding power in negotiations and why power is critical to negotiation.
2. Explore different sources or bases of power in negotiation.
3. Consider different strategic approaches for negotiators who have more power and for dealing with others who have more power.

In this chapter, we focus on power in negotiation. By *power*, we mean the capabilities negotiators can assemble to give themselves an advantage or increase the probability of achieving their objectives. All negotiators want power; they want to know what they can do to put pressure on the other party, persuade the other to see it their way, get the other to give them what they want, get one up on the other, or change the other's mind. Note that, according to this definition, we have already talked about many power tactics in Chapters 2 and 3. The tactics of distributive bargaining and integrative negotiation are *leverage tactics*—tactics used to exert influence over the other party in the service of achieving the best deal for one or both parties.

We begin by defining the nature of power and discussing some of the dynamics of its use in negotiation. We focus on the power sources that give negotiators capacity to exert influence. Of the many sources of power that exist, we consider three major ones in this chapter: information and expertise, control over resources, and one's position in an organization or network.[1]

Why Is Power Important to Negotiators?

Most negotiators believe that power is important in negotiation because it gives one negotiator an *advantage* over the other party. Negotiators who have this advantage usually want to use it to secure a greater share of the outcomes or achieve their preferred solution. Seeking power in negotiation usually arises from one of two perceptions:

1. The negotiator believes he or she currently has *less power* than the other party. In this situation, a negotiator believes the other party already has some advantage that can and will be used, so he or she *seeks power to offset or counterbalance the other's advantage.*

2. The negotiator believes he or she needs *more power* than the other party to increase the probability of securing a desired outcome. In this context, the negotiator believes that added power is necessary to *gain or sustain one's own advantage in the upcoming negotiation.*

Embedded in these two beliefs are significant questions of tactics and motives. The tactics may be designed to enhance the negotiator's own power or to diminish the other's power, and to create a state of either power equalization (both parties have relatively equal or countervailing power) or power difference (one's power is greater than the other's). The motive questions relate to why the negotiator is using the tactics. Most commonly, negotiators employ tactics designed to create power equalization as a way to level the playing field. The goal is to minimize either side's ability to dominate the relationship. This lays the groundwork for moving discussions toward a compromising or collaborative, integrative agreement. In contrast, negotiators also employ tactics designed to create power difference as a way to gain advantage or to block the other party's power moves. Such tactics enhance the capacity for one side to dominate the relationship, paving the way for a competing or dominating strategy and a distributive agreement. Box 7.1 presents a framework on the merits of using power as a negotiating tactic (compared with the focus on interests or an emphasis on "rights" in a dispute).

In general, negotiators who don't care about their power or who have matched power—equally high or low—find that their deliberations proceed with greater ease and simplicity toward a mutually satisfying and acceptable outcome. In contrast, negotiators who do care about their power and seek to match or exceed the other's power are probably seeking a solution in which they either do not lose the negotiation (a defensive posture) or dominate the negotiation (an offensive posture).

Power is implicated in the use of many of the competitive and collaborative negotiation tactics described earlier, such as hinting to the other party that you have good alternatives (a strong BATNA) in order to increase your leverage. Relatively few research studies have focused specifically on power and influence tactics in negotiation, and we integrate those that have into our discussion. However, much of the work on power discussed in this chapter is also drawn from broader studies of how managers influence one another in organizations, and we apply those findings to negotiation situations as appropriate.

A Definition of Power

In a broad sense, people have power when they have "the ability to bring about outcomes they desire" or "the ability to get things done the way [they want] them to be done."[2] Presumably, a party with power can induce another to do what the latter otherwise would not do.[3]

But there is a problem here: the definition we have developed so far seems to focus on power as absolute and coercive, which is too restrictive for understanding how power is used in negotiation. In fact, there are really two perspectives on power: power used to dominate and control the other (more likely in a distributive bargaining context) and power used to work together with the other (more likely in an integrative negotiation context.[4] From the powerholder's point of view, the first perspective fits the *power over* definition, implying that this power is fundamentally dominating and coercive in nature. From the other party's point of view, this use of power implies *powerlessness and dependence* on the receiving

One way of thinking about the role of power in negotiation is in relation to other, alternative strategic options. In Chapter 5 we introduced a framework developed by Ury, Brett, and Goldberg (1993) that compares three different strategic approaches to negotiation: interests, rights, and power.

- Negotiators focus on interests when they strive to learn about each other's interests and priorities as a way to work toward a mutually satisfying agreement that creates value.

- Negotiators focus on rights when they seek to resolve a dispute by drawing upon decision rules or standards grounded in principles of law, community standards of fairness, or perhaps an existing contract.

- Negotiators focus on power when they use threats or other means to try to coerce the other party into making concessions.

This framework assumes that all three approaches can potentially exist in a single situation; negotiators make choices about where to place their focus. But do negotiators really use all three? Should they? These questions were addressed in a study by Anne Lytle, Jeanne Brett, and Debra Shapiro.

Lytle and her colleagues found that most negotiators cycled through all three strategies—interests, rights, and power—during the same encounter. They also found that negotiators tended to reciprocate these strategies. A coercive power strategy, for example, may be met with a power strategy in return, which can lead to a negative conflict spiral and a poor (or no) agreement. They developed some important implications for the use of power in negotiation:

- Starting a negotiation by conveying your own power to coerce the other party could bring a quick settlement if your threat is credible. If the other party calls your bluff, however, you are left to either carry out your threat or lose face, both of which may be undesirable.

- Power tactics (and rights tactics) may be most useful when the other party refuses to negotiate or when negotiations have broken down and need to be restarted. In these situations, not much is risked by making threats based on rights or power, but the threat itself may help the other party appreciate the severity of the situation.

- The success of power tactics (and rights tactics) depends to a great extent on how they are implemented. To be effective, threats must be specific and credible, targeting the other party's high-priority interests. Otherwise, the other party has little incentive to comply. Make sure that you leave an avenue for the other party to "turn off" the threat, save face, and reopen the negotiations around interests.

Source: Adapted from A. L. Lytle, J. M. Brett, and D. L. Shapiro, "The Strategic Use of Interests, Rights, and Power to Resolve Disputes," *Negotiation Journal* 15, no. 1 (1999), pp. 31–51.

end. The dynamics of this power relationship can range from "benign and supportive (as in many mentoring relationships) to oppressive and abusive (as with a dictatorial parent)."[5]

From the second perspective, the actor's view of power suggests *power with*,[6] implying that the power holder jointly develops and shares power with the other. The receiver experiences this power as *empowered and independent,* and its dynamics reflect the benefits of empowerment, such as better employee participation, broad delegation of authority, and a greater capacity to act with autonomy and personal integrity. This view of power fits a view of power that contrasts with the *power over* definition:

> an actor . . . has power in a given situation (situational power) to the degree that he can satisfy the purposes (goals, desires, or wants) that he is attempting to fulfill in that situation. Power is a relational concept; it does not reside in the individual but rather in the relationship of the person to his environment. Thus, the power of an actor in a given situation is determined by the characteristics of the situation as well as by his own characteristics.[7]

There has been a tendency for others to view power as an attribute of the actor only. This tendency ignores those elements of power that are derived from the situation or context in which the actor operates. The statement "A is more powerful than B" should be viewed from three distinct yet often interrelated perspectives: environmental power, or "A is more usually able to favorably influence his overall environment and/or to overcome its resistance than is B;" relationship power, or "A is usually more able to influence B favorably and/or to overcome B's resistance than B is able to do with A;" and personal power, or "A is usually more able to satisfy his desires than is B."[8]

Before moving forward, we want to draw attention to the weakness of any discussion of power. It would be nice to be able to write a chapter that comprehensively reviews the power sources available to negotiators, the major configurations of power bases assembled as influence strategies, and the conditions under which each should be used. Unfortunately, such a task is not just daunting but impossible, for two principal reasons. First, the effective use of power requires a sensitive and deft touch, and its consequences may vary greatly from one person to the next. In the hands of one user, the tools of power can craft a benevolent realm of prosperity and achievement, whereas in the hands of another, they may create a nightmare of tyranny and disorder.[9] Second, not only do the key actors and targets change from situation to situation, but the context in which the tools of power operate changes as well. As a result, the best we can do is to identify a few key sources of power.

Sources of Power—How People Acquire Power

Understanding the different ways in which power can be exercised is best accomplished by looking first at the various sources of power. In their seminal work on power, French and Raven identified five major types: expert power, reward power, coercive power, legitimate power, and referent power.[10] Most of these are relatively self evident in nature:

- *Expert power:* derived from having unique, in-depth information about a subject.
- *Reward power:* derived by being able to reward others for doing what needs to be done.
- *Coercive power:* derived by being able to punish others for not doing what needs to be done.
- *Legitimate power:* derived from holding an office or formal title in some organization and using the powers that are associated with that office (e.g., a vice president or director).
- *Referent power:* derived from the respect or admiration one commands because of attributes like personality, integrity, interpersonal style, and the like. A is said to have referent power over B to the extent that B identifies with or wants to be closely associated with A.

Many contemporary discussions of power are still grounded in this typology (and Raven has elaborated the typology several times since it was proposed over 50 years ago). In this chapter, we take a broader perspective on power as it relates to negotiation and aggregate the major sources of power into five different groupings (see Table 7.1):

- Informational sources of power.
- Personal sources of power.

TABLE 7.1 | Major Sources of Power

Source of Power	Description
Informational	• Information: the accumulation and presentation of data intended to change the other person's point of view or position on an issue. • Expertise: an acknowledged accumulation of information, or mastery of a body of information, on a particular problem or issue. Expertise power can be positive (we believe the other because of their acknowledged expertise) or negative (we so distrust the other that their claimed expertise leads us to pursue a course of action opposite to the one they advocate).
Personality and individual differences	Power derived from differences in • Psychological orientation (broad orientations to power use). • Cognitive orientation (ideologies about power). • Motivational orientation (specific motives to use power). • Dispositions and skills (orientations to cooperation/competition). • Moral orientation (philosophical orientations to power use).

Position-based power	Power derived from being located in a particular position in an organizational or communication structure; leads to several different kinds of leverage:
	• Legitimate power, or formal authority, derived from occupying a key position in a hierarchical organization. However, legitimate power can also influence social norms, such as
	  Reciprocity, or the expected exchange of favors.
	  Equity, or the expected return when one has gone out of one's way for the other.
	  Dependence, of the expected obligation one owes to others who cannot help themselves.
	• Resource control, or the accumulation of money, raw material, labor, time, and equipment that can be used as incentives to encourage compliance or as punishments for noncompliance. Resource control is manifested in
	  Reward power, the use of tangible rewards or personal approval to gain the other's compliance.
	  Punishment power, the use of tangible punishments or withholding of personal approval to gain the other's compliance.

Relationship-based power	• Goal interdependence—how the parties view their goals Referent power—based on an appeal to the other based on common experiences, group membership, status, etc. Referent power can also be positive (we believe the other because we respect them) or negative (we so disrespect the other that we pursue a course of action opposite to the one they advocate). • Access to or control over information, resources supply flows, or access, derived from location within flows in a network.
Contextual power	Power derived from the context in which negotiations take place. Common sources of contextual power include • Availability of BATNAs. • Organizational and national culture. • Availability of agents, constituencies, and audiences who can directly or indirectly affect the outcomes of the negotiation.

- Power based on position in an organization.
- Relationship-based sources of power.
- Contextual sources of power.

As we regularly note, these categories are not rigid or absolute. Power can be created in many different ways in many different contexts, and a source of leverage can shift from one category to another over time. As we elaborate on these approaches, we also indicate how the French and Raven model has been revised and updated.

Informational Sources of Power

Within the context of negotiation, information is perhaps the most common source of power. Information power is derived from the negotiator's ability to <u>assemble and organize facts and data to support his or her position, arguments, or desired outcomes</u>. Negotiators may also use information as a tool to challenge the other party's position or desired outcomes or to undermine the effectiveness of the other's negotiating arguments. Even in the simplest negotiation, the parties take a position and then present arguments and facts to support that position. I want to sell a used motorcycle for $1,500; you say it is worth only $1,000. I proceed to tell you how much I paid for it, point out what good condition it is in and what attractive features it has, and explain why it is worth $1,500. You point out that it is five years old; emphasize the nicks, dents, and rust spots; and comment that the tires are worn and need to be replaced. You also tell me that you can't afford to spend $1,500. After 20 minutes of discussion about the motorcycle, we have exchanged extensive information about its original cost, age, use, depreciation, and current condition, as well as your financial situation and my need to raise cash. We then settle on a price of $1,300, including a "loan" of $300 I have given you. (See Box 7.2 on the ways that the power of information, now available through the Internet, has changed the ways people buy new cars.)

The exchange of information in negotiation is also at the heart of the concession-making process. As each side presents information, a common definition of the situation emerges. The amount and kind of information shared, and the way the negotiators share it, allow both parties to derive a common (and hopefully realistic) picture of the current condition of the motorcycle, its market worth, and the preferences of each side. Moreover, this information need not be 100 percent accurate to be effective; bluffs, exaggerations, omissions, and outright lies may work just as well. I may tell you I paid $2,200 for the bike when I paid only $2,000; I may not tell you that the clutch needs to be replaced. You may not tell me that you actually can pay $1,500 but simply don't want to spend that much or that you plan to buy this bike regardless of what you have to pay for it. (We return to these issues of bluffing and misrepresentation in Chapter 8 when we discuss the ethics of lying and deception.)

Power derived from expertise is a special form of information power. The power that comes from information is available to anyone who assembles facts and figures to support arguments, but expert power is accorded to those who are seen as having achieved some level of command and mastery of a body of information. Experts are accorded respect, deference, and credibility based on their experience, study, or accomplishments. One or

Before the age of the Internet, many consumers approached buying a car with the same enthusiasm as visiting the dentist. Customers knew their role was to scoff at the asking price, threaten to walk away from the vehicle, and generally engage in tough negotiation postures in order to get the best deal. Still, after they drove the car off the lot, nagging doubts remained about whether or not they paid too much for their new car.

Savvy customers have always known that they should determine their real requirements for an automobile, find several cars that meet their objectives, determine the book value of each car, contact current owners to determine their satisfaction, and keep from becoming emotionally attached to a particular automobile. These strategies certainly have helped people prepare for negotiations with their local dealer. However, customers still had to rely largely on guesswork to determine what price offers would be acceptable to the dealership.

Today, however, price information on new and used cars is readily available through the Internet and other sources. Customers can enter negotiations with car dealers armed with accurate facts and figures about the car's cost to the dealership, the actual price for various options, prices in neighboring states, and the customer and dealer incentives in place at a given time. Car buyers who take the time to gather information about "real" prices report saving hundreds or even thousands of dollars on automobiles. This wealth of information gives consumers more power in negotiations with dealers. Ultimately, that power leads to lower prices on new automobiles.[11]

both parties in a negotiation will give experts' arguments more credibility than those of nonexperts—but only to the extent that the expertise is seen as functionally relevant to the persuasion situation.[12] For example, someone knowledgeable about cars may not be an expert on motorcycles. Thus, a negotiator who would like to take advantage of his or her expertise will often need to demonstrate that this expertise (1) actually exists and (2) is relevant to the issues under discussion.

Power Based on Personality and Individual Differences

Personal Orientation　Individuals have different psychological orientations to social situations. Three such orientations are paramount: "cognitive, motivational and moral orientations to a given situation that serve to guide one's behavior and responses to that situation."[13] These are stable individual differences—personality traits, if you will—that affect how individuals acquire and use power. We now briefly discuss these orientations.

Cognitive Orientation　Individual differences in ideological frames of reference—one way to represent a cognitive orientation—are central to their approach to power. There are three types of ideological frames:

- The unitary frame, characterized by beliefs that society is an integrated whole and that the interests of individuals and society are one, such that power can be largely ignored or, when needed, be used by benevolent authorities to benefit the good of all (a view common to many "communal" societies and cultures).
- The radical frame, characterized by beliefs that society is in a continual clash of social, political, and class interests, and that power is inherently and structurally imbalanced (a view common to Marxist individuals and cultures).

- The pluralist frame, characterized by beliefs that power is distributed relatively equally across various groups, which compete and bargain for a share of the continually evolving balance of power (a view common to many liberal democracies).[14]

Each ideological perspective operates as a "frame" (see Chapter 5) or perspective on the world, shaping expectations about what one should pay attention to, how events will evolve, and how one should engage situations of power. The ideological perspective has also been shown to affect the way individuals process social information about power: "whether it is limited or expandable, competitive or cooperative, or equal or unequal," and how the orientation affects people's willingness to share power when they have authority.[15]

Motivational Orientation   A second orientation focuses on differences in individual motivations—that is, differences rooted more in needs and "energizing elements" of the personality rather than in ideology. Individual differences in "power motive," or the disposition of some people to have high needs to influence and control others and to seek out positions of power and authority. More dramatically, in the era following World War II and the notorious empire-building dispositions of Hitler and Mussolini, personality theorists described "the authoritarian personality," as an individual who has a strong need to dominate others and yet, at the same time, to identify with and submit to those in high authority.[16] These orientations are likely to play out in either the "power over" or "powerless" situations of power, depending on the status of the other party.

Dispositions and Skills   Several authors have suggested that orientations to power are broadly grounded in individual dispositions to be cooperative or competitive (e.g., the dual concerns model, Chapter 1).[17] Competitive dispositions and skills may emphasize the "power over" approach and suggest that people with these dispositions maintain skills such as sustaining energy and stamina; maintaining focus; and having high expertise, strong self-confidence, and high tolerance for conflict. Cooperative dispositions and skills are more allied with the "power with" approach, emphasizing skills such as sensitivity to others, flexibility, and ability to consider and incorporate the views of others into an agreement.

Moral Orientation   Finally, individuals differ in their moral views about power and its use. One researcher has noted that there is a significant positive relationship between people's implicit ideals regarding egalitarianism—a deep-seated belief in the ideal of equality of power for all—and their willingness to share power with low power parties.[18] In Chapter 8, we show how differences in moral orientation broadly affect the use of ethical and unethical tactics in negotiation.

Power Based on Position in an Organization

We discuss two major sources of power based on position in an organization: (1) legitimate power, which is grounded in the title, duties, and responsibilities of a job description and "level" within an organization hierarchy; and (2) power based on the control of resources (budget, funding, etc.) associated with that position.

Legitimate Power   Legitimate power is derived from occupying a particular job, office, or position in an organizational hierarchy. In this case, the power resides in the title, duties, and responsibilities of the job itself, and the "legitimacy" of the officeholder comes from the title and duties of the job description within that organization context. Thus, a newly promoted vice president acquires some legitimate power merely from holding the title of vice president.

There are times when people respond to directions from another, even directions they do not like, because they feel it is proper (legitimate) for the other to direct them and proper (obligatory) for them to obey. This is the effect of legitimate power.

Legitimate power is at the foundation of our social structure. When individuals and groups organize into any social system—a small business, a combat unit, a union, a political action organization, a sports team, a task force—they almost immediately create some form of structure and hierarchy. They elect or appoint a leader and may introduce formal rules about decision making, work division, allocation of responsibilities, and conflict management. Without this social order, either the group can take little coordinated action (chaos prevails), or everyone is required to participate in every decision and group coordination takes forever. Social structures are efficient and effective, and this fact creates the basis for legitimate power. People are willing to give up their right to participate in every decision by vesting authority in someone who can act on their behalf (a president, leader, or spokesperson). By creating a group structure that gives one person a power base, group members generate a willingness within themselves to obey that person's directives.

People can acquire legitimate power in several ways. First, it may be acquired at birth. Elizabeth II has the title of Queen of the United Kingdom of Great Britain and Northern Ireland and all the stature the title commands. She also controls a great deal of the personal wealth of the monarchy. However, she has little actual power in terms of her ability to run the day-to-day affairs of Britain, a situation that has created controversy and resentment in recent years. Second, legitimate power may be acquired by election to a designated office: the President of the United States has substantial legitimate power derived from the constitutional structure of the American government. Third, legitimate power is derived simply by appointment or promotion to some organizational position. Thus, holding the title of Director or General Manager entitles a person to all the rights, responsibilities, and privileges that go with that position. Finally, some legitimate authority comes to an individual who occupies a position for which other people simply show respect. Usually, such respect is derived from the intrinsic social good or important social values of that person's position or organization. In many societies, the young listen to and obey the old. People also listen to college presidents or the members of the clergy. They follow their advice because they believe it is proper to do so. While clergy members, college presidents, and many others may have precious little they can actually give to individuals as rewards or use against them as coercive punishments, they still have considerable legitimate power.[19]

The effectiveness of formal authority is derived from the willingness of followers to acknowledge the legitimacy of the organizational structure and the system of rules and regulations that empowers its leaders.[20] In short, legitimate power cannot function without obedience or the consent of the governed. If enough British citizens question the legitimacy of the Queen and her authority—even given the hundreds of years of tradition and law on which the monarchy is founded—her continued rule will be in serious jeopardy. If enough Catholics challenge the Pope's rulings on abortion, birth control, or other social policy, the

NON SEQUITUR   BY WILEY

Pope's authority will erode. If the President's cabinet members and key advisers are unwilling to act on presidential orders, then the President's effectiveness is nullified. When enough people begin to distrust the authority or discredit its legitimacy, they will begin to defy it and thereby undermine its potential as a power source.

Because legitimate power can be undermined if followers choose to no longer recognize the powerholder's authority, it is not uncommon for powerholders to accumulate other power sources (such as resource control or information) to fortify their power base. Resource control and information power frequently accompany a title, position, or job definition. Legitimate power is often derived from manipulating these other sources of power. Military officers have known this for a long time. All military-style organizations (soldiers, police, etc.) still drill their personnel, even though military units no longer march into battle as they once did. There are several reasons for this: a drill is an easy place to give instructions, teach discipline and obedience, closely monitor large numbers of people, and quickly punish or reward performance. Drilling gets large numbers of people used to accepting orders from a specific person, without question. Those who follow orders are rewarded, whereas those who do not are quickly and publicly punished. After a while, the need for reward and punishment drops off, and it seems natural or legitimate for the soldier to accept orders from an officer without asking why or inquiring about the consequences.

Although we have been talking about organizational structures and positions as conferring "legitimacy," it is also possible to apply the notion of legitimacy to certain social norms or conventions that exert strong control over people.[21] Examples include the following:

1. The legitimate power of reciprocity, a very strong social norm that suggests that if one person does something positive or favorable for the other, the gesture or favor is expected to be returned ("I did you a favor; I expect you to do one for me").

2. The legitimate power of equity, another strong social norm, in which the agent has a right to request compensation from the other if the agent goes out of his or her way or endures suffering for the other ("I went out of my way for you; this is the least you could do for me").

3. The legitimate power of responsibility or dependence, a third strong social norm that says we have an obligation to help others who cannot help themselves and are

dependent on us ("I understood that the other really needed help on this and could not do it themselves").

Resource Control   People who control resources have the capacity to give them to someone who will do what they want and withhold them (or take them away) from someone who doesn't do what they want. Resources can be many things. Particular resources are more useful as instruments of power to the extent that they are highly valued by participants in the negotiation. In an organizational context, some of the most important resources are the following:

1. *Money,* in its various forms: cash, salary, budget allocations, grants, bonus money, expense accounts, and discretionary funds.
2. *Supplies:* raw materials, components, pieces, and parts.
3. *Human capital:* available labor supply, staff that can be allocated to a problem or task, temporary help.
4. *Time:* free time, the ability to meet deadlines, the ability to control a deadline. If time pressure is operating on one or both parties, the ability to help someone meet or move a deadline can be extremely powerful (we discussed deadlines in negotiation in Chapter 3).
5. *Equipment:* machines, tools, technology, computer hardware and software, vehicles.
6. *Critical services:* repair, maintenance, upkeep, installation and delivery, technical support, and transportation.
7. *Interpersonal support:* verbal praise and encouragement for good performance or criticism for bad performance. This is an interesting resource because it is available to almost anyone, does not require significant effort to acquire, and the impact of receiving it is quite powerful on its own.

The ability to control and dispense resources is a major power source in organizations. Power also comes from creating a resource stockpile in an environment where resources appear to be scarce. In his book *Managing with Power,*[22] Jeffrey Pfeffer illustrated how powerful political and corporate figures build empires founded on resource control. During his early years in Congress, Lyndon Johnson took over the "Little Congress" (a speaker's bureau for clerical personnel and aides to members of Congress) and leveraged it into a major power base that led him to become Speaker of the House of Representatives and eventually President. Similarly, Robert Moses, beginning as the parks commissioner of New York City, built a power empire that resulted in the successful construction of 12 bridges, 35 highways, 751 playgrounds, 13 golf courses, 18 swimming pools, and more than 2 million acres of park land in the New York metropolitan area—a base he used to become a dominant power broker in the city.

To use resources as a basis for power, negotiators must develop or maintain control over some desirable reward that the other party wants—such as physical space, jobs, budget authorizations, or raw materials—or control over some punishment the other seeks to avoid. As noted, these rewards and punishments could be tangible or intangible, such as liking, approval, respect, and so on. Successful control over resources also requires that the other party deal directly with the powerholder. Finally, the powerholder must be willing to

BOX | 7.3 | **Power Relationships in Salary Negotiation**

Salary and negotiation expert Paul Barada from Monster.com points out that power is one of the most overlooked but important dynamics in negotiation. He says that power relationships aren't like blackjack, but there is one parallel: power will determine who has the better hand. The employer often has the better hand because he or she has something the candidate wants: the job opening, and there are probably lots of candidates who want the job (a good BATNA). But if the candidate has unique skills that the employer wants, or if there is a shortage of talent in a particular field, the candidate can have a lot of power (and hence a good hand). A job candidate can increase his or her power as follows:

- Determine what skills he or she has, and which ones can be transferred to the job one has applying for.

- Do homework on the demand for those skills in various jobs and industries.

- Know what is a fair and reasonable salary for this job, given the market conditions and the geographic area in which the job is located.

- Be prepared to make a convincing set of arguments for the value one will bring to your new employer.

- Determine a fair compensation rate (target) and a threshold below which one will not go (walkaway point).

If the candidate determines that he or she does not have the appropriate skills, education or experience, he or she should consider how to gain those skills or experience to give him or her more power in job negotiations.

Source: P. W. Barada, "Power Relationships and Negotiation." (2008). http://www.career-advice.monster.com/salary-negotiation/Power-Relationships-and-Negotiation/home.asp.

allocate resources depending on the other's compliance or cooperation with the power-holder's requests. The increasing scarcity of resources of all kinds has led to the new golden rule of organizations: "whoever has the gold makes the rules."

Power Based on Relationships

Three types of power are discussed here: goal interdependence, referent power, and power based on relationships with others in personal and professional networks.

Goal Interdependence   How the parties view their goals—and how much achievement of their goal depends on the behavior of the other party—has a strong impact on how likely parties will be to constructively use power. Cooperative goals tend to shape the "power with" orientation, even between superiors and subordinates; these goals induce "higher expectations of assistance, more assistance, greater support, more persuasion and less coercion and more trusting and friendly attitudes."[23] In contrast, competitive goals lead the parties to pursue a "power over" orientation; to reinforce or enhance existing power differences; and to use that power to maximize one's own goals, often at the expense of the other.[24] For example, relationships and goal interdependence are key sources of power in salary negotiations (see Box 7.3).

Referent Power   As defined earlier, referent power is derived from the respect or admiration one commands because of attributes like personality, integrity, interpersonal style, and the like. A is said to have referent power over B to the extent that B identifies with or wants to be closely associated with A. Referent power is often based on an appeal to common experiences, common past, common fate, or membership in the same groups. Referent power is made *salient* when one party identifies the dimension of commonality in an effort to increase his or her power (usually persuasiveness) over the other. Thus, a negotiator might start getting to know the other in order to discover commonalities (home town, college, favorite sports team, political perspective) that, when discovered, will hopefully create a bond between the parties that will facilitate agreement. Like expert power, referent power can also have negative forms. Negative referent power is often used, particularly when parties seek to create distance or division between themselves and others or to label the other. Thus, political rivals often label each other as "liberals" or "right wingers" in an effort to make the other a less attractive candidate in an upcoming election.[25]

Networks The third type of relational power also comes from location in an organizational structure, but not necessarily a hierarchical structure. In this case, power is derived from whatever flows through that particular location in the structure (usually information and resources, such as money). The person occupying a certain position may not have a formal title or office; his or her leverage comes from the ability to control and manage what "flows" through that position. For example, before China modernized in the 1980s, automobile chauffeurs held enormous power even though their title was not prestigious. If a chauffeur did not like a passenger or did not feel like driving to a certain location, he could make life very difficult and impose serious consequences for the passenger (e.g., delayed departure time, driving very slowly, taking a roundabout route, etc.).

This example shows that even without a lofty position or title, individuals can become powerful because of the way their actions and responsibilities are embedded in the flows of information, goods and services, or contacts. For example, individuals such as clerks or data-entry operators, who have access to a large amount of information or who are responsible for collecting, managing, and allocating vital resources (money, raw materials, permissions and authorizations) may become very powerful.[26] The job may not have a fancy title, a large staff, or a large corner office, but it can confer a significant amount of power by virtue of the amount of information and resources that pass through it.

Understanding power in this way is derived from conceptualizing organizations and their functioning not as a hierarchy, but as a network of interrelationships. Network schemas represent key individuals as circles or nodes and relationships between individuals as lines of transaction. (See Figure 7.1 for an example of a network as compared with an organizational hierarchy).

These lines *(ties)* connect individuals or groups *(nodes)* who interact or need to interact with each other in the organization. Through information and resources as the primary focus of transactions, personal relationships, referent power, and "pressure" may also be negotiated across network lines. In formal hierarchy terms, authority is directly related to how high the position is on the vertical organization chart and how many people report to that individual from lower levels. In network terms, in contrast, power is determined by location within the set of relationships and the flows that occur through that node in the network. Several key aspects of networks shape power: tie strength, tie content, and network structure (including node centrality, criticality, flexibility, and visibility).

FIGURE 7.1 | Comparing Organization Hierarchies and Networks

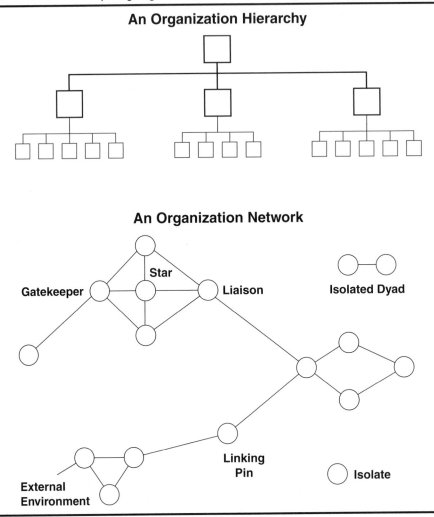

Tie Strength   This is an indication of the strength or quality of relationships with others. Quality might be measured by how close you are, how much personal information you share with the other, or how much one person is willing to go out of his or her way for the other. Strength of ties between individuals can be determined by how often the parties interact, how long they have known each other, how close the personal relationship is with the other, how many different ways the two parties interact with each other, and how much reciprocity or mutuality there is in the relationship so that each contributes equally to the give-and-take. Stronger ties with another usually indicate greater power to have the other accede to requests.

Tie Content   Content is the resource that passes along the tie with the other person. This could be money or other resources, information, support, emotion, and the like. The more the content of the ties builds a strong personal relationship and the more they create trust and respect for each other, the stronger the tie will be.[27]

Network Structure   While tie strength and content relate to an individual relationship within a network, network structure refers to the overall set of relationships within a social system (e.g., a workplace, department, school, or other social environment). Some aspects of network structure that determine power in a role include:

1. *Centrality*. The more central a node is in a network of exchanges and transactions, the more power that node's occupant will have. Centrality may be determined by the amount of information or total number of transactions that pass through a node or by the degree to which the node is central to managing information flow. In the network depicted in Figure 7.1, the star has greater centrality and therefore more power. Researchers have shown that being in the center of information flows—the workflow network, the informal communication network, and the friendship network—is particularly important to being promoted.[28] A new faculty member might decide to volunteer to head up the "speakers" program for faculty seminars because it would put him or her in the center of many communications about the weekly presentations.

2. *Criticality and relevance*. A second source of network power is the criticality of the node. Although a large amount of information or resources may not flow through a particular node, what does may be essential to the organization's mission, major task, or key product. People who depend highly on others may become critical to the degree that they are charged with assembling information from many locations; that is, they may be in frequent contact with many important people and may be required to integrate information from those contacts into a recommendation, action strategy, or decision. In Figure 7.1, liaisons and linking pins perform this role. Employees who want to succeed rapidly are frequently counseled to find jobs with high centrality and criticality in an organization so they can get the experience and visibility necessary for rapid promotion. Being critical—even irreplaceable—is a core part of getting and maintaining power.

3. *Flexibility*. A third source of network power lies in the position's flexibility, or the degree to which the key individual can exercise discretion in how certain decisions are made or who gains access. Flexibility is often related to criticality (see the preceding discussion). A classic example of flexibility is the role of gatekeeper (Figure 7.1), the person in a network who controls the access to a key figure or group. Anyone who wants to get to the star has to go through the gatekeeper. If you want to see the boss, you have to get permission and access from the secretary.

4. *Visibility*. Nodes differ in their degree of visibility—that is, how visible the task performance is to others in the organization. If a negotiator gains significant concessions from the other party while being watched, the team will give that negotiator a great deal of affirmation. A node with high centrality and criticality may not be visible, but if it is not, it is much less likely to be recognized and rewarded.

5. *Membership in a coalition*. Finally, as a node in a network, you can be a member of one or more subgroups or coalitions. Coalitions often act together to represent a point

of view or promote action or change; the more coalitions you belong to, the more likely you will be to find "friends" who can help you meet key people, obtain important (often "inside") information, and accomplish objectives.

Contextual Sources of Power

Finally, while power can be located within individuals and their relationships, power is also based in the context, situation, or environment in which negotiations take place. While these forms of power often go unrecognized in the short term (because of our tendency to see power as an individual quality rather than embedded in the structure or context of a conflict), these sources are just as critical.

BATNAs   In Chapters 3 and 4, we discussed the role of a best alternative to a negotiated agreement—that is, an alternative deal that a negotiator might pursue if she or he does not come to agreement with the current other party. The availability of a BATNA offers a negotiator significant power because he or she now has a choice between accepting the other party's proposal or the alternative deal. Any viable BATNA gives the negotiator the choice to walk away from the current deal or to use the BATNA as leverage to strike a better agreement in the current discussions. Students who have two financial aid offers from different graduate schools will have significantly more power to increase the quality of that aid package offer from either university than students who have only one financial aid offer.

Culture   Culture determines the "meaning system" of a social environment. Culture often shapes what kinds of power are seen as legitimate and illegitimate or how people use influence and react to influence. For example, in one organization known to the authors of this book, the chief executive officer (CEO) introduced ideas for major changes in business strategy in management team meetings. Senior managers made very few critical comments about these ideas in the meeting, but they then actively expressed their disagreement with the idea in one-to-one conversations with each other or the CEO. This public lack of openness and honesty—a cultural value in this organization—contributed to many decisions that were apparently made by consensus, but then consistently undermined in private by the very people who were part of the decision. Cultures often contain many implicit "rules" about use of power and whether "power over" or "power with" processes are seen as more or less appropriate.[29]

We explore this approach in greater depth in our treatment of international negotiation in Chapter 11.

Finally, culture—both organizational and national—often translates into deeply embedded structural inequalities in a society. The degree to which women, religious or ethnic groups, certain social classes, or other minority interests are treated unjustly in a society reflect longstanding historical evolution of power inequalities in social structures and institutions. Many significant social problems and negotiations about how to change them can be traced to the historical evolution of these dispositions within a culture, and they require significant effort and attention over many years to introduce meaningful change.

Agents, Constituencies, and External Audiences   Most negotiations that we describe in this book take place one-to-one—just you and the other negotiator. But negotiations become significantly more complex when negotiators are representing others' views (e.g., acting as an agent representing their organization or being represented by another person) and when there are multiple parties, the public media, and/or audiences present to observe, critique, and evaluate the negotiations. When all of these other parties are present in a negotiation, they can become actively involved to formally or informally pressure others as part of the negotiation process, which changes the power dynamics.

Dealing with Others Who Have More Power

Thus far, we have been focusing on the numerous ways that negotiators can assemble and use power to their advantage in a negotiation. However, negotiators are often on the receiving end of that power. Very little research has focused on how parties can deal with others who have significantly more power (from one or more of the sources we have mentioned in this chapter). We end this chapter with some advice to negotiators who are in a low-power position. Michael Watkins[30] specifically addresses the problem of "dancing with elephants" (striking a deal with an opponent much bigger than you) and highlights ways that lower-power parties can deal with the big players in business deals and partnerships. Here is some of his advice:

1. *Never do an all-or-nothing deal.* Relying on a single party and creating a make-or-break deal with them leaves the low-power party highly vulnerable. For example, a small business that agrees to let Walmart stores be its only customer runs the risk of being completely controlled by Walmart. Low-power parties should attempt to diversify their risk by entering into deals with several other partners so that no single high-power player could wipe the low-power partner out.

2. *Make the other party smaller.* In dealing with a high-power party, particularly if it is a group or organization, one should attempt to establish multiple relationships and engage in multiple negotiations. By dealing with a variety of different individuals and departments in the high-power party, one may be able to "divide and conquer" by diversifying the relationships and the multiple interests that may be served in working with these different subgroups.

3. *Make yourself bigger.* Similarly, low-power players should attempt to build coalitions with other low-power players so as to increase their collective bargaining power.

4. *Build momentum through doing deals in sequence.* Early deals can be done to build a relationship, strengthen the relationship with the high-power party, and perhaps acquire resources (information, technology, seed capital, etc.). Select those high-power targets that have the most to gain, and maximize visibility of those deals to other parties.

5. *Use the power of competition to leverage power.* This is a variation on the power of a BATNA. If you have something to offer, make sure you offer it to more than one high-power party. If you can get them competing against each other for what you want, some may actually do a deal with you simply to keep you from doing a deal with one of their competitors.

6. *Constrain yourself.* Tie your hands by limiting the ways that you can do business or who you can do business with. However, while these constraints might drive away your competition, they also have the liability of constraining you as well.

7. *Good information is always a source of power.* Seek out information that strengthens your negotiating position and case. Anticipate the information that would be most compelling or persuasive to the other side; organize it so that you can draw on it quickly and assemble it to be maximally persuasive.

8. *Ask lots of questions to gain more information.* Research shows that negotiators with less power ask more diagnostic than leading questions and constantly showed their willingness to cooperate—and that these behaviors resulted in better outcomes.[31]

9. *Do what you can to manage the process.* If the high-power party controls the negotiation process (the agenda, the cadence, the timing, and the location), he or she will do it in a way to assure outcomes he or she wants. If the low-power party controls the process, he or she is more likely to be able to steer the deal in an advantageous direction.[32]

Chapter Summary

In this chapter, we discussed the nature of power in negotiation. We suggested that there were two major ways to think about power: "power over," which suggests that power is fundamentally dominating and coercive in nature, and "power with," suggesting that power is jointly shared with the other party to collectively develop joint goals and objectives. There is a great tendency to see and define power as the former, but as we have discussed in this chapter and our review of the basic negotiation strategies, "power with" is critical to successful integrative negotiation.

We reviewed five major sources of power:

- Informational sources of power (information and expertise).

- Personal sources of power (psychological orientation, cognitive orientation, motivational orientation, certain dispositions, and moral orientation and skills).

- Position-based sources of power (legitimate power and resource control).

- Relationship-based power (goal interdependence and referent power and networks).

- Contextual sources of power (availability of BATNAs, availability of agents, and the organizational or national culture in which the negotiation occurs).

In closing, we wish to stress two key points. First, while we have presented many vehicles for attaining power in this chapter, it must be remembered that power can be highly elusive and fleeting in negotiation. Almost anything can be a source of power if it gives the negotiator a temporary advantage over the other party (e.g., a BATNA or a piece of critical information). Second, power is only the capacity to influence; using that power and skillfully exerting influence on the other requires a great deal of sophistication and experience.

Endnotes

[1] French and Raven, 1959; Pfeffer, 1992.

[2] Salancik and Pfeffer, 1977.

[3] Dahl, 1957; Kotter, 1979.

[4] Coleman, 2000.

[5] Ibid, p. 111.

[6] Follett, 1942.

[7] Deutsch, 1973, pp. 84–95.

[8] Ibid, p. 85.

[9] Researchers have defined an individual difference called communication competency (Spitzberg and Cupach, 1984). Individuals who are high in communication competency are likely to have strong verbal ability, are able to strategize about the way they communicate from one situation to the next, and can easily take the perspective of the other party. Individuals who are strong in communication competence are able to adapt to different situations and do what is most necessary and desirable in any given situation.

[10] French and Raven, 1959.

[11] Blumenstein, 1997; McGraw, 1997.

[12] Cronkhite and Liska, 1976, 1980.

[13] Deutsch, 1985, p. 74.

[14] Burrell and Morgan, 1979.

[15] Coleman, 2000, p. 116.

[16] McClelland, 1975; McClelland and Burnham, 1976; Adorno, Frenkl-Brunswick, Levinson, and Sanford, 1950.

[17] Pfeffer, 1992; Frost, 1987.

[18] Coleman, 1997.

[19] See Cialdini, 2001, on the illusions of authority.

[20] Barnard, 1938.

[21] Raven, 1993; Raven, Schwartzwald, and Koslowski, 1998.

[22] Pfeffer and Salancik, 1974; Pfeffer, 1992.

[23] Tjosvold, 1997, p. 297.

[24] Deutsch, 1973; Howard, Gardner, and Thompson, 2007.

[25] Raven and Rubin, 1976.

[26] See Charan, 1991; Kaplan, 1984; Krackhardt and Hanson, 1993.

[27] Ibarra and Andrews, 1993.

[28] Brass, 1984.

[29] Schein, 1988.

[30] Watkins, 2002.

[31] de Dreu and Van Kleef, 2004.

[32] Watkins, 2002.

CHAPTER

Ethics in Negotiation

Objectives

1. Understand commonly accepted approaches to ethical standards and ethical reasoning.
2. Explore factors that determine how ethics affect negotiation processes.
3. Consider different types of ethically problematic tactics and how they are perceived.
4. Gain an understanding of how marginally ethical tactics will be received by others in a negotiation and how to detect and cope with others' use of deceptive tactics.

In this chapter, we explore the question of whether there are, or should be, accepted ethical standards for behavior in negotiations. This topic has received increased attention from researchers in recent years. It is our view that fundamental questions of ethical conduct arise in every negotiation. The effective negotiator must recognize when the questions are relevant and what factors must be considered to answer them. We identify the major ethical dimensions raised in negotiations, describe how people tend to think about these ethical choices, and provide a framework for making informed ethical decisions.

But before we dive head first into all of that, let's set the stage with a few hypothetical dilemmas.

A Sampling of Ethical Quandaries

Consider the following situations:

1. You are trying to sell your stereo to raise money for an upcoming trip overseas. The stereo works great, and an audiophile friend tells you that if he were in the market for stereo equipment (which he isn't), he'd give you $500 for it. A few days later the first potential buyer comes to see the stereo. The buyer looks it over and asks a few questions about how it works. You assure the buyer that the stereo works well. When asked how much, you tell the buyer that you have already had an offer for $500. The buyer buys the stereo for $550.

    Is it ethical to have said what you said about having another offer?

2. You are an entrepreneur interested in acquiring a business that is currently owned by a competitor. The competitor, however, has not shown any interest in either selling his business or merging with your company. To gain inside knowledge of his firm, you hired a consultant you know to call contacts in your competitor's business and ask if the company is having any serious problems that might threaten its viability.

If there are such problems, you might be able to use the information to either hire away the company's employees or get the competitor to sell.

Is this an ethical course of action? Would you be likely to do it if you were the entrepreneur?

3. You are a vice president of human resources, negotiating with a union representative for a new labor contract. The union refuses to sign a new contract unless the company agrees to raise the number of paid holidays from six to seven. Management estimates it will cost approximately $220,000 for each paid holiday, and argues that the company cannot afford to meet the demand. However, you know that, in reality, money is not the issue— the company simply doesn't think the union's demand is justified. To convince the union leaders that they should withdraw their demand, you have been considering these alternatives: *(a)* tell the union that the company simply can't afford it, without further explanation; *(b)* prepare erroneous financial statements that show that it will cost about $300,000 per paid holiday, which you simply can't afford; and *(c)* offer union leaders an all-expenses-paid "working" trip to a Florida resort if they will simply drop the demand.

Do any of the strategies raise ethical concerns? Which ones? Why?

4. You are about to graduate from the MBA program of a leading university. You special-ized in management information systems (MIS) and will start a job with a company that commercially develops Web pages. You own a personal computer that is a couple of years old. You have decided to sell it and buy new equipment later after you see what kinds of projects your employer has you working on. So you post a flyer on campus bulletin boards about the computer for sale. You have decided not to tell prospective buyers that your hard drive acts like it is about to fail and that the computer occasion-ally crashes without warning.

Is this ethical? Would you be likely to do this if you were this particular student?

5. You buy a new pair of shoes on sale. The printed receipt states very clearly that the shoes are not returnable. After you get them home, you wear the shoes around the house for a day and decide that they just don't fit you correctly. So you take the shoes back to the store. The clerk points to the message on the receipt, but you don't let that deter you. You start to yell angrily about the store's poor quality service so that peo-ple in the store start to stare. The clerk calls the store manager; after some discussion, the manager agrees to give you your money back.

Is this ethical? Would you be likely to do this if you were this customer?

These situations are hypothetical; however, the problems they present are real ones for negotiators. People in and out of organizations are routinely confronted with important de-cisions about the strategies they will use to achieve important objectives, particularly when a variety of influence tactics are open to them. These decisions frequently carry ethical im-plications. In this chapter, we address the major ethical issues that arise in negotiation through consideration of these questions:

1. What are ethics, and why do they apply to negotiation?
2. What questions of ethical conduct are likely to arise in negotiation?

3.   What motivates unethical behavior, and what are the consequences?

4.   How can negotiators deal with the other party's use of deception?

What Do We Mean by "Ethics," and Why Do They Matter in Negotiation?

Ethics Defined

Ethics are broadly applied social standards for what is right or wrong in a particular situation, or a process for setting those standards. They differ from morals, which are individual and personal beliefs about what is right and wrong. Ethics grow out of particular philosophies, which purport to (1) define the nature of the world in which we live and (2) prescribe rules for living together. Different philosophies adopt distinct perspectives on these questions, which means in practice that they may lead to different judgments about what is right and wrong in a given situation. The "hard work" of ethics in practice is figuring out how ethical philosophies differ from one another, deciding which approaches are personally preferable, and applying them to real-world situations at hand.

Our goal is to distinguish among different criteria, or standards, for judging and evaluating a negotiator's actions, particularly when questions of ethics might be involved. Although negotiation is our focus, the criteria involved are really no different than might be used to evaluate ethics in business generally. An ethical dilemma exists for a negotiator when possible actions or strategies put the potential economic benefits of doing a deal in conflict with one's social obligations to other involved parties or one's broader community.

Many writers on business ethics have proposed frameworks that capture competing ethical standards (these typically map onto classical theories of ethical philosophy that have been around a long time). Drawing on some of these writers, here are four standards for evaluating strategies and tactics in business and negotiation:[1]

- Choose a course of action on the basis of results I expect to achieve (e.g., greatest return on investment).

- Choose a course of action on the basis of my duty to uphold appropriate rules and principles (e.g., the law).

- Choose a course of action on the basis of the norms, values, and strategy of my organization or community (e.g., the usual way we do things at this firm).

- Choose a course of action on the basis of my personal convictions (e.g., what my conscience tells me to do).

Each of these approaches reflects a fundamentally different approach to ethical reasoning. The first may be called *end-result ethics*, in that the rightness of an action is determined by evaluating the pros and cons of its consequences. The second is an example of what may be called *duty ethics*, in that the rightness of an action is determined by one's obligation to adhere to consistent principles, laws, and social standards that define what is right and wrong and where the line is. The third represents a form of *social contract ethics*, in that the rightness of an action is based on the customs and norms of a particular community. Finally, the fourth may be called *personalistic ethics*, in that the rightness of the action is based on one's own conscience and moral standards. See Table 8.1 for an overview of these four approaches.

TABLE 8.1 | Four Approaches to Ethical Reasoning

Ethical System	Definition	Major Proponent	Central Tenets	Major Concerns
End-result ethics	Rightness of an action is determined by considering consequences.	Jeremy Bentham (1748–1832) John Stuart Mill (1806–1873)	• One must consider all likely consequences. • Actions are more right if they promote more happiness, more wrong as they produce unhappiness. • Happiness is defined as presence of pleasure and absence of pain. • Promotion of happiness is generally the ultimate aim. • Collective happiness of all concerned is the goal.	• How does one define happiness, pleasure, or utility? • How does one measure happiness, pleasure, or utility? • How does one trade off between short-term vs. long-term happiness? • If actions create happiness for 90% of the world and misery for the other 10%, are they still ethical?
Duty ethics	Rightness of an action is determined by considering obligations to apply universal standards and principles.	Immanuel Kant (1724–1804)	• Human conduct should be guided by primary moral principles, or "oughts." • Individuals should stand on their principles and restrain themselves by rules. • The ultimate good is a life of virtue (acting on principles) rather than pleasure. • We should not adjust moral law to fit our actions, but adjust our actions to fit moral law.	• By what authority do we accept particular rules or the "goodness" of those rules? • What rule do we follow when rules conflict? • How do we adapt general rules to fit specific situations? • How do rules change as circumstances change? • What happens when good rules produce bad consequences? • Are there rules without any exceptions?

(Continued)

TABLE 8.1 | *(Concluded)*

Ethical System	Definition	Major Proponent	Central Tenets	Major Concerns
Social contract ethics	Rightness of an action is determined by the customs and norms of a community.	Jean-Jacques Rousseau (1712–1778)	• People must function in a social, community context to survive. • Communities become "moral bodies" for determining ground rules. • Duty and obligation bind the community and the individual to each other. • What is best for the common good determines the ultimate standard. • Laws are important, but morality determines the laws and standards for right and wrong.	• How do we determine the general will? • What is meant by the "common good"? • What do we do with independent thinkers who challenge the morality of the existing social order (e.g., Jefferson, Gandhi, Martin Luther King)? • Can a state be corrupt and its people still be "moral" (e.g., Nazi Germany)?
Personalistic ethics	Rightness of an action is determined by one's conscience.	Martin Buber (1878–1965)	• Locus of truth is found in human existence. • Conscience within each person calls them to fulfill their human-ness and to decide between right and wrong. • Personal decision rules are the ultimate standards. • Pursuing a noble goal by ignoble means leads to an ignoble end. • There are no absolute formulas for living. • One should follow one's group but also stick up for what one individually believes.	• How could we justify ethics other than by saying, "It felt like the right thing to do"? • How could we achieve a collective definition of what is ethical if individuals disagreed? • How could we achieve cohesiveness and consensus in a team that only fosters personal perspectives? • How could an organization assure some uniformity in ethics?

Source: Derived from W. Hitt, *Ethics and Leadership: Putting Theory into Practice* (Columbus, OH: Battelle Press, 1990).

Applying Ethical Reasoning to Negotiation

Each of these approaches could be used to analyze the five hypothetical situations at the beginning of the chapter. For instance, in the first situation involving selling a stereo and the statement to a prospective buyer about the existence of another potential buyer:

- If you believed in *end-result* ethics, then you might do whatever was necessary to get the best possible outcome (including lie about an alternative buyer).

- If you believed in *duty* ethics, you might perceive an obligation never to engage in subterfuge, and might therefore reject a tactic that involves an outright lie.

- If you believed in *social contract* ethics, you would base your tactical choices on your view of appropriate conduct for behavior in your community; if others would use deception in a situation like this, you lie.

- If you believed in *personalistic* ethics, you would consult your conscience and decide whether your need for cash for your upcoming trip justified using deceptive or dishonest tactics.

What this example shows is that the approach to ethical reasoning you favor affects the kind of ethical judgment you make, and the consequent behavior you choose, in a situation that has an ethical dimension to it.

Ethics versus Prudence versus Practicality versus Legality

Discussions of business ethics frequently confuse what is *ethical* (appropriate as determined by some standard of moral conduct) versus what is *prudent* (wise, based on trying to understand the efficacy of the tactic and the consequences it might have on the relationship with the other) versus what is *practical* (what a negotiator can actually make happen in a given situation) versus what is *legal* (what the law defines as acceptable practice).[2] In earlier chapters, we evaluated negotiation strategies and tactics by the prudence and practicality criteria; in this chapter, the focus is on evaluating negotiation strategies and tactics by ethical criteria.

Figure 8.1 presents a helpful way to think about what it means to comprehend and analyze an ethical dilemma. The figure shows a model of the process of analyzing a moral

FIGURE 8.1 | Analytical Process for the Resolution of Moral Problems

Understand all moral standards	Define complete moral problem	Determine the economic outcomes	Propose convincing moral solution
Recognize all moral impacts: • Benefits to some • Harms to others • Rights exercised • Rights denied		Consider the legal requirements Evaluate the ethical duties	

Source: L.T. Hosmer (2003). *The Ethics of Management* (4th ed.). New York: McGraw-Hill/Irwin.

problem developed by Larue Hosmer, a writer on business ethics.[3] According to Hosmer, before one can ponder solutions, the first step is developing a complete understanding of the moral problem at hand. Looking at the left side of Figure 8.1, this means grasping the various subjective standards (norms, beliefs, values, etc.) in play among involved parties and recognizing the mix of potential harms, benefits, and rights that are involved in the situation. With the problem fully defined, the path to a convincing solution travels through the three modes of analysis shown on the right side of the figure: (1) a determination of economic outcomes of potential courses of action, (2) a consideration of legal requirements that bear on the situation, and (3) an assessment of the ethical obligations to other involved parties regarding what is "'right' and 'just' and 'fair.'"[4] This last element—ethical reasoning— refers to the basic ethical frameworks mentioned earlier (see again Table 8.1).

What Questions of Ethical Conduct Arise in Negotiation?

Why do some negotiators choose to use tactics that may be unethical? The first answer that occurs to many people is that such negotiators are corrupt, degenerate, or immoral. However, that answer is much too simplistic. As we discussed in Chapter 5, people tend to regard *other people's* unsavory behavior as caused by disposition or personality, while attributing the causes of their *own* behavior to factors in the social environment.[5] Thus, a negotiator might consider an adversary who uses an ethically questionable tactic unprincipled, profit-driven, or willing to use any tactic to get what he or she wanted. In contrast, when attempting to explain why you as the negotiator might use the same tactic, you would tend to say that you are highly principled but had very good reasons for deviating from those principles just this one time.

In this section we discuss negotiation tactics that bring issues of ethicality into play. We first discuss what we mean by tactics that are "ethically ambiguous," and we link negotiator ethics to the fundamental issue of truth telling. We then describe research that has sought to identify and classify such tactics and analyze people's attitudes toward their use. We also distinguish between active and passive forms of deception—lies of omission versus commission. The section concludes with a model that portrays the negotiator's decision-making process with respect to the possible use of such tactics.

Ethically Ambiguous Tactics: It's (Mostly) All about the Truth

Here we discuss what kinds of tactics are ethically ambiguous and how they can work to afford a temporary strategic advantage. Our use of the phrase *ethically ambiguous* reflects a carefully considered choice of words. One dictionary defines "ambiguous" as "open to more than one interpretation . . . doubtful or uncertain."[6] We are interested in tactics that may or may not be improper, depending on an individual's ethical reasoning and circumstances.

Most of the ethics issues in negotiation are concerned with standards of truth telling— how honest, candid, and disclosing a negotiator should be. The attention here is more on what negotiators *say* (communicate about) or what they say they will do (and how they say it) than on what they actually *do* (although negotiators may act unethically as well). Some negotiators may cheat (violate formal and informal rules—e.g., claiming that rules about deadlines or procedures don't apply to them) or steal (e.g., break into the other party's or competitor's database or headquarters to secure confidential documents or briefing memoranda), but most of the attention in negotiator ethics has been on lying behavior.

Most negotiators would probably place a high value on a reputation for being truthful. Yet what does being truthful mean? Questions about truth telling are straightforward, but the answers are not so clear. First, how does one define *truth*? Do you follow a clear set of rules, determine what the social contract is for truth in your group or organization, or follow your conscience? Second, how does one define and classify deviations from the truth? Are all deviations lies, no matter how small and minor they are? Finally, one can add a relativistic dimension to these questions: should a person tell the truth all the time, or are there times when not telling the truth is an acceptable (or even necessary) form of conduct? These are questions of major concern to negotiators (and philosophers since time immemorial!) who are trying to decide what they can and cannot say and still remain ethical.

A number of articles in business journals have addressed the ethical issues surrounding truth telling. For example, a businessman named Carr argued over 40 years ago in a controversial *Harvard Business Review* article titled "Is Business Bluffing Ethical?" that strategy in business is analogous to strategy in a game of poker.[7] He advocated that, short of outright cheating (the equivalent of marking cards or hiding an ace up your sleeve), businesspeople ought to play the game as poker players do. Just as good poker playing often involves concealing information and bluffing (convincing others that you have the cards when you really don't), so do many business transactions. From time to time, most executives find themselves compelled, for their own interests or the interests of their companies, to practice some form of deception in their dealings with customers, suppliers, labor unions, government officials, or even other key executives. Through conscious misstatements, concealment of pertinent facts, or exaggeration—in short, bluffing—they seek to persuade others to agree with them. Carr argues that if an executive refuses to bluff periodically—if he or she feels obligated to tell the truth, the whole truth, and nothing but the truth all the time—he or she is probably ignoring opportunities permitted under the rules of business and is probably at a heavy disadvantage in business dealings.[8]

Bluffing, exaggeration, and concealment or manipulation of information, Carr maintained, are legitimate ways for both individuals and corporations to maximize their self-interest. Such strategies may be either advantageous or disadvantageous. An executive might plead poverty in a contract negotiation with a key employee and thereby save a significant amount of money for the company. However, a similar cost-cutting focus might lead the same executive to fail to make safety or quality improvements on one of the company's products, which could have severe long-term business consequences. As you can well imagine, Carr's position sparked lively debate among *Harvard Business Review* readers. A number of critics argued that individual businesspeople and corporations should be held to higher standards of ethical conduct, and they took Carr to task for his position.[9]

Questions and debate regarding the ethical standards for truth telling in negotiation are ongoing. As we pointed out when we discussed interdependence (Chapter 1), negotiation is based on information dependence—the exchange of information regarding the true preferences and priorities of the other negotiator.[10] Arriving at a clear, precise, effective negotiated agreement depends on the willingness of the parties to share accurate information about their own preferences, priorities, and interests. At the same time, because negotiators may also be interested in maximizing their self-interest, they may want to disclose as little as possible about their positions—particularly if they think they can do better by manipulating the information they disclose to the other party (see Chapter 3). This results in fundamental negotiation dilemmas involving trust and honesty. The *dilemma of trust* is that a negotiator who

BOX 8.1   When Is It Legal to Lie?

Although a major focus in the ethics of negotiation is on the morality of using deception in negotiation, it also behooves the effective negotiator to be familiar with the *legality* of doing so. Richard Shell, a lawyer and professor who writes about and teaches negotiation, offered an interpretation of U.S. law in his article "When Is It Legal to Lie in Negotiation?"

Shell starts with a basic "common law" definition of fraud: "a *knowing misrepresentation* of a *material fact* on which the victim reasonably *relies* and which *causes* damage" (p. 94; emphasis added).

A closer look at the meaning of the key (italicized) words in this definition brings legal issues involving lying in negotiation into focus.

A *misrepresentation*. An affirmative misstatement of something.

A *knowing* misrepresentation. Shell says a misrepresentation is "knowing" when you know that what you say is false when you say it. Does this mean you can skirt liability by avoiding coming into contact with the knowledge involved? Shell says no—courts would regard that as reckless disregard for the truth.

A *fact*. To be illegal, in theory, the thing being misrepresented generally has to be an objective fact. But in practice, Shell points out that misstating an opinion or an intention can get you into trouble if it builds on factual misrepresentation or is particularly egregious—especially if you know the falsity at the time you make the statement or promise.

A *material* fact. Not all "facts" are objective or material. Shell says that by the standards of legal practice in the United States, demands and reservation points are not regarded as "material" to the deal, so it is not actionable fraud to bluff about them. He cautions, however, that lying about alternatives or other offers or other buyers can get you into trouble. It's not clear that these are always material, but this kind of thing may be left up to a jury to decide if a claim of fraud went to trial.

Reliance/causation. For a deceptive statement to be legally fraudulent, the receiver must prove that he or she relied on the information and that doing so caused harm.

Does this mean that illegal deception always involves affirmative statements that are false? Will silence protect you from legal liability? Shell says no: there are conditions under which you are legally bound to share truthful information. For instance, you are obligated to disclose in these situations:

- If you make a partial disclosure that would be misleading.
- If the parties stand in fiduciary relationship to one another.
- If the nondisclosing party has "superior information" that is "vital."
- In cases involving certain specialized transactions, such as insurance contracts.

Source: Adapted from G. Richard Shell, "When Is It Legal to Lie in Negotiations?" *Sloan Management Review* 32, no. 3 (1991), pp. 93–101.

---

believes everything the other says can be manipulated by dishonesty. The *dilemma of honesty* is that a negotiator who tells the other party all of his exact requirements and limits will, inevitably, never do better than his walkaway point. Sustaining the bargaining relationship means choosing a middle course between complete openness and complete deception.[11]

As a final point on the subject of truth telling, there is, beyond ethics, the matter of *legal* obligations to be truthful. Deception in negotiation can rise to the level of legally actionable fraud. The law on this subject (like on most subjects!) is complex and often hard to pin down. See Box 8.1 for a guide to the (il)legality of lying in negotiation.[12]

Identifying Ethically Ambiguous Tactics and Attitudes toward Their Use

What Ethically Ambiguous Tactics Are There?   Deception and subterfuge may take several forms in negotiation. Researchers have been working to identify the nature of these tactics, and their underlying structure, for almost 20 years.[13] They have extensively explored the nature and conceptual organization of ethically ambiguous negotiating tactics. The general approach has been to ask students and executives to rate a list of tactics on several dimensions: the appropriateness of the tactic, the rater's likelihood of using the tactic, and/or the perceived efficacy of using the tactic. Analyzing these questionnaire results, six clear categories of tactics emerged and have been confirmed by additional data collection and analysis.[14] These categories are listed in Table 8.2. It is interesting to note that of the six categories, two—emotional manipulation and the use of "traditional competitive bargaining" tactics—are viewed as generally appropriate and likely to be used. These tactics, therefore, while mildly inappropriate, are nevertheless seen as appropriate and effective in successful distributive bargaining. The other four categories of tactics—misrepresentation, bluffing, misrepresentation to opponent's network, and inappropriate information collection—are generally seen as inappropriate and unethical in negotiation.

Is It All Right to Use Ethically Ambiguous Tactics?   Research suggests that there are tacitly agreed-on rules of the game in negotiation. In these rules, some minor forms of untruths—misrepresentation of one's true position to the other party, bluffs, and emotional manipulations—may be seen by some negotiators as ethically acceptable and within the rules (but not by others). In contrast, outright deception and falsification are generally seen as outside the rules. However, we must place some strong cautionary notes on these

TABLE 8.2 | Categories of Marginally Ethical Negotiating Tactics

Category	Example
Traditional competitive bargaining	Not disclosing your walkaway; making an inflated opening offer
Emotional manipulation	Faking anger, fear, disappointment; faking elation, satisfaction
Misrepresentation	Distorting information or negotiation events in describing them to others
Misrepresentation to opponent's networks	Corrupting your opponent's reputation with his or her peers
Inappropriate information gathering	Bribery, infiltration, spying, etc.
Bluffing	Insincere threats or promises

Sources: Adapted from R. Robinson, R. J. Lewicki, and E. Donahue, "Extending and Testing a Five Factor Model of Ethical and Unethical Bargaining Tactics: The SINS Scale," *Journal of Organizational Behavior* 21 (2000), pp. 649–64; and B. Barry, I. S. Fulmer, and A. Long, *Ethically Marginal Bargaining Tactics: Sanction, Efficacy, and Performance.* Presented at the annual meeting of the Academy of Management, Toronto, August, 2000.

conclusions. First, these statements are based on ratings by large groups of people (mostly business students); in no way do they, or should they, predict how any one individual negotiator will perceive and use the tactics or how any one target who experiences them will rate them. (We discuss reactions from the "victim's" perspective later in this chapter.) Second, these observations are based primarily on what people said they would do, rather than what they actually did. Perceptions and reactions may well be different when the parties are making decisions in an actual negotiation, rather than rating the tactics on a questionnaire removed from any direct experience with another person in a meaningful social context. Third, by engaging in research on ethically ambiguous tactics (as the authors of this book have) and reporting these results, we do not mean to endorse the use of any marginally ethical tactic. Instead, our objective is to focus debate among negotiators on exactly when these tactics might be appropriate or should be used. Finally, we acknowledge that this is a Western view, in which individuals determine what is ethically acceptable; in some other cultures (e.g., Asia), a group or organization would decide on ethics, while in other cultures (e.g., some nations with emerging free markets), ethical constraints on negotiated transactions may be minimal or hard to determine clearly, and "let the buyer beware" at all times!

Deception by Omission versus Commission

The use of deceptive tactics can be active or passive. To illustrate, consider a study that examined the tendency for negotiators to misrepresent their interests on a common-value issue—an issue for which both parties are seeking the same outcome.[15] A negotiator using this tactic deceives the other party about what she wants on the common-value issue and then (grudgingly) agrees to accept the other party's preference, which in reality matches her own. By making it look as though she has made a concession, she can seek a concession from the other party in return. Overall, 28 percent of subjects in the study misrepresented the common-value issue in an effort to obtain a concession from the other party. The researchers discovered that negotiators used two forms of deception in misrepresenting the common-value issue: misrepresentation by *omission* (failing to disclose information that would benefit the other) and misrepresentation by *commission* (actually lying about the common-value issue).

In another set of studies, students took part in a role-play involving the sale of a car with a defective transmission.[16] Students could lie by omission—by simply failing to mention the defective transmission—or by commission—by denying that the transmission was defective even when asked by the other party. Far more students were willing to lie by omission (not revealing the whole truth) than by commission (falsely answering a question when asked). This finding points to an important insight into human nature: many people are willing to let another person continue to operate under false premises, but will stop short of assertively making a false statement themselves. It clearly reinforces the norm of caveat emptor (let the buyer beware), suggesting that it is up to each party to ask the right questions and be appropriately skeptical when accepting the other's pitch.

The Decision to Use Ethically Ambiguous Tactics: A Model

We conclude this section of the chapter with a relatively simple model that helps explain how a negotiator decides whether to employ one or more deceptive tactics (see Figure 8.2). The model casts a negotiator in a situation where he or she needs to decide which tactics to use to influence the other party. The individual identifies possible influence tactics that could be effective in a given situation, some of which might be deceptive, inappropriate, or otherwise marginally ethical. Once these tactics are identified, the individual may decide to actually use one or more of them. The selection and use of a given tactic is likely to be influenced by the negotiator's own motivations and his or her perception/judgment of the tactic's appropriateness. Once the tactic is employed, the negotiator will assess consequences on three standards: (1) whether the tactic worked (produced the desired result), (2) how the negotiator feels about him- or herself after using the tactic, and (3) how the individual may be judged by the other party or by neutral observers. Negative or positive conclusions on any of these three standards may lead the negotiator to try to explain or justify use of the tactic, but they will also eventually affect a decision to employ similar tactics in the future.

Why Use Deceptive Tactics? Motives and Consequences

In the preceding pages we discussed at length the nature of ethics and the kinds of tactics in negotiation that might be regarded as ethically ambiguous. Now we turn to a discussion of why such tactics are tempting and what the consequences are of succumbing to that temptation. We begin with motives, and motives inevitably begin with power.

The Power Motive

The purpose of using ethically ambiguous negotiating tactics is to increase the negotiator's power in the bargaining environment. Information is a major source of leverage in negotiation. Information has power because negotiation is intended to be a rational activity involving the exchange of information and the persuasive use of that information. Often, whoever has better information, or uses it more persuasively, stands to "win" the negotiation.

FIGURE 8.2 | A Simple Model of Deception in Negotiation

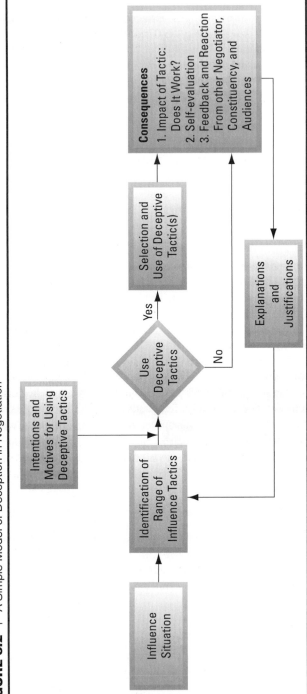

Such a view assumes that the information is accurate and truthful. To assume otherwise—that it is not truthful—is to question the very assumptions on which daily social communication is based and the honesty and integrity of the presenter of that information. Of course, raising such questions openly might insult the others and reduce the implied trust we placed in them. Moreover, investigating someone else's truthfulness and honesty is time and energy consuming. So any inaccurate and untruthful statements (i.e., lies) introduced into this social exchange manipulate information in favor of the introducer. Through the tactics we described earlier—bluffing, falsification, misrepresentation, deception, and selective disclosure—the liar gains advantage. In fact, it has been demonstrated that individuals are more willing to use deceptive tactics when the other party is perceived to be uninformed or unknowledgable about the situation under negotiation; particularly when the stakes are high.[17]

Other Motives to Behave Unethically

The motivation of a negotiator can clearly affect his or her tendency to use deceptive tactics. A person's "motivational orientation"—whether negotiators are motivated to act cooperatively, competitively, or individualistically toward each other—can affect the strategies and tactics they pursue. In one study, researchers manipulated negotiators' motivational orientation to the situation, predisposing parties to either a competitive or a cooperative orientation toward the other.[18] Competitive negotiators—those looking to maximize their own outcome, regardless of the consequences for the other—were more likely to use misrepresentation as a strategy. Cultural differences may also map onto motivational influences: There is evidence that individuals in a highly individualistic culture (the United States) are more likely to use deception for personal gain than those in a more collectivist culture (Israel).[19]

But the impact of motives may be more complex. In one study on tactics, negotiators were asked about their predisposition to use ethically ambiguous tactics.[20] Different versions of the questionnaire explicitly told respondents to assume either a competitive or a cooperative motivational orientation toward the other party and to assume that the other party would be taking either a competitive or a cooperative motivational orientation. The researchers predicted that competitive motivations would elicit the strongest endorsement of ethically ambiguous tactics. The results revealed that differences in the negotiators' *own* motivational orientation—cooperative rather than competitive—did *not* cause differences in their view of the appropriateness of using the tactics, but the negotiators' perception of the *other's* expected motivation did! In other words, negotiators were significantly more likely to see the ethically ambiguous tactics as appropriate if they anticipated that the other party would be competitive rather than cooperative. This finding suggests that negotiators may rationalize the use of marginally ethical tactics in anticipation of the other's expected conduct rather than take personal responsibility for using these tactics in the service of their own competitive orientation.

The Consequences of Unethical Conduct

A negotiator who employs an unethical tactic will experience consequences that may be positive or negative, based on three aspects of the situation: (1) whether the tactic is effective; (2) how the other person, his or her constituencies, and audiences evaluate the tactic; and (3) how the negotiator evaluates the tactic. We discuss each in turn.

Effectiveness   Let us first consider the consequences that occur based on whether the tactic is successful or not. Clearly, a tactic's effectiveness will have some impact on whether it is more or less likely to be used in the future (essentially, a simple learning and reinforcement process). If using the tactic allows a negotiator to attain rewarding outcomes that would be unavailable if he had behaved ethically, and if the unethical conduct is not punished by others, the frequency of unethical conduct is likely to increase because the negotiator believes he or she can get away with it. Thus, real consequences—rewards and punishments that arise from using a tactic or not using it—should not only motivate a negotiator's present behavior but also affect his or her predisposition to use similar strategies in similar circumstances in the future. (For the moment, we will ignore the consequences of these tactics on the negotiator's reputation and trustworthiness, an impact that most deceptive negotiators unfortunately ignore in the short term.)

These propositions have not been tested in negotiating situations, but they have been tested extensively in other research studies on ethical decision making. For example, when research participants expected to be rewarded for making an unethical decision by participating in a laboratory-simulated kickback scheme, they not only participated but also were willing to participate again when a second opportunity arose.[21] Moreover, when there were also strong pressures on the research subjects to compete with others—for example, announcing how well each person had done on the task and giving a prize to the one with the highest score—the frequency of unethical conduct increased even further.

Reactions of Others   A second set of consequences may arise from judgments and evaluations by the person who was the "target" of the tactic, by constituencies, or by audiences that can observe the tactic. Depending on whether these parties recognize the tactic and whether they evaluate it as proper or improper to use, the negotiator may receive a great deal of feedback. If the target person is unaware that a deceptive tactic was used, he or she may show no reaction other than disappointment at having lost the negotiation. However, if the target discovers that deception has occurred, he or she is likely to react strongly. People who discover that they have been deceived or exploited are typically angry. In addition to perhaps having "lost" the negotiation, they feel foolish for having allowed themselves to be manipulated or deceived by a clever ploy. The victim is unlikely to trust the unethical

NON SEQUITUR © Wiley Miller. Dist. by UNIVERSAL PRESS SYNDICATE. Reprinted with permission. All rights reserved.

negotiator again, may seek revenge from the negotiator in future dealings, and may also generalize this experience to negotiations with others.

These negative consequences were apparent in a research showing that victims had strong emotional reactions to deception when they had an intimate relationship with the subject, when the information at stake was very important, and when they saw lying as an unacceptable type of behavior for that relationship (i.e., when strong expectations of truth telling were clearly violated).[22] In a majority of cases, the discovery of the lie was instrumental in an eventual termination of the relationship with the other person, and in most cases the termination was initiated by the victim. The more the deception was serious, personal, and highly consequential for trust between the parties, the more destructive it was to the relationship. In a similar vein, there is also evidence that individuals who are deceptive are regarded as less truthful and less desirable for future interactions.[23] We emphasize here that damage to one's reputation can be difficult to repair. One study revealed that the effects of untrustworthy actions on one's credibility can be remedied with subsequent truthful behavior, as long as the untrustworthy actions that breached trust did not involve deception. But when deception is the cause of the rift, attempts to restore trust through an apology or other behavior apology are ineffective.[24] In sum, although the use of unethical tactics may create short-term success for the negotiator, it may also create an adversary who is distrustful or, even worse, bent on revenge and retribution.

Reactions of Self Under some conditions—such as when the other party has truly suffered—a negotiator may feel some discomfort, stress, guilt, or remorse. This can lead a negotiator to seek ways to reduce the psychological discomfort. In one study, individuals who had lied to their partner during the course of a simulated business negotiation made larger concessions later in the negotiation to compensate.[25] This compensation for an earlier lie was especially common among study participants who rated themselves highly on "moral attributes" (e.g., honest, fairness, benevolence) and among those who told they were negotiating on behalf of an organization that "prides itself on being fair and honest in its business dealings."

Of course, negotiators who see no problem with using deceptive tactics may be inclined to use them again and may begin to ponder how to use them more effectively. On the one hand, although the use of ethically questionable tactics may have severe consequences for the negotiator's reputation and trustworthiness, parties seldom appear to take these outcomes into consideration in the short term. On the other hand, and particularly if the tactic has worked, the negotiator may be able to rationalize and justify the use of the tactic. We explore these rationalizations and justifications next.

Explanations and Justifications

When a negotiator has used an ethically ambiguous tactic that may elicit a reaction—as we described earlier—the negotiator must prepare to defend the tactic's use to himself (e.g., "I see myself as a person of integrity, and yet I have decided to do something that might be viewed as unethical"), to the victim, or to constituencies and audiences who may express their concerns. The primary purpose of these explanations and justifications is to rationalize, explain, or excuse the behavior—to verbalize some good, legitimate reason why this tactic was necessary. Some examples include:[26]

- *The tactic was unavoidable.* Negotiators frequently justify their actions by claiming that the situation made it necessary for them to act the way they did. The negotiator may feel that she was not in full control of her actions or had no other option; hence she should not be held responsible. Perhaps the negotiator had no intent to hurt anyone but was pressured to use the tactic by someone else.

- *The tactic was harmless.* The negotiator may say that what he did was really trivial and not very significant. People tell white lies all the time. For example, you may greet your neighbor with a cheery "Good morning, nice to see you" when, in fact, it may not be a good morning, you are in a bad mood, and you wish you hadn't run into your neighbor because you are angry about his dog barking all night. Exaggerations, bluffs, or peeking at the other party's private notes during negotiations can all be easily explained away as harmless actions. Note, however, that this particular justification interprets the harm from the actor's point of view; the victim may not agree and may have experienced significant harm or costs as a result.

- *The tactic will help to avoid negative consequences.* When using this justification, negotiators are arguing that the ends justify the means. In this case, the justification is that the tactic helped to avoid greater harm. It is okay to lie to an armed robber about where you have hidden your money to avoid being robbed. Similarly, negotiators may see lying (or any other means–ends tactic) as justifiable if it protects them against even more undesirable consequences should the truth be known.

- *The tactic will produce good consequences, or the tactic is altruistically motivated.* Again, the end justifies the means, but in a positive sense. A negotiator who judges a tactic on the basis of its consequences is acting in accord with the tenets of utilitarianism— that the quality of any given action is judged by its consequences. Utilitarians may argue that certain kinds of lies or means–ends tactics are appropriate because they may provide for the larger good—for example, Robin Hood tactics in which someone robs from the rich to make the poor better off. In reality, most negotiators use deceptive tactics for their own advantage, not for the general good.

- *"They had it coming," or "They deserve it," or "I'm just getting my due."* These are all variations on the theme of using lying and deception either against an individual who may have taken advantage of you in the past or against some generalized source of authority (i.e., "the system"). Polls have noted an erosion of honesty in the United States—people increasingly think it appropriate to take advantage of the system in various ways, including tax evasion, petty theft, shoplifting, improper declaration of bankruptcy, journalistic excesses, and distortion in advertising.[27]

- *"They were going to do it anyway, so I will do it first."* Sometimes a negotiator legitimizes the use of a tactic because he or she anticipates that the other intends to use similar tactics. One study found that people were most willing to use deception when negotiating with a partner who had a reputation for being unethical.[28] Another study linked one's own inclination to deceive and judgments of the other party's integrity. The more an individual was tempted to engage in misrepresentation, the more he or she believed that the other would also misrepresent information.[29] Thus, one's own temptation to misrepresent creates a self-fulfilling logic in which one believes one needs to misrepresent because the other is likely to do it as well. At the same time, subjects in this study consistently rated themselves as more ethical than the other party, which suggests that people experience some combination of positive illusions about themselves and their own behavior, and negative illusions about the other and the other's likely behavior.

- *"He started it."* This is a variation on the last point. In this case, the rationale is that others have *already* violated the rules, therefore legitimizing the negotiator's right to violate them as well. In such cases, unethical tactics are employed in a tit-for-tat manner, to restore balance, or to give others their due.

- *The tactic is fair or appropriate to the situation.* This approach uses a kind of moral (situational) relativism as a rationale or justification. Most social situations, including negotiations, are governed by a set of generally well-understood rules of proper conduct and behavior. For example, recall the earlier arguments that business is a game and that the game has a special ethos to it that legitimizes normally unethical actions.[30] Others have countered these arguments, contending that deceit in business is just as immoral as it is in other areas of life and that the game analogy of business no more legitimizes unethical conduct than other analogies.[31] As a general matter, ethical relativism—the idea that moral standards shift with changing circumstances—frequently comes under fire as an unacceptable take on morality. As one writer put it, "If all ethical systems are equally valid, then no firm moral judgments can be made about individual behavior, and we are all on our own to do as we like to others, within economic limits and legal constraints."[32] We leave it to the reader to decide if this is a good thing or a bad thing.

As self-serving rationalizations for one's own conduct, explanations allow the negotiator to convince others—particularly the victim—that conduct that would ordinarily be wrong in a given situation is acceptable. Explanations and justifications help people rationalize the behavior to themselves as well. But there is a risk: we surmise that the more frequently negotiators engage in this self-serving process, the more their judgments about ethical standards and values will become biased, diminishing their ability to see the truth for what it is. The tactics involved may have been used initially to gain power in a negotiation, but negotiators who use them frequently may experience a loss of power over time. These negotiators will be seen as having low credibility or integrity, and they will be treated accordingly as people who will act exploitatively if the opportunity arises. Good reputations are easier to maintain than to restore once damaged.

How Can Negotiators Deal with the Other Party's Use of Deception?

People lie—quite frequently, in fact[33]—so a chapter such as this would be incomplete without briefly noting some of the things that you can do as a negotiator when you believe the other party is using deceptive tactics. Table 8.3 presents some verbal strategies for trying to determine if others are being deceptive. And what if they are? Here are some options:

Ask Probing Questions   Many negotiators fail to ask enough questions, yet asking questions can reveal a great deal of information, some of which the negotiator might otherwise have intentionally left undisclosed.[34] In an experimental simulation of a negotiation over the sale of a computer, buyers were either strongly prompted to ask questions of the seller

TABLE 8.3 | Detecting Deception

Researchers have identified a number of verbal tactics that you can use to determine whether the other party is acting deceptively.

Tactic	Explanation and Examples
Intimidation	Force the other to admit he is using deception by intimidating him into telling the truth. Make a no-nonsense accusation of the other. Criticize the other. Hammer the other with challenging questions. Feign indifference to what he has to say ("I'm not interested in anything you have to say on the matter").
Futility portrayal	Emphasize the futility and impending danger associated with continued deceit: "The truth will come out someday," "Don't dig the hole deeper by trying to cover it up," "If you try to cover it up, it will only be worse in the future," "You are all alone in your deception."
Discomfort and relief	State the maxim, "Confession is good for the soul." Help the other reduce the tension and stress associated with being a known deceiver.
Bluffing	Lie to the other to make her believe you have uncovered her deception: "Your sins are about to be uncovered." Indicate that you know what she knows but will not discuss it.
Gentle prods	Encourage the other to keep talking so that he gives you information that may help you separate true facts from deceptions. Ask him to elaborate on the topic being discussed. Ask questions but indicate that you are asking because "other people want to know." Play devil's advocate and ask playful questions. Praise the other so as to give him confidence and support that may lead to information sharing.
Minimization	Play down the significance of any deceptive act. Help the other find excuses for why she was deceptive; minimize the consequences of the action; indicate that others have done worse; shift the blame to someone else.
Contradiction	Get the other to tell his story fully in order to discover more information that will allow you to discover inconsistencies and contradictions in his comments or reports. Point out and ask for explanations about apparent contradictions. Ask the speaker the same question several times and look for inconsistencies in his response. Present contradictions back and ask the speaker to explain. Put pressure on the speaker and get him to slip up or say things he doesn't want to say.
Altered information	Alter information and hopefully trick the other into revealing deception. Exaggerate what you believe is the deception, hoping that the other will jump in to "correct" the statement. Ask the suspected deceiver a question containing incorrect information and hope she corrects you.
A chink in the defense	Try to get the other to admit a small or partial lie about some information, and use this to push for admission of a larger lie: "If you lied about this one little thing, how do I know you have not lied about other things?"
Self-disclosure	Reveal a number of things about yourself, including, perhaps, dishonesty on your own part, hoping the other will begin to trust you and reciprocate with disclosures of dishonesty.

(Continued)

TABLE 8.3 | (*Concluded*)

Point of deception cues	Point out behaviors you detect in the other that might be an indication he is lying: sweating, nervousness, change of voice, inability to make eye contact, and so on.
Concern	Indicate your true concern for the other's welfare: "You are important to me," "I care deeply about you," "I feel your pain."
Keeping the status quo	Admonish the other to be truthful in order to maintain her good name. "What will people think?" Appeal to her pride and desire to maintain a good reputation.
Direct approach	"Simply tell me the truth." "Let's be honest here." "Surely you have no objection to telling me everything you know."
Silence	Create a "verbal vacuum" that makes the other uncomfortable and gets him to talk and disclose information. When he tells a lie, simply maintain direct eye contact but remain silent.

Source: Adapted from Pamela J. Kalbfleisch, "The Language of Detecting Deceit," *Journal of Language and Social Psychology* 13, no. 4 (1994), pp. 469–96.

about the condition of the computer, or not prompted to ask questions.[35] Across the board, asking questions about the condition of the computer reduced the number of the seller's deceptive comments (lies of commission). However, under some conditions, asking questions also increased the seller's use of lies of omission about other aspects of the computer. Thus, while questions can help a negotiator determine whether another is being deceptive, cross-examination may actually increase the seller's tendency to be deceptive in areas where questions are not being asked. (Refer back to Chapter 6 for a more extensive examination of asking good questions.)

Phrase Questions in Different Ways   Robert Adler, a scholar in law and ethics, points out that what negotiators engaged in deception are usually doing is not outright lying (which risks liability for fraud); instead, "they dodge, duck, bob, and weave around the truth, assuming that their statements will be misconstrued or not challenged."[36] A question posed a certain way may elicit an answer that is technically true, but skirts the actual truth the questioner seeks to uncover. Consider this example: as a prospective house buyer I ask, "How is the heating system?" and the seller replies, "It works fine," so I draw the conclusion that there's no problem. Alternatively, I could have asked, "When was the last time the heating system was inspected, and what was the result?" (and perhaps gone even further and asked for written documentation of the inspection). I might learn that although the system is in reasonable working order at the moment ("it works fine"), the inspection revealed it's on its last legs and will need replacement within the next year. Different question, different answer, and less of an evasion.

Force the Other Party to Lie or Back Off   If you suspect the other party is being cagey or deceptive about an issue but is not making a clear statement in plain language, pose a question that forces him or her to tell a direct lie (if the assertion is false) or else abandon or qualify the assertion. For instance, if the seller of a piece of property alludes to other interested buyers and implies there are other offers, ask a question about other offers in a clear way that

BOX | 8.2 | Is There Such a Thing as an "Honest Face"?

Although people in general are not particularly good at spotting lies, some people continue to believe that they can tell by looking into someone's face if that person is inclined to be dishonest or truthful on a regular basis. But how accurate are such assessments?

A study asked participants to view photographs of the same people as children, adolescents, and adults and to rate their attractiveness and honesty based on an assessment of their faces. These results were compared to self-reports of honest behavior provided by the people in the photographs. The results demonstrated that structural qualities of the face, such as attractiveness, "baby-faceness," eye size, and symmetry each individually contributed to perceptions of greater honesty in observers. The self-reports revealed that men who

looked more honest early in life actually were more honest as they grew older. On the other hand, women whose behavior was less honest when they were young grew to appear more honest as they aged, even though their behavior did not change significantly. Study participants were able to correctly identify the most honest men in the group as they aged, but their assessment of women was largely inaccurate. The researchers concluded that men's faces accurately reflected their tendency toward honesty, but women's faces were not particularly valid indicators of their truthfulness.

Source: Adapted from L. A. Zebrowitz, L. Voinescu, and M. A. Collins, "Wide-Eyed and Crooked-Faced: Determinants of Perceived and Real Honesty across the Life Span," *Personality and Social Psychology Bulletin* 22 (1996), pp. 1258–69.

calls for a yes or no answer. This can be a useful strategy because, as we noted earlier, research shows people are more inclined to lie by omission than by commission. Some people are comfortable being cagey or misleading, but they will run headlong into their conscience if forced to flatly lie while looking someone in the eye. Conscience aside, this kind of question may also make the other party nervous about liability for fraudulent negotiator behavior. Hence the timely use of a sharp, direct question will induce some adversaries to back off rather than fib to your face. (Granted, the pathological liar may well rise to the challenge.)

Test the Other Party   Not sure if the other party is the kind of person who would lie? Consider asking a question to which you already know the answer.[37] If the answer you get is evasive or deceptive, you have learned something important about the other party and his or her trustworthiness. And when you do think your opponent's allegiance to the truth is shaky, take good notes during the negotiation (and invite the other side to confirm the accuracy of your notes) in order to create and preserve accountability later.

"Call" the Tactic   Indicate to the other side that you know he is bluffing or lying. Do so tactfully but firmly, and indicate your displeasure. Keep in mind, however, that spotting lies is not always easy—see Box 8.2. Mistakenly calling the other party a liar or an unethical negotiator is certainly not the path to a constructive process and fruitful outcome.

Ignore the Tactic   If you are aware that the other party is bluffing or lying, simply ignore it, especially if the deception concerns a relatively minor aspect of the negotiation. Some may lie or bluff out of an expectation that this is what they "should" be doing—that it's part of the ritual or dance of negotiation—rather than out of a sinister sense of ethics or morality. Negotiators at times make unwise commitments—statements they later regret promising things or ruling out options—and it is sometimes in the best interest of the other party to help that negotiator "escape" the commitment and save face. A similar logic can apply to deceptive statements when the motive is closer to naïveté than depravity: let it pass, avoid embarrassing the other person, and move on. (Table 8.3 has additional suggestions for dealing with situations where you suspect that the other party is engaged in deception.)

Discuss What You See and Offer to Help the Other Party Shift to More Honest Behaviors   This is a variation on calling the tactic, but it tries to assure the other party that telling the truth is, in the long term, more likely to get him what he wants than any form of bluffing or deception will.

Respond in Kind   If the other party bluffs, you bluff more. If she misrepresents, you misrepresent. We do not recommend this course of action at all, because it simply escalates the destructive behavior and drags you into the mud with the other party, but if she recognizes that you are lying too, she may also realize that the tactic is unlikely to work. Of course, if the other party's lies are so direct and extreme as to constitute legally actionable fraud, then it is not an approach you would want to mimic under any circumstances. In general, the "respond in kind" approach is best treated as a "last resort" strategy.

Chapter Summary

In this chapter, we have discussed factors that negotiators consider when they decide whether particular tactics are deceptive and unethical. We approached the study of ethically ambiguous tactics from a decision-making framework, examining the ethical overtones of the choices that negotiators make.

We began by drawing on a set of hypothetical scenarios to show how ethical questions are inherent in the process of negotiation, and then presented four fundamental approaches to ethical reasoning that might be used to make decisions about what is ethically appropriate. We proposed that a negotiator's decision to use ethically ambiguous (or flatly unethical) tactics typically grows out of a desire to increase one's negotiating power by manipulating the landscape of (presumably accurate) information in the negotiation. We discussed the different forms that ethically ambiguous tactics take, and we analyzed the motives for and consequences of engaging in unethical negotiation behavior. Finally, we addressed how negotiators can respond to another party that may be using tactics of deception or subterfuge.

In closing, we suggest that negotiators who are considering the use of deceptive tactics ask themselves the following questions:

- Will they really enhance my power and help me achieve my objective?

- How will the use of these tactics affect the quality of my relationship with the other party in the future?

- How will the use of these tactics affect my personal and professional reputation as a negotiator?

Negotiators frequently overlook the fact that, although unethical or expedient tactics may get them what they want in the short run, these same tactics typically lead to tarnished reputations and diminished effectiveness in the long run.

Endnotes

[1] Green, 1994; Hitt, 1990; Hosmer, 2003.

[2] Missner, 1980.

[3] Hosmer, 2003.

[4] Ibid., p. 87.

[5] Miller and Ross, 1975.

[6] *The American Heritage Dictionary of the English Language* (3rd edition), Houghton Mifflin.

[7] Carr, 1968.

[8] Ibid., p. 144.

[9] For example, Allhoff, 2003; Koehn, 1997.

[10] Kelley and Thibaut, 1969.

[11] Rubin and Brown, 1975.

[12] The accompanying box (8.1) on the legality of lying in negotiation addresses U.S. law. Obviously, legal systems vary from country to country, and so too will legal doctrine regarding deception and fraud in negotiation.

[13] See Lewicki, 1983; Lewicki and Robinson, 1998; Lewicki and Spencer, 1990; Lewicki and Stark, 1995.

[14] Robinson, Lewicki, and Donahue, 2000; Barry, Fulmer, and Long, 2000.

[15] O'Connor and Carnevale, 1997.

[16] Schweitzer, 1997; Schweitzer and Croson, 1999.

[17] Boles, Croson, and Murnighan, 2000.

[18] O'Connor and Carnevale, 1997.

[19] Sims, 2002.

[20] Lewicki and Spencer, 1991.

[21] Hegarty and Sims, 1978.

[22] McCornack and Levine, 1990.

[23] Boles, Croson, and Murnighan, 2000.

[24] Schweitzer, Hershey, and Bradlow, 2006.

[25] Aquino and Becker, 2005.

[26] Examples are drawn from Bok, 1978.

[27] For example, Patterson and Kim, 1991; Yankelovich, 1982.

[28] Volkema and Fleury, 2002.

[29] Tenbrunsel, 1998.

[30] Carr, 1968.

[31] Bowie, 1993; Koehn, 1997.

[32] Hosmer, 2003, p. 89.

[33] Adler, 2007

[34] Schweitzer, 1997; Schweitzer and Croson, 1999.

[35] Schweitzer, Brodt and Croson, 2002.

[36] Adler, 2007, p. 72.

[37] Adler, 2007.

CHAPTER 9

Relationships in Negotiation

Objectives

1. Understand how negotiation within an existing relationship changes the nature of negotiation dynamics.
2. Explore the different forms of relationships in which negotiation can occur.
3. Consider the critical roles played by reputations, trust, and fairness in any negotiating relationship.
4. Gain insight into how to rebuild trust and repair damaged relationships.

Up to this point in this text, we have described the negotiation process as though it occurred between two parties who had no prior relationship or knowledge of each other, came together to do a deal, and had no relationship once the deal was done. In other words, it was just a "snapshot" taken out of time and context. But this is clearly not the way many actual negotiations unfold. Negotiations occur in a rich and complex social environment that has a significant impact on how the parties interact and how the process evolves.

One major way that context affects negotiation is that people act within a relationship, and these relationships have a past, present, and future. In this chapter, we focus on the ways these past and future relationships impact present negotiations. Our treatment of relationships will come in two major sections. First, we examine how a past, ongoing, or future relationship between negotiators affects the negotiation process. This discussion challenges many of the general assumptions that have been made about the theory and practice of negotiation—assumptions that have not taken into account a relationship between the parties—and provides a critical evaluation of the adequacy of negotiation theory for understanding and managing negotiations within relationships. We present a taxonomy of different kinds of relationships and the negotiations that are likely to occur within them and broadly describe research studies that have examined negotiation processes within existing relationships. Finally, we look at three major themes—reputations, trust, and justice—that are particularly critical to effective negotiations within a relationship.

The Adequacy of Established Approaches to Research for Understanding Negotiation within Relationships

Traditionally, researchers have studied the negotiation process in two ways. On the one hand, they have studied actual negotiations with real negotiators in "live" field situations such as labor relations.[1] On the other hand, researchers have simulated complex negotiations by simplifying them in a research laboratory. They create simplified negotiating games and simulations, find college students who are willing to be research participants, and explore negotiating problems and situations under controlled laboratory conditions. This latter approach has dominated the research process in the negotiation field for the past 40 years.

There are, however, serious problems with this strong laboratory research tradition. Most of our conclusions about what is effective in *complex* negotiations have been drawn from studies using a limited set of fairly *simple* bargaining games and classroom simulations. Findings from simple laboratory research has been extensively used to prescribe how negotiators should behave in complex situations; thus, rather than just describe what people actually do in negotiations (real and simulated), many books (including this one) have used that theory to guide negotiators about what they *should* do and how they *should* negotiate. One can reasonably question whether such extensive prescriptions are fully accurate or appropriate, because most negotiations occur between people who are in a relationship with the other party and thus have a significant past history and expect to be together in the future. Only recently have researchers begun to examine actual negotiations in a rich relationship context in order to offer better prescriptions on how to negotiate when the parties are deeply embedded in a relationship.

One group of authors has discussed the inadequacy of existing theory to explain negotiation within ongoing relationships. They provided the following examples:

> A recently married couple discusses whose parents they will be spending Christmas vacation with. Procter & Gamble and Wal-Mart discuss who will own the inventory in their new relationship. Price Waterhouse discusses a cost overrun with an extremely important audit client. Members of a new task force discuss their new roles only to discover that two wish to serve the same function. Each of these discussions could be modeled quite well as a single issue, distributive negotiation problem. There are two parties: A single, critical dimension and opposing positions. A great portion of each discussion will entail searching for the other's walkaway point and hiding of one's own. But the discussions are also more complicated than the single distributive problem.[2]

As we noted, the problem, they argue, is that researchers have been too quick to generalize from simple research studies ("transactional negotiations") to negotiating in complex relationships. Here are several ways that an existing relationship context changes negotiation dynamics:

1. *Negotiating within relationships takes place over time.* In Chapter 3, we noted that one way of turning a distributive negotiation into an integrative one is for the parties to take turns in reaping a benefit or reward. Within a relationship, parties can do this easily. Husband and wife can agree to visit each other's parents on alternate holidays. Time becomes an important variable in negotiating in relationships; understanding how parties package or trade off issues over time may be critical to managing difficult situations.

2. *Negotiation is often not a way to discuss an issue, but a way to learn more about the other party and increase interdependence.* In a transactional negotiation, the parties seek to get information about each other so they can strike a better deal. The short time span

of a transaction requires a party to either act simply on their own preferences or to gather small bits of information about the other before deciding how to act. In a relationship, gathering information about the *other's* ideas, preferences, and priorities is often the most important activity; this information is usually used to learn about and understand the other's thinking, work habits, and so forth, and thus enhance the party's ability to coordinate activities and enhance the ongoing relationship. In short, in a transactional negotiation, the most important issue is usually the deal; in a relationship negotiation, the most important issue is preserving or enhancing the relationship.

3. *Resolution of simple distributive issues has implications for the future.* While time can be an asset, it can also be a curse. The settlement of any one negotiation issue can create undesired or unintended precedents for the future. How Procter & Gamble handles one inventory question may have implications for how similar inventory questions are handled in the future. Alternating holiday visits to their parents in the first two years does not mean the married couple can never change the visitation schedule or that they have to take turns on every issue on which they disagree. But they may have to discuss explicitly when certain precedents apply or do not apply and explain their decisions to others. These negotiations may also shift the power and dependence dynamics in their future relationship. The more the parties learn about each other, the more they may become vulnerable or dependent on each other. Distributive dynamics now can create reputation problems for both parties in the future, and we explicitly address the impact of reputations later in this chapter.

4. *Distributive issues within relationship negotiations can be emotionally hot.* If one party feels strongly about the issues or the other acts provocatively, the parties can become angry with each other. Expressing that anger clearly makes negotiating over other issues difficult (we discussed how emotion affects negotiation in Chapter 5). The parties may say things they don't mean, make hurtful comments, cut off discussions, and even refuse to speak further. At a minimum, the parties may have to cool off or apologize before they can proceed. In extreme cases, the parties can continue feuds for years, carrying emotional baggage from one fight to another that never gets resolved and never permits them to talk about issues important to the relationship.

5. *Negotiating within relationships may never end.* One of the advantages of negotiating in a game or simulation is that there is a defined end. In fact, many participants in laboratory negotiating experiments may develop a specific strategy for how they are going to play "the end game"; often, they abandon cooperative strategies in favor of getting the other on the last move. In many relationships, however, negotiations are never over; parties are often constantly trying to renegotiate old agreements or issues that were never firmly settled (or settled in favor of one party but not the other). This may have several consequences:

   • *Parties may defer negotiations over tough issues in order to start on the right foot.* If the married couple thought their relationship would be over in two years, they would make sure they each got what they wanted while they were married; in addition, they would probably negotiate a very specific agreement about who was to get what when the relationship was over. But if the couple expects the marriage to last forever, they may simply mingle all of their assets and property in the hope that "everything will work out" in the future.

- *Attempting to anticipate the future and negotiate everything up front is often impossible.* Two young entrepreneurs who decide to go into business together can't possibly anticipate all the dimensions of where their common efforts will take them or what issues they should consider if they decide to separate in five years. Who knows now how successful the business will be or what might be the most important issues? At best, all they can do is pledge to communicate with each other and discuss problems as they arise.

- *Issues on which parties truly disagree may never go away.* As we suggested earlier, some negotiations in relationships are never over. Two roommates who have different standards of cleanliness—one is neat, the other messy—may never settle the question of whose preference is going to govern the living arrangements in their apartment. The messy one will always be disposed to leave things out and around, while the clean one will always be bothered by things left out and around. As long as they live together, the issue may confront them; agreements about cleanliness may regularly get broken, even though they may go through a range of different possible solutions as they try to accommodate each other's preferences and habits.

6. *In many negotiations, the other person* is *the focal problem.* A well-known prescriptive theory of integrative negotiation teaches that in order to be effective, negotiators must "separate the person from the problem."[3] But what happens if the other person *is* the problem? Return to some of our earlier examples: when one combines a set of emotion-laden issues with people who have major differences in values or preferred lifestyles, there is a recipe for a fight that goes beyond a single-issue negotiation. In the situation of the two roommates, the neatnik's passion for cleanliness may lead her to see the other's messiness not as a simple issue of lifestyle differences, but as intentional and even provocative: "She leaves a mess because she knows how angry I get when this place looks like a dump! She does it just to spite me!" This is no longer a problem of how often to clean or of whether one cares enough to tolerate the other's idiosyncrasies; this is now a problem of one party seeing the other as spiteful and provocative, causing the problem simply by her very coexistence in the living space. While the parties might engage in extensive efforts to "separate the person from the problem" and find viable solutions, the very fact that one party's existence, preferences, lifestyle, or behavior irritates the other can create an intractable negotiation problem for which permanent separation or relationship dissolution may be the only solution.

7. *In some negotiations, relationship preservation is the overarching negotiation goal, and parties may make concessions on substantive issues to preserve or enhance the relationship.* A potential resolution to the "person-is-the-problem" negotiation is that one or both parties may actually make major concessions on substantive issues simply to preserve the relationship. Parties in traditionally distributive market transactions usually make concessions by starting high or low on an issue and moving toward the middle. Even logrolling concessions can be fairly well understood because the parties equate their benefits on two separate issues and then trade one off against the other. However, it is difficult to understand how parties trade off the value of the relationship against specific goals on tangible issues. Suppose I have a used car that has a market value of $5,000. However, I decide to sell it to my mother, who needs a car only for occasional

International negotiation expert Jeswald Salacuse (1998) suggests three important rules for negotiating a relationship:

- Don't rush prenegotiation. Spend ample time getting to know the other party, visiting with him, learning about him, and spending time with him. This process enhances your information gathering and builds a relationship that may include trust, information sharing, and productive discussions. In particular, North American executives have a tendency to rush through things in order to get down to business, which compromises this critical stage for relationship building.

- Recognize a long-term business deal as a continuing negotiation. Change and uncertainty are constants in any business deal. The discussions do not end when the contract is signed; they continue as the parties perform according to the contract, during which time they often have to meet to work out problems and renegotiate specific parts of the agreement.

- Consider mediation or conciliation. Finally, consider the roles that can usefully be played by third parties. A third party can help monitor the deal, work out disagreements about contract violations, and assure that the agreement does not go sour because the parties cannot resolve differences in interpretation or enforcement.

Source: Adapted from J. Salacuse, "So, What's the Deal Anyway? Contracts and Relationships as Negotiating Goals," *Negotiation Journal* 14, no. 1 (1998), pp. 5–12.

---

trips around town or visits to her grandchildren. This is not a simple market transaction! Can I convince my mother that she should pay the same price that I would quote to a stranger off the street? Can I convince *myself* of that? Clearly, the value I place on the past and future relationships between my mother and me will dictate the answer to that question at least as much as (and quite possibly far more than) the market value of the car. In Chapter 1, we discussed *accommodation* as a strategic choice most likely to be pursued when the relationship with the other party is important but the substantive issues are not; accommodation is far more likely as a strategy in relationship negotiations than it is in market transactions.[4]

In summary, we have identified several issues that make negotiating in relationships different from and more challenging than conducting either distributive or integrative negotiations between parties who have no past or intended future relationship. It is not always clear how the prescriptive lessons learned from market transactions apply to negotiation within relationships. For example, see Box 9.1.

Negotiations in Communal Relationships

Studies have shown that compared with those in other kinds of negotiations, parties who are in a communal-sharing relationship (or who expect to have future interaction):

- Are more cooperative and empathetic.[5]
- Craft better quality agreements.[6]
- Perform better on both decision making and motor tasks.[7]
- Focus their attention on the other party's outcomes as well as their own.[8]
- Focus more attention on the norms that develop about the way that they work together.[9]

BOX 9.2   Balancing Inquiry with Advocacy

Researchers have studied how to minimize interpersonal conflicts in working relationships and how to resolve them effectively when they do arise. They suggest that the key is to balance advocacy skills—what most managers are trained to do—with inquiry skills—the ability to ask questions—in order to promote mutual learning. Guidelines for balancing inquiry and advocacy include the following:

When advocating your own view,

- Make your reasoning explicit.
- Encourage others to explore your view.
- Encourage others to provide different views.
- Actively inquire into others' views that differ from your own.

When inquiring into others' views,

- State your assumptions clearly and acknowledge that they are assumptions.
- Share the "data" on which your assumptions are based.

- Don't ask questions if you are not genuinely interested in the others' responses.

When you arrive at an impasse,

- Ask what logic or data might change the others' views.
- Ask if there is any way you might jointly design a technique that might provide more information.

When you or others are hesitant to express views or experiment with alternative ideas,

- Encourage them (or yourself) to think out loud about what might be making it difficult.
- If mutually desirable, jointly brainstorm ideas about overcoming any barriers.

Source: Adapted from L. A. Hill (1997), "Building Effective One-on-One Work Relationships" (Harvard Business School Note 9-497-028); and P. Senge, *The Fifth Discipline: The Art and Practice of the Learning Organization* (New York: Doubleday Currency, 1990).

- Are more likely to share information with the other and less likely to use coercive tactics.[10]
- Are more likely to use indirect communication about conflict issues and develop a unique conflict structure.[11]
- May be more likely to use compromise or problem solving as strategies for resolving conflicts.[12]

It is unclear, however, whether parties in close relationships produce better solutions than other negotiators do. Some studies found that parties who did *not* have a close relationship produced better integrative solutions.[13] It may be that parties in a relationship may not push hard for a preferred solution in order to minimize the conflict level in the relationship or, alternatively, may sacrifice their own preferences in order to preserve the relationship.[14] Some describe this tension as a process of balancing inquiry and advocacy (see Box 9.2).[15]

Finally, studies are beginning to explore the way parties in a relationship might enact different relationship forms, and the consequences of those differences. In a study of Israeli married couples who chose to participate in divorce mediation, men tended to use arguments that were based on principles of law and customary practice for handling problems and conflicts in the marriage dissolution, while women tended to use more arguments that were based on personal responsibility of parties to each other. Men tended to be more unemotional and reserved, while women tended to express deeper feelings of insult and pain.[16] For deeper insight into conflict management in relationships, see Box 9.3.

Conflict Resolution in Intense, Complex Relationships

BOX 9.3

Psychologist John Gottman has been studying conflict resolution in marriages throughout his career. By videotaping thousands of couples as they talk about challenging problems in their marriages, he offers the following insights into what make a relationship effective:

1. Successful couples look for ways to stay positive, and say "yes" as often as possible. They constantly affirm the other's ideas, contributions, opinions and preferences. This is particularly important for men who often may not accept a woman's influence.

2. They embrace conflict as a way to work through differences, rather than try to avoid it or give in all the time. Typical conflicts in a relationship are about different preferences for working and relaxing, punctuality, and the way they resolve a dispute when they disagree about something important.

3. Good relationships are not only about how to fight, but how to repair a relationship after a fight. Humor, affection, apologies, and other forms of "positive emotion" that allow for true "connection" with the other are critical. Gottman stresses that these are not large, complex events in a relationship—they are often brief, fleeting, and almost trivial moments but critical for relationship management.

4. Successful long-term relationships are characterized by continuing to stress what one likes, values, appreciates and respects in the other. In contrast, the best predictors that a relationship will not last are frequent incidents of criticism of the other, defensiveness when the other is critical, stonewalling and refusing to yield or compromise, and contempt or disgust for the other and their views. Gottman views contempt as the most toxic element that can quickly turn a relationship from good to bad.

Sources: Adapted from John M. Gottman, *The Seven Principles for Making Marriage Work;* and "Making Relationships Work: A Conversation with Psychologist John Gottman," *Harvard Business Review,* December 2007, pp. 45–50.

Key Elements in Managing Negotiations within Relationships

Reputation, trust, and justice are three elements that become more critical and pronounced when they occur within a negotiation. In this section, we discuss how the effects of these elements become intensified in negotiations within relationships.

Reputation

Your reputation is how other people remember their past experience with you. Reputation is the legacy that negotiators leave behind after a negotiation encounter with another party. Reputation is a "perceptual identity, reflective of the combination of salient personal characteristics and accomplishments, demonstrated behavior and intended images preserved over time, as observed directly and/or as reported from secondary sources."[17] Based on this definition, we can say several things about the importance of reputations:

- Reputations are perceived and highly subjective in nature. It is not how we would *like* to be known by others, or how we think we are known—it is what they *actually think* of us, and their judgment, that count. Once a reputation is formed, it acts as a lens or "schema" by which people form their expectations for future behavior (refer back to our discussion of perception in Chapter 5).[18]

- An individual can have a number of different, even conflicting, reputations because she may act quite differently in different situations. She may distributively bargain with the person who runs the yard sale down the road but be quite integrative with the person who regularly services her computer. While individuals can elicit different reputations in different contexts, most commonly a reputation is a single and consistent image from many different persons across many contexts—in most cases, there is generally shared agreement on who we are and how we are seen.

- Reputations are shaped by past behavior. On the one hand, we may know someone's reputation based on our own past experience with him (e.g., a history of cooperative or competitive behavior). On the other hand, our expectations may be shaped by the way the other behaves with other people. Thus, "direct" reputations (from our own experience) may be different from "hearsay" reputations (based on others' experience). Individuals tend to trust more those with better experiential reputations, and rely more on experiential reputations than hearsay reputations in deciding whether to trust another.[19]

- Reputations are also influenced by an individual's personal characteristics and accomplishments. These may include qualities such as age, race, and gender; education and past experience; and personality traits, skills, and behaviors. All of these work together over time to create a broad reputation—how other people remember us in general—as well as a specific reputation that comes from how we, or others, have experienced this particular other person in the past.

- Reputations develop over time; once developed, they are hard to change. Our early experiences with another—or what we have heard about them from other people—shape our views of them, which we bring to new situations in the form of expectations about the other. These expectations are then confirmed or disconfirmed by the next set of experiences. Thus, first impressions and early experiences with others are powerful in shaping others' expectations; once these expectations are shaped, they become hard to change. A negotiator who develops a reputation as a distributive "shark" early on will thus have a difficult time convincing the current other negotiator that he is honest and trustworthy and wants to work toward a mutually acceptable agreement.[20]

- Others' reputations can shape emotional states as well as their expectations. Good hearsay reputations create positive emotional responses from others, and bad hearsay reputations elicit negative emotional responses from others.[21]

- Finally, negative reputations are difficult to "repair." The more long-standing the negative reputation, the harder it is to change that reputation to a more positive one. Reputations need to be actively defended and renewed in others' eyes. Particularly when an event is likely to be seen by others in a negative light, we must work hard to defend and protect our reputation and to make sure that others do not remember the experience in a negative way. How we account for past behavior, how we apologize and ask another person to overlook or discount the past, or how we use excuses or justifications to explain why we did something the other views as unfavorable will have a major impact on how others remember us and their experience with us. We say more about the role of apologies, excuses, and other "accounts" in the next section, on trust.

Trust

Many of the scholars who have written about relationships have identified trust as central to any relationship.[22] Daniel McAllister defined the word *trust* as "an individual's belief in and willingness to act on the words, actions and decisions of another."[23] There are three things that contribute to the level of trust one negotiator may have for another: the individual's chronic disposition toward trust (i.e., individual differences in personality that make some people more trusting than others), situation factors (e.g., the opportunity for the parties to communicate with each other adequately), and the history of the relationship between the parties.

Recent Research on Trust and Negotiation   Many researchers have explored trust in negotiation.[24] These early studies were often conducted with very primitive conceptualizations of trust and in reasonably primitive experimental settings; hence, the findings were rather limited in nature. As one might expect, this early research generally showed that higher levels of trust make negotiation easier, while lower levels of trust make negotiation more difficult. Similarly, integrative processes tend to increase trust, while more distributive processes are likely to decrease trust.[25] Some of the more recent research on trust has revealed somewhat more complex relationships between trust and negotiation behavior. Here is a summary of those findings:

- Many people approach a new relationship with an unknown other party with remarkably high levels of trust. Thus, while people in new relationships might be expected to start their trust of the other at "zero," in fact, most of us assume that the other can be trusted and are remarkably willing to trust the other even with very little information or knowledge about the other.[26]

- Trust tends to cue cooperative behavior. Parties who trust each other approach each other with cooperative dispositions. Thus, trust tends to cue a more communal orientation to a relationship and more cooperative behavior.[27]

- Individual motives also shape both trust and expectations of the other's behavior. Parties who are more cooperatively motivated report higher initial trust of the other party and more positive initial impressions of the other party than those who are individually motivated.[28]

- Trustors, and those trusted, may focus on different things as trust is being built. Trustors may focus primarily on the risks of being trusted (e.g., how vulnerable they are), while those being trusted focus on the benefits to be received from the trust. Here we see a negotiator framing bias (Chapter 5) by both the sender and receiver that shapes how trust actions are viewed. Trustors are more likely to trust when the risk is low, but their willingness to trust does not seem to depend on the amount of benefit received by the person being trusted. However, the receiver is more likely to trust when the benefits to be received from the trust are high, but their trust does not seem to depend on the amount of vulnerability feared by the trustor. Moreover, each party reported that they were not particularly sensitive to the factors that affected their counterpart's decision. Thus, trust building might be greatly facilitated if parties could communicate more clearly and directly about the vulnerabilities to be felt or the benefits to be received, and how to manage these effectively.[29]

- The nature of the negotiation task (distributive versus integrative) can shape how parties judge the trust. In a more distributive context, trustors tend to focus on the risks they face, while those who are in a position to receive and then reciprocate the others' trust focus on the benefits that the trustors have provided them. Given the framing biases just mentioned, however, neither party tends to consider the other's point of view prior to making a decision whether to reciprocate the other's trust. As a result, the possibilities for trust to break down or not be completed may increase because neither party truly understands the risks or rewards as perceived by the other. More reciprocity occurs among individuals who are better at taking the perspective of the other in a negotiation, and reciprocity can be increased by coaching a negotiator to consider the views of the other party in their decision making.[30]

- Greater expectations of trust between negotiators leads to greater information sharing with the other party, similarly, greater expectations of distrust lead to less information sharing.[31]

- Greater information sharing tends to enhance effectiveness in achieving a good negotiation outcome, and less information sharing tends to diminish effectiveness in achieving a good outcome—although this effectiveness may *not* necessarily be the result of greater trust.[32]

- Distributive processes lead negotiators to see the negotiation dialogue, and critical events in the dialogue, as largely about the nature of the negotiation task (i.e., how to divide the pie). Distributive processes also lead people to judge the other party with negative characterization frames (see our discussion of frames in Chapter 5). Both of these perspectives tend to reduce trust. In contrast, integrative processes lead negotiators to see the dialogue as largely about interests, relationships, and positive affect and to see the other party with positive characterization frames; these perspectives tend to increase trust.[33]

- Trust increases the likelihood that negotiation will proceed on a favorable course over the life of a negotiation. As described in Chapter 4, researchers have begun to examine turning points in negotiation—or key events, comments, or behaviors that turn the negotiation in a more positive (or more negative) direction. One study has generally shown that trust increases the likelihood of more facilitative turning points around interests and the relationship and decreases the number of inhibitory turning points around discussion of a distributive task or negative characterization of the other party. These processes subsequently lead to higher levels of trust at the end of the negotiation and lower levels of mistrust.[34]

- Face-to-face negotiation encourages greater trust development than negotiation online. There is evidence that parties anticipating an online negotiation expect less trust before the negotiations begin, are less satisfied with their negotiation outcomes, are less confident in the quality of their performance during the negotiation, trust the other less after the negotiation, and have less desire for a future interaction with the other party.[35]

- Negotiators who are representing others' interests, rather than their own interests, tend to behave in a less trusting way (be less trustworthy) and tend to expect that the other will be less trusting. As a result of being less trustworthy, negotiators engage in less give-and-take with the other party and expect the other party to engage in less give-and-take.[36]

Pepper . . . and Salt
THE WALL STREET JOURNAL

**"Let's offer an apology but
without expressing contrition,
regret or responsibility."**

From *The Wall Street Journal.* Used with permission of Cartoon Features Syndicate.

Trust Repair   The preceding review of research clearly indicates that trust improves negotiation processes, leads to more integrative negotiation processes, and frequently produces better negotiation outcomes; and that *dis*trust hinders negotiation processes, leads to more distributive negotiations, and frequently diminishes strong negotiation outcomes. Because trust and positive negotiation processes and outcomes appear to be so critical, we should comment on ways that broken trust can be repaired in order to return negotiations toward a more productive direction.

A number of studies have begun to investigate the ways that trust can be repaired.[37] A sampling of these results reveals the following:

- The more severe the breach of trust (the greater the costs incurred by the other party), the more difficult it is to repair trust and reconcile the relationship.
- If the parties had a good past relationship, it was easier to repair trust than if the past relationship had been poor.
- The sooner an apology occurs after the breach of trust, the more effective the apology is likely to be.
- The more sincerely an apology is expressed, the more effective it was in repairing trust.
- Apologies in which the actor took personal responsibility for having created the breach were more effective than those apologies in which the actor tried to blame external causes for the breach. Apologies were even more effective when the actor took personal responsibility *and* the apology was viewed as sincere.
- Apologies were more effective when the trust breach appeared to be an isolated event rather than habitual and repetitive for the other party.[38]

Recent studies have also shown that following a period of untrustworthy behavior, trust is more likely to be repaired if the trust violation was not accompanied by deception.

Deception appears to harm trust far more than untrustworthy actions, and hence trust is much harder to repair if deception has occurred.[39]

Justice

The third major issue in relationships is the question of what is fair or just. Again, justice has been a major issue in the organizational sciences; individuals in organizations often debate whether their pay is fair, whether they are being fairly treated, or whether the organization might be treating some group of people (e.g., women, minorities, people from other cultures) in an unfair manner.

Justice can take several forms:[40]

- *Distributive justice* is about the distribution of outcomes. Parties may be concerned that one party is receiving more than he or she deserves, that outcomes should be distributed equally, or that outcomes should be distributed based on needs.[41] One study showed that outcome fairness is often determined in a distributive negotiation as the point midway between the opening position of the two parties (what is often known as a "split-the-difference" settlement—see Chapter 2). The presence of such an obvious settlement point appears to increase both concession making and the likelihood of settlement.[42]

- *Procedural justice* is about the process of determining outcomes. Parties may be concerned that they were not treated fairly during the negotiation, that they were not given a chance to offer their point of view or side of the story, or that they were not treated with respect. Because negotiation is an environment in which parties are offered an opportunity to shape the outcome they receive, procedural fairness is generally high in most negotiations. Concerns about procedural fairness are more likely to arise when negotiators are judging the behavior of third parties: viewing the third party as neutral, seeing them as trustworthy, accepting their decisions, and in the case of formal authorities such as police, voluntarily accepting their decisions and directives.[43]

- *Interactional justice* is about how parties treat each other in one-to-one relationships. Research has shown that people have strong expectations about the ways another party should treat them; when those standards are violated, parties feel unfairly treated. When the other party practices deception, is not candid and forthcoming, acts rudely, asks improper questions, makes prejudicial and discriminatory statements, or makes decisions or takes precipitous actions without justification, negotiators feel that fairness standards have been violated.[44]

- Finally, *systemic justice* is about how organizations appear to treat groups of individuals and the norms that develop for how they should be treated. When some groups are discriminated against, disfranchised, or systematically given poorer salaries or working conditions, the parties may be less concerned about specific procedural elements and more concerned that the overall system may be biased or discriminatory in its treatment of certain groups and their concerns.

The issue of fairness is beginning to receive some systematic investigation in negotiation dynamics. The following conclusions can be drawn from a number of recent studies:

- Involvement in the process of helping to shape a negotiation strategy increases commitment to that strategy and willingness to pursue it. This is the familiar "procedural justice effect," in that parties involved in the process of shaping a decision are more committed to that decision. Negotiators who helped develop a group negotiation strategy were more committed to it and to the group's negotiation goals.[45]

- Negotiators (buyers in a market transaction) who are encouraged ("primed") to think about fairness are more cooperative in distributive negotiations. They make greater concessions, act more fairly and reach agreement faster, and have stronger positive attitudes toward the other party. They also demand fair treatment from the other party in return. However, when the other party did not reciprocate the negotiator's cooperative behavior, the negotiator actively retaliated and punished the other's competitive behavior. Thus, stating one's own intention to be fair and encouraging the other party to be fair may be an excellent way to support fair exchanges; but watch out for the negotiator whose fairness gestures are double-crossed.[46]

- Similarly, parties who receive offers they perceive as unfair may reject them out of hand, even though the amount offered may be better than the alternative settlement, which is to receive nothing at all. Here we see the role of intangibles entering into a negotiation. Economists would predict that any deal better than zero should be accepted (if the only alternative is zero), but research has shown that negotiators will often reject these small offers. Clearly, a less-than-fair small offer creates feelings of anger and wounded pride, and negotiators will often act spitefully to sink the entire deal rather than accept a token settlement.[47]

- Establishment of some objective standard of fairness has a positive impact on negotiations and satisfaction with the outcome. We discussed the role of setting an "objective standard" for fairness in Chapter 3.[48] Among students who participated in a simulation of a corporate takeover, buyers who knew what a fair selling price would be for the company were more satisfied with those offered selling prices, more willing to buy the company, and more willing to do business with the other party in the future. Also, knowledge of an opponent's BATNA, as well as information about estimated market prices for the negotiated object, most strongly determine negotiator's judgments of fairness.[49]

- Judgments about fairness are subject to the type of cognitive biases described earlier. For example, most negotiators have an egocentric bias, which is the tendency to regard a larger share for oneself as fair, even if the obvious fairness rule is an equal split. Recent research has shown that this egocentric bias can be diminished by strong interactional justice. That is, recognizing the need to treat the other person fairly, and actually treating the other fairly, lead to a smaller egocentric bias, a more even split of the resources, quicker settlements, and fewer stalemates.[50]

- Not unsurprisingly, these egocentric biases vary across cultures. At least one study has shown that egocentric biases are stronger in cultures that are individualistic (e.g., the United States), where the self is served by focusing on one's positive attributes in order to stand out and be better than others, compared with more collectivist cultures (e.g., Japan) where the self is served by focusing on one's negative characteristics, so as to blend in with others.[51]

Given the pervasiveness of concerns about fairness—how parties view the distribution of outcomes, how they view the process of arriving at that decision, or how they treat each other—it is remarkable that more research has not explicitly addressed justice issues

BOX 9.4 **The Idiosyncratic Deal: Flexibility versus Fairness**

Professor Denise Rousseau of Carnegie Mellon University has long studied the changing nature of employment relationships and "psychological contracts" between employees and employers. In a 2001 article, she discussed the "idiosyncratic deal"—the unique ways that employers may come to treat certain employees compared to others in the same office or environment. Many idiosyncratic deals are now negotiated in the workplace (e.g., educational leaves, flextime, working at home, working on one's own separate project while on the job, doing volunteer work on company time). While idiosyncratic deals were once available only to individuals with long seniority or to jobs with more discretionary job descriptions, Rousseau observes that idiosyncratic deals are much more common today, and they are not reserved only for a special few. Thus, while idiosyncratic deals are a new source of flexibility and innovation in the workplace, they also raise major concerns about fairness and consistent treatment of classes of employees. Here are some observations about idiosyncratic deals:

1. They are more common when workers

   - Are highly marketable (e.g., have a good BATNA in the job market).
   - Are willing to negotiate.
   - Have strong market and business knowledge.
   - Are located in small or start-up firms.
   - Work in more knowledge-oriented firms (specialize in information or services rather than specific products).

2. They are more common in certain countries, such as the United States, the United Kingdom, and New Zealand.

3. Idiosyncratic deals are more likely to work effectively when

   - There is a high-quality relationship between the worker and manager.
   - Responsibilities and role requirements are well understood and accepted.
   - Performance criteria are clear and well specified.
   - Workers trust the performance appraisal process.
   - There is shared understanding of performance criteria among co-workers.
   - Co-workers have mutually supportive relations.
   - Co-workers trust the manager.
   - When flexibility is limited, legitimate reasons are stated and clear. Such deals are viewed as a source of innovation that can be shared and adopted by others in the firm.

Source: D. Rousseau, "The Idiosyncratic Deal: Flexibility vs. Fairness?" *Organizational Dynamics* 29, no. 4 (2001), pp. 260–73.

in negotiation contexts. For example, justice issues are also raised when individuals negotiate inside their organizations, such as to create a unique or specialized set of job duties and responsibilities. These "idiosyncratic deals" have to be managed effectively in order to make sure that they can continue to exist without disrupting others' sense of fairness about equal treatment (see Box 9.4). And they may not always be as fair as they seemed at the outset. One might expect that negotiated exchanges are seen as procedurally fair because the parties collectively make the decision, know the terms in advance, give mutual assent to the process, and make binding decisions. Yet at least one study has shown that after such agreements are struck, negotiators perceive their partners as *less* fair and are unwilling to engage in future exchanges with them. Thus, rather than making things more fair, negotiated exchanges may serve to emphasize the conflict between actors who are blind to their own biases and inclined to see the other party's motives and characteristics in an unfavorable light.[52]

Relationships among Reputation, Trust, and Justice

Not only are various forms of justice interrelated, but reputations, trust, and justice all interact in shaping expectations of the other's behavior. For example, when one party feels the other has acted fairly in the past or will act fairly in the future, he or she is more likely to trust the other.[53] We would also predict that acting fairly leads to being trusted and also enhances a positive reputation. Conversely, several theoretical and empirical works have shown that when parties are unfairly treated, they often become angry and retaliate against either the injustice itself or those who are seen as having caused it. Unfair treatment is likely to lead to distrust and a bad reputation.[54] Trust, justice, and reputation are all central to relationship negotiations and feed each other; we cannot understand negotiation within complex relationships without prominently considering how we judge the other (and ourselves) on these dimensions.

Repairing a Relationship

There are many steps to repairing a relationship. Trying to overcome a bad reputation, rebuilding trust, or restoring fairness to a relationship are much easier to talk about than to actually do! Fisher and Ertel suggest the following diagnostic steps in beginning to work on improving a relationship:

1. *What might be causing any present misunderstanding, and what can I do to understand it better?* If the relationship is in difficulty, what might have caused it, and how can I gather information or perspective to improve the situation?

2. *What might be causing a lack of trust, and what can I do to begin to repair trust that might have been broken?* Trust repair is a long and slow process. It requires adequate explanations for past behavior, apologies, and perhaps even reparations (see Box 9.5).

3. *What might be causing one or both of us to feel coerced, and what can I do to put the focus on persuasion rather than coercion?* How can we take the pressure off each other so that we can give each other the freedom of choice to talk about what has happened and what is necessary to fix it?

4. *What might be causing one or both of us to feel disrespected, and what can I do to demonstrate acceptance and respect?* How can we begin to appreciate each other's contributions and the positive things that we have done together in the past? How can we restore that respect and value each other's contributions?

5. *What might be causing one or both of us to get upset, and what can I do to balance emotion and reason?* How can we surface the deeply felt emotions that have produced anger, frustration, rejection, and disappointment? How can we effectively vent these emotions, or understand their causes, so that we can move beyond them?[55]

These are important questions. If the relationship problem is not significant or long lasting, the parties may be able to work them out on their own. If the problem has persisted for a time, or the breakdown creates serious costs for one or both sides, third parties will probably have to intervene.

BOX 9.5 JetBlue Apologizes

On February 14, 2007 (Valentine's Day in the United States), airline JetBlue suffered a major crisis. Two inches of snow and ice at New York's JFK airport led to 1,000 flight cancellations, massive delays, and passengers stranded on planes for up to nine hours. The event received massive media visibility, and it took almost a week for JetBlue to resume normal operations. While other airlines also suffered service disruptions because of the storm, JetBlue received most of the visibility for the breakdown—largely because in its seven-year history it had inspired much higher expectations of good treatment from its loyal customers.

JetBlue founder and CEO David Neeleman was faced with the challenge of how to repair the public's trust in a way that would strengthen the strong brand identity that the company had created. In the week following the crisis, he appeared in every local and national news media. He accepted responsibility for bad decisions and organizational problems. He apologized repeatedly, promised refunds for stranded passengers, and promised to fix the problems that created the disaster. He also introduced a customer "bill of rights." Two weeks after the meltdown, 43 percent of a sample of people visiting JetBlue's Web site said the airline was still their number-one favorite.

In a time when most airlines enjoy very little customer confidence, Neeleman's successful handling of the crisis has been highlighted as an example of creating a trustworthy brand identity—and being able to sustain it in a time of crisis. Bruce Blythe, CEO of Crisis Management International, sums it up well: "The single most important thing that a company needs to show in a crisis is that it cares. That's not a feeling. It's a behavior."

Source: C. Salter, "Lessons from the Tarmac," *Fast Company,* May 2007, pp. 31–32.

Chapter Summary

In this chapter, we explored the way that existing relationships shape negotiation. Much of negotiation theory and research is based on what we have learned in experimental research settings, consisting of two negotiating parties who don't know each other, don't expect to deal with each other in the future, and are engaged in a market transaction over price and quantity. Yet much of the professional negotiations conducted in business, law, government, communities, and international affairs occur in a context in which the parties have a past (and future) relationship and in which their relationship strongly affects the negotiation process.

In addition, we cannot assume that negotiators are involved only in arm's-length market transactions about the exchange of fees for goods and services. Many negotiations concern how to work (and live) together more effectively over time, how to coordinate actions and share responsibilities, or how to manage problems that have arisen in the relationship. In this chapter, we evaluated the status of previous negotiation research—which has focused almost exclusively on market-exchange relationships—and evaluated its status for different types of relationships, particularly communal-sharing and authority-ranking relationships. Within relationships, we see that parties shift their focus considerably, moving away from a sole focus on price and exchange to also attend to the future of the relationship, including the level of trust between the parties and questions of fairness, and to build strong positive reputations. We argue that most negotiations occur within these relationship contexts, and future work must attend to their unique complexities.

We turn next in Chapter 10 to another aspect of negotiations involving relationships: how things change when negotiators are representing the interests of others rather than their own interests and when more than two parties are actively involved in the negotiation process.

Endnotes

[1] Douglas, 1962; Friedman, 1994.

[2] Sheppard and Tuchinsky, 1996a, pp. 132–33.

[3] Fisher, Ury, and Patton, 1991.

[4] Sheppard and Tuchinsky, 1996a, b.

[5] Greenhalgh and Gilkey, 1993.

[6] Sondak, Neale, and Pinkley, 1995.

[7] Shah and Jehn, 1993.

[8] Loewenstein, Thompson, and Bazerman, 1989.

[9] Macneil, 1980.

[10] Greenhalgh and Chapman, 1996; Greenhalgh and Kramer, 1990.

[11] Tuchinsky, 1998.

[12] Dant and Schul, 1992; Ganesan, 1993.

[13] Fry, Firestone, and Williams, 1983; Thompson, Peterson, and Brodt, 1996.

[14] Barry and Oliver, 1996; Tripp, Sondak, and Bies, 1995.

[15] Senge, 1990; Argyris and Schön 1996.

[16] Pines, Gat, and Tal, 2002.

[17] Ferris, Blass, Douglas, Kolodinsky, and Treadway, 2005, p. 215.

[18] Fiske and Taylor, 1991.

[19] Goates, 2008.

[20] Ferris et al., 2005.

[21] Goates, 2008.

[22] Greenhalgh, 2001; Greenhalgh and Chapman, 1996; and Tuchinsky, Edson Escalas, Moore, and Sheppard, 1994.

[23] McAllister, 1995.

[24] For example, Butler, 1991; Kimmel, Pruitt, Magenau, Konar-Goldband, and Carnevale, 1980; Lindskold, Bentz, and Walters, 1986; Schlenker, Helm, and Tedeschi, 1973; and Zand, 1972, 1977.

[25] As we noted earlier, a problem with much of this research is that it tends to view trust as a simple, unidimensional construct characteristic of market exchanges (Kimmel et al. 1980; Tedeschi, Heister, and Gahagan, 1969). Because relationships are complex, changing over time, and often grounded in compatibility of personalities, interpersonal styles and values, it would appear likely that the more complex models of trust we suggest in this chapter really operate in close communal relationships the same as in arm's-length market transactions.

[26] Kramer, 1994; Myerson, Weick, and Kramer, 1996.

[27] Butler, 1995, 1999.

[28] Olekalns, Lau, and Smith, 2007.

[29] Malhotra, 2004.

[30] Malhotra, 2003.

[31] Butler, 1995, 1999.

[32] Butler, 1999; Olekalns and Smith, 2001.

[33] Olekalns and Smith, 2001; see also Koeszegi, 2004, for a description of the process of trust building in interorganizational relationships.

[34] Olekalns and Smith, 2001, 2005.

[35] Naquin and Paulson, 2003.

[36] Song, 2004.

[37] See Bottom, Gibson, Daniels, and Murnighan, 2002; Kim, Dirks, Cooper, and Ferrin, 2006; Schweitzer, Hershey, and Bradlow, 2006; Tomlinson, Dineen, and Lewicki, 2004.

[38] Tomlinson, Dineen, and Lewicki, 2004.

[39] Schweitzer, Hershey, and Bradlow, 2006.

[40] See Sheppard, Lewicki, and Minton, 1992, and Greenberg and Colquitt, 2005 for reviews of justice issues in organizations; and Albin, 1993 for a commentary on the role of fairness in negotiation.

[41] Deutsch, 1985; See also Loewenstein, Thompson, and Bazerman, 1989.

[42] Benton and Druckman, 1974.

[43] Tyler and Blader, 2004.

[44] Bies and Moag, 1986.

[45] Jones and Worchel, 1992.

[46] Maxwell, Nye, and Maxwell, 1999, 2003.

[47] Pillutla and Murnighan, 1996.

[48] Fisher, Ury, and Patton, 1991.

[49] Buelens and Van Poucke, 2004.

[50] Leung, Tong, and Ho, 2004.

[51] Gelfand et al., 2002.

[52] Molm, Takahashi, and Peterson, 2003.

[53] Lewicki, Wiethoff, and Tomlinson, 2005.

[54] See Greenberg, 1990; Sheppard, Lewicki, and Minton, 1992; and Skarlicki and Folger, 1997.

[55] Fisher and Ertel, 1995.

CHAPTER

Multiple Parties and Teams

Objectives

1. Understand the ways negotiations become more complex when there are more than two negotiators at the bargaining table.
2. Describe the key elements of an effective group as they apply to negotiation processes in groups.
3. Spell out the key stages in managing an effective multiparty negotiation.

The purpose of this chapter is to understand how the negotiation process changes when there are more than two parties at the table simultaneously. Most of what has been addressed in earlier chapters assumed a "one-on-one" negotiation situation. In this chapter, we examine how dynamics change when groups, teams, and task forces have to present individual views and come to a collective agreement about a problem, plan, or future course of action.

The Nature of Multiparty Negotiations

We define a *multiparty negotiation* as one in which more than two parties are working together to achieve a collective objective. To illustrate the nature of a multiparty negotiation, take the following example. A group of four students is selling a stereo system and puts up notices in the dorm and dining areas. A year ago, each put in $200 to buy the system; now they have different preferences for what they should do with it. Aaron (A) wants to sell it and simply split up the money because he wants to buy a new bike for himself; Bill (B) wants to sell it and buy a newer but inexpensive stereo system; Chuck (C) wants to sell it and buy a super-high-quality system that will require each of them to chip in a lot more money; and Dan (D) doesn't want to sell it at all and thinks the whole thing is a dumb idea. Each party has his own preferences and priorities, and the roommates must collectively decide what to do as a group if and when the system is sold. They might agree to make a single collective decision about what to do next, or they might agree to align together in subgroups to pool their money, or each might go his separate way. When the parties agree to hold a meeting to discuss the options and make a collective decision, this is a multiparty negotiation that involves unique dynamics in a collective decision-making process.

The general model for a multiparty negotiation is represented in Figure 10.1. Each of the parties (there can be three or more) is representing his or her own interests. In a different

FIGURE 10.1 | A Multiparty Negotiation

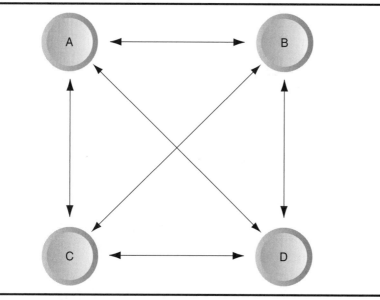

situation (e.g., they might be representatives of different departments meeting together as a task force), they could be representing the interests of others (see Figure 10.2). Most of the complexities described in this section increase linearly, if not exponentially, as more parties, constituencies, and audiences are added.

In this chapter, we note the factors that make multiparty negotiations more difficult to manage than one-on-one negotiations. We comment on some of the key stages and phases of multiparty deliberations. For each phase, we consider a variety of strategies that can be used to manage multiparty negotiations effectively. We show the ways that multiparty negotiations are complex and highly susceptible to breakdown and show that managing them effectively requires a conscious commitment from the parties and a facilitator as they work toward an effective multiparty agreement.[1]

Differences between Two-Party Negotiations and Multiparty Negotiations

Multiparty negotiations differ from two-party deliberations in several important ways. In every case, the differences are what make multiparty negotiations more complex, challenging, and difficult to manage.

Number of Parties   The first difference is the most obvious one: multiparty negotiations have more negotiators at the table. Thus, negotiations simply become bigger. This creates challenges for managing several different perspectives and ensuring that each party has adequate time to speak and be heard. Each party may be acting as a principal—that is, representing his or her own interests (Figure 10.1)—or an agent—representing the interests of at least one other party (the constituency; Figure 10.2). In addition, parties may have different

FIGURE 10.2 | A Multiparty Negotiation with Constituents

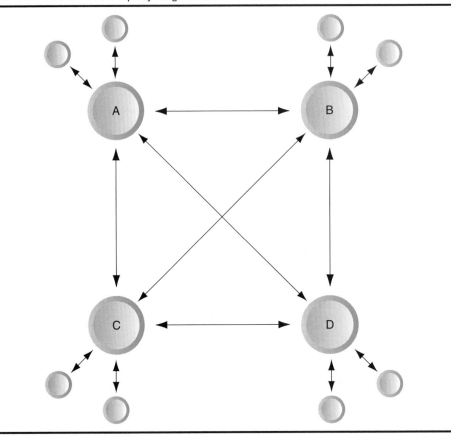

social roles outside the negotiation (e.g., president, vice president, director, board chairman) that may lead to either equal or unequal levels of power and status in the negotiation (see Chapter 7). If the parties are all equals (e.g., all vice presidents), the exchange within the negotiation should be more open than if one party has higher status or power than the others.

Informational and Computational Complexity   A second difference in multiparty negotiations is that more issues, more perspectives on issues, and more total information (facts, figures, viewpoints, arguments, documentary support) are introduced. "One of the most fundamental consequences of increasing the number of parties is that the negotiation situation tends to become less lucid, more complex, and therefore, in some respects, more demanding. As size increases, there will be more values, interests, and perceptions to be integrated or accommodated."[2] Keeping track of all this information, the perspectives of each side, and the parameters into which a solution must fit becomes a major challenge for the negotiators.

Social Complexity   A third difference is that as the number of parties increases, the social environment changes from a one-on-one dialogue to a small-group discussion. As a result, all the dynamics of small groups begin to affect the way the negotiators behave. First, how the process evolves may depend on the motivational orientation of the parties toward each other. Parties with a cooperative (versus an individualistic) motivational orientation were much more likely to achieve a higher-quality outcome in their deliberations and that cooperatively motivated parties were more trusting and engaged in less argumentation than individualistic ones.[3] This orientation also seemed to affect the way the parties discussed the issues (discussed later).

Second, social pressures may develop for the group to act cohesively, yet the members are in conflict with each other and cannot be cohesive unless they can find an acceptable solution. Members compare themselves with one another, evaluate themselves against one another, and try to use a variety of influence tactics to persuade one another toward their point of view. Strong pressures for conformity develop as members pressure other members to adopt a common perspective or definition of the problem or to endorse a particular solution. In addition, the group can develop dysfunctional group dynamics. Fiascoes such as the U.S. invasion of the Bay of Pigs in Cuba during the Kennedy administration or NASA's decision to launch the *Challenger* space shuttle were caused by dynamics in the key decision-making groups that left group members hesitant to create conflict and express their real reservations about going ahead with the project. This hesitancy led to an illusion of consensus in which each party believed that he was the only dissenting member in a fairly strong emerging agreement about what actions to take. Afraid to express their dissent for fear of looking weak and foolish (note the face-saving dynamics), group members self-censored their reservations and concerns, thereby reinforcing the apparent surface consensus and leading to a decision with disastrous consequences.[4]

Procedural Complexity   A fourth way in which multiparty negotiations are more complex than two-party ones is that the process they have to follow is more complicated. In one-on-one negotiations, the parties simply take turns in presenting their issues and perspectives, challenging the other's perspectives, or moving the negotiation along from its early stages to the later ones. When more parties are involved, the procedural rules become far less clear. Whose turn is it to do what? How do the parties coordinate where they are in the negotiations (e.g., opening statements, presentation of viewpoints, moving toward agreement)? There are several consequences of this procedural complexity. First, negotiations will take longer,[5] so more time must be allowed. Second, the greater the number of parties, the more complex and out of control the process can become—particularly if some parties choose to adopt a strategy of tough positional bargaining and dominate the process in an effort to railroad through their particular viewpoints.[6] Third, as a result of the first two elements, negotiators will probably have to devote explicit discussion time to how they will manage the process to arrive at the type of solution or agreement they want. Finally, the parties must decide how they want to approach multiple issues on the table. Parties who discussed multiple issues simultaneously—considering all the issues at once and looking for ways to trade one off against another—achieved higher—quality agreements and increased the likelihood of achieving agreement compared with groups that approached the issues sequentially (one at a time, in a fixed or negotiated sequence). Groups that approached issues simultaneously also exchanged more information and had greater insight into the preferences and priorities of the other parties at the table.[7]

Strategic Complexity   Finally, multiparty negotiations are more strategically complex than two-party ones. In one-on-one negotiations, the negotiator need only attend to the behavior of the other negotiator; strategy is therefore driven by the negotiator's objectives, the other party's actions, and the tactics they each use. In a group negotiation, complexity increases significantly. The negotiator must consider the strategies of all the other parties at the table and decide whether to deal with each of them separately or as a group. The actual process of dealing with each of them usually evolves into a series of one-on-one negotiations—but conducted within the view of all the other group members. Viewed in this manner, this series of one-on-one negotiations can have several consequences.

First, these exchanges are subject to surveillance by the audience. Negotiators will be sensitive to being observed and may feel the need to be tough to show their firmness and resolve (both to the other party and to bystanders or audiences). As a result, the social milieu may lead negotiators to adopt distributive strategies and tactics—even if they did not intend to do so—simply to show their toughness and resolve to others. The short-term result is that negotiators in the group may become strongly positional unless specific actions are taken to manage the group beyond this competitive escalation. A related dynamic is that once the parties have become strongly positional, negotiators will have to find satisfactory ways to explain modification of their positions—concession making or movement toward compromises and consensus—to their constituencies without the face-threatening dynamics discussed earlier. Even without constituencies, negotiators will not want to lose face with the other negotiators present. This will be particularly true in the situation shown in Figure 10.2, when negotiators have constituencies.

Second, negotiators who have some way to control the number of parties at the table (or even in the room) may begin to act strategically, using this control to serve their objectives. The tactic used will be determined by the strategic interests to be served by adding other parties. Additional parties may be invited to add support or credence to the negotiator's position, to provide "independent" testimony or support to a point of view, or simply to present a show of force. For example, when communities are in dispute about whether to build a new shopping center or school, change a zoning law, or present a new tax package, it is not uncommon for the agents who will publicly speak about the issue to pack the audience with a large number of supporters who will occasionally show their enthusiasm and support (or opposition) for a position. Thus, negotiators can strategically add parties to the negotiation, either to enhance their perceived power through sheer numbers or the prestige of the supporters or to present some credible threat about the consequences that will occur if the negotiators do not get their way.

Third, negotiators can explicitly engage in coalition building as a way to marshal support. Parties may explicitly or implicitly agree to support each other's positions in order to add collective weight to their combined view and then use this coalition to either dominate the negotiation process or shape the desired settlement. Coalitions may be explicitly formed prior to negotiations or during negotiation recesses and breaks, or they may emerge as the discussion proceeds. Members of coalitions can exert their strength in multiparty negotiations in a number of ways: by expressing solidarity with each other, by agreeing to help each other achieve their common or individual objectives, by dominating discussion time, and by agreeing to support each other as particular solutions and negotiated agreements emerge. One author has suggested that the emergence of consensus in decision-making groups proceeds as a "snowballing coalition." Coalitions are built one party at a time. Thus, in a group discussion, as parties share information and then deliberate possible solutions, a few people will emerge with a common perspective and then tacitly or explicitly agree to support each other's views. Other individuals then negotiate with the emerging coalition to incorporate their own views. Those who may be unwilling to negotiate or modify their views are eventually rejected and left out of the group decision.[8]

The risk for those on the outside of an influential coalition is that they will not be an active participant in the discussions, some of which may occur in caucuses away from the main negotiating table. Negotiators who are excluded from part of a multiparty negotiation receive a lesser share of the outcome than those who are present for the duration. This is particularly damaging to the excluded party when he or she misses the second half of the discussion. The lesson seems to be that simply being present when key discussions occur is important, especially in the later stages as the parties hone in on a final settlement.[9]

Finally, relationships are the most significant force in shaping which parties will enter coalitions with each other in a multiparty negotiation. When a relationship is in place, parties extensively incorporate the time dimension into their deliberations and side negotiations with each other. Thus, what the parties have done for each other in the past, and/or what they think they can do for each other in the future, has a strong impact on the current discussions.[10] In addition, as we noted in Chapter 9, relationships may lead the parties to have similar preferences, to have strong concern for the others and a desire to help the others achieve their outcomes, and to create and sustain strong trust among group members.

Summary

There are five ways in which the complexity increases as three or more parties simultaneously engage in negotiation. First, there are simply more parties involved in the negotiation, which increases the number of speakers, increases the demand for discussion time, and increases the number of different roles the parties may play. Second, more parties bring more issues and positions to the table; thus, more perspectives must be presented and discussed. Third, negotiations become socially more complex—social norms emerge that affect member participation, and there may be stronger pressures to conform and suppress disagreement. Fourth, negotiations become procedurally more complex, and the parties may have to negotiate a new process that allows them to coordinate their actions more effectively. Finally, negotiations become more strategically complex because the parties must monitor the moves and actions of several other parties in determining what each will do next. In addition, the possibility of coalitions increases the likelihood that decisions will not be made by a comprehensive negotiated consensus but by some subgroup that can dominate the discussion and decision-making processes.

What Is an Effective Group?

Multiparty negotiation looks a lot like group decision making because it involves a group of parties trying to reach a common solution in a situation where the parties' preferences may diverge. Consequently, understanding multiparty negotiation means, in part, understanding the attributes of an effective group. Effective groups and their members do the following things:

1. *Test assumptions and inferences.* In effective groups, each individual member makes his or her assumptions and inferences clear by articulating them and checking them out with others. Unchecked assumptions and inferences can lead to unfounded conclusions.

2. *Share as much relevant information as possible.* In a competitive negotiation, parties are likely to use information strategically—sharing very little with other parties while attempting to gain much information from others. However, effective groups require the type of information sharing that occurs in integrative negotiation in order to maximize the information available to the group to find solutions that meet the interests of all parties. Thus, parties should discuss their interests, but not disclose their walkaway or BATNA.

3. *Focus on interests, not positions.* As in an integrative negotiation, group deliberations should use procedures that surface the underlying interests of individual members, rather than just their stated positions: sharing information, asking questions, and probing for underlying interests or needs.

4. *Explain the reasons behind one's statements, questions, and answers.* Disclosing interests requires that we be clear to others about what is most important and that we indicate the reasons *why* those things are important.

5. *Be specific—use examples.* Parties should attempt to talk in specific terms about directly observable behaviors, people, places, and events. Generalities can lead to misunderstandings or ambiguity that can send problem solving off the track.

6. *Agree on the meaning of important words.* Participants should be careful to fully explain and define key words or language that may be part of the agreement. For example, if group members agree that all decisions will be made by *consensus*, they should all have the same definition of what will constitute "consensus" in the group—voting procedures, general support by most members, or full support by 100 percent of the members.

7. *Disagree openly with any member of the group.* If parties withhold their disagreement, conflict is forced underground, which may ultimately lead to an inability to reach consensus or to implement a plan to which the group might agree. Disagreement can be productive without being offensive.

8. *Make statements, then invite questions and comments.* Diversity of viewpoints should not just be reserved for disagreeing with another, but it should also be invited *from* others: encourage others to clarify their own understanding of your interests and needs.

9. *Jointly design ways to test disagreements and solutions.* Develop a process for confirming facts, verifying interpretations of events, and surfacing the reasons for disagreements so that problem solving can move forward. This process can be facilitated

by anyone who is not directly involved in the central debate. We return to this point later in the chapter.

10. *Discuss undiscussable issues.* Groups often have a number of issues that they consider undiscussable: group members who are not performing up to expectations (or who are behaving badly) or challenges to a boss in the room. Getting these issues on the table may be critical for the group to be productive. One approach is to discuss openly the undiscussability of an important norm, rule, or problem and to state the implied consequences of discussing that topic openly. As Schwartz notes, "If members can be assured that their fears will not be realized, they will be more willing to talk openly about previously undiscussable issues" (p. 82).

11. *Keep the discussion focused.* Team leaders should make sure that the conversation stays on track until everyone has been heard. Develop an agenda, and have the chair manage the process to ensure that discussions don't wander all over the map.

12. *Do not take cheap shots or otherwise distract the group.* Distractions, sarcasm, irrelevant stories, and humor are all distractions that take the group off task and off focus. Although some of this behavior is perhaps inevitable, both in groups that like each other a lot and those that have strong conflict, effective groups try to keep distractions to a minimum.

13. *Expect to have all members participate in all phases of the process.* All group members must be willing to contribute to all phases of the group process—sharing relevant information, working to help the group arrive at a solution, or helping manage the process.

14. *Exchange relevant information with nongroup members.* If outsiders are invited in as experts or important sources of information, they should be fully briefed on the group's ground rules for operation and asked to comply with them.

15. *Make decisions by consensus.* Although it is not always possible for groups to make unanimous decisions, groups should strive for consensus whenever possible. We return to discuss group decision rules later in the chapter.

16. *Conduct a self-critique.* Finally, in between decisions or major deliberations, groups should spend some time in a postmortem evaluating their process and effectiveness. Paradoxically, groups that do not work well together seldom take the time to evaluate their process, probably because they hope to avoid the anticipated conflict that might arise from discussing the dysfunctionality. Not surprisingly, not discussing the dysfunctionality usually makes it worse.[11]

Managing Multiparty Negotiations

Given the additional complexity that occurs in a multiparty negotiation, what is the most effective way to cope? There are three key stages that characterize multilateral negotiations: the prenegotiation stage, managing the actual negotiations, and managing the agreement stage. In addressing these three stages, we also identify what a single negotiator can do when:

- The individual is simply one of the parties in a multiparty negotiation and wants to ensure that his or her own issues and interests are clearly incorporated into the final agreement.
- The individual wants to ensure that the group reaches the highest quality and best possible final agreement.
- The individual is responsible for managing a multiparty negotiation process to ensure that many of the strategic and procedural complexities are effectively managed.[12]

The Prenegotiation Stage

This stage is characterized by a great deal of informal contact among the parties. The parties tend to work on a number of important issues.

Participants   The parties must agree on who is going to be invited to the talks. If the group is already an intact one, this is an easy question. However, many complex international negotiations give a great deal of time to the question of who will be recognized and who can speak for others. Issues about participants can be decided on the basis of the following:

- Who must be included if a deal is to be reached (key coalition members)?
- Who could spoil the deal if they were excluded (possible veto players)?
- Whose presence is likely to help other parties achieve their objectives (desirable coalition members)?
- Whose presence is likely to keep other parties from achieving their objectives (key coalition blockers)?
- Whose status will be enhanced simply by being at the table? (This was often a key issue in the Palestinian–Israeli talks in the Middle East and in the Paris Peace Talks to end the Vietnam War—when the Viet Cong were invited to the table as a fully recognized party.)

Coalitions   It is not uncommon for coalitions to exist before negotiations begin or for coalitions to organize in anticipation of the meeting of all the parties. Naturally, coalitions will form to either promote or block a particular agenda.

Defining Group Member Roles   If the group already has a structure, then roles—leaders, mediators, recordkeepers, and so on—will already have been determined. But if the group has not met before, then parties may begin to jockey for key roles. Some may want to lead, participate actively, and promote a particular agenda; others may wish to stay silent and be invisible; still others may wish to take a third-party role such as mediator or facilitator. Group members can play a number of different roles in a group. Table 10.1 describes three types of roles that members can play—*task roles*, which move the group along toward a decision or conclusion; *relationship roles*, which manage and sustain

TABLE 10.1 | Roles Commonly Played by Members of a Group

Task-Oriented Roles	Relationship-Oriented Roles	Self-Oriented Roles
Initiating/offering—offering new ideas	Encouraging—supporting others' comments, contributions	Blocking—act negatively, active and frequent disagreement with others
Information seeking—asking others for their views	Harmonizing—smoothing over conflict, reinforcing "we-ness" of the group	Recognition seeker—draw the group's attention to themselves, seek approval from others
Opinion seeking—asking others for their opinions, judgments	Compromising—shifting one's own position in order to find a middle ground of opinion between people	Dominator—speak frequently, dominate the conversation, manipulate the group toward their preferred outcome
Elaborating—clarifying, expanding on the topic	Gatekeeping—encouraging participation from those who do not speak often, discouraging participation from those who speak frequently	Avoider—remain quiet and disengaged, withhold contributions on either task or relationship issues
Evaluating—offering judgments about the topic	Standard setting—Asking for or offering standards for judging the team's effectiveness	
Coordinating—pulling together ideas proposed by others		
Energizing—creating excitement about the topic being discussed		

Source: Based on K. D. Benne and P. Sheats. "Functional Roles of Group Members," *Journal of Social Issues* 4 (1948), 41–49.

good relationships between group members, and *self-oriented roles*, which serve to bring attention to the individual group member, often at the expense of group effectiveness.

Understanding the Costs and Consequences of No Agreement   Negotiators need to understand the costs and consequences that will ensue if the group fails to agree. Earlier in this volume, we made that suggestion to negotiators in one-on-one encounters, in the discussion of a BATNA (cf. Chapters 2, 3, and 4). For example, suppose a group of vice presidents in a computer company is trying to decide which models of a new line of personal computers should be built next year, and the quantities of each one. To make this decision effectively, they must include in their decision options a consideration of what will happen if they fail to agree on what to do. Will someone else (i.e., the president) step in and decide for them? How will the president feel about the group if the members can't agree? Are the costs of impasse the same for every negotiator? Usually this is not the case—different agents have different costs associated with no agreement. For example, if the vice presidents cannot agree, the president may mandate the model line and quantities, which may have greater costs for the engineering and manufacturing departments (which would have to change over) than for the marketing and sales departments (which would have to design a new marketing and ad campaign regardless of what was done). The group members with the better impasse alternatives are likely to have more power in the negotiation because they care less about whether the group reaches a particular solution relative to no agreement.[13] Finally, do group members perceive their agreement and no-agreement options accurately? There is much evidence that negotiators are prone to perceptual biases that lead them to believe they are better than others (refer back to Chapter 5), their options are better than others' options, they are more likely to achieve their outcomes than others, and they have more control over shaping an outcome than others.[14] In multiparty negotiations, these biases are likely to affect negotiators by inflating their sense of power and ability to win—leading them to believe that the no-agreement alternative is much better than it really is. Reality checking with others is important in keeping these biases under control: are group members really willing to live with the possible costs of no agreement, and at what point will the group be ready to endorse that possibility?

Learning the Issues and Constructing an Agenda   Finally, parties spend a great deal of time familiarizing themselves with the issues, absorbing information, and trying to understand one another's interests. They also spend time constructing an agenda. There are many reasons an agenda can be an effective decision aid:

- It establishes the issues to be discussed.
- Depending on how the issues are worded, it can also define how each issue is positioned and framed (refer back to our discussion of framing in Chapter 5).
- It can define the order in which issues are discussed.
- It can be used to introduce process issues (decision rules, discussion norms, member roles, discussion dynamics), as well as substantive issues, simply by including them.
- It can assign time limits to various items, thereby indicating the importance of the different issues.

In addition to creating an agenda, parties in the process might also agree to abide by a set of "ground rules"—ways to conduct themselves during the negotiation. The Connect Model is a proven approach to building effective team relationships. Table 10.2 overviews the four key requirements and steps in this process model.[15]

TABLE 10.2 | The Connect Model and the Requirements for Building a Relationship

Four Requirements	Process Model
1. Can we agree to have a constructive conversation?	**C**ommit to the relationship—signal that you are ready to work on the problem and it is worth doing. **O**ptimize safety—you will do your best to not make the other feel defensive, and you will try to appreciate the other's point of view.
2. Can our conversation be productive enough to make a difference?	**N**arrow the discussion to one issue—identify one issue at a time in a nonthreatening way. **N**eutralize defensiveness—minimize using words, terms, or descriptions that make the other defensive.
3. Can we understand and appreciate each other's perspective?	**E**xplain and echo each perspective—tell the other what you observe, how it makes you feel, and the long-term consequences.
4. Can we all commit to making improvements?	**C**hange one behavior each—agree that each of you is going to change one behavior. **T**rack it!—determine ways to monitor progress.

Source: From F.M.S. LaFasto and C. Larson, *When teams work best* (Thousand Oaks, CA: Sage Publications, 2001), p. 51.

The Formal Negotiation Stage—Managing the Group Process and Outcome

Much of the multiparty negotiation process is a combination of the group discussion, bilateral negotiation, and coalition-building activities described earlier in this volume. It also incorporates a great deal of what we know about how to structure a group discussion so as to achieve an effective and endorsed result. The following approaches are likely to ensure a high-quality group decision.

Appoint an Appropriate Chair   Multiparty negotiations will proceed more smoothly when it is clear to everyone involved who is chairing or facilitating the process. Often this role will be played by one of the interested parties, but multiparty negotiations can be greatly facilitated by the presence of a neutral chairperson who can implement many of the tactics described here. When feasible, the parties should seriously consider designating a chair who has little stake in the specific outcome but a strong interest in ensuring that the group works toward achieving the best possible outcome. As a practical matter, it is frequently the case that the chair will be drawn from within the circle of interested parties. Keep in mind that if a chairperson is also advocating a particular position or preferred outcome, it will be most difficult for that individual to act or be seen as neutral because the solution the person wants to obtain on the issues is likely to compromise (or be perceived to compromise) his or her neutrality or objectivity with respect to facilitating the process. See Box 10.1 for an inventory of constructive approaches to acting as a chair in multiparty negotiations.

Use and Restructure the Agenda   A critical way to control the flow and direction of negotiation is through an agenda. Either the chair or the parties to the negotiation may introduce and coordinate the agenda. An agenda adds a high degree of structure, organization, and coordination to a discussion. Agendas provide low-power or disadvantaged groups a vehicle for getting their issues heard and addressed, assuming that they can get them on the agenda. However, the manner in which an agenda is built (by collective consensus at the beginning of a meeting versus by one person prior to the meeting) and who builds it will have a great deal of impact on the flow of the negotiation. Unless group members feel comfortable challenging the person who introduces a preemptive agenda, the agenda will go unquestioned and hence the implicit discussion structure and format it suggests will prevail. Negotiators entering a multiparty negotiation for which an (unacceptable) agenda has been created in advance should consider letting other parties know ahead of time that they view the agenda itself as open to discussion or change. In other words, make sure that possible modifications to the agenda are part of the agenda.

Although an agenda may add needed structure to a complex negotiation, a drawback is that it may artificially partition related issues; as a result, issues may be discussed separately rather than coupled or traded off to exploit integrative potential. The parties using an agenda must be sensitive to the implicit structure it imposes, and they must be willing to challenge and reconfigure it if doing so will facilitate the emergence of an integrative, consensus-based agreement.

Ensure a Diversity of Information and Perspectives   A third way to facilitate the negotiation is to ensure that the group receives a wide variety of different perspectives about the

BOX 10.1 Chairing a Multiparty Negotiation

Chairpersons of multiparty negotiations must be sensitive to keeping tight control over the group process while not directly affecting the group's outcome. When a group wants to achieve a consensus or unanimous decision, the responsibility of the chair is to be constantly attentive to the group process. Some pointers for how to chair a multiparty negotiation effectively include these:

1. Explicitly describe the role you will take as chair. Be clear that you are there only to manage process and that the group will determine the outcome.

2. Introduce the agenda or build one based on the group's issues, concerns, and priorities. Make sure the group has an opportunity to discuss, modify, or challenge the agenda before you begin.

3. Make logistical arrangements that will help the negotiation process. Does the physical setup of the room offer the best possible configuration for constructive discussion? Arrange for a flip chart, whiteboard, or overhead projector to write down issues and interests. Many negotiators find they benefit from common visual access to issues, proposals, and other information during the discussion.

4. Introduce necessary ground rules or let the parties suggest them. How long will the group meet? What is the expected output or final product? Will minutes be taken? Will the group take breaks? Where will negotiations take place? How and when can group members consult with their constituents?

5. Create or review decision standards and rules. Find standards for what parties believe will be a fair or reasonable settlement. What criteria will be used to assess whether a particular solution is fair, reasonable, and effective? How will the group ultimately decide to adopt an agreement?

6. Assure individual members that they will have an opportunity to make opening statements or other ways of placing their individual concerns and issues on the table. Be clear that once parties are familiar with the issues, simultaneous discussion of several issues can take place. This will permit trade-offs among issues rather than forcing a compromise on each individual issue.

7. Be an active gatekeeper. Make sure that people have a chance to speak and that the more vocal people do not dominate so that the less vocal people become silent and drop out. Ask the more vocal people to hold back and explicitly invite the more silent people to make comments and input. Often, as a group moves toward some form of agreement or consensus, some people participate less. Make sure that they have chosen not to participate, rather than simply dropped out because they don't think their views are worthwhile or important.

8. Listen for interests and commonalities. Encourage people to express interests, mirror them back, and encourage people to identify not only what they want, but also why they want it. Listen for priorities and concerns. Once the issues and interests have been identified, explicitly set aside a time for inventing options. Use brainstorming and other group decision-making techniques to generate options and evaluate them.

9. Introduce external information (studies, reports, statistics, facts, testimony from experts) that will help illuminate the issues and interests. Ask for hard data to support assertions (but be careful to refrain from engaging in aggressive "cross-examination" that will compromise your neutrality).

10. Summarize frequently, particularly when conversation becomes stalled, confused, or tense. State where you think the group is, what has been accomplished, and what needs to be done. Paraphrasing and summarizing brings the group back to reality and back on task.

task and different sources of information. Because the nature of the information changes depending on the group's task—for example, designing and implementing a change, finding the best possible solution to a problem, or simply finding a solution that is politically acceptable to several constituencies—it is difficult to prescribe what information is critical and how to ensure that the group is exposed to it. This can simply be a matter of making sure that the voices of all participants are heard.

If there is a chair, he or she can ensure that the group receives input from each group member; that various constituencies and stakeholders have an opportunity to provide input (through written comments or opportunities for open testimony before the group); and that relevant reports, documents, or statistical analyses are circulated and discussed. There are five key process steps that a chair can implement to ensure having an effective, amicable disagreement on a team:

1. *Collect your thoughts and composure before speaking.* Avoid the temptation to "shoot from the hip" with emotion rather than reasoned arguments.

2. *Try to understand the other person's position.* In Chapters 6 and 9, we discussed techniques such as listening skills, mirroring, and role reversal to understand the other.

3. *Try to think of ways that you both can win.*

4. *Consider how important this issue is to you.* Is this your most important issue in the negotiation? Can you afford to sacrifice all or part of your position on this issue for gains elsewhere?

5. *Remember that you will probably have to work together with these people in the future.* Even out of anger and frustration, don't use tactics that will make you regret the conversation tomorrow.[16]

Ensure Consideration of All the Available Information   One way to ensure that the group discusses all available information is to monitor discussion norms. Discussion norms reflect the way the group engages in sharing and evaluating the information introduced.[17]

Although it would be highly desirable to do so, groups seldom consider in advance what discussion norms they are going to follow. In most cases, this failure is probably due to a lack of understanding about how much deliberations can be improved by following norms and rules that will enhance discussion. Several group norms can undermine an effective discussion:

- *Unwillingness to tolerate conflicting points of view and perspectives.* There may be many reasons for this: one or more members dislike conflict, are afraid that conflict will be uncontrollable, or see conflict as destructive to group cohesiveness. But as we noted earlier, the absence of conflict can also lead to disastrous decisions.

- *Side conversations.* Side conversations between two or three members of a group can sometimes be beneficial and sometimes detrimental. While people can often have a more comfortable conversation with one or two other people compared with an entire group, side conversations can also destroy the sense of unity in the group and the ability to come to agreement when consensus is critical. When a decision can benefit from unique perspectives and creative input, side conversations can be beneficial; however, when a group must remain unified and collectively embrace the outcome, side conversations may create more disruption and reduce the likelihood of achieving that unity.[18]

- *No means for defusing an emotionally charged discussion.* Unless there is a way to release it, anger, frustration, or resentment can become mixed in with the substantive issues and hamper the group's efforts. Although a great deal of negotiation literature suggests that parties should simply be calm and rational at all times, doing so is simply not humanly possible. The more the parties care about a particular issue and are invested in it, the more likely it is that emotions will creep in. Vehicles must exist to allow the parties to vent their emotions productively.

- *Coming to a meeting unprepared.* Unfortunately, preparation for a meeting often consists of either no preparation at all or simply preparing one's own position. Attention to the others' positions or to assessing underlying interests and priorities requires thorough preparation.

Several strategies may be used to manage each of these three potentially destructive discussion norms. The parties must generate and exchange ideas in a manner that permits full exploration and allows everyone to have some input, yet avoids some of the destructive conflict and emotions that can occur. There are several group decision-making and brainstorming techniques that are frequently used to achieve this objective:

The Delphi Technique A moderator structures an initial questionnaire and sends it out to all parties, asking for input. Parties provide their input and send it back to the moderator. The moderator summarizes the input and sends it back to the parties. Parties then evaluate the report, make further input, and return it to the moderator. Over a number of rounds, through the questions and inquiries shaped by the moderator, the parties can exchange a great deal of information and share different perspectives.

Brainstorming In brainstorming, the parties are instructed to define a problem and then to generate as many solutions as possible without criticizing any of them. We discussed brainstorming in Chapter 3. Box 10.2 offers a list of critical rules to be used in brainstorming.

Nominal Group Technique The nominal group technique typically follows brainstorming. Once the brainstormed list of solution options is created, group members can rank, rate, or evaluate the alternatives in terms of the degree to which each alternative solves the problem. The leader collects, posts, and records these ratings so that all group members have an opportunity to formally evaluate the options and vote on the ones they consider to be most effective.[19]

Manage Conflict Effectively As implied by many of the suggestions offered throughout this section, groups must generate many ideas and approaches to a problem—which usually creates conflict—while not allowing that conflict to either disrupt the information flow or create personal animosity. When done well, conflict is a natural part of group life that improves members' ability to complete tasks, work together, and sustain these relationships. When done poorly, conflict actively disrupts all of these processes. One study examined the development and management of conflict over time in high-performance task groups. The

- **No criticism is allowed.** No other member can say whether an idea is good or bad.

- **Questions can be asked only for clarification of an idea.**

- **Free-wheeling is a plus.** Wild and crazy ideas are welcome, and in fact they may help trigger other ideas from team members. Don't worry about whether the idea you voice is good, bad, silly, or realistic; just say it.

- **Go for quantity.** The more ideas you get from team members, the better this team effort will be.

- **Combine and improve ideas.** It is certainly fine to build on someone else's idea.

Source: C. C. Manz, Christopher P. Neck, James Mancuso, and K. P. Manz, *For Team Members Only* (New York: AMACOM, 1997), p. 135.

---

authors examined three kinds of conflict typical to work groups: relationship conflict (interpersonal incompatibilities; dislike among group members; and feelings of tension, friction, annoyance, frustration, and dislike), task conflicts (awareness of difference in viewpoints about the group's task), and process conflict (awareness of controversies about how task accomplishment will proceed—who will do what, how much one should get from a result, etc.). High-performing teams were characterized by low, but increasing, levels of process conflict; low levels of relationship conflict with a rise near the deadline; and moderate levels of task conflict at the midpoint of the interaction. Those teams that were able to create this ideal conflict profile had similar preestablished work-related value systems among the group members, high levels of trust and respect, and open discussion norms around conflict during the middle stages of the interaction. Effective groups both anticipate that they will have to deal with conflict and have developed multiple strategies for dealing with them when they arise.[20]

Review and Manage the Decision Rules　In addition to monitoring the discussion norms and managing the conflict processes effectively, the parties also need to manage the decision rules—that is, the way the group will decide what to do. In decision-making groups, the dominant view is to assume that the majority rules and, at some point, take a vote of all members, assuming that any settlement option that receives more than 50 percent of the votes will be the one adopted. Obviously, this is not the only option. Groups can make decisions by dictatorship (one person decides); oligarchy (a dominant minority coalition decides); simple majority (one more person than half the group decides); two-thirds majority; quasi-consensus (most of the group agrees, and those who dissent agree not to protest or raise objections); and true unanimity, or consensus (everyone agrees). Determining the group's decision rule before deliberations begin also significantly affects the group process. For example, if a simple majority will make the decision in a five-person group, then only three people need to agree. Thus, any three people can get together and form a coalition during or even prior to the meeting. In contrast, if the decision rule will be consensus, or unanimity, then the group must meet and work hard enough to ensure that all parties' interests are raised, discussed, and incorporated into the group decision. Deciding whether a coalition-building strategy or a complete sharing of positions, interests, and problem solving is necessary requires significantly different approaches.[21]

Strive for a First Agreement   Finally, if the objective is consensus or the best quality solution, negotiators should not strive to achieve it all at once. Rather, they should strive for a *first agreement* that can be revised, upgraded, and improved. As we have discussed, the additional complexity of multiparty negotiations increases the complexity of the events, the likelihood of communication breakdown, and the likelihood that the parties will negotiate more positionally (either because of the competitive dynamics or the consequences of audience or constituency dynamics). Given these conditions, achieving true consensus among the parties becomes much more difficult, even if a true consensus solution exists. As a result, it is often better to set a more modest objective for these negotiations: to reach a preliminary agreement or a tentative consensus that can then be systematically improved through "renegotiation," using the first agreement as a plateau that can be modified, reshaped, tweaked, and improved upon in a follow-up negotiation effort.

The drawback, of course, is that many group members may be satisfied with the first solution—either because it already incorporates their views or because the difficulty of achieving it may sap their enthusiasm for exerting any time and energy to improve it. First agreements typically reflect the position of a group's majority or the views of a small number of powerful group members. These parties may not be open to dissenting views that would otherwise stimulate consideration of a wider set of possible alternative outcomes.[22]

This resistance to further deliberations by parties who are happy with the first agreement may be overcome by taking a break after the first agreement is reached, encouraging the group to critique and evaluate the first agreement, and explicitly planning to come back with a commitment to try second-agreement negotiations (renegotiations). In addition, if the group has been through a great deal of divisive and unproductive conflict to reach the first agreement, then the renegotiations must specifically attend to changing and managing the conflict process.[23]

Manage Problem Team Members   Finally, the behaviors of individual team members may be a source of difficulty for group process. Members may show up late for meetings, fail to prepare adequately, distract the group with side comments and humor, or neglect to put in their fair share of work. Unfortunately, there is a tendency for many groups to try to ignore these individuals rather than to address their behavior and try to change it. Here are some tactics for dealing with problem team members:

1. Be specific about the problem behavior—offer clear, specific examples.

2. Phrase the problem as one that is affecting the entire team, rather than just you. Use "we" instead of "you," which sounds much more accusatory and is likely to make the other defensive.

3. Focus on behaviors the other can control. The purpose is not to criticize or embarrass, but to focus on specific behaviors that the individual can control and modify.

4. Wait to give constructive criticism until the individual can truly hear and accept it. Consult with the problem person in private, and when he or she is not pressured to go elsewhere or deal with some major problem.

5. Keep feedback professional. Use a civil tone and describe the offending behavior and its impact specifically. Make the tenor of the conversation adult to adult, not parent to child.

6. Make sure the other has heard and understood your comments. Ask him or her to repeat or rephrase so that you know you have been heard.[24]

The Agreement Stage

The third and final stage in managing multiparty negotiations is the agreement stage. During the agreement stage, the parties must select among the alternatives on the table. They are also likely to encounter some last-minute problems and issues, such as deadline pressures, the discovery of new issues that were not previously addressed, the need for more information on certain problems or concerns, and the tendency for some parties to threaten veto power while they lobby to get their specific pet idea or project included in the final group agreement. Four key problem-solving steps occur during this phase:

- *Select the best solution.* The group must weigh the alternatives they have considered and either select a single alternative or combine alternatives into a package that will satisfy as many members as possible.

- *Develop an action plan.* This increases the likelihood that the solution will be implemented completely, effectively, and on time. For example, a good action plan might include a list of key steps, the objectives to be achieved at each step, when the step should be started and completed, what resources are needed to complete the step, and who has responsibility for completing the step. Working on this plan can also cause ambiguities or omissions from the earlier discussion to surface, thus preventing greater conflict down the road when implementation has begun.

- *Implement the action plan.* This is likely to take place after the group disbands or outside the scope of the group, but it needs to follow the guidelines established by the group. Without an effective action plan, the problems that might have been recognized at this point are sure to occur.

- *Evaluate outcomes and the process.* Conducting an evaluation of the process and the outcome can be critical for surfacing data about the group's working effectiveness. This evaluation need not occur at the same time or place as the decision meeting, but it should not be deferred or omitted. If team members are unwilling to raise criticisms publicly, anonymous questionnaires can be completed, summarized, and sent back to the group by the leader or a neutral facilitator, who can then use the data to highlight specific concerns about faulty process or incomplete outcomes.[25]

What the Chair Can Do to Help   In addition to the list of chair responsibilities outlined in Box 10.1, here are some things a group facilitator can do to keep the group moving toward a successful completion:

- *Move the group toward selecting one or more of the options.* Use the process rules we discussed earlier, as well as the wide variety of techniques for achieving an integrative agreement presented in Chapter 3. Listen for the emergence of a tentative consensus among key members. Permit and encourage packaging and trade-offs among multiple issues or modification of the first agreement or tentative agreement reached earlier. If the decision is particularly laden with conflict, pursue a first agreement with the understanding that the group will take a break and come back to renegotiate the agreement at a later date.

- *Shape and draft the tentative agreement.* Write it down. Work on language. Write the wording on a whiteboard, flip chart, or overhead projection that can be displayed to the entire group, so that all can see it and edit it freely. Test to make sure all parties understand the agreement and its implications and consequences. Remember that the person who does the writing often has more power than others because he or she gets to write the agreement in his or her own language and may bias or selectively remember some points and omit others.

- *Discuss whatever implementation and follow-up or next steps need to occur.* Make sure that individuals who have a role in this process understand what they need to do. Make assignments to individuals to ensure that key action steps are designed and executed. Schedule a follow-up meeting. Plan for another meeting in the future to evaluate how the agreement is working.

- *Thank the group for their participation, their hard work, and their efforts.* If the discussion has been particularly difficult or required a large time commitment, a small group celebration and formal thank-you notes or gifts may be in order. Have dinner or a party together to celebrate all the hard work.

- *Organize and facilitate the postmortem.* Have group members discuss the process and the outcome and evaluate what they might do better or differently the next time. This will ensure learning for both the group members and the chair.

Chapter Summary

Most negotiation theory has been developed under the assumption that negotiation is a bilateral process—that there are only two focal negotiators or teams of negotiators opposing each other. Yet many negotiations are multilateral or group deliberations—more than two negotiators are involved, each with his or her own interests and positions, and the group must arrive at a collective agreement regarding a plan, decision, or course of action. In this chapter, we explored the dynamics of two forms of multiparty negotiations: when multiple parties must work together to achieve a collective decision or consensus and when two or more teams are opposing each other in a negotiation.

One theme that runs through all forms of multiparty negotiation is the need to actively monitor and manage negotiation process situations that are significantly more complex than two-party negotiations. We present here a brief set of questions that any participant in negotiations involving coalitions, multiple parties, or teams should keep in mind:

- What are the consequences of the parties failing to agree due to the increased complexities? What happens if there is no agreement?

- How will the parties involved actually make a decision? That is, what decision rules will be used? Why are these the best possible rules?

- How can the parties use iterations—multiple rounds of discussion—to achieve their objectives? (This may be particularly appropriate when the decision rule is consensus—or the best-quality agreement—because consensus may not be achievable in a single iteration.)

- Do we need a designated chair or facilitator? Should it be a neutral outsider, or can one of the parties fill this role? What tactics can a facilitator use to manage group process in order to ensure that the best decision is reached? (These tactics might include ensuring that the group is exposed to a variety of information sources, managing the process to make sure that the group considers and discusses all available information thoroughly, and structuring the group's agenda with care.)

If these issues are raised and thoughtfully considered, the parties involved are considerably more likely to feel better about the process and to arrive at an effective outcome than if these factors are left to chance.

Endnotes

[1] This chapter draws heavily on the works of Bazerman, Mannix, and Thompson, 1988; Brett, 1991; and Kramer, 1991, who have provided solid overviews of the problems and challenges of multiparty negotiation.

[2] Midgaard and Underal, 1977, p. 332 as quoted in Kramer, 1991.

[3] Weingart, Bennett, and Brett, 1993.

[4] Tompkins, 1993.

[5] Sebenius, 1983.

[6] Bazerman, Mannix, and Thompson, 1988.

[7] Weingart, Bennett, and Brett, 1993.

[8] Murnighan, 1986.

[9] Kim, 1997.

[10] Polzer, Mannix, and Neale, 1995, 1998.

[11] Schwartz, 1994.

[12] Touval, 1988.

[13] Brett, 1991.

[14] Taylor and Brown, 1988; Tyler and Hastie, 1991.

[15] LaFasto and Larson, 2001.

[16] Manz, Neck, Mancuso, and Manz, 1997.

[17] Brett, 1991.

[18] Swaab, Phillips, Diermeier, and Medvec, 2008.

[19] Bazerman, Mannix, and Thompson, 1988.

[20] Jehn and Mannix, 2001; for additional ideas on managing conflict in groups, see Cloke and Goldsmith, 2005.

[21] Brett, 1991.

[22] Ibid.; Nemeth, 1986, 1989.

[23] Brett, 1991.

[24] Manz, Neck, Mancuso, and Manz, 1997.

[25] Schwartz, 1994.

International and Cross-Cultural Negotiation

Objectives

1. Understand how international and cross-cultural negotiations are different from domestic or same-culture negotiations.

2. Explore different definitions and meanings of a culture.

3. Consider how culture affects negotiation dynamics.

4. Gain strategies that negotiators can adapt to another party's cultural style.

Although there has been an interest in international negotiation for centuries, the frequency of international negotiation has increased rapidly in the past 20 years.[1] People today travel more frequently and farther, and business is more international than ever before. For many people and organizations, international negotiation has become the norm rather than an exotic activity that only occurs occasionally. Numerous books and articles—from both academic and practitioner perspectives—have been written about the complexities of negotiating across borders, be it with a person from a different country, culture, or region. Although the term *culture* has many possible definitions, we use it to refer to the shared values, beliefs, and behaviors of a group of people. Countries can have more than one culture, and cultures can span national borders. As we discussed in Chapter 1, negotiating is a social process that is embedded in a much larger context. This context increases in complexity when more than one culture or country is involved, making international negotiation a highly complicated process.[2]

This chapter is organized in the following manner.[3] First we discuss the art and science of cross-cultural negotiation. Next, we consider some of the factors that make international negotiation different, including both the environmental context (macropolitical factors) and the immediate context (microstrategic factors). We then turn to a discussion of the most frequently studied aspect of international negotiation: the effect of culture, be it national, regional, or organizational. We discuss how culture has been conceptualized and discuss four approaches to culture used by academics and practitioners. Next we examine the influence of culture on negotiations, discussing this from managerial and research perspectives. The chapter concludes with a discussion of culturally responsive strategies available to the international negotiator. Boxes throughout the chapter present examples of factors to think about when negotiating with people from other cultures.[4]

International Negotiation: Art and Science

The notion that negotiation is both art and science is especially valid at the cross-cultural or international level. The science of negotiation provides research evidence to support broad trends that often, but not always, occur during negotiation. The art of negotiation is deciding which strategy to apply when and choosing which models and perspectives to apply to increase cross-cultural understanding. This is especially challenging because cross-cultural and international negotiations add a level of complexity significantly greater than within-culture negotiations. There are two implications of this complexity for this chapter.

First, we present many different models and perspectives on cross-cultural negotiation. They vary in comprehensiveness and usefulness across different situations. No one model will explain every cross-cultural negotiation situation—there is simply not the level of knowledge to create such a model, and likely never will be. This complexity is a source of frustration for many cross-cultural negotiators, who would like clearer practical guidance when negotiating across borders.

No simple cookbook exists. The models and approaches we present in this chapter allow cross-cultural negotiators to build a strong portfolio of tools to draw upon when they are negotiating cross-culturally. From reading and studying the effects of these tools negotiators will be able to hone their artistry in the domain of cross-cultural negotiation.

The second implication of the complexity of cross-cultural negotiation is the tendency for negotiators to undervalue the amount of *within-culture variation* that exists. It is important to remember that negotiation outcomes, both domestically and internationally, are determined by several different factors. While cultural differences are clearly important, negotiators must guard against assigning too much responsibility to them.[5] Dialdin, Kopelman, Adair, Brett, Okumura, and Lytle have labeled the tendency to overlook the importance of situational factors in favor of cultural explanations the *cultural attribution error*.[6]

In summary, cross-cultural and international negotiations are much more complex than domestic negotiations. This complexity is also a source of energy, excitement, and frustration when negotiating across borders and will challenge negotiators to understand the science of negotiation while developing their artistry.

What Makes International Negotiation Different?

Phatak and Habib suggest that two overall contexts have an influence on international negotiations: the environmental context and the immediate context (see Figure 11.1).[7] The *environmental context* includes environmental forces that neither negotiator controls that influence the negotiation. The *immediate context* includes factors over which negotiators appear to have some control. Understanding the role of factors in both the environmental and the immediate contexts is important to grasping the complexity of international negotiation processes and outcomes.

FIGURE 11.1 | The Contexts of International Negotiations

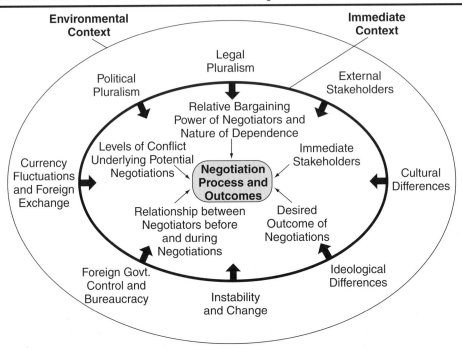

Source: Adapted from A. V. Phatak and M. H. Habib, "The Dynamics of International Business Negotiations," *Business Horizons* 39 (1996), pp. 30–38; and J. W. Salacuse, "Making Deals in Strange Places: A Beginner's Guide to International Business Negotiations," *Negotiation Journal* 4 (1988), pp. 5–13.

Environmental Context

Salacuse identified six factors in the environmental context that make international negotiations more challenging than domestic negotiations: political and legal pluralism, international economics, foreign governments and bureaucracies, instability, ideology, and culture.[8] (Culture has received by far the most attention by those examining international negotiation, and it is discussed in a separate section later in this chapter.) Phatak and Habib have suggested an additional factor: external stakeholders.[9] These factors can act to limit or constrain organizations that operate internationally, and it is important that negotiators understand and appreciate their effects.

Political and Legal Pluralism   Firms conducting business in different countries are working with different legal and political systems. There may be implications for taxes that an organization pays, labor codes or standards that must be met, and different codes of contract law and standards of enforcement (e.g., case law versus common law versus no functioning legal system). In addition, political considerations may enhance or detract from business negotiations in various countries at different times. For instance, the open business environment in the former Soviet republics in the 1990s is quite different than the closed environment of the 1960s, and conducting business in China today is quite different than even 10 years ago.

International Economics   The exchange value of international currencies naturally fluctuates, and this factor must be considered when negotiating in different countries. In which currency will the agreement be made? The risk is typically greater for the party who must pay in the other country's currency.[10] The less stable the currency, the greater the risk for both parties. In addition, any change in the value of a currency (upward or downward) can significantly affect the value of the agreement for both parties, changing a mutually valuable deal into a windfall profit for one and a large loss for the other. Many countries also control the currency flowing across their borders. Frequently, purchases within these countries may be made only with hard currencies that are brought into the country by foreign parties, and domestic organizations are unable to purchase foreign products or negotiate outcomes that require payment in foreign currencies.

Foreign Governments and Bureaucracies   Countries differ in the extent to which the government regulates industries and organizations. Firms in the United States are relatively free from government intervention, although some industries are more heavily regulated than others (e.g., power generation, defense) and some states have tougher environmental regulations than others. Generally, business negotiations in the United States occur without government approval and the parties to a negotiation decide whether or not to engage in an agreement based on business reasons alone. In contrast, the governments of many developing and (former) communist countries closely supervise imports and joint ventures,[11] and frequently an agency of the government has a monopoly in dealing with foreign organizations.[12] In addition, political considerations, such as the effect of the negotiation on the government treasury and the general economy of the country, may influence the negotiations more heavily than what businesses in developed countries would consider legitimate business reasons.

Instability   Businesses negotiating within North America are accustomed to a degree of stability that is not present in many areas of the world. Instability may take many forms, including a lack of resources that Americans commonly expect during business negotiations (paper, electricity, computers), shortages of other goods and services (food, reliable transportation, potable water), and political instability (coups, sudden shifts in government policy, major currency revaluations). The challenge for international negotiators is to anticipate changes accurately and with enough lead time to adjust for their consequences. Salacuse suggests that negotiators facing unstable circumstances should include clauses in their contracts that allow easy cancellation or neutral arbitration and consider purchasing insurance policies to guarantee contract provisions.[13] This advice presumes that contracts will be honored and that specific contract clauses will be culturally acceptable to the other party.

Ideology   Negotiators within the United States generally share a common ideology about the benefits of individualism and capitalism. Americans believe strongly in individual rights, the superiority of private investment, and the importance of making a profit in business.[14] Negotiators from other countries do not always share this ideology. For example, negotiators from some countries (e.g., China, France) may instead stress group rights as more important than individual rights and public investment as a better allocation of resources than private investment; they may also have different prescriptions for earning and sharing profit. Ideological clashes increase the communication challenges in international negotiations in the broadest sense because the parties may disagree at the most fundamental levels about what is being negotiated.

Culture   People from different cultures appear to negotiate differently.[15] In addition to behaving differently, people from different cultures may also interpret the fundamental processes of negotiations differently (such as what factors are negotiable and the purpose of the negotiations). According to Salacuse, people in some cultures approach negotiations deductively (they move from the general to the specific) whereas people from other cultures are more inductive (they settle on a series of specific issues that become the area of general agreement).[16] In some cultures, the parties negotiate the substantive issues while considering the relationship between the parties to be more or less incidental. In other cultures, the relationship between the parties is the main focus of the negotiation, and the substantive issues of the deal itself are more or less incidental.[17] There is also evidence that preference for conflict resolution models varies across cultures.[18]

External Stakeholders   Phatak and Habib defined external stakeholders as "the various people and organizations that have an interest or stake in the outcome of the negotiations."[19] These stakeholders include business associations, labor unions, embassies, and industry associations, among others.[20] For example, a labor union might oppose negotiations with foreign companies because of fears that domestic jobs will be lost. International negotiators can receive a great deal of promotion and guidance from their government via the trade section of their embassy and from other businesspeople via professional associations (e.g., a Chamber of Commerce in the country in which they are negotiating).

Immediate Context

At many points throughout this book we have discussed aspects of negotiation that relate to immediate context factors, but without considering their international implications. In this section, we will discuss the concepts from the Phatak and Habib model of international negotiation, highlighting that the immediate context can have an important influence on negotiation.[21]

Relative Bargaining Power   One aspect of international negotiations that has received considerable research attention is the relative bargaining power of the two parties involved. Joint ventures have been the subject of a great deal of research on international negotiation, and relative power has frequently been operationalized as the amount of equity (financial and other investment) that each side is willing to invest in the new venture.[22] The presumption is that the party who invests more equity has more power in the negotiation and therefore will have more influence on the negotiation process and outcome. Research by Yan and Gray questions this perspective, however, and suggests that relative power is not simply a function of equity, but appears to be due to management control of the project, which was found to be heavily influenced by negotiating.[23] In addition, several factors seem to be able to influence relative power, including special access to markets (e.g., in current or former communist countries), distribution systems (e.g., in Asia, where creating a new distribution system is so expensive that it may be a barrier to entering markets), or managing government relations (e.g., where the language and culture are quite different).

Levels of Conflict   The level of conflict and type of interdependence between the parties to a cross-cultural negotiation will also influence the negotiation process and outcome. High-conflict situations—those based on ethnicity, identity, or geography—are more difficult to resolve.[24] Ongoing conflicts in Zimbabwe, the Middle East, and Sudan are but a few examples. There is historical evidence, however, that civil wars concluded through a comprehensive, institutionalized agreement that prohibits the use of coercive power and promotes the fair distributions of resources and political power lead to more stable settlements.[25] Also important is the extent to which negotiators frame the negotiation differently or conceptualize what the negotiation concerns (see Chapters 4 and 5 for extended discussions of framing), and this appears to vary across cultures,[26] as do the ways in which negotiators respond to conflict.[27] For example, Fisher, Ury, and Patton discuss how conflicts in the Middle East were difficult to deal with for several years because the different parties had such different ways of conceptualizing what the dispute was about (e.g., security, sovereignty, historical rights).[28] Diplomatic "back-channel" negotiations conducted in secret may help resolve high conflict situations, but their success is not guaranteed.[29]

Relationship between Negotiators   Phatak and Habib suggest that the relationships developed among the principal negotiating parties before the actual negotiations will also have an important impact on the negotiation process and outcome.[30] Negotiations are part of the larger relationship between two parties. The history of relations between the parties will influence the current negotiation (e.g., how the parties frame the negotiation), just as the current negotiation will become part of any future negotiations between the parties. (See Chapter 9 for a detailed discussion of this point.)

Desired Outcomes   Tangible and intangible factors also play a large role in determining the outcomes of international negotiations. Countries often use international negotiations to achieve both domestic and international political goals. For instance, one of the main goals of the North Vietnamese during the Paris Peace Talks to end the war in Vietnam was to be recognized formally by the other parties to the negotiation. Similarly, in recent ethnic conflicts around the world, numerous parties have threatened that unless they are recognized at the formal negotiations they will disrupt the successful resolution of the conflict (e.g., Northern Ireland). Ongoing tension can exist between one party's short-term objectives for the current negotiations and its influence on the parties' long-term relations. In trade negotiations between the United States and Japan, both sides often settle for less than their desired short-term outcomes because of the importance of the long-term relationship.[31]

Immediate Stakeholders   The immediate stakeholders in the negotiation include the negotiators themselves as well as the people they directly represent, such as their managers, employers, and boards of directors.[32] Stakeholders can influence negotiators in many ways (see Chapter 9). The skills, abilities, and international experience of the negotiators themselves clearly can have a large impact on the process and outcome of international negotiations. In addition, the personal motivations of the principal negotiators and the other immediate stakeholders can have a large influence on the negotiation process and outcomes. People may be motivated by several intangible factors in the negotiation, including how the process or outcome will make them look in the eyes of both the other party and their own superiors, as well as other intangible factors like their personal career advancement.[33]

Section Summary

In summary, models such as Phatak and Habib's are very good devices for guiding our thinking about international negotiation.[34] It is always important to remember, however, that negotiation processes and outcomes are influenced by many factors, and that the influence of these factors can change in magnitude over time.[35] The challenge for every international negotiator is to understand the simultaneous, multiple influences of several factors on the negotiation process and outcome and to update this understanding regularly as circumstances change. This also means that planning for international negotiations is especially important, as is the need to adjust as new information is obtained through monitoring the environmental and immediate contexts.

Conceptualizing Culture and Negotiation

The most frequently studied aspect of international negotiation is culture, and the amount of research on the effects of culture on negotiation has increased substantially in the past 20 years.[36] There are many different meanings of the concept of culture, but all definitions share two important aspects.[37] First, culture is a group-level phenomenon. That means that a defined group of people shares beliefs, values, and behavioral expectations. The second common element of culture is that cultural beliefs, values, and behavioral expectations are learned and passed on to new members of the group.

Robert Janosik identified four ways that culture has been conceptualized in international negotiation: as learned behavior, as shared values, as dialectic, and in context.[38] While there are similarities and differences among the four approaches, each stresses the importance of understanding how culture affects negotiation.

Culture as Learned Behavior

One approach to understanding the effects of culture documents the systematic negotiation behavior of people in different cultures. Rather than focusing on why members of a given culture behave in certain ways, this pragmatic, nuts-and-bolts approach concentrates on creating a catalogue of behaviors that foreign negotiators should expect when entering a host culture.[39] Many popular books and articles on international negotiation treat culture as learned behavior, providing lists of dos and don'ts to obey when negotiating with people from different cultures. For instance, Solomon suggests that international negotiators should recognize that Chinese negotiators will begin negotiations with a search for broad principles and building a relationship.[40] This will be followed by a long period of assessment in which the boundaries of the relationship will be explored; a decision about whether or not to strike an agreement will eventually be made, and this agreement will form the foundation for further concessions and modifications. Research consistent with this perspective has examined the effects of culture on displaying emotion during negotiation,[41] and on face-saving behavior.[42]

Culture as Shared Values

The second approach to conceptualizing culture concentrates on understanding central values and norms and then building a model for how these norms and values influence negotiations within that culture.[43] Cross-cultural comparisons are made by finding the important norms and values that distinguish one culture from another and then understanding how these differences will influence international negotiation.

Hofstede's Model of Cultural Dimensions   Geert Hofstede conducted an extensive program of research on cultural dimensions in international business.[44] Hofstede examined data on values that had been gathered from more than 100,000 IBM employees around the world, and more than 50 cultures were included in the initial study. Statistical analysis of these data suggests that four dimensions could be used to describe the important differences among the cultures in the study: individualism/collectivism, power distance, career success/quality of life, and uncertainty avoidance.[45] Cultures ranking in the top 10 on each of these dimensions are listed in Table 11.1, and each dimension is discussed next.

1. Individualism/Collectivism   The individualism/collectivism dimension describes the extent to which a society is organized around individuals or the group. Individualistic societies encourage their young to be independent and to look after themselves. Collectivistic societies

TABLE 11.1 | Cultures Ranking in the Top 10 on the Cultural Dimensions Reported by Hofstede (1991)

Individualism	Power Distance	Quality of Life	Uncertainty Avoidance
1. United States	1. Malaysia	1. Sweden	1. Greece
2. Australia	2. Guatemala	2. Norway	2. Portugal
3. Great Britain	Panama	3. Netherlands	3. Guatemala
4. Canada	4. Philippines	4. Denmark	4. Uruguay
Netherlands	5. Mexico	5. Costa Rica	5. Belgium
6. New Zealand	Venezuela	Yugoslavia	El Salvador
7. Italy	7. Arab countries	7. Finland	7. Japan
8. Belgium	8. Ecuador	8. Chile	8. Yugoslavia
9. Denmark	Indonesia	9. Portugal	9. Peru
10. France	10. India	10. Thailand	10. Argentina
Sweden	West Africa		Chile
			Costa Rica
			Panama
			Spain

Source: Based on G. Hofstede, *Culture and Organizations: Software of the Mind* (London: McGraw-Hill, 1991). Reproduced with permission of The McGraw-Hill Companies.

integrate individuals into cohesive groups that take responsibility for the welfare of each individual. Hofstede suggests that the focus on relationships in collectivist societies plays a critical role in negotiations—negotiations with the same party can continue for years, and changing a negotiator changes the relationship, which may take a long time to rebuild. Contrast this with individualistic societies, in which negotiators are considered interchangeable and competency (rather than relationship) is an important consideration when choosing a negotiator. The implication is that negotiators from collectivist cultures will strongly depend on cultivating and sustaining a long-term relationship, whereas negotiators from individualistic cultures may be more likely to swap negotiators, using whatever short-term criteria seem appropriate.

2. Power Distance   The power distance dimension describes "the extent to which the less powerful members of organizations and institutions (like the family) accept and expect that power is distributed unequally."[46] According to Hofstede, cultures with greater power distance will be more likely to concentrate decision making at the top, and all important decisions will have to be finalized by the leader. Cultures with low power distance are more likely to spread the decision making throughout the organization, and while leaders are respected, it is also possible to question their decisions. The consequences for international negotiations are that negotiators from comparatively high power distance cultures may need to seek approval from their supervisors more frequently, and for more issues, leading to a slower negotiation process.

3. Career Success/Quality of Life   Hofstede found that cultures differed in the extent to which they held values that promoted career success or quality of life. Cultures promoting career success were characterized by "the acquisition of money and things, and not caring for others, the quality of life, or people."[47] Cultures promoting quality of life were characterized by concern for relationships and nurturing. According to Hofstede, this dimension influences negotiation by increasing the competitiveness when negotiators from career success cultures meet; negotiators from quality of life cultures are more likely to have empathy for the other party and to seek compromise.[48]

4. Uncertainty Avoidance   Uncertainty avoidance "indicates to what extent a culture programs its members to feel either uncomfortable or comfortable in unstructured situations."[49] Unstructured situations are characterized by rapid change and new situations, whereas structured situations are stable and secure. Negotiators from high uncertainty avoidance cultures are less comfortable with ambiguous situations and are more likely to seek stable rules and procedures when they negotiate. Negotiators from low uncertainty avoidance cultures are likely to adapt to quickly changing situations and will be less uncomfortable when the rules of the negotiation are ambiguous or shifting.

Hofstede's model has become a dominant force in cross-cultural research in international business, although the model is not without its skeptics.[50] The most important criticism of the model is that the research was conducted with a sample of participants that was not truly representative of the richness of different cultures because there were proportionally too many males, members of the middle class were overrepresented, the education levels were higher than average, and the participants came from one company (IBM). In other words, there is some concern that Hofstede's model underestimates the true richness of value differences across cultures.

Schwartz's 10 Cultural Values   The work of Shalom Schwartz and his colleagues provides a very comprehensive example of the culture-as-values perspective (see Figure 11.2).[51] Schwartz concentrated on identifying the motivational goal underlying cultural values and found 10 fundamental values (see the values within the circle in Figure 11.2). These 10 values may conflict or be compatible with each other, and the values on the opposite side of the circle from a given value are most likely to be in conflict. Schwartz also proposed that the 10 values may be represented in two bipolar dimensions: openness to change/conservatism and self-transcendence/self-enhancement (see the outer wheel in Figure 11.2). Schwartz's cultural values and the two bipolar dimensions provide the most comprehensive exploration of cultural values to date, and they have been validated with extensive research. While this work has been slow to appear in the study of cross-cultural negotiation, references to it have started to appear.[52] The advantage of Schwartz's 10 values is the richness with which they can be used to describe a culture. The disadvantage is while this richness may increase cultural understanding, it does not provide clear managerial advice about negotiating across cultures.

FIGURE 11.2 | Schwartz's 10 Cultural Values

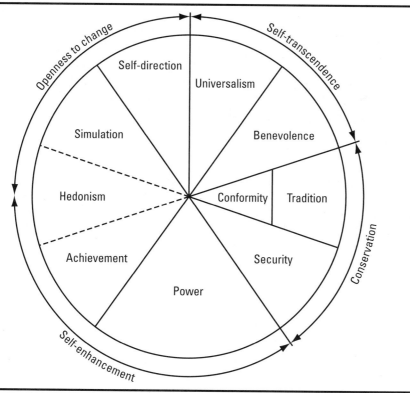

The presumption is that negotiators who better understand another culture will be more successful negotiating within that culture.

Section Summary

The culture-as-shared-value perspective provides explanations for why cross-cultural negotiations are difficult and have a tendency to break down. For example, a central value in the United States is individualism. Americans are expected to make individual decisions, defend their points of view, and take strong stands on issues that are important to them. Contrast this with a central value of the Chinese—collectivism.[53] Chinese negotiators are expected to make group decisions, defend the group above the individual, and take strong stands on issues important to the group. When Americans and Chinese negotiate, differences in the individualism/collectivism cultural value may influence negotiation in many ways. For instance, (1) the Chinese will likely take more time when negotiating because they have to gain the consensus of their group before they strike a deal; (2) Chinese use of multiple lines of authority will lead to mixed signals about the true needs of the group, and no single individual may understand all the requirements; and (3) because power is shared by many different people and offices, it may be difficult for foreigners to identify their appropriate counterpart in the Chinese bureaucracy.[54]

Culture as Dialectic

The third approach to using culture to understand international negotiation identified by Janosik recognizes that all cultures contain dimensions or tensions that are called *dialectics*.[55] These tensions are nicely illustrated in parables from the Judeo-Christian tradition. Consider the following examples: "too many cooks spoil the broth" and "two heads are better than one." These adages offer conflicting guidance for those considering whether to work on a task alone or in a group. This reflects a dialectic, or tension, within the Judeo-Christian tradition regarding the values of independence and teamwork. Neither complete independence nor complete teamwork works all the time; each has advantages and disadvantages that vary as a function of the circumstances (e.g., the type of decision to be made or task to be addressed). According to Janosik, the culture-as-dialectic approach has advantages over the culture-as-shared-values approach because it can explain variations within cultures (i.e., not every person in the same culture shares the same values to the same extent).[56] The culture-as-dialectic approach does not provide international negotiators with simple advice about how to behave in a given negotiation. Rather, it suggests that negotiators who want to have successful international negotiations need to appreciate the richness of the cultures in which they will be operating.

The culture as dialectic perspective starts with a deep understanding of a culture and uses that understanding to create negotiation metaphors to have a rich understanding of how negotiations unfold within a culture. Negotiators with stronger understanding of the negotiation metaphor within a culture are more likely to succeed in negotiations.

Culture in Context

Proponents of the fourth approach to using culture to understand international negotiations recognize that human behavior is not determined by a single cause. Rather, all behavior may be understood at many different levels simultaneously, and a social behavior as complex as negotiation is determined by many different factors, one of which is culture. Other factors that may be important determinants of negotiation behavior include personality, social context, and environmental factors.[57] Proponents of the culture-in-context approach recognize that negotiation behavior is multiply determined, and using culture as the sole explanation of behavior is oversimplifying a complex social process. Kumar and Worm make this point succinctly: "while negotiations are always in the present they are influenced by what looms in the past and are constrained by the shadow of the future."[58]

Recent theory and research in international negotiation has taken a culture-in-context approach. For instance, Tinsley, Brett, Shapiro, and Okumura proposed a *cultural complexity theory* in which they suggest that cultural values will have a direct effect on negotiations in some circumstances and a moderated effect in others.[59] Values are proposed to have a direct effect when they have strong effects across several different contexts (e.g., American individuality), whereas values that have a moderated effect are those that have different contextual instigators in the culture. For example, France has both monarchical and democratic traditions, both of which can influence negotiation behavior depending on the context.[60] Fang suggests that traditions of Mao, Confucius, and Sun Tzu provide multiple influence on Chinese negotiators that can vary by context. Another example of the culture-in-context approach comes from Adair and Brett,[61] who found that communication patterns were different for negotiators from high- and low-context cultures at different stages of the negotiation.[62]

The culture-in-context models are becoming more and more complex in order to explain nuanced differences in cross-cultural negotiations. As this complexity increases, however, they become less useful for practitioners of cross-cultural negotiation to put into practice.[63] Their strength, however, is in forging a deeper understanding of how cross-cultural negotiations work and using that understanding to prepare and engage more effectively in international negotiation.

The Influence of Culture on Negotiation: Managerial Perspectives

Cultural differences have been suggested to influence negotiation in several different ways. In this section we discuss 10 different ways that culture can influence negotiations.[64]

Definition of Negotiation

The fundamental definition of negotiation, what is negotiable, and what occurs when we negotiate can differ greatly across cultures.[65] For instance, "Americans tend to view negotiating as a competitive process of offers and counteroffers, while the Japanese tend to view the negotiation as an opportunity for information-sharing."[66]

Negotiation Opportunity

Culture influences the way negotiators perceive an opportunity as distributive versus integrative. Negotiators in North America are predisposed to perceive negotiation as being fundamentally distributive.[67] This is not the case outside North America, however, as there appears to be a great deal of variation across cultures in the extent to which negotiation situations are initially perceived as distributive or integrative.[68] Cross-cultural negotiations are influenced by the extent that negotiators in different cultures have fundamental agreement or disagreement about whether or not the situation is distributive or integrative.

Selection of Negotiators

The criteria used to select who will participate in a negotiation is different across cultures. These criteria can include knowledge of the subject matter being negotiated, seniority, family connections, gender, age, experience, and status. Different cultures weigh these criteria differently, leading to varying expectations about what is appropriate in different types of negotiations. For instance, in China it is important to establish relationship connections early in the negotiation process, and selection of the appropriate negotiators can help with this.[69]

Protocol

Cultures differ in the degree to which protocol, or the formality of the relations between the two negotiating parties, is important. American culture is among the least formal cultures in the world. A familiar communication style is quite common; first names are used, for example, while titles are ignored. Contrast this with other cultures. Many European countries (e.g., France, Germany, England) are very formal, and not using the proper title when addressing someone (e.g., Mr., Dr., Professor, Lord) is considered insulting.[70] The formal calling cards or business cards used in many countries in the Pacific Rim (e.g., China, Japan) are essential for introductions there. Negotiators who forget to bring business cards or who write messages on them are frequently breaching protocol and insulting their counterpart.[71] Even the way that business cards are presented, hands are shaken, and dress codes are observed are subject to interpretation by negotiators and can be the foundation of attributions about a person's background and personality.

Communication

Cultures influence how people communicate, both verbally and nonverbally. There are also differences in body language across cultures; a behavior that may be highly insulting in one culture may be completely innocuous in another.[72] To avoid offending the other party in negotiations, the international negotiator needs to observe cultural rules of communication carefully. For example, placing feet on a desk in the United States signals power or relaxation; in Thailand, it is considered very insulting. Clearly, there is a lot of information about how to communicate that an international negotiator must remember in order not to insult, anger, or embarrass the other party during negotiations. Culture-specific books and articles can provide considerable advice to international negotiators about how to communicate in various cultures; seeking such advice is an essential aspect of planning for international negotiations.[73]

Time Sensitivity

Cultures largely determine what time means and how it affects negotiations.[74] In the United States, people tend to respect time by appearing for meetings at an appointed hour, being sensitive to not wasting the time of other people, and generally holding that "faster" is better than "slower" because it symbolizes high productivity. Other cultures have quite different views about time. In more traditional societies, especially in hot climates, the pace is slower than in the United States. This tends to reduce the focus on time, at least in the short term. Arab-speaking Islamic cultures appear to focus more on event-time than clock-time where "in clock-time cultures people schedule events according to the clock; in event-time cultures, events schedule people."[75] Americans are perceived by other cultures as enslaved by their clocks because they watch time carefully and guard it as a valuable resource. In some cultures, such as China and Latin America, time per se is not important. The focus of negotiations is on the task, regardless of the amount of time it takes. The opportunity for misunderstandings because of different perceptions of time is great during cross-cultural negotiations. Americans may be perceived as always being in a hurry and as flitting from one task to another, while Chinese or Latin American negotiators may appear to Americans to be doing nothing and wasting time.

Risk Propensity

Cultures vary in the extent to which they are willing to take risks. Some cultures tend to produce bureaucratic, conservative decision makers who want a great deal of information before making decisions. Other cultures produce negotiators who are more entrepreneurial and who are willing to act and take risks when they have incomplete information (e.g., "nothing ventured, nothing gained"). According to Foster, Americans fall on the risk-taking end of the continuum, as do some Asian cultures, while some European cultures are quite conservative (e.g., Greece).[76] The orientation of a culture toward risk will have a large effect on what is negotiated and the content of the negotiated outcome. Negotiators in risk-oriented cultures will be more willing to move early on a deal and will generally take more chances. Those in risk-avoiding cultures are more likely to seek further information and take a wait-and-see stance.

Groups versus Individuals

Cultures differ according to whether they emphasize the individual or the group. The United States is very much an individual-oriented culture, where being independent and assertive is valued and praised. Group-oriented cultures, in contrast, favor the superiority of the group and see individual needs as second to the group's needs. Group-oriented cultures value fitting in and reward loyal team players; those who dare to be different are socially ostracized—a large price to pay in a group-oriented society. This cultural difference can have a variety of effects on negotiation. Americans are more likely to have one individual who is responsible for the final decision, whereas group-oriented cultures like the Japanese are more likely to have a group responsible for the decision. Decision making in group-oriented cultures involves consensus and may take considerably more time than American negotiators are used to. In addition, because so many people can be involved in the negotiations in group-oriented cultures, and because their participation may be sequential rather than simultaneous, American negotiators may be faced with a series of discussions over the same issues and materials with many different people. In a negotiation in China, one of the authors of this book met with more than six different people on successive days, going over the same ground with different negotiators and interpreters, until the negotiation was concluded.

Nature of Agreements

Culture also has an important effect both on concluding agreements and on what form the negotiated agreement takes. In the United States, agreements are typically based on logic (e.g., the low-cost producer gets the deal), are often formalized, and are enforced through the legal system if such standards are not honored. In other cultures, however, obtaining the deal may be based on who you are (e.g., your family or political connections) rather than on what you can do. In addition, agreements do not mean the same thing in all cultures. Foster notes that the Chinese frequently use memorandums of agreement to formalize a relationship and to signal the start of negotiations (mutual favors and compromise).[77] Frequently, however, Americans will interpret the same memorandum of agreement as the completion of the negotiations that is enforceable in a court of law. Again, cultural differences in how to close an agreement and what exactly that agreement means can lead to confusion and misunderstandings.

Emotionalism

Culture appears to influence the extent to which negotiators display emotions.[78] These emotions may be used as tactics, or they may be a natural response to positive and negative circumstances during the negotiation.[79] While personality likely also plays a role in the expression of emotions, there also appears to be considerable cross-cultural differences, and the rules that govern general emotional displays in a culture are likely to be present during negotiation.[80]

In summary, a great deal of practical advice has been written about the importance of culture in international negotiations. Although the word culture has been used to mean several different things, it is clearly a critical aspect of international negotiation that can have a broad influence on many aspects of the process and outcome of international negotiation. We now turn to examining research perspectives on how culture influences negotiation.

Culturally Responsive Negotiation Strategies

Although a great deal has been written about the challenge of international and cross-cultural negotiations, far less attention has been paid to what negotiators should do when faced with negotiating with someone from another culture. The advice by many theorists in this area, either explicitly or implicitly, has been, "When in Rome, act as the Romans do."[81] In other words, negotiators are advised to be aware of the effects of cultural differences on negotiation and to take them into account when they negotiate. Many theorists appear to assume implicitly that the best way to manage cross-cultural negotiations is to be sensitive to the cultural norms of the other negotiator and to modify one's strategy to be consistent with behaviors that occur in that culture.

Several factors suggest that negotiators should *not* make large modifications to their approach when negotiating cross-culturally, however:

1. Negotiators may not be able to modify their approach effectively. It takes years to understand another culture deeply, and negotiators typically do not have the time necessary to gain this understanding before beginning a negotiation. Although a little understanding of another culture is clearly better than ignorance, it may not be

enough to enable negotiators to make effective adjustments to their negotiation strategy. Attempting to match the strategies and tactics used by negotiators in another culture is a daunting task that requires fluency in their language as well as deep cultural understanding. Even simple words may be translated in several different ways with different nuances, making the challenge of communicating in different languages overwhelming.[82]

2. Even if negotiators can modify their approach effectively, it does not mean that this will translate automatically into a better negotiation outcome. It is quite possible that the other party will modify his or her approach too. The results in this situation can be disasterous, with each side trying to act like the other "should" be acting, and both sides not really understanding what the other party is doing. Consider the following example contrasting typical American and Japanese negotiation styles. Americans are more likely to start negotiations with an extreme offer in order to leave room for concessions. Japanese are more likely to start negotiations with gathering information in order to understand with whom they are dealing and what the relationship will be. Assume that both parties understand their own and the other party's cultural tendencies (this is a large assumption that frequently is not met). Now assume that each party, acting out of respect for the other, decides to "act like the Romans do" and to adopt the approach of the other party. The possibilities for confusion are endless. When the Americans gather information about the Japanese, are they truly interested or are they playing a role? It will be clear that they are not acting like Americans, but the strategy that they are using may not be readily identified. How will the Americans interpret the Japanese behavior? The Americans have prepared well for their negotiations and understand that the Japanese do not present extreme positions early in negotiations. When the Japanese do present an extreme position early in negotiations (in order to adapt to the American negotiation style), how should the Americans interpret this behavior? The Americans likely will think, "That must be what they really want, because they don't typically open with extreme offers." Adopting the other party's approach does not guarantee success, and in fact it may lead to more confusion than acting like yourself (where at least your behavior is understood within your own cultural context).

3. Research suggests that negotiators may naturally negotiate differently when they are with people from their own culture than when they are with people from other cultures.[83] The implications of this research are that a deep understanding of how people in other cultures negotiate, such as Costa Ricans negotiating with each other, may not help an American negotiating with a Costa Rican.[84]

4. Research by Francis suggests that moderate adaptation may be more effective than "acting as the Romans do."[85] In a simulation study of Americans' responses to negotiators from other countries, Francis found that negotiators from a familiar culture (Japan) who made moderate adaptations to American ways were perceived more positively than negotiators who made no changes or those who made large adaptations. Although these findings did not replicate for negotiators from a less familiar culture (Korea), more research needs to be conducted to understand why. At the very least, the results of this study suggest that large adaptations by international negotiators will not always be effective.

Recent research findings have provided some specific advice about how to negotiate cross-culturally. Rubin and Sander suggest that during preparation, negotiators should concentrate on understanding three things: (1) their own biases, strengths, and weaknesses; (2) the other negotiator as an individual; and (3) the other negotiator's cultural context.[86] Brett and her colleagues suggest that cross-cultural negotiators should go further and ask themselves a series of questions about how culture may influence information sharing and the negotiation process (e.g., Does this culture share information directly or indirectly?[87] Is it monochronic or polychronic?). Learning about how another culture shares information and structures the negotiation process may help negotiators plan more strategically for the negotiation.[88] Finally, Adair, Okumura, and Brett suggest that both parties in a cross-cultural negotiation need to be prepared to communicate in the other party's culturally preferred method of direct or indirect communication in order to increase the chances of a successful negotiation outcome.[89]

Stephen Weiss has proposed a useful way of thinking about the options we have when negotiating with someone from another culture.[90] Weiss observes that negotiators may choose from among eight different culturally responsive strategies. These strategies may be used individually or sequentially, and the strategies can be switched as the negotiation progresses. When choosing a strategy, negotiators should be aware of their own and the other party's culture in general, understand the specific factors in the current relationship, and predict or try to influence the other party's approach.[91] Weiss's culturally responsive strategies may be arranged into three groups, based on the level of familiarity (low, moderate, high) that a negotiator has with the other party's culture. Within each group there are some strategies that the negotiator may use individually (unilateral strategies) and others that involve the participation of the other party (joint strategies).

Low Familiarity

Employ Agents or Advisers (Unilateral Strategy)   One approach for negotiators who have very low familiarity with the other party's culture is to hire an agent or adviser who is familiar with the cultures of both parties. This relationship may range from having the other party conduct the negotiations under supervision (agent) to receiving regular or occasional advice during the negotiations (adviser). Although agents or advisers may create other challenges, they may be quite useful for negotiators who have little awareness of the other party's culture and little time to prepare.

Bring in a Mediator (Joint Strategy)   Many types of mediators may be used in cross-cultural negotiations, ranging from someone who conducts introductions and then withdraws to someone who is present throughout the negotiation and takes responsibility for managing the negotiation process. Interpreters will often play this role, providing both parties with more information than the mere translation of words during negotiations. Mediators may encourage one side or the other to adopt one culture's approaches or a third cultural approach (the mediator's home culture).

Induce the Other Negotiator to Use Your Approach (Joint Strategy)   Another option is to persuade the other party to use your approach. There are many ways to do this, ranging from making a polite request to asserting rudely that your way is best. More subtly, negotiators can continue to respond to the other party's requests in their own language because they "cannot express themselves well enough" in the other's language. Although this strategy has many advantages for the negotiator with low familiarity, there are also some disadvantages. For instance, a Japanese party may become irritated or insulted by having to make the extra effort to deal with a Canadian negotiator on Canadian cultural terms. In addition, the other negotiator may also have a strategic advantage because he or she may now attempt more extreme tactics and excuse their use on the basis of his or her "cultural ignorance" (after all, negotiators can't expect the other party to understand everything about how they negotiate).

Moderate Familiarity

Adapt to the Other Negotiator's Approach (Unilateral Strategy)   This strategy involves negotiators making conscious changes to their approach so that it is more appealing to the other party. Rather than trying to act like the other party, negotiators using this strategy maintain a firm grasp on their own approach but make modifications to help relations with the other party. These modifications may include acting in a less extreme manner, eliminating some behaviors, and adopting some of the other party's behaviors. The challenge in using this strategy is to know which behaviors to modify, eliminate, or adopt. In addition, it is not clear that the other party will interpret modifications in the way that negotiators have intended.

Coordinate Adjustment (Joint Strategy)   This strategy involves both parties making mutual adjustments to find a common process for negotiation. Although this can be done implicitly, it is more likely to occur explicitly ("How would you like to proceed?"), and it can be thought of as a special instance of negotiating the process of negotiation. This strategy requires a moderate amount of knowledge about the other party's culture and at least some facility with his or her language (comprehension, if not the ability to speak). Coordinate adjustment occurs on a daily basis in Montreal, the most bilingual city in North America (85 percent of Montrealers understand both English and French). It is standard practice for businesspeople in Montreal to negotiate the process of negotiation before the substantive discussion begins. The outcomes of this discussion are variations on the theme of whether the negotiations will occur in English or French, with a typical outcome being that either party may speak either language. Negotiations often occur in both languages, and frequently the person with the best second-language skills will switch languages to facilitate the discussion. Another outcome that occasionally occurs has both parties speaking in their second language (i.e., the French speaker will negotiate in English while the English speaker will negotiate in French) to demonstrate respect for the other party. Another type of coordinate adjustment occurs when the two negotiating parties adopt aspects of a third culture to facilitate their negotiations. For instance, during a trip to Latin America, one of the authors of this book conducted discussions in French with a Latin American colleague who spoke Spanish and French, but not English. On a subsequent trip to China, negotiations were conducted in French, English, and Chinese because each of the six participants spoke two of the three languages.

High Familiarity

Embrace the Other Negotiator's Approach (Unilateral Strategy)   This strategy involves completely adopting the approach of the other negotiator. To be used successfully, the negotiator needs to be completely bilingual and bicultural. In essence, the negotiator using this strategy doesn't act *like* a Roman; he or she *is* a Roman. This strategy is costly in preparation time and expense, and it places the negotiator using it under considerable stress because it is difficult to switch back and forth rapidly between cultures. However, there is much to gain by using this strategy because the other negotiator can be approached and understood completely on his or her own terms.

Improvise an Approach (Joint Strategy)   This strategy involves crafting an approach that is specifically tailored to the negotiation situation, other negotiator, and circumstances. To use this approach, both parties to the negotiation need to have high familiarity with the other party's culture and a strong understanding of the individual characteristics of the other negotiator. The negotiation that emerges with this approach can be crafted by adopting aspects from both cultures when they will be useful. This approach is the most flexible of the eight strategies, which is both its strength and weakness. Flexibility is a strength because it allows the approach to be crafted to the circumstances at hand, but it is a weakness because there are few general prescriptive statements that can be made about how to use this strategy.

Effect Symphony (Joint Strategy)   This strategy allows negotiators to create a new approach that may include aspects of either home culture or adopt practices from a third culture. Professional diplomats use such an approach when the customs, norms, and language they use transcend national borders and form their own culture (diplomacy). Use of this strategy is complex and involves a great deal of time and effort. It works best when the parties are familiar with each other and with both home cultures and have a common structure (like that of professional diplomats) for the negotiation. Risks of using this strategy include costs due to confusion, lost time, and the overall effort required to make it work.

Chapter Summary

This chapter examined various aspects of a growing field of negotiation that explores the complexities of international and cross-cultural negotiation. We began the chapter with a discussion of the art and science of negotiation. Next we considered some of the factors that make international negotiations different. Phatak and Habib suggest that both the environmental and the immediate context have important effects on international negotiations.[92] We then discussed Salacuse's description of the environmental factors that influence international negotiations: (1) political and legal pluralism, (2) international economics, (3) foreign governments and bureaucracies, (4) instability, (5) ideology, and (6) culture.[93] We added one more environmental factor—external stakeholders—from Phatak and Habib.[94] Phatak and

Habib's five immediate context factors were discussed next: (1) relative bargaining power, (2) levels of conflict, (3) relationship between negotiators, (4) desired outcomes, and (5) immediate stakeholders. Each of these environmental and immediate context factors acts to make international negotiations more difficult, and effective international negotiators need to understand how to manage them.

Next, we turned to a discussion of how to conceptualize culture. Robert Janosik suggests that researchers and practitioners of negotiation use culture in at least four different ways: (1) culture as learned behavior, (2) culture as shared values, (3) culture as dialectics, and (4) culture in context.[95] We then examined two perspectives on how cultural differences can influence negotiations. From the managerial perspective, we discussed 10 ways that culture can influence negotiation: (1) the definition of negotiation, (2) the negotiation opportunity, (3) the selection of negotiators, (4) protocol, (5) communication, (6) time sensitivity, (7) risk propensity, (8) groups versus individuals, (9) the nature of agreements, and (10) emotionalism.

The chapter concluded with a discussion of how to manage cultural differences in negotiation. Weiss presents eight different culturally responsive strategies that negotiators can use with a negotiator from a different culture. Some of these strategies may be used individually, whereas others are used jointly with the other negotiator. Weiss indicates that one critical aspect of choosing the correct strategy for a given negotiation is the degree of familiarity (low, moderate, or high) that a negotiator has with the other culture. However, even those with high familiarity with another culture are faced with a daunting task if they want to modify their strategy completely when they deal with the other culture.

Endnotes

[1] Hopmann, 1995; Weiss, 2006.

[2] Sebenius, 2002a.

[3] It is important to recognize that this book has been written from a North American perspective, and that this cultural filter has influenced how we think about negotiation (Brett and Gelfand, 2004), both in our choices about what we discuss and because we use Americans as the base from which to make comparisons to other cultures. That is not to say that all Americans share the same culture. Descriptions of the American negotiation style may be found in Druckman, 1996; Koh, 1996; Le Poole, 1989; and McDonald, 1996. At some level, however, Americans do share (more or less) a common culture that is different from that of other countries. While recognizing the differences within the United States, we will use some common aspects of American culture in our discussion of international and cross-cultural negotiation.

[4] For more examples see Acuff, 1993; Hendon and Hendon, 1990; and Kennedy, 1985.

[5] Rubin and Sander, 1991; Sebenius, 2002b; Weiss, 2003.

[6] Dialdin, Kopelman, Adair, Brett, Okumura, and Lytle, 1999; also see Huang and van de Vliert, 2004; Matsumoto and Yoo, 2006.

[7] Phatak and Habib, 1996.

[8] Salacuse, 1988.

[9] Phatak and Habib, 1996.

[10] Salacuse, 1988.

[11] See Brouthers and Bamossy, 1997; Derong and Faure, 1995; Pfouts, 1994.

[12] Salacuse, 1988.

[13] Ibid.

[14] Ibid.

[15] For example Graham and Mintu-Wimsat, 1997; Metcalf, Bird, Shankarmahesh, Aycan, Larmio, and Valdelamar, 2006; Metcalf, Bird, Peterson, Shankarmahesh, and Lituchy, 2007.

[16] Palich, Carini, and Livingstone, 2002; Xing, 1995.

[17] See Tinsley, 1997.

[18] Tinsley, 1997, 1998, 2001.

[19] Phatak and Habib, 1996, p. 34.

[20] See Sebenius, 2002a.

[21] Phatak and Habib, 1996; also see Lin and Miller, 2003.

[22] See Yan and Gray, 1994, for a review.

[23] Ibid.

[24] See Agha and Malley, 2002; Isajiw, 2000; Ross, 2000; Rubinstein, 2003; Stein, 1999; and Zartman, 1997.

[25] Hartzell, 1999.

[26] Abu-Nimer, 1996.

[27] Ohbuchi and Takahashi, 1994; Tinsley, 1998; and see Weldon and Jehn, 1995, for a review.

[28] Fisher, Ury, and Patton, 1991.

[29] Wanis-St. John, 2006.

[30] Phatak and Habib, 1996.

[31] Ibid.

[32] Ibid.

[33] Ibid.

[34] Ibid.

[35] See Stark, Fam, Waller, and Tian, 2005; Yan and Gray, 1994.

[36] For reviews of this work see Brett, 2001; and Gelfand and Dyer, 2000.

[37] See Avruch, 2000.

[38] Janosik, 1987.

[39] Ibid.

[40] Solomon, 1987.

[41] George, Jones, and Gonzalez, 1998.

[42] Ogawa, 1999; Ting-Toomey and Kurogi, 1998.

[43] Faure, 1999; Sebenius, 2002a.

[44] Hofstede, 1980a, 1980b, 1989, 1991.

[45] Hofstede labeled career success/quality of life as masculine–feminine, but we have adopted gender neutral labels for this dimension (Adler, 2002). Subsequent research by Hofstede and Bond (1988) suggested that a fifth dimension, labeled Confucian Dynamism, be added. Confucian Dynamism contains three elements: work ethic, time, and commitment to traditional Confucian values. The dimension has received little attention in the negotiation literature (cf., Chan, 1998).

[46] Hofstede, 1989, p. 195.

[47] Hofstede, 1980a, p. 46.

[48] Hofstede, 1989.

[49] Ibid., p. 196.

[50] See, for example, Kale and Barnes, 1992; Schwartz, 1994; Triandis, 1982.

[51] See Schwartz, 1992, 1994; Schwartz and Bilsky, 1990; and Smith and Schwartz, 1997.

[52] See Gelfand and Dyer, 2000; Kozan and Ergin, 1999.

[53] See Faure, 1999, for systematic analysis of the effects of culture on the Chinese negotiation style.

[54] Pye, 1992.

[55] Janosik, 1987.

[56] Ibid.

[57] Rubin and Sander, 1991.

[58] Kumar and Worm, 2004, p. 305.

[59] Tinsley, Brett, Shapiro, and Okumura, 2004.

[60] Brett et al., 1998.

[61] Fang, 2006.

[62] Adair and Brett, 2003.

[63] Janosik, 1987.

[64] The discussion that follows is based on the work of Foster, 1992; Hendon and Hendon, 1990; Moran and Stripp, 1991; Salacuse, 1998; and Weiss and Stripp, 1985.

[65] See Ohanyan, 1999; Yook and Albert, 1998.

[66] Foster, 1992, p. 272.

[67] Thompson and Hastie, 1990b.

[68] Salacuse, 1998.

[69] See Zhu, McKenna, and Sun, 2007.

[70] See Braganti and Devine, 1992.

[71] Foster, 1992.

[72] Axtell, 1990, 1991, 1993.

[73] For example, see Binnendijk, 1987; Graham and Sano, 1989; Pye, 1992; and Tung, 1991.

[74] See Macduff, 2006; Mayfield, Mayfield, Martin, and Herbig, 1997.

[75] Alon and Brett, 2007, p. 58.

[76] Foster, 1992.

[77] Ibid.

[78] Salacuse, 1998.

[79] See Kumar, 2004.

[80] Salacuse, 1998.

[81] See Francis, 1991; and Weiss, 1994, for reviews of the oversimplification of this advice.

[82] See Adachi, 1998.

[83] Adler and Graham, 1989; Natlandsmyr and Rognes, 1995.

[84] See Drake, 1995; Weldon and Jehn, 1995.

[85] Francis, 1991.

[86] Rubin and Sander, 1991.

[87] Brett et al., 1998.

[88] Adair et al., 2004.

[89] Adair, Okumura, and Brett, 2001.

[90] Weiss, 1994.

[91] Ibid.

[92] Phatak and Habib, 1996.

[93] Salacuse, 1988.

[94] Phatak and Habib, 1996.

[95] Janosik, 1987.

CHAPTER 12

Best Practices in Negotiations

Objectives

1. Appreciate the extent to which negotiation is both an art and a science.
2. Explore the 10 best practices that all negotiators can follow to achieve a successful negotiation.

Negotiation is an integral part of daily life and the opportunities to negotiate surround us. While some people may look like born negotiators, negotiation is fundamentally a skill involving analysis and communication that everyone can learn. The purpose of this book is to provide students of negotiation with an overview of the field of negotiation, perspective on the breadth and depth of the subprocesses of negotiation, and an appreciation for the art and science of negotiation. In this final chapter we reflect on negotiation at a broad level by providing 10 best practices for negotiators who wish to continue to improve their negotiation skills (see Table 12.1).

1. Be Prepared

We cannot overemphasize the importance of preparation, and we strongly encourage all negotiators to prepare properly for their negotiations (see Chapter 4). Preparation does not have to be a time-consuming or arduous activity, but it should be right at the top of the best practices list of every negotiator. Negotiators who are better prepared have numerous

TABLE 12.1 | 10 Best Practices for Negotiators

1.	Be prepared.
2.	Diagnose the fundamental structure of the negotiation.
3.	Work the BATNA.
4.	Be willing to walk away.
5.	Master paradoxes.
6.	Remember the intangibles.
7.	Actively manage coalitions.
8.	Savor and protect your reputation.
9.	Remember that rationality and fairness are relative.
10.	Continue to learn from the experience.

advantages, including the ability to analyze the other party's offers more effectively and efficiently, to understand the nuances of the concession-making process, and to achieve their negotiation goals. Preparation should occur *before* the negotiation begins so that the time spent negotiating is more productive. Good preparation means understanding one's own goals and interests as well as possible and being able to articulate them to the other party skillfully. It also includes being ready to understand the other party's communication in order to find an agreement that meets the needs of both parties. Few negotiations are going to conclude successfully without both parties achieving at least some of their goals, and solid work up front to identify your needs and to understand the needs of the other party is a critical step to increasing the odds of success.

Good preparation also means setting aspirations for negotiation outcomes that are high but achievable. Negotiators who set their sights too low are virtually guaranteed to reach an agreement that is suboptimal, while those who set them too high are more likely to stalemate and end the negotiation in frustration. Negotiators also need to plan their opening statements and positions carefully so they are especially well prepared at the start of negotiations. It is important to avoid preplanning the complete negotiation sequence, however, because while negotiations do follow broad stages, they also ebb and flow at irregular rates. Overplanning the tactics for each negotiation stage in advance of the negotiation is not a good use of preparation time. It is far better that negotiators prepare by understanding their own strengths and weaknesses, their needs and interests, the situation, and the other party as well as possible so that they can adjust promptly and effectively as the negotiation proceeds.

2.   Diagnose the Fundamental Structure of the Negotiation

Negotiators should make a conscious decision about whether they are facing a fundamentally distributive negotiation, an integrative negotiation, or a blend of the two, and choose their strategies and tactics accordingly. Using strategies and tactics that are mismatched will lead to suboptimal negotiation outcomes. For instance, using overly distributive tactics in a fundamentally integrative situation will likely result in reaching agreements that leave integrative potential untapped because negotiators tend not to readily share the information needed to succeed in integrative negotiations when confronted with distributive tactics. In these situations, money and opportunity are often left on the table.

Similarly, using integrative tactics in a distributive situation may not lead to optimal outcomes either. For instance, one of the authors of this book was recently shopping for a new car and the salesman spent a great deal of time and effort asking questions about the author's family and assuring him that he was working hard to get the highest possible value for his trade-in. Unfortunately, the salesman met the author's requests for clarification about the list price of the car and information about recently advertised manufacturer incentives with silence or by changing the topic of conversation. This was a purely distributive situation for the author, who was not fooled by the salesman's attempt to bargain "integratively." The author bought a car from a different dealer who was able to provide the requested information in a straightforward manner—and whose price was $1,500 lower than the first dealer for the same car!

Negotiators also need to remember that many negotiations will consist of a blend of integrative and distributive elements and that there will be distributive and integrative phases to these negotiations. It is especially important to be careful when transitioning between these phases within the broader negotiation because missteps in these transitions can confuse the other party and lead to impasse.

Finally, there are also times when accommodation, avoidance, and compromise may be appropriate strategies (see Chapter 1). Strong negotiators will identify these situations and adopt appropriate strategies and tactics.

3. Identify and Work the BATNA

One of the most important sources of power in a negotiation is the alternatives available to a negotiator if an agreement is not reached. One alternative, the best alternative to a negotiated agreement (BATNA), is especially important because this is the option that likely will be chosen should an agreement not be reached. Negotiators need to be vigilant about their BATNA. They need to know what their BATNA is relative to a possible agreement and consciously work to improve the BATNA so as to improve the deal. Negotiators without a strong BATNA may find it difficult to achieve a good agreement because the other party may try to push them aggressively, and hence they may be forced to accept a settlement that is later seen as unsatisfying.

For instance, purchasers who need to buy items from sole suppliers are acutely aware of how the lack of a positive BATNA makes it difficult to achieve positive negotiation outcomes. Even in this situation, however, negotiators can work to improve their BATNA in the long term. For instance, organizations in a sole-supplier relationship have often vertically integrated their production and started to build comparable components inside the company, or they have redesigned their products so they are less vulnerable to the sole supplier. These are clearly long-term options and would not be available in a current negotiation. However, it may be possible to refer to these plans when negotiating with a sole supplier in order to remind them that you will not be dependent forever.

Negotiators also need to be aware of the other negotiator's BATNA and to identify how it compares to what you are offering. Negotiators have more power in a negotiation when their potential terms of agreement are significantly better than what the other negotiator can obtain with his or her BATNA. On the other hand, when the difference between your terms and the other negotiator's BATNA is small, then negotiators have less room to maneuver. There are three things negotiators should do with respect to the other negotiator's BATNA: (1) monitor it carefully in order to understand and retain your competitive advantage over the other negotiator's alternatives; (2) remind the other negotiator of the advantages your offer has relative to her BATNA; and (3) in a subtle way, suggest that the other negotiator's BATNA may not be as strong as he or she thinks it is (this can be done in a positive way by stressing your strengths or in a negative way by highlighting competitors' weaknesses).

4. Be Willing to Walk Away

The goal of most negotiations is achieving a valued outcome, not reaching an agreement *per se.* Strong negotiators remember this and are willing to walk away from a negotiation when no agreement is better than a poor agreement or when the process is so offensive that the deal isn't worth the work. While this advice sounds easy enough to take in principle, in practice, negotiators can become so focused on reaching an agreement that they lose sight of the real goal, which is to reach a good outcome (and not necessarily an agreement). Negotiators can ensure that they don't take their eyes off the goal by making regular comparisons with the targets they set during the planning stage and by comparing their progress during their negotiation against their walkaway and BATNA. While negotiators are often optimistic about goal achievement at the outset, they may need to reevaluate these goals during the negotiation. It is important to continue to compare progress in the current negotiation with the target, walkaway, and BATNA and to be willing to walk away from the current negotiation if their walkaway or BATNA becomes the truly better choice.

5.   Master the Key Paradoxes of Negotiation

Excellent negotiators understand that negotiation embodies a set of paradoxes—seemingly contradictory elements that actually occur together. We discuss five common paradoxes that negotiators face. The challenge for negotiators in handling these paradoxes is to strive for *balance* in these situations. There is a natural tension in choosing between one or the other alternative in the paradox, but the best way to manage paradox is to achieve a balance between the opposing forces. Strong negotiators know how to manage this tension.

Claiming Value versus Creating Value

All negotiations have a value-*claiming* stage, where parties decide who gets how much of what, but many negotiations also have a value-*creation* stage, where parties work together to expand the resources under negotiation. The skills and strategies appropriate to each stage are quite different; in general terms, distributive skills are called for in the value-claiming stage and integrative skills are useful in value creation. Typically, the value-creation stage will precede the value-claiming stage, and a challenge for negotiators is to balance the emphasis on the two stages and the transition from creating to claiming value. There is no signpost to mark this transition, however, and negotiators need to manage it tactfully to avoid undermining the open brainstorming and option-inventing relationship that has developed during value creation. One approach to manage this transition is to publicly label it. For instance, negotiators could say something like, "It looks like we have a good foundation of ideas and alternatives to work from. How can we move on to decide what is a fair distribution of the expected outcomes?" In addition, research shows that most negotiators are overly biased toward thinking that a negotiation is more about claiming value rather than creating value, so managing this paradox will likely require an overemphasis on discussing the creating value dynamics.

Sticking by Your Principles versus Being Resilient to the Flow

The pace and flow of negotiations can move from an intense haggle over financial issues to an equally intense debate over deeply held principles about what is right or fair or just. These transitions often create a second paradox for negotiators. On the one hand, effective negotiation requires flexible thinking and an understanding that an assessment of a situation may need to be adjusted as new information comes to light; achieving any deal will probably require both parties to make concessions. On the other hand, core principles are not something to back away from easily in the service of doing a deal. Effective negotiators are thoughtful about the distinction between issues of principle, where firmness is essential, and other issues where compromise or accommodation are the best route to a mutually acceptable outcome.

Sticking with the Strategy versus Opportunistic Pursuit of New Options

New information will frequently come to light during a negotiation, and negotiators need to manage the paradox between sticking with their prepared strategy and pursuing a new opportunity that arises during the process. This is a challenging paradox for negotiators to manage because new "opportunities" may in fact be Trojan horses harboring unpleasant surprises. On the other hand, circumstances do change and legitimate one-time, seize-the-moment deals do occur. The challenge for negotiators is to distinguish phantom opportunities from real ones; developing the capacity to recognize the distinction is another hallmark of the experienced negotiator.

Strong preparation is critical to being able to manage the "strategy versus opportunism" paradox. Negotiators who have prepared well for the negotiation and who understand the circumstances are well positioned to make this judgment. We also suggest that negotiators pay close attention to their intuition. If a deal doesn't feel right, if it seems too good to be true, then it probably *is* too good to be true and is not a viable opportunity. If negotiators feel uneasy about the direction the negotiation is taking, then it is best to take a break and consult with others about the circumstances. Often explaining the "opportunity" to a colleague, friend, or constituent will help distinguish real opportunities from Trojan horses.

We are not suggesting that negotiators become overly cautious, however. Frequently, there are genuinely good opportunities that occur during a negotiation, legitimately caused by changes in business strategy, market opportunities, excess inventory, or a short-term cash flow challenge. Negotiators who have prepared well will be able to take full advantage of real opportunities when they arise and reduce the risk presented by Trojan horses.

Honest and Open versus Closed and Opaque

Negotiators face the *dilemma of honesty*: how open and honest should I be with the other party? Negotiators who are completely open and tell the other party everything expose themselves to the risk that the other party will take advantage of them. In fact, research suggests that too much knowledge about the other party's needs can actually lead to suboptimal negotiation outcomes. On the other hand, being completely closed will not only have a negative effect on your reputation (discussed later), but it is also an ineffective negotiation strategy because you don't disclose enough information to create the groundwork for agreement. The challenge of this paradox is deciding how much information to reveal and how much to conceal—both for pragmatic and ethical reasons.

Strong negotiators have considered this paradox and understand their comfort zone, which will likely vary depending on the other party. We suggest that negotiators should remember that negotiation is an ongoing process. As the negotiators make positive progress, they should be building trust and hopefully feeling more comfortable about revealing more information to the other party. That said, there is some information that should probably not be revealed (e.g., the bottom line in a distributive negotiation) regardless of how well the negotiation is progressing.

Trust versus Distrust

As a mirror image of the dilemma of honesty, negotiators also face the *dilemma of trust*: how much to trust what the other party tells them. Negotiators who believe everything the other party tells them make themselves vulnerable to being taken advantage of by the other party. On the other hand, negotiators who do not believe anything the other party tells them will have a very difficult time reaching an agreement. As with the dilemma of honesty, we suggest that negotiators remember that negotiation is a process that evolves over time. First, as we noted, trust can be built by being honest and sharing information with the other side, which hopefully will lead to reciprocal trust and credible disclosure by the other side. Moreover, there will be individual differences in trust. Some negotiators will start off by being more trusting, but become less trusting if information comes to light showing that the other party is not trustworthy. Other negotiators will be more comfortable having the other party earn their trust and will be more skeptical early in negotiations. There is no right or wrong approach to managing this dilemma. Strong negotiators are aware of this dilemma, however, and consciously monitor how they are managing this challenge.

6.   Remember the Intangibles

It is important that negotiators remember the intangible factors while negotiating and re-main aware of their potential effects. Intangibles frequently affect negotiation in a negative way, and they often operate out of the negotiator's awareness. As noted in Chapter 1, intan-gibles are deep psychological factors that motivate negotiators and they include winning, avoiding loss, looking tough or strong to others, not looking weak, being fair, and so on. For instance, if the other party is vying with his archrival at the next desk for a promotion, he may be especially difficult when negotiating with you in front of his boss in order to look tough and impress his boss. It is unlikely that the other negotiator will tell you this is what he is doing, and in fact he may not even be aware of it himself. The best way to iden-tify the existence of intangible factors is to try to see what is not there. In other words, if your careful preparation and analysis of the situation reveals no tangible explanation for the other negotiator's behavior—adamant advocacy of a certain point, refusal to yield another one, or behavior that just doesn't make sense—then it is time to start looking for the intan-gibles driving his behavior.

For example, several years ago one of the authors of this book was helping a friend buy a new car, and the price offered from the dealer was $2,000 less than any other dealer in town. The only catch was that the car had to be sold that day. On the surface this looked like a trick (see "Strategy versus Opportunism"), but there was no obvious tangible factor that explained this special price. The friend had never purchased from the dealer before, the car was new and fully covered by a good warranty, and the friend had price shopped at several dealers and knew this price was substantially lower. As they continued to discuss the po-tential deal, the salesman became more and more agitated. Sweat was literally falling from his brow. The friend decided to purchase the car, and as soon as he signed, the salesman was simultaneously relieved and excited. He asked for a moment to telephone his wife to share with her some good news. It turned out that the salesman had just won a complicated incentive package offered by the dealer which included a two-week all expenses paid Caribbean vacation for his family of four. The incentive package required that a total of 10 vehicles, one from each category of vehicle at the dealership, be sold in a month. The salesman, who specialized in selling trucks, felt immense pressure when the friend hesitated because he had given the friend a huge discount on a sports car to close the deal.

The intangible factor of trying to win the vacation package explained the salesman's agitated behavior in the preceding example. The buyer learned of this only when the salesman could no longer contain his excitement and shared the good news with his family. Often, negotiators do not learn what intangible factors are influencing the other negotiator unless the other chooses to disclose them. Negotiators can see evidence of their existence, however, by looking for changes in the other negotiator's behavior from one negotiation to another, as well as by gathering information about the other party before negotiation begins. For instance, if you find out that the other party has a new boss that she doesn't like and she is subsequently more difficult to deal with in the negotiation, the intangible of the new boss may be to blame.

There are at least two more ways to discover intangibles that might be affecting the other. One way to surface the other party's intangibles is to ask questions. These questions should try to get the other party to reveal why he or she is sticking so strongly to a given point. It is important to remember that strong emotions and/or values are the root of many intangibles, so surfacing intangibles may result in the discussion of various fears and anxieties. The question-asking process should also be gentle and informal; if the questioning is aggressive, it may only make the other defensive, adding another intangible to the mix and stifling effective negotiations! A second way is to take an observer or listener with you to the negotiation. Listeners may be able to read the other's emotional tone or nonverbal behavior, focus on roadblock issues, or try to take the other's perspective and put themselves in the other's shoes (role reversal). A caucus with this listener may then help refocus the discussion so as to surface the intangibles and develop a new line of questions or offers.

Negotiators also need to remember that intangible factors influence their own behavior (and that it is not uncommon for us to not recognize what is making us angry, defensive, or zealously committed to some idea). Are you being particularly difficult with the other party because he does not respect you, are you trying to teach a subordinate a lesson, or do you want to win this negotiation to look better than another manager? Without passing judgment on the legitimacy of these goals, we strongly urge negotiators to be aware of the effect of intangible factors on their own aspirations and behavior. Often talking to another person—a sympathetic listener—can help the negotiator figure these out. Strong negotiators are aware of how both tangible and intangible factors influence negotiation, and they weigh both factors when evaluating a negotiation outcome.

7. Actively Manage Coalitions

Coalitions can have very significant effects on the negotiation process and outcome. Negotiators should recognize three types of coalitions and their potential effects: (1) coalitions against you; (2) coalitions that support you; and (3) loose, undefined coalitions that may materialize either for or against you. Strong negotiators assess the presence and strength of coalitions and work to capture the strength of the coalition for their benefit. If this is not possible, negotiators need to work to prevent the other party from capturing a loose coalition for their purposes. When negotiators are part of a coalition, communicating with the coalition is critical to ensuring that the power of the coalition is aligned with their goals. Similarly, negotiators who are agents or representatives of a coalition must take special care to manage this process.

Successfully concluding negotiations when a coalition is aligned against a negotiator is an extremely challenging task. It is important to recognize when coalitions are aligned against you and to work consciously to counter their influence. Frequently this will involve a divide-and-conquer strategy, where negotiators try to increase dissent within the coalition by searching for ways to breed instability.

Coalitions occur in many formal negotiations, such as environmental assessments and reaching policy decisions in an industry association. Coalitions may also have a strong influence in less formal settings, such as work teams and families, where different subgroups of people may not have the same interests. Managing coalitions is especially important when negotiators need to rely on other people to implement an agreement. It may be possible for negotiators to forge an agreement when the majority of people influenced are not in favor, but implementing the outcomes of that agreement will be very challenging. Strong negotiators need to monitor and manage coalitions proactively, and while this may take considerable time throughout the negotiation process, it will likely lead to large payoffs at the implementation stage.

8.   Savor and Protect Your Reputation

Reputations are like eggs—fragile, important to build, easy to break, and very hard to rebuild once broken. Reputations travel fast, and people often know more about you than you think that they do. Starting negotiations with a positive reputation is essential, and negotiators should be vigilant in protecting their reputations. Negotiators who have a reputation for breaking their word and not negotiating honestly will have a much more difficult time negotiating in the future than those who have a reputation for being honest and fair. Consider the following contrasting reputations: "tough but fair" versus "tough and underhanded." Negotiators prepare differently for others with these contrasting reputations. Negotiating with a tough but fair negotiator means preparing for potentially difficult negotiations while being aware that the other party will push hard for her perspective but will also be rational and fair in her behavior. Negotiating with a tough but underhanded other party means that negotiators will need to verify what the other says, be vigilant for dirty tricks, and be more guarded about sharing information.

How are you perceived as a negotiator? What is your reputation with others at this point? What reputation would you like to have? Think about the negotiators you respect the most and their reputation. What is it about their behavior that you admire? Also think about the negotiators who have a bad reputation. What would it take for them to change your image of them?

Rather than leaving reputation to chance, negotiators can work to shape and enhance their reputation by acting in a consistent and fair manner. Consistency provides the other party with a clear set of predictable expectations about how you will behave, which leads to a stable reputation. Fairness sends the message that you are principled and reasonable. Strong negotiators also periodically seek feedback from others about the way they are perceived and use that information to strengthen their credibility and trustworthiness in the marketplace.

9.   Remember That Rationality and Fairness Are Relative

Research on negotiator perception and cognition is quite clear (Chapter 5): people tend to view the world in a self-serving manner and define the rational thing to do or a fair outcome or process in a way that benefits themselves. First, negotiators need to be aware of this tendency in both themselves and the other party. Negotiators can do three things to manage these perceptions proactively. First, they can question their own perceptions of fairness and ground them in clear principles. Second, they can find external benchmarks and examples that suggest fair outcomes. Finally, negotiators can illuminate definitions of fairness held by the other party and engage in a dialogue to reach consensus on which standards of fairness apply in a given situation.

Moreover, negotiators are often in the position to collectively define what is right or fair as a part of the negotiation process. In most situations, neither side holds the keys to what is absolutely right, rational, or fair. Reasonable people can disagree, and often the most important outcome that negotiators can achieve is a common, agreed-upon perspective, definition of the facts, agreement on the right way to see a problem, or standard for determining what is a fair outcome or process. Be prepared to negotiate these principles as strongly as you prepare for a discussion of the issues.

10.   Continue to Learn from Your Experience

Negotiation epitomizes lifelong learning. The best negotiators continue to learn from the experience—they know there are so many different variables and nuances when negotiating that no two negotiations are identical. These differences mean that for negotiators to remain sharp, they need to continue to practice the art and science of negotiation regularly. In addition, the best negotiators take a moment to analyze each negotiation after it has concluded, to review what happened and what they learned. We recommend a three-step process:

- Plan a personal reflection time after each negotiation.
- Periodically take a lesson from a trainer or coach.
- Keep a personal diary on strengths and weaknesses and develop a plan to work on weaknesses.

This analysis does not have to be extensive or time consuming. It should happen after every important negotiation, however, and it should focus on *what* and *why* questions: what happened during this negotiation, why did it occur, and what can I learn? Negotiators who take the time to pause and reflect on their negotiations will find that they continue to refine their skills and that they remain sharp and focused for their future negotiations.

Moreover, even the best athletes—in almost any sport—have one or more coaches on their staff and stop to take a lesson, when necessary. Negotiators have access to seminars to enhance their skills, books to read, and coaches who can help refine their skills. This book should be seen as one step along the way to sharpening and refining your negotiation skills, and we encourage you to continue to learn about the art and science of negotiation. We wish you the best of luck in all of your future negotiations!

Aaronson, K. (1989). *Selling on the fast track.* New York: Putnam.

Abu-Nimer, M. (1996). Conflict resolution approaches: Western and Middle Eastern lessons and possibilities. *American Journal of Economics and Sociology, 55* (1), 35–52.

Acuff, F. L. (1993). *How to negotiate anything with anyone anywhere around the world.* New York: AMACOM.

Adachi, Y. (1998). The effects of semantic difference on cross-cultural business negotiation: A Japanese and American case study. *Journal of Language for International Business, 9,* 43–52.

Adair, W., Brett, J., Lempereur, A., Okumura, T., Shikhirev, P., Tinsley, C., & Lytle, A. (2004). Culture and negotiation strategy. *Negotiation Journal, 20,* 87–110.

Adair, W. L., & Brett, J. M. (2005). The negotiation dance: Time, culture, and behavioral sequences in negotiation. *Organization Science, 16* (1), 33–51.

Adair, W. L., Okumura, T., & Brett, J. M. (2001). Negotiation behavior when cultures collide: The United States and Japan. *Journal of Applied Psychology, 86,* 371–85.

Adler, N. J. (2002). *International dimensions of organizational behavior* (4th ed.). Cincinnati, OH: South-Western.

Adler, N. J., & Graham, J. L. (1989). Cross-cultural interaction: The international comparison fallacy? *Journal of International Business Studies, 20,* 515–37.

Adler, R. S. (2007). Negotiating with liars. *MIT Sloan Management Review, 48* (4), 69–74.

Adler, R., Rosen, B., & Silverstein, E. (1996). Thrust and parry: The art of tough negotiating. *Training and Development, 50,* 42–48.

Adorno, T. W., Frenkl-Brunswick, E., Levinson, D. J., & Sanford, R. N. (1950). *The authoritarian personality.* New York: HarperCollins.

Agha, H., & Malley, R. (2002). The last negotiation: How to end the Middle East peace process. *Foreign Affairs, 81* (3), 10–18.

Albin, C. (1993). The role of fairness in negotiation. *Negotiation Journal, 9,* 223–43.

Alexander, J. F., Schul, P. L., & Babakus, E. (1991). Analyzing interpersonal communications in industrial marketing negotiations. *Journal of the Academy of Marketing Science, 19,* 129–39.

Allhoff, F. (2003). Business bluffing reconsidered. *Journal of Business Ethics, 45,* 283–89.

Allred, K. G. (1999). Anger-driven retaliation: Toward an understanding of impassioned conflict in organizations. In R. J. Bies, R. J. Lewicki, & B. H. Sheppard (Eds.), *Research on negotiation in organizations* (Vol. 7), Greenwich, CT: JAI Press.

Allred, K. G., Mallozzi, J. S., Matsui, F., & Raia, C. P. (1997). The influence of anger and compassion on negotiation performance. *Organizational Behavior and Human Decision Processes, 70,* 175–87.

Alon, I., & Brett, J. M. (2007). Perceptions of time and their impact on negotiations in the Arabic-speaking Islamic world. *Negotiation Journal, 23,* 55–73.

Aquino, K., & Becker, T. E. (2005). Lying in negotiation: How individual and situational factors influence the use of neutralization strategies. *Journal of Organizational Behavior, 26,* 661–79.

Argyris, C., & Schön, D. (1996). *Organizational learning II: Theory, method, and practice.* Reading, MA: Addison-Wesley Longman.

Asherman, I. G., & Asherman, S. V. (1990). *The negotiation sourcebook.* Amherst, MA: Human Resource Development Press.

Avruch, K. (2000). Culture and negotiation pedagogy. *Negotiation Journal, 16,* 339–46.

Axtell, R. E. (1990). *Do's and taboos of hosting international visitors.* New York: John Wiley and Sons.

Axtell, R. E. (1991). *Gestures: The do's and taboos of body language around the world.* New York: John Wiley and Sons.

Axtell, R. E. (1993). *Do's and taboos around the world* (3rd ed.). New York: John Wiley and Sons.

Babcock, L., & Loewenstein, G. (1997). Explaining bargaining impasse: The role of self-serving biases. *Journal of Economic Perspectives 11* (1) 109–26.

Babcock, L., Wang, X., & Loewenstein, G. (1996). Choosing the wrong pond: Social comparisons in negotiations that reflect a self-serving bias. *Quarterly Journal of Economics, 111* (1), 1–19.

Ball, S. B., Bazerman, M. H., & Carroll, J. S. (1991). An evaluation of learning in the bilateral winner's curse. *Organizational Behavior and Human Decision Processes, 48,* 1–22.

Baranowski, T. A., & Summers, D. A. (1972). Perceptions of response alternatives in a prisoner's dilemma game. *Journal of Personality and Social Psychology, 21,* 35–40.

Barki, H., & Hartwick, J. (2004). Conceptualizing the construct of interpersonal conflict. *The International Journal of Conflict Management, 15* (3), 216–44.

Barnard, C. (1938). *The functions of the executive.* Cambridge, MA: Harvard University Press.

Baron, R. A. (1990). Environmentally induced positive affect: Its impact on self efficacy and task performance, negotiation and conflict. *Journal of Applied Social Psychology, 20,* 368–84.

Barry, B. (1999). The tactical use of emotion in negotiation. In R. Bies, R. J. Lewicki, & B. H. Sheppard (Eds.), *Research on negotiation in organizations* (Vol. 7, pp. 93–121), Stamford, CT: JAI Press.

Barry, B., & Fulmer, I. S. (2004). The medium and the message: The adaptive use of communication media in dyadic influence. *Academy of Management Review, 2,* 272–92.

Barry, B., Fulmer, I. S., & Goates, N. (2006). Bargaining with feeling: Emotionality in and around negotiation. In L.Thompson (Ed.), *Negotiation Theory and Research* (pp. 99–127). New York: Psychology Press.

Barry, B., Fulmer, I. S., & Long, A. (2000). Ethically marginal bargaining tactics: Sanction, efficacy, and performance. Presented at the annual meeting of the Academy of Management, Toronto.

Barry, B., Fulmer, I. S., & Van Kleef, G. A. (2004). I laughed, I cried, I settled: The role of emotion in negotiation. In M. Gelfand and J. Brett (Eds.), *Culture and Negotiation: Integrative Approaches to Theory and Research.* Stanford University Press, Stanford, CA.

Barry, B., & Oliver, R. L. (1996). Affect in dyadic negotiation: A model and propositions. *Organizational Behavior and Human Decision Processes, 67,* 127–43.

Bateson, B. (1972). *Steps to an ecology of mind.* New York: Ballantine Books.

Bazerman, M. H., & Carroll, J. S. (1987). Negotiator cognition. In B. M. Staw & L. L. Cummings. *Research in organizational behavior* (Vol. 9, pp. 247–88), Greenwich, CT: JAI Press.

Bazerman, M. H., Curhan, J. R., Moore, D. A., & Valley, K. L. (2000). Negotiation. *Annual Review of Psychology, 51,* 279–314.

Bazerman, M. H., & Gillespie, J. J. (1999). Betting on the future: The virtues of contingent contracts. *Harvard Business Review,* Sept–Oct, 155–60.

Bazerman, M. H., Magliozzi, T., & Neale, M. A. (1985). Integrative bargaining in a competitive market. *Organizational Behavior and Human Decision Processes, 35,* 294–313.

Bazerman, M. H., Mannix, E. A., & Thompson, L. L. (1988). Groups as mixed motive negotiations. In E. J. Lawler & B. Markovsky (Eds.), *Advances in group processes* (Vol. 5, pp. 195–216). Greenwich, CT: JAI Press.

Bazerman, M. H., Moore, D. A., & Gillespie, J. J. (1999). The human mind as a barrier to wiser environmental agreements. *American Behavioral Scientist, 42,* 1277–1300.

Bazerman, M. H., & Neale, M. A. (1992). *Negotiating rationally.* New York: Free Press.

Bazerman, M. H., & Samuelson, W. F. (1983). I won the auction but don't want the prize. *Journal of Conflict Resolution, 27,* 618–34.

Bazerman, M. H., Tenbrunsel, A.E., & Wade-Benzoni, K. (1998). Negotiating with yourself and losing: Making decisions with competing internal preferences. *Academy of Management Review, 23* (2), 225–241.

Beckhard, R. (1978, July–September). The dependency dilemma. *Consultants' Communique, 6,* 1–3.

Beckman, N. (1977). *Negotiations.* Lexington, MA: Lexington Books.

Beebe, S. A. (1980). Effects of eye contact, posture, and vocal inflection upon credibility and comprehension. *Australian SCAN: Journal of Human Communication, 7–8,* 57–70.

Beisecker, T., Walker, G., & Bart, J. (1989). Knowledge versus ignorance in bargaining strategies: The impact of knowledge about other's information level. *Social Science Journal, 26,* 161–72.

Benton, A. A., & Druckman, D. (1974). Constituent's bargaining orientation and intergroup negotiations. *Journal of Applied Social Psychology, 4,* 141–50.

Berkowitz, L. (1989). The frustration-aggression hypothesis: An examination and reformulation. *Psychological Bulletin, 106,* 59–73.

Bies, R., & Moag, J. (1986). Interactional justice: Communication criteria of fairness. In R. J. Lewicki, B. H. Sheppard, and M. H. Bazerman (Eds.), *Research on negotiation in organizations* (Vol. 1, pp. 43–55). Greenwich, CT: JAI Press.

Bies, R., & Shapiro, D. (1987). Interactional fairness judgments: The influence of causal accounts. *Social Justice Research, 1,* 199–218.

Bies, R., & Tripp, T. (1998). Revenge in organizations: The good, the bad and the ugly. In R. W. Griffin, A. O'Leary-Kelly, & J. Collins (Eds.), *Dysfunctional behavior in organizations,* Vol. 1: *Violent behavior in organizations* (pp. 49–68). Greenwich, CT: JAI Press.

Binnendijk, H. (1987). *National negotiating styles.* Washington, DC: Foreign Service Institute, Department of State.

Bless, H., Bohner, G., Schwarz, N., & Strack, F. (1988). Happy and mindless: Moods and the processing of persuasive communication. Unpublished manuscript, Mannheim, GR.

Blumenstein, R. (1997, December 30). Haggling in cyberspace transforms car sales. *The Wall Street Journal,* pp. B1, B6.

Bok, S. (1978). *Lying: Moral choice in public and private life.* New York: Pantheon.

Boles, T. L., Croson, R. T. A., & Murnighan, J. K. (2000). Deception and retribution in repeated ultimatum bargaining. *Organizational Behavior and Human Decision Processes, 83,* 235–59.

Bottom, W. P., Gibson, K., Daniels, S. & Murnighan, J. K. (2002). When talk is not cheap: Substantive penance and expressions of intent in the reestablishment of cooperation. *Organization Science, 13,* 497–513.

Bottom, W. P., & Paese, P. W. (1999). Judgment accuracy and the asymmetric cost of errors in distributive bargaining. *Group Decision and Negotiation, 8,* 349–64.

Bowie, N. (1993). Does it pay to bluff in business? In T. L. Beauchamp & N. E. Bowie (Eds.), *Ethical theory and business* (pp. 449–54). Englewood Cliffs, NJ: Prentice Hall.

Braganti, N. L., & Devine, E. (1992). *European customs and manners: How to make friends and do business in Europe* (rev. ed.). New York: Meadowbrook Press.

Brass, D. J. (1984). Being in the right place: A structural analysis of individual influence in an organization. *Administrative Science Quarterly, 29,* 518–39.

Brett, J. (1991). Negotiating group decisions. *Negotiation Journal, 7,* 291–310.

Brett, J., Adair, W., Lempereur, A., Okumura, T., Shikhirev, P., Tinsley, C., & Lytle, A. (1998). Culture and joint gains in negotiation. *Negotiation Journal, 14* (1), 61–86.

Brett, J., & Gelfand, M. (2004). *A cultural analysis of the underlying assumptions of negotiation theory.* Unpublished paper, Dispute Resolution Research Center, Northwestern University, Evanston, IL.

Brett, J. M. (2001). *Negotiating globally.* San Francisco: Jossey-Bass.

Brett, J. M., Shapiro, D. L., & Lytle, A. L. (1998). Breaking the bonds of reciprocity in negotiation. *Academy of Management Journal, 41,* 410–24.

Brockner, J. (1992). The escalation of commitment to a failing course of action: Toward theoretical progress. *Academy of Management Review, 17,* 39–61.

Brodt, S. E. (1994). "Inside information" and negotiator decision behavior. *Organizational Behavior and Human Decision Processes, 58,* 172–202.

Brodt, S. E., & Tuchinsky, M. (2000). Working together but in opposition: An examination of the "Good-Cop/Bad-Cop" negotiating team tactic. *Organizational Behavior and Human Decision Processes, 81* (2), 155–77.

Brooks, E., & Odiorne, G. S. (1984). *Managing by negotiations.* New York: Van Nostrand.

Brouthers, K. D., & Bamossy, G. J. (1997). The role of key stakeholders in international joint venture negotiations: Case studies from Eastern Europe. *Journal of International Business Studies, 28,* 285–308.

Bruner, J. S., & Tagiuri, R. (1954). The perception of people. In G. Lindzey (Ed.), *The handbook of social psychology* (Vol. 2, pp. 634–54). Reading, MA: Addison-Wesley.

Buechler, S. M. (2000). *Social movements in advanced capitalism.* New York: Oxford University Press.

Buelens, M., & Van Poucke, D. (2004). Determinants of a negotiator's initial opening offer. *Journal of Business and Psychology, 19,* 23–35.

Burgoon, J. K., Coker, D. A., & Coker, R. A. (1986). Communication of gaze behavior: A test of two contrasting explanations. *Human Communication Research, 12,* 495–524.

Burnstein, D. (1995). *Negotiator pro.* Beacon Expert Systems, 35 Gardner Road, Brookline, MA.

Burrell, G., & Morgan, G. (1979). *Sociological paradigms and organizational analysis: Elements of the sociology of corporate life.* London: Heinemann.

Butler, J. K., Jr. (1991). Toward understanding and measuring conditions of trust: Evolution of a conditions of trust inventory. *Journal of Management, 17,* 643–63.

Butler, J. K., Jr. (1995). Behaviors, trust and goal achievement in a win-win negotiation role play. *Group & Organization Management, 20,* 486–501.

Butler, J. K., Jr. (1996). Two integrative win-win negotiating strategies. *Simulation and Gaming, 27,* 387–92.

Butler, J. K., Jr. (1999). Trust expectations, information sharing, climate of trust, and negotiation effectiveness and efficiency. *Group and Organization Management, 24,* 217–38.

Carnevale, P. J. (2006). Creativity in the outcomes of conflict. In M. Deutsch et al. (Eds.), *The handbook of conflict resolution: Theory and practice,* 2nd ed., (pp. 414–35). San Francisco: Jossey-Bass.

Carnevale, P. J., & Isen, A. M. (1986). The influence of positive affect and visual access on the discovery of integrative solutions in bilateral negotiation. *Organizational Behavior and Human Decision Processes, 37,* 1–13.

Carnevale, P. J. D., & Pruitt, D. G. (1992). Negotiation and mediation. In M. Rosenberg & L. Porter (Eds.), *Annual Review of Psychology* (Vol. 43, pp. 531–82). Palo Alto, CA: Annual Reviews, Inc.

Carnevale, P. J. D., Pruitt, D. G., & Seilheimer, S. D. (1981). Looking and competing: Accountability and visual access in integrative bargaining. *Journal of Personality and Social Psychology, 40,* 111–20.

Carr, A. Z. (1968, January–February). Is business bluffing ethical? *Harvard Business Review, 46,* 143–53.

Carroll, J., Bazerman, M., & Maury, R. (1988). Negotiator cognitions: A descriptive approach to negotiators' understanding of their opponents. *Organizational Behavior and Human Decision Processes, 41,* 352–70.

Carroll, J., Delquie, P., Halpern, J., & Bazerman, M. (1990). *Improving negotiators' cognitive processes.* Working paper, Massachusetts Institute of Technology, Cambridge, MA.

Carver, C. S., & Scheir, M. E. (1990). Origins and foundations of positive and negative affect: A control process view. *Psychological Review, 97,* 19–35.

Cellich, C. (1997). Closing your business negotiations. *International Trade Forum, 1,* 14–17.

Chan, C. W. (1998). Transfer pricing negotiation outcomes and the impact of negotiator mixed-motives and culture: Empirical evidence from the U.S. and Australia. *Management Accounting Research, 9,* 139–61.

Charan, R. (1991). How networks reshape organizations—for results. *Harvard Business Review, 69* (5), Sept./Oct., pp. 104–15.

Chertkoff, J. M., & Conley, M. (1967). Opening offer and frequency of concessions as bargaining strategies. *Journal of Personality and Social Psychology, 7,* 181–85.

Cialdini, R. B. (2001). *Influence: Science and practice* (4th ed.). Boston: Allyn and Bacon.

Cialdini, R. B., & Goldstein, N. J. (2004). Social influence: Compliance and conformity. *Annual Review of Psychology, 55,* 591–621.

Cloke, K., & Goldsmith, J. (2005). *Resolving Conflicts at Work.* Second Edition. San Francisco: Jossey-Bass.

Clyman, D. R., & Tripp, T. M. (2000). Discrepant values and measures of negotiator performance. *Group Decision and Negotiation, 9,* 251–74.

Cohen, H. (1980). *You can negotiate anything.* Secaucus, NJ: Lyle Stuart.

Cohen, H. (2003). *Negotiate this!* New York: Warner Books.

Coleman, P. (1997). Refining ripeness: A social-psychological perspective. *Peace and Conflict: Journal of Peace Psychology, 3,* 81–103.

Coleman, P. (2000). Power and conflict. In M. Deutsch, & P. Coleman, *Handbook of conflict resolution.* San Francisco: Jossey-Bass.

Conlon, D. E., & Hunt, C. S. (2002). Dealing with feeling: The influence of outcome representations on negotiation. *International Journal of Conflict Management, 13,* 38–58.

Cooper, W. (1981). Ubiquitous halo. *Psychological Bulletin, 90,* 218–44.

Coser, L. (1956). *The functions of social conflict.* New York: Free Press.

Cronkhite, G., & Liska, J. (1976). A critique of factor analytic approaches to the study of credibility. *Communication Monographs, 32,* 91–107.

Cronkhite, G., & Liska, J. (1980). The judgment of communicant acceptability. In M. E. Roloff & G. R. Miller (Eds.), *Persuasion: New directions in theory and research* (pp. 101–39). Beverly Hills, CA: Sage.

Croson, R. T. A. (1999). Look at me when you say that: An electronic negotiation simulation. *Simulation & Gaming, 30,* 23–37.

Crumbaugh, C. M., & Evans, G. W. (1967). Presentation format, other persons' strategies and cooperative behavior in the prisoner's dilemma. *Psychological Reports, 20,* 895–902.

Curhan, J. R., Neale, M. A., & Ross, L. (2004). Dynamic valuation: Preference changes in the context of face-to-face negotiation. *Journal of Experimental Social Psychology, 40,* 142–151.

Curhan, J. R., & Pentland, A. (2007). Thin slides of negotiation: Predicting outcomes from conversational dynamics within the first 5 minutes. *Journal of Applied Psychology, 92,* 802–811.

Dahl, R. A. (1957). The concept of power. *Behavioral Science, 2,* 201–15.

Daly, J. (1991). The effects of anger on negotiations over mergers and acquisitions. *Negotiation Journal, 7,* 31–39.

Dant, R. P., & Schul, P. L. (1992). Conflict resolution processes in contractual channels of distribution. *Journal of Marketing, 56,* 38–54.

de Dreu, C. K. W. (1995). Coercive power and concession making in bilateral negotiation. *Journal of Conflict Resolution, 39,* 646–70.

de Dreu, C. K. W. (2003). Time pressure and closing of the mind in negotiation. *Organizational Behavior and Human Decision Processes, 91,* 280–95.

de Dreu, C. K. W., Carnevale, P. J. D., Emans, B. J. M., & van de Vliert, E. (1994). Effects of gain-loss frames in negotiation: Loss aversion, mismatching, and frame adoption. *Organizational Behavior and Human Decision Processes, 60,* 90–107.

de Dreu, C. K. W., Nauta, A., & van de Vliert, E. (1995). Self-serving evaluations of conflict behavior and escalation of the dispute. *Journal of Applied Social Psychology, 25,* 2049–66.

de Dreu, C. K. W., & Van Kleef, G. A. (2004). The influence of power on the information search, impression formation and demands in negotiation. *Journal of Experimental Social Psychology, 40,* 303–19.

de Dreu, C. K. W., & van Lange, P. A. M. (1995). The impact of social value orientation on negotiator cognition and behavior. *Personality and Social Psychology Bulletin, 21,* 1178–88.

Deep, S., & Sussman, L. (1993). *What to ask when you don't know what to say: 555 powerful questions to use for getting your way at work.* Englewood Cliffs, NJ: Prentice Hall.

Dennis, A. R., & Reinicke, B. A. (2004). Beta versus VHS and the acceptance of electronic brainstorming technology. *MIS Quarterly, 28,* 1–20.

Derong, C., & Faure, G. O. (1995). When Chinese companies negotiate with their government. *Organization Studies, 16,* 27–54.

Deutsch, M. (1958). Trust and suspicion. *Journal of Conflict Resolution, 2,* 265–79.

Deutsch, M. (1962). Cooperation and trust: Some theoretical notes. In M. R. Jones (Ed.), *Nebraska symposium on motivation* (pp. 275–318). Lincoln, NE: University of Nebraska Press.

Deutsch, M. (1973). *The resolution of conflict.* New Haven, CT: Yale University Press.

Deutsch, M. (1985). *Distributive justice: A social-psychological perspective.* New Haven, CT: Yale University Press.

Devine, P. G. (1989). Stereotypes and prejudice: Their automatic and controlled components. *Journal of Personality and Social Psychology, 56,* 5–18.

Dialdin, D., Kopelman, S., Adair, W., Brett, J. M., Okumura, T., & Lytle, A. (1999). *The distributive outcomes of*

cross-cultural negotiations. DRRC working paper. Evanston, IL: Northwestern University.

Diekmann, K. A., Tenbrunsel, A. E., Shah, P. P., Schroth, H. A., & Bazerman, M. H. (1996). The descriptive and prescriptive use of previous purchase price in negotiations. *Organizational Behavior and Human Decision Processes, 66,* 179–91.

Donohue, W. A. (1981). Analyzing negotiation tactics: Development of a negotiation interact system. *Human Communication Research, 7,* 273–87.

Donohue, W. A., & Roberto, A. J. (1996). An empirical examination of three models of integrative and distributive bargaining. *International Journal of Conflict Management, 7,* 209–99.

Douglas, A. (1962). *Industrial peacemaking.* New York: Columbia University Press.

Drake, L. E. (1995). Negotiation styles in intercultural communication. *International Journal of Conflict Management, 6,* 72–90.

Drolet, A. L., & Morris, M. W. (2000). Rapport in conflict resolution: Accounting for how face-to-face contact fosters mutual cooperation in mixed-motive conflicts. *Journal of Experimental Social Psychology, 36,* 26–50.

Druckman, D. (1996). Is there a U.S. negotiating style? *International Negotiation, 1,* 327–34.

Druckman, D., & Broome, B. (1991). Value difference and conflict resolution: Familiarity or liking? *Journal of Conflict Resolution, 35* (4), 571–93.

Eyuboglu, N., & Buja, A. (1993). Dynamics of channel negotiations: Contention and reciprocity. *Psychology & Marketing, 10,* 47–65.

Fang, T. (2006). Negotiation: The Chinese style. *The Journal of Business & Industrial Marketing, 21* (1), 50–60.

Faure, G. O. (1999). The cultural dimension of negotiation: The Chinese case. *Group Decision and Negotiation, 8,* 187–215.

Felstiner, W. L. F., Abel, R. L., & Sarat, A. (1980–81). The emergence and transformation of disputes: Naming, blaming, and claiming. *Law and Society Review, 15,* 631–54.

Ferris, G. R., Blas, F. R., Douglas, C., Kolodinsky, R. W., & Treadway, D. C. (2005). Personal reputation in organizations. In J. Greenberg (Ed.), *Organizational behavior: The state of the science.* Mahwah, NJ: Lawrence Erlbaum.

Filley, A. C. (1975). *Interpersonal conflict resolution.* Glenview, IL: Scott Foresman.

Fisher, R., & Ertel, D. (1995). *Getting ready to negotiate: The getting to yes workbook.* New York: Penguin.

Fisher, R., Ury, W., & Patton, B. (1991). *Getting to yes: Negotiating agreement without giving in* (2nd ed.). New York: Penguin.

Fiske, S. T., & Taylor, S. W. E. (1991). *Social cognition.* Reading, MA: Addison-Wesley.

Folger, J. P., Poole, M. S., & Stutman, R. K. (1993). *Working through conflict: Strategies for relationships, groups and organizations* (2nd ed.). New York: HarperCollins.

Follett, M. P. (1940). *Dynamic administration: The collected papers of Mary Parker Follett.* H. C. Metcalf & L. Urwick (Eds.). New York: Harper & Brothers.

Follett, M. P. (1942). Constructive conflict. In H. C. Metcalf & L. Urwick (Eds.), *Dynamic administration: The collected papers of Mary Parker Follett* (pp. 30–49). New York: Harper & Brothers.

Foo, M. D., Elfenbein, H. A., Tan, H. H., & Aik, V. C. (2004). Emotional intelligence and negotiation: The tension between creating and claiming value. *International Journal of Conflict Management, 15,* 411–29.

Foreman, P., & Murnighan, J. K. (1996). Learning to avoid the winner's curse. *Organizational Behavior and Human Decision Processes, 67,* 170–80.

Forgas, J. P. (1992). Affect in social judgments and decisions: A multiprocess model. *Advances in Experimental Social Psychology, 25,* 227–75.

Forgas, J. P., & Fiedler, K. (1996). Us and them: Mood effects on intergroup discrimination. *Journal of Personality and Social Psychology, 70,* 28–40.

Foster, D. A. (1992). *Bargaining across borders: How to negotiate business successfully anywhere in the world.* New York: McGraw-Hill.

Fragale, A. R., & Heath, C. (2004). Evolving informational credentials: The (mis)attribution of believable facts to credible sources. *Personality and Social Psychology Bulletin, 30,* 225–36.

Francis, J. N. P. (1991). When in Rome? The effects of cultural adaptation on intercultural business negotiations. *Journal of International Business Studies, 22,* 403–28.

Friedman, Raymond A. (1994). *Front Stage, Backstage: The Diamatic Structure of Labor Negotiations.* Cambridge, MA: Massachusetts Institute of Technology.

Friedman, R., Anderson, C., Brett, J., Olekalns, M., Goates, N., & Lisco, C. C. (2004). The positive and negative effects of anger on dispute resolution: Evidence from electronically mediated disputes. *Journal of Applied Psychology, 89,* 369–76.

French, J. R. P., & Raven, B. (1959). The bases of social power. In D. Cartwright (Ed.), *Studies in social power.* Ann Arbor, MI: Institute for Social Research.

Froman, L. A., & Cohen, M. D. (1970). Compromise and logrolling: Comparing the efficiency of two bargaining processes. *Behavioral Sciences, 15,* 180–83.

Frost, P. (1987). Power, politics and influence. In F. M. Jablin, *Handbook of organizational communication.*, Newbury Park, CA: Sage., pp. 403–548.

Fry, W. R., Firestone, I. J., & Williams, D. L. (1983). Negotiation process and outcome of stranger dyads and dating couples: Do lovers lose? *Basic and Applied Social Psychology, 4,* 1–16.

Galinsky, A. D., Seiden, V. L., Kim, P. H., & Medvec, V. H. (2002). The dissatisfaction of having your first offer accepted: The role of counterfactual thinking in negotiations. *Personality and Social Psychology Bulletin, 28* (2), 271–83.

Gallupe, R. B., & Cooper, W. H. (1993). Brainstorming electronically. *Sloan Management Review, 35* (1), 27–36.

Ganesan, S. (1993). Negotiation strategies and the nature of channel relationships. *Journal of Marketing Research, 30,* 183–203.

Gelfand, M. J., & Dyer, N. (2000). A cultural perspective on negotiation: Progress, pitfalls, and prospects. *Applied Psychology: An International Review, 49,* 62–99.

Gelfand, M., Higgins, M., Nishii, L. H., Raver, J. L., Dominguez, A., Murakami, F., Yamaguchi, S., and Toyama, M. (2002). Culture and egocentric perceptions of fairness in conflict and negotiation. *Journal of Applied Psychology, 87* (5), pp. 833–45.

Gentner, J., Loewenstein, J., & Thompson, L. (2003). Learning and transfer: A general role for analogical encoding. *Journal of Educational Psychology, 95,* 393–408.

George, J. M., Jones, G. R., & Gonzalez, J. A. (1998). The role of affect in cross-cultural negotiations. *Journal of International Business Studies, 29,* 749–72.

Ghosh, D. (1996). Nonstrategic delay in bargaining: An experimental investigation. *Organizational Behavior and Human Decision Processes, 67,* 312–25.

Gibb, J. (1961). Defensive communication. *Journal of Communication, 3,* 141–48.

Gillespie, J. J., & Bazerman, M. H. (1997). Parasitic integration: Win-win agreements containing losers. *Negotiation Journal, 13,* 271–82.

Gillespie, J. J., & Bazerman, M. H. (1998, April). Pre-settlement settlement (PreSS): A simple technique for initiating complex negotiations. *Negotiation Journal, 14,* 149–59.

Girard, J. (1989). *How to close every sale.* New York: Warner Books.

Goates, N. (2008, August). Reputation as a basis for trust: Social information, emotional state and trusting behavior. Paper presented to the Academy of Management Annual Meetings.

Goffman, E. (1969). *Strategic interaction.* Philadelphia, PA: University of Philadelphia Press.

Goffman, E. (1974). *Frame analysis.* New York: Harper & Row.

Gonzalez, R. M., Lerner, J. S., Moore, D. A., & Babcock, L. C. (2004). Mad, mean, and mistaken: The effects of anger on strategic social perception and behavior. Paper presented at the annual meeting of the International Association for Conflict Management, Pittsburgh.

Gordon, T. (1977). *Leader effectiveness training.* New York: Wyden Books.

Graham, J. L., & Mintu-Wimsat, A. (1997). Culture's influence on business negotiations in four countries. *Group Decision and Negotiation, 6,* 483–502.

Graham, J. L., & Sano, Y. (1989). *Smart bargaining.* New York: Harper Business.

Gray, B. (1991). The framing of disputes: Partners, processes and outcomes in different contexts. Paper presented at the annual conference of the International Association of Conflict Management, Den Dolder, The Netherlands.

Gray, B. (1994). The gender-based foundation of negotiation theory. In B. H. Sheppard, R. J. Lewicki, & R. J. Bies (Eds.), *Research in negotiation in organizations* (Vol. 4, pp. 3–36). Greenwich, CT: JAI Press.

Gray, B. (1997). Framing and reframing of intractable environmental disputes. In R. J. Lewicki, R. J. Bies & B. Sheppard (Eds.), *Research on negotiation in organizations* (Vol. 6, pp. 163–88). Greenwich, CT: JAI Press.

Gray, B., & Donnellon, A. (1989). *An interactive theory of reframing in negotiation.* Unpublished manuscript.

Green, R. M. (1994). *The ethical manager: A new method for business ethics.* Upper Saddle River, NJ: Prentice Hall.

Greenberg, J. (1990). Organizational justice: Yesterday, today, tomorrow. *Journal of Management, 16,* 299–432.

Greenberg, J., & Colquitt, J. (2005). *Handbook of organizational justice.* Mahwah, NJ: Lawrence Erlbaum Associates.

Greenhalgh, L. (2001). *Managing strategic relationships.* New York: Free Press.

Greenhalgh, L., & Chapman, D. (1996). Relationships between disputants: Analysis of their characteristics and impact. In S. Gleason (Ed.), *Frontiers in dispute resolution and human resources* (pp. 203–28). East Lansing, MI: Michigan State University Press.

Greenhalgh, L., & Gilkey, R. W. (1993). The effect of relationship orientation on negotiators cognitions and tactics. *Group Decision and Negotiation, 2,* 167–86.

Greenhalgh, L., & Kramer, R. M. (1990). Strategic choice in conflicts: The importance of relationships. In K. Zald (Ed.), *Organizations and nation states: New perspectives on conflict and cooperation* (pp. 181–220). San Francisco: Jossey-Bass.

Gruder, C. L., & Duslak, R. J. (1973). Elicitation of cooperation by retaliatory and nonretaliatory strategies in a mixed-motive game. *Journal of Conflict Resolution, 17,* 162–174.

Hall, J. (1969). *Conflict management survey: A survey of one's characteristic reaction to and handling conflict between himself and others.* Conroe, TX: Telemetrics International.

Harinck, F., de Dreu, C. K. W., & Van Vianen, A. E. M. (2000). The impact of conflict issues on fixed-pie perceptions, problem solving, and integrative outcomes in negotiation. *Organizational Behavior and Human Decision Processes, 81,* 329–58.

Hartzell, C. A. (1999). Explaining the stability of negotiated settlements to intrastate wars. *Journal of Conflict Resolution, 43,* 3–22.

Hegarty, W., & Sims, H. P. (1978). Some determinants of unethical decision behavior: An experiment. *Journal of Applied Psychology, 63,* 451–57.

Hegtvedt, K. A., & Killian, C. (1999). Fairness and emotions: Reactions to the process and outcomes of negotiations. *Social Forces, 78,* 269–303.

Heider, F. (1958). *The psychology of interpersonal relations.* New York: John Wiley and Sons.

Hendon, D. W., & Hendon, R. A. (1990). *World-class negotiating: Dealmaking in the global marketplace.* New York: John Wiley and Sons.

Higgins, E. T. (1987). Self discrepancy theory: A theory relating self and affect. *Psychological Review, 94,* 319–40.

Hilty, J. A., & Carnevale, P. J. (1993). Black-hat/white-hat strategy in bilateral negotiation. *Organizational Behavior and Human Decision Processes, 55,* 444–69.

Hinton, B. L., Hamner, W. C., & Pohlan, N. F. (1974). Influence and award of magnitude, opening bid and concession rate on profit earned in a managerial negotiating game. *Behavioral Science, 19,* 197–203.

Hitt, W. (1990). *Ethics and leadership: Putting theory into practice.* Columbus, OH: Battelle Press.

Hochberg, A. M., & Kressel, K. (1996). Determinations of successful and unsuccessful divorce negotiations. *Journal of Divorce and Remarriage, 25,* 1–21.

Hocker, J. L., & Wilmot, W. W. (1985). *Interpersonal conflict* (2nd ed.). Dubuque, IA: Wm. C. Brown.

Hofstede, G. (1980a). Motivation, leadership, and organization: Do American theories apply abroad? *Organizational Dynamics, 9,* 42–63.

Hofstede, G. (1980b). *Culture's consequences: International differences in work related values.* Beverly Hills, CA: Sage.

Hofstede, G. (1989). Cultural predictors of national negotiation styles. In. F. Mautner-Markhof (Ed.), *Processes of international negotiations* (pp. 193–201). Boulder, CO: Westview Press.

Hofstede, G. (1991). *Culture and organizations: Software of the mind.* London, UK: McGraw-Hill.

Hofstede, G., & Bond, M. H. (1988). Confucius and economic growth: New trends in culture's consequences. *Organizational Dynamics, 16,* 4–21.

Holaday, L. C. (2002). Stage development theory: A natural framework for understanding the mediation process. *Negotiation Journal, 18* (3), 191–210.

Homans, G. C. (1961). *Social behavior: Its elementary forms.* New York: Harcourt, Brace & World Co.

Hopmann, P. T. (1995). Two paradigms of negotiation: Bargaining and problem solving. *Annals of the American Academy, 542,* 24–47.

Hosmer, L. T. (2003). *The ethics of management* (4th ed.). Boston: McGraw-Hill/Irwin.

Howard, E. S., Gardner, W. L., & Thompson, L. (2007). The role of the self-concept and the social context in determining the behavior of power holders: Self-construal in intergroup versus dyadic dispute resolution negotiations. *Journal of Personality and Social Psychology, 93,* 614–31.

Huang, X., & van de Vliert, E. (2004). A multilevel approach to investigating cross-national differences in negotiation processes. *International Negotiation, 9,* 471–484.

Hunt, C. S., & Kernan, M. C. (2005). Framing negotiations in affective terms: Methodological and preliminary theoretical findings. *International Journal of Conflict Management, 16,* 128–156.

Ibarra, H., & Andrews, S. (1993). Power, social influence and sense making: Effects of network centrality and proximity on employee perceptions. *Administrative Science Quarterly, 38,* 277–303.

Ikle, F. C. (1964). *How nations negotiate.* New York: Harper & Row.

Isajiw, W. W. (2000). Approaches to ethnic conflict resolution: paradigms and principles. *International Journal of Inter-Cultural Relations, 24,* 105–24.

Isen, A. M., & Baron, R. A. (1991). Positive affect as a factor in organizational behavior. In B. M. Staw & L. L. Cummings (Eds.), *Research in organizational behavior* (Vol. 13, pp. 1–53). Greenwich, CT: JAI Press.

Ivey, A. E., & Simek-Downing, L. (1980). *Counseling and psychotherapy.* Englewood Cliffs, NJ: Prentice Hall.

Jacobs, A. T. (1951). Some significant factors influencing the range of indeterminateness in collective bargaining negotiations. Unpublished doctoral dissertation, University of Michigan, Ann Arbor, MI.

Janosik, R. J. (1987). Rethinking the culture-negotiation link. *Negotiation Journal, 3,* 385–95.

Jehn, E., & Mannix, E. (2001). The dynamic nature of conflict: A longitudinal study of intragroup conflict and group performance. *Academy of Management Journal, 44* (2), 238–51.

Jensen, L. (1995). Issue flexibility in negotiating internal war. *Annals of the American Academy of Political and Social Science, 542,* 116–30.

Johnson, D. W. (1971). Role reversal: A summary and review of the research. *International Journal of Group Tensions, 1,* 318–34.

Johnston, R. W. (1982, March–April). Negotiation strategies: Different strokes for different folks. *Personnel, 59,* 36–45.

Jones, E. E., & Nisbett, R. E. (1976). The actor and the observer: Divergent perceptions of causality. In J. W. Thibaut, J. T. Spence, & R. C. Carson (Eds.), *Contemporary topics in social psychology* (pp. 37–52). Morristown, NJ: General Learning Press.

Jones, M., & Worchel, S. (1992). Representatives in negotiation: "Internal" variables that affect "external" negotiations. *Basic and Applied Social Psychology, 13* (3), 323–36.

Kahneman, D., Knetsch, J. L., & Thaler, R. H. (1990). Experimental tests of the endowment effect and the Coase Theorem. *Journal of Political Economy, 98,* 1325–48.

Kahneman, D., & Tversky, A. (1979). Prospect theory: An analysis of decisions under risk. *Econometrica, 47,* 263–91.

Kale, S. H., & Barnes, J. W. (1992). Understanding the domain of cross-national buyer-seller interactions. *Journal of International Business Studies, 23,* 101–32.

Kaplan, Robert. (1984, Spring). Trade routes: The manager's network of relationships. *Organizational Dynamics, 12,* 37–52.

Karrass, C. L. (1974). *Give and take.* New York: Thomas Y. Crowell.

Karrass, G. (1985). *Negotiate to close: How to make more successful deals.* New York: Simon & Schuster.

Kellerman, J. L., Lewis, J., & Laird, J. D. (1989). Looking and loving: The effects of mutual gaze on feelings of romantic love. *Journal of Research in Personality, 23,* 145–61.

Kelley, H. H. (1966). A classroom study of the dilemmas in interpersonal negotiation. In K. Archibald (Ed.), *Strategic interaction and conflict: Original papers and discussion* (pp. 49–73). Berkeley, CA: Institute of International Studies.

Kelley, H. H., & Thibaut, J. (1969). Group problem solving. In G. Lindzey & E. Aronson (Eds.), *Handbook of social psychology* (2nd ed.), (Vol. 4, pp. 1–101). Reading, MA: Addison-Wesley.

Kemp, K. E., & Smith, W. P. (1994). Information exchange, toughness, and integrative bargaining: The roles of explicit cues and perspective-taking. *International Journal of Conflict Management, 5,* 5–21.

Kennedy, G. (1985). *Doing business abroad.* New York: Simon & Schuster.

Kim, P. H. (1997). Strategic timing in group negotiations: The implications of forced entry and forced exit for negotiators with unequal power. *Organizational Behavior and Human Decision Processes, 71,* 263–86.

Kim, P. H., Dirks, K. T., Cooper, C. D., & Ferrin, D. L. (2006). When more blame is better than less; The implications of internal vs. external attributions for the repair of trust after a competence- vs. integrity-based trust violation. *Organizational Behavior and Human Decision Processes*, *99,* 49–65.

Kim, P. H., Pinkley, R. L. & Fragale, A. R. (2005). Power dynamics in negotiation. *Academy of Management Review, 30,* (4), 799–822.

Kimmel, M. J., Pruitt, D. G., Magenau, J. M., Konar-Goldband, E., & Carnevale, P. J. D. (1980). Effects of trust aspiration and gender on negotiation tactics. *Journal of Personality and Social Psychology, 38,* 9–23.

Kleinke, C. L. (1986). Gaze and eye contact: A research review. *Psychological Bulletin, 100,* 78–100.

Koehn, D. (1997). Business and game playing: The false analogy. *Journal of Business Ethics, 16,* 1447–52.

Koeszegi, S. (2004). Trust building strategies in inter-organizational negotiations. *Journal of Managerial Psychology, 19,* (6), 640–660.

Koh, T. T. B. (1996). American strengths and weaknesses. *Negotiation Journal, 12,* 313–17.

Kolb, D. (1985). *The mediators.* Cambridge, MA: MIT Press.

Kolb, D. M., & Putnam, L. L. (1997). Through the looking glass: Negotiation theory refracted through the lens of gender. In S. Gleason (Ed.), *Frontiers in dispute resolution in labor relations and human resources* (pp. 231–57). East Lansing, MI: Michigan State University Press.

Komorita, S. S., & Brenner, A. R. (1968). Bargaining and concessions under bilateral monopoly. *Journal of Personality and Social Psychology, 9,* 15–20.

Kopelman, S., Rosette, A. S., & Thompson, L. (2006). The three faces of Eve: Strategic display of positive, negative, and neutral emotions in negotiations. *Organizational Behavior and Human Decision Processes, 99,* 81–101.

Kotter, J. (1979). *Power in management.* New York: AMACOM.

Kozan, M. K., & Ergin, C. (1999). The influence of intra-cultural value differences on conflict management processes. *International Journal of Conflict Management, 10,* 249–67.

Krackhardt, D., & Hanson, J. R. (1993, July–August). Informal networks: The company behind the chart. *Harvard Business Review, 71,* 104–11.

Kramer, R. (1994). The sinister attribution error: Paranoid cognition and collective distrust in organizations. *Motivation and Emotion, 18,* 199–203.

Kramer, R. M. (1991). The more the merrier? Social psychological aspects of multiparty negotiations in organizations. In M. H. Bazerman, R. J. Lewicki, & B. H. Sheppard, *Research on negotiation in organizations* (Vol. 3, pp. 307–32). Greenwich, CT: JAI Press.

Kramer, R. M., Pommerenke, P., & Newton, B. (1993). The social context of negotiation: Effects of trust, aspiration and gender on negotiation tactics. *Journal of Personality and Social Psychology, 38* (1), 9–22.

Kristensen, H., & Garling, T. (1997). The effects of anchor points and reference points on negotiation process and outcome. *Organizational Behavior and Human Decision Processes, 71,* 85–94.

Kristensen, H., & Garling, T. (2000). Anchor points, reference points, and counteroffers in negotiations. *Group Decision and Negotiation, 9,* 493–505.

Ku, G. (2008). Learning to de-escalate: The effects of regret in escalation of commitment. *Organizational Behavior and Human Decision Processes, 105,* 221–232.

Kumar, R. (1997). The role of affect in negotiations: An integrative overview. *Journal of Applied Behavioral Science, 3* (1), 84–100.

Kumar, R. (2004). Brahmanical idealism, anarchical individualism, and the dynamics of Indian negotiating behavior. *International Journal of Cross Cultural Management, 4,* 39–58.

Kumar, R., & Worm, V. (2004). Institutional dynamics and the negotiation process: comparing India and China. *International Journal of Conflict Management, 15* (3), 304–334.

Kwon, S., & Weingart, L. R. (2004). Unilateral concessions from the other party: Concession behavior, attributions, and negotiations judgments. *Journal of Applied Psychology, 89,* 263–278.

LaFasto, F. M. J., & Larson, C. E. (2001). *When teams work best.* Thousand Oaks, CA: Sage Publications, Inc.

Landon, E. L., Jr. (1997). For the most fitting deal, tailor negotiating strategy to each borrower. *Commercial Lending Review, 12,* 5–14.

Larrick, R. P., & Wu, G. (2007). Claiming a large slice of a small pie: Asymmetric disconfirmation in negotiation. *Journal of Personality and Social Psychology, 93,* 212–233.

Lax, D., & Sebenius, J. (1986). *The manager as negotiator: Bargaining for cooperation and competitive gain.* New York: Free Press.

Lax, D. A., & Sebenius, J. K. (2002). Dealcrafting: The substance of three-dimensional negotiations. *Negotiation Journal, 18,* 5–28.

Le Poole, S. (1989). Negotiating with Clint Eastwood in Brussels. *Management Review, 78,* 58–60.

Leung, K., Tong, K., & Ho, S. S. (2004). Effects of interactional justice on egocentric bias in resource allocation decisions. *Journal of Applied Psychology, 89* (3), 405–15.

Levinson, J. C., Smith, M. S. A., & Wilson, O. R. (1999). *Guerilla negotiating.* New York: John Wiley.

Lewicki, R., Wiethoff, C., & Tomlinson, E. (2005). What is the role of trust in organizational justice? In Greenberg, J. and Colquitt, J. *Handbook of organizational justice* (pp. 247–72). Mahwah, NJ: Lawrence Erlbaum Associates.

Lewicki, R. J. (1983). Lying and deception: A behavioral model. In M. H. Bazerman & R. J. Lewicki (Eds.), *Negotiating in organizations* (pp. 68–90). Beverly Hills, CA: Sage.

Lewicki, R. J. (1992). Negotiating strategically. In A. Cohen (Ed.), *The portable MBA in management* (pp. 147–89). New York: John Wiley and Sons.

Lewicki, R. J., & Dineen, B. R. (2002). Negotiating in virtual organizations. In Heneman, R. L. & Greenberger, D. B. *Human resource management in virtual organizations.* New York: John Wiley and Sons.

Lewicki, R. J., Gray, B., & Elliott, M. (2003). *Making sense of intractable environmental disputes.* Washington, DC: Island Press.

Lewicki, R. J., & Hiam, A. (1999). *The fast forward MBA in negotiation and dealmaking.* New York: John Wiley and Sons.

Lewicki, R. J., Hiam, A., & Olander, K. (1996). *Think before you speak: The complete guide to strategic negotiation.* New York: John Wiley and Sons.

Lewicki, R. J., & Robinson, R. (1998). A factor-analytic study of negotiator ethics. *Journal of Business Ethics, 18,* 211–28.

Lewicki, R. J., & Spencer, G. (1990, June). Lies and dirty tricks. Paper presented at the annual meeting of the International Association for Conflict Management, Vancouver, B. C., Canada.

Lewicki, R. J., & Spencer, G. (1991, August). Ethical relativism and negotiating tactics: Factors affecting their perceived ethicality. Paper presented at the annual meeting of the Academy of Management, Miami, FL.

Lewicki, R. J., & Stark, N. (1995). What's ethically appropriate in negotiations: An empirical examination of bargaining tactics. *Social Justice Research, 9,* 69–95.

Lewicki, R. J., Weiss, S., & Lewin, D. (1992). Models of conflict, negotiation and third-party intervention: A review and synthesis. *Journal of Organizational Behavior, 13,* 209–52.

Liebert, R. M., Smith, W. P., & Hill, J. H. (1968). The effects of information and magnitude of initial offer on interpersonal negotiation. *Journal of Experimental Social Psychology, 4,* 431–41.

Lim, R. G. (1997). Overconfidence in negotiation revisited. *International Journal of Conflict Management, 8,* 52–70.

Lim, R. G., & Murnighan, J. K. (1994). Phases, deadlines, and the bargaining process. *Organizational Behavior and Human Decision Processes, 58,* 153–71.

Lin, X., & Miller, S. J. (2003). Negotiation approaches: Direct and indirect effects of national culture. *International Marketing Review, 20,* 286–303.

Lindskold, S., Bentz, B., & Walters, P. D. (1986). Trust development, the GRIT proposal and the effects of conciliatory acts on conflict and cooperation. *Psychological Bulletin, 85,* 772–93.

Locke, E., & Latham, G. (1984). *Goal setting: A motivational technique that works!* Englewood Cliffs, NJ: Prentice Hall.

Loewenstein, G. F., Thompson, L., & Bazerman, M. H. (1989). Social utility and decision making in interpersonal contexts. *Journal of Personality and Social Psychology, 57* (3), 426–41.

Loewenstein, J., Morris, M.W., Chakravarti, A., Thompson, L., & Kopelman, S. (2005). At a loss for words: Dominating the conversation and the outcome in negotiation as a function of intricate arguments and communication media. *Organizational Behavior and Human Decision Processes, 98,* 28–38.

Loewenstein, J., & Thompson, L. (2000). The challenge of learning. *Negotiation Journal, 16,* 399–408.

Loewenstein, J., Thompson, L., & Gentner, D. (1999). Analogical encoding facilitates knowledge transfer in organizations. *Psychonomic Bulletin and Review, 6,* 586–97.

Loewenstein, J., Thompson, L., & Gentner, D. (2003). Analogical learning in negotiation teams: Comparing cases promotes learning and transfer. *Academy of Management Learning and Education, 2,* 119–27.

Macduff, I. (2006). Your pace or mine? Culture, time, and negotiation. *Negotiation Journal, 22* (1), 31–45.

Macneil, I. R. (1980). *The new social contract.* New Haven, CT: Yale University Press.

Malhotra, D. K. (2003). Reciprocity in the context of trust: The differing perspective of trustors and trusted parties. *Dissertation Abstracts, 63,* 11–18.

Malhotra, D. K. (2004). Trust and reciprocity decisions: The differing perspectives of trustors and trusted parties. *Organizational Behavior and Human Decision Processes, 94* (2), 61–73.

Malhotra, D., & Bazerman, M. H. (2007). Investigative negotiation. *Harvard Business Review, 85,* 72–78.

Manz, C. C., Neck, C. P., Mancuso, J., & Manz, K. P. (1997). *For team members only.* New York: AMACOM.

Matsumoto, D., & Yoo, S. H. (2006). Toward a new generation of cross-cultural research. *Perspectives on Psychological Science, 1* (3), 234–250.

Maxwell, S., Nye, P., & Maxwell, N. (1999). Less pain, some gain: The effects of priming fairness in price negotiations. *Psychology and Marketing, 16* (7), pp. 545–62.

Maxwell, S., Nye, P., & Maxwell, N. (2003). The wrath of the fairness-primed negotiator when the reciprocity is violated. *Journal of Business Research, 56* (5), pp. 399–409.

Mayer, J. D., Salovey, P., & Caruso, D. (2000). Emotional intelligence. In R. Sternberg (Ed.), *Handbook of intelligence* (pp. 396–420). Cambridge: Cambridge University Press.

Mayfield, M., Mayfield, J., Martin, D., & Herbig, P. (1997). Time perspectives of the cross-cultural negotiations process. *American Business Review, 15,* 78–85.

McAllister, D. J. (1995). Affect- and cognition-based trust as foundations for interpersonal cooperation in organizations. *Academy of Management Journal, 38,* 24–59.

McClelland, D. C. (1975). *Power: The inner experience.* New York: Irvington.

McClelland, D. C., & Burnham, D. H. (1976). Power is the great motivator. *Harvard Business Review, 43* (2), 100–110.

McCornack, S. A., & Levine, T. R. (1990). When lies are uncovered: Emotional and relational outcomes of discovered deception. *Communication Monographs, 57,* 119–38.

McDonald, J. W. (1996). An American's view of a U.S. negotiating style. *International Negotiation, 1,* 323–26.

McGraw, D. (1997, October 20). Will he own the road? *U.S. News & World Report,* pp. 45–54.

Metcalf, L. E., Bird, A., Peterson, M. F., Shankarmahesh, M., & Lituchy, T. R. (2007). Cultural influences in negotiations: A four country comparative analysis. *International Journal of Cross Cultural Management, 7* (2), 147–68.

Metcalf, L. E., Bird, A., Shankarmahesh, M., Aycan, Z., Larimo, J., & Valdelamar, D. D. (2006). Cultural tendencies in negotiation: A comparison of Finland, India, Mexico, Turkey, and the United States. *Journal of World Business, 41,* 382–94.

Midgaard, K., & Underal, A. (1977). Multiparty conferences. In D. Druckman (Ed.), *Negotiations: Social psychological perspectives* (pp. 329–45). Beverly Hills, CA: Sage.

Miller, D. T., & Ross, M. (1975). Self-serving bias in the attribution of causality: Fact or fiction? *Psychological Bulletin, 82,* 213–25.

Mintzberg, H., & Quinn, J. B. (1991). *The strategy process: Concepts, contexts, cases* (2nd ed.). Englewood Cliffs, NJ: Prentice Hall.

Missner, M. (1980). *Ethics of the business system.* Sherman Oaks, CA: Alfred Publishing Company.

Molm, L., Takahashi, N., & Peterson, G. (2003). In the eye of the beholder: Procedural justice in social exchange. *American Sociological Review, 68* (1), pp. 128–52.

Moran, R. T., & Stripp, W. G. (1991). *Dynamics of successful international business negotiations.* Houston, TX: Gulf Publishing.

Moran, S., & Ritov, I. (2002). Initial perceptions in negotiations: Evaluation and response to "logrolling" offers. *Journal of Behavioral Decision Making, 15,* 101–24.

Morley, I., & Stephenson, G. (1977). *The social psychology of bargaining.* London: Allen and Unwin.

Morris, M., Nadler, J., Kurtzberg, T., & Thompson, L. (2000). Schmooze or lose: Social friction and lubrication in e-mail negotiations. *Group Dynamics-Theory Research and Practice, 6,* 89–100.

Mosterd, I., & Rutte, C. G. (2000). Effects of time pressure and accountability to constituents on negotiation. *International Journal of Conflict Management, 11* (3), 227–47.

Mouzas, S. (2006). Negotiating umbrella agreements. *Negotiation Journal, 22* (3), 279–301.

Murnighan, J. K. (1986). Organizational coalitions: Structural contingencies and the formation process. In R. J. Lewicki, B. H. Sheppard, & M. H. Bazerman

(Eds.), *Research on negotiation in organizations* (Vol. 1, pp. 155–73). Greenwich, CT: JAI Press.

Myerson, D., Weick, K. E., & Kramer, R. M. (1996). Swift trust and temporary groups. In R. M. Kramer & T. Tyler (Eds.), *Trust in organizations: Frontiers of theory and research* (pp. 166–95). Thousand Oaks, CA: Sage Publications, Inc.

Nadler, J., Thompson, L., & Van Boven, L. (2003). Learning negotiation skills: Four models of knowledge creation and transfer. *Management Science, 49,* 529–40.

Naquin, C. E. (2002). The agony of opportunity in negotiation: Number of negotiable issues, counterfactual thinking, and feelings of satisfaction. *Organizational Behavior and Human Decision Processes, 91,* 97–107.

Naquin, C. E., & Paulson, G. D. (2003). Online bargaining and interpersonal trust. *Journal of Applied Psychology, 88* (1), 113–20.

Nash, J. F. (1950). The bargaining problem. *Econometrica, 18,* 155–62.

Natlandsmyr, J. H., & Rognes, J. (1995). Culture, behavior, and negotiation outcomes: A comparative and cross-cultural study of Mexican and Norwegian negotiators. *International Journal of Conflict Management, 6,* 5–29.

Neale, M., & Bazerman, M. H. (1983). The role of perspective-taking ability in negotiating under different forms of arbitration. *Industrial and Labor Relations Review, 36,* 378–88.

Neale, M., & Bazerman, M. H. (1985). The effects of framing and negotiator overconfidence on bargaining behaviors and outcomes. *Academy of Management Journal, 28,* 34–49.

Neale, M., & Bazerman, M. H. (1991). *Cognition and rationality in negotiation.* New York: Free Press.

Neale, M. A., & Bazerman, M. H. (1992a). Negotiator cognition and rationality: A behavioral decision theory perspective. *Organizational Behavior and Human Decision Processes, 51,* 157–75.

Neale, M., & Bazerman, M. H. (1992b). Negotiating rationally: The power and impact of the negotiator's frame. *Academy of Management Executive, 6* (3), 42–51.

Neale, M., Huber, V., & Northcraft, G. (1987). The framing of negotiations: Contextual vs. task frames. *Organizational Behavior and Human Decision Processes, 39,* 228–41.

Neale, M. A., & Northcraft, G. B. (1986). Experts, amateurs, and refrigerators: Comparing expert and amateur negotiators in a novel task. *Organizational Behavior and Human Decision Processes, 38,* 305–17.

Neale, M. A., & Northcraft, G. B. (1991). Behavioral negotiation theory: A framework for conceptualizing dyadic bargaining.

In L. L. Cummings & B. M. Staw (Eds.), *Research in organizational behavior* (Vol. 13, pp. 147–90). Greenwich, CT: JAI Press.

Nelson, D., & Wheeler, M. (2004). Rocks and hard places: Managing two tensions in negotiation. *Negotiation Journal, 20,* 113–125.

Nemeth, C. J. (1986). Differential contributions to majority and minority influence. *Psychological Review, 93,* 23–32.

Nemeth, C. J. (1989). The stimulating properties of dissent. Paper presented at the first annual Conference on Group Process and Productivity, Texas A & M University, College Station, TX.

Nierenberg, G. (1976). *The complete negotiator.* New York: Nierenberg & Zeif Publishers.

Nierenberg, G., & Calero, H. (1971). *How to read a person like a book.* New York: Simon & Schuster.

Northcraft, G. B., & Neale, M. A. (1987). Experts, amateurs, and real estate: An anchoring and adjustment perspective on property pricing decisions. *Organizational Behavior and Human Decision Processes, 39,* 228–41.

Novemsky, N., & Schweitzer, M. E. (2004). What makes negotiators happy? The differential effects of internal and external social comparisons on negotiator satisfaction. *Organization Behavior and Human Decision Processes, 95,* 186–97.

O'Connor, K. M. (1997). Motives and cognitions in negotiation: A theoretical integration and an empirical test. *International Journal of Conflict Management, 8,* 114–31.

O'Connor, K. M., & Arnold, J. A. (2001). Distributive spirals: Negotiation impasses and the moderating role of disputant self-efficacy. *Organizational Behavior and Human Decision Processes, 84,* 148–76.

O'Connor, K. M., & Carnevale, P. J. (1997). A nasty but effective negotiation strategy: Misrepresentation of a common-value issue. *Personality and Social Psychology Bulletin, 23,* 504–15.

Ogawa, N. (1999). The concept of facework: Its function in the Hawaii model of mediation. *Mediation Quarterly, 17,* 5–20.

Ohanyan, A. (1999). Negotiation culture in a post-Soviet context: An interdisciplinary perspective. *Mediation Quarterly, 17,* 83–104.

Ohbuchi, K., & Takahashi, Y. (1994). Cultural styles of conflict management in Japanese and Americans: Passivity, covertness, and effectiveness of strategies. *Journal of Applied Social Psychology, 24,* 1345–66.

Olekalns, M. (2002). Negotiation as social interaction. *Australian Journal of Management, 27,* 39–46.

Olekalns, M., Lau, F., & Smith, P. L. (2007). Resolving the empty core: Trust as a determinant of outcomes in three-party negotiation. *Group Decision and Negotiation, 16,* 527–538.

Olekalns, M., & Smith, P. (2001). Metacognition in negotiation: The identification of critical events and their role in shaping trust and outcomes. Melbourne Business School Working Paper 2001–15.

Olekalns, M., & Smith, P. (2005). Moments in time: Metacognitions, trust and outcomes in dyadic negotiations. *Personality and Social Psychology Bulletin, 31* (12), 1696–707.

Olekalns, M., Smith, P. L., & Walsh, T. (1996). The process of negotiating: Strategy and timing as predictors of outcomes. *Organizational Behavior and Human Decision Processes, 68,* 68–77.

Oliver, R. L., Balakrishnan, P. V., & Barry, B. (1994). Outcome satisfaction in negotiation: A test of expectancy disconfirmation. *Organizational Behavior and Human Decision Processes, 60,* 252–75.

Palich, L. E., Carini, G. R., & Livingstone, L. P. (2002). Comparing American and Chinese negotiating styles: The influence of logic paradigms. *Thunderbird International Business Review, 44,* 777–98.

Parrott, W. (1994). Beyond hedonism: Motives for inhibiting good moods and for maintaining bad moods. In D. M. Wegner & J. W. Pennebaker (Eds.), *Handbook of mental control* (pp. 278–305). Englewood Cliffs, NJ: Prentice Hall.

Parrott, W. G. (2001). Emotions in social psychology: Volume overview. In W. G. Parrott (Ed.), *Emotions in social psychology* (pp. 1–19). Philadelphia: Psychology Press.

Patterson, J., & Kim, P. (1991). *The day America told the truth.* New York: Prentice Hall.

Pfeffer, J. (1992). *Managing with power.* Boston, MA: Harvard Business School Press.

Pfeffer, J., & Salancik, G. R. (1974). Organizational decision making as a political process: The case of a university budget. *Administrative Science Quarterly, 19,* 135–51.

Pfouts, R. W. (1994). Buying a pig when both buyer and seller are in a poke. *Atlantic Economic Journal, 22,* 80–85.

Phatak, A. V., & Habib, M. H. (1996). The dynamics of international business negotiations. *Business Horizons, 39,* 30–38.

Pillutla, M. M., & Murnighan, J. K. (1996). Unfairness, anger and spite: Emotional rejections of ultimatum offers. *Organizational Behavior and Human Decision Processes, 68* (3), 208–24.

Pines, A. M., Gat, H., & Tal, Y. (2002). Gender differences and content and style of argument between couples during divorce mediation. *Conflict Resolution Quarterly, 20* (1), 23–50.

Pinkley, R. L. (1992). Dimensions of conflict frame: Relation to disputant perceptions and expectations. *International Journal of Conflict Management, 3,* 95–113.

Pinkley, R. L. (1995). Impact of knowledge regarding alternatives to settlement in dyadic negotiations: Whose knowledge counts? *Journal of Applied Psychology, 80,* 403–17.

Pinkley, R. L., Griffith, T. L., & Northcraft, G. B. (1995). "Fixed pie" a la mode: Information availability, information processing, and the negotiation of suboptimal agreements. *Organizational Behavior and Human Decision Processes, 62,* 101–12.

Pinkley, R. L., Neale, M. A., & Bennett, R. J. (1994). The impact of alternatives to settlement in dyadic negotiation. *Organizational Behavior and Human Decision Processes, 57,* 97–116.

Pinkley, R. L., & Northcraft, G. B. (1994). Cognitive interpretations of conflict: Implications for dispute processes and outcomes. *Academy of Management Journal, 37,* 193–205.

Polzer, J. T., Mannix, E. A., & Neale, M. A. (1995). Multiparty negotiations in a social context. In R. Kramer & D. Messick (Eds.), *Negotiation as a social process* (pp. 123–42). Thousand Oaks, CA: Sage.

Polzer, J. T., Mannix, E. A., & Neale, M. A. (1998). Interest alignment and coalitions in multiparty negotiation. *Academy of Management Journal, 41* (1), 42–54.

Provis, C. (1996). Interests vs. positions: A critique of the distinction. *Negotiation Journal, 12,* 305–23.

Pruitt, D. G. (1981). *Negotiation behavior.* New York: Academic Press.

Pruitt, D. G. (1983). Strategic choice in negotiation. *American Behavioral Scientist, 27,* 167–94.

Pruitt, D. G., & Carnevale, P. J. D. (1993). *Negotiation in social conflict.* Pacific Grove, CA: Brooks-Cole.

Pruitt, D. G., & Lewis, S. A. (1975). Development of integrative solutions in bilateral negotiation. *Journal of Personality and Social Psychology, 31,* 621–33.

Pruitt, D. G., & Rubin, J. Z. (1986). *Social conflict: Escalation, stalemate and settlement.* New York: Random House.

Pruitt, D. G., & Syna, H. (1985). Mismatching the opponent's offers in negotiation. *Journal of Experimental Social Psychology, 21,* 103–13.

Putnam, L. L. (1994). Productive conflict: Negotiation as implicit coordination. *International Journal of Conflict Management, 5,* 284–98.

Putnam, L. L., & Holmer, M. (1992). Framing, reframing, and issue development. In L. Putnam & M. Roloff (Eds.), *Communication and negotiation* (pp. 128–55). Newbury Park, CA: Sage.

Putnam, L. L., & Jones, T. S. (1982). Reciprocity in negotiations: An analysis of bargaining interaction. *Communication Monographs, 49,* 171–91.

Putnam, L. L., & Wilson, S. R. (1989). Argumentation and bargaining strategies as discriminators of integrative outcomes. In M. A. Rahim (Ed.), *Managing conflict: An interdisciplinary approach* (pp. 121–31). New York: Praeger.

Putnam, L., Wilson, S., & Turner, D. (1990). The evolution of policy arguments in teachers' negotiations. *Argumentation, 4,* 129–52.

Pye, L. W. (1992). *Chinese negotiating style.* New York: Quorum Books.

Quinn, J. B. (1991). Strategies for change. In H. Mintzberg & J. B. Quinn (Eds.), *The strategy process: Concepts, contexts, cases* (2nd ed., pp. 4–12). Englewood Cliffs, NJ: Prentice Hall.

Rahim, M. A. (1983). A measure of styles of handling interpersonal conflict. *Academy of Management Journal, 26,* 368–76.

Rahim, M. A. (1992). *Managing conflict in organizations* (2nd ed.). Westport, CT: Praeger.

Raiffa, H. (1982). *The art and science of negotiation.* Cambridge, MA: Belknap Press of Harvard University Press.

Rapoport, A. (1964). *Strategy and conscience.* New York: Harper & Row.

Rapoport, A., Erev, I., & Zwick, R. (1995). An experimental study of buyer-seller negotiation with one-sided incomplete information and time discounting. *Management Science, 41,* 377–94.

Raven, B. (1993). The bases of power: Origins and recent developments. *Journal of Social Issues, 49* (4), 227–51.

Raven, B., Schwartzwald, J. & Koslowski, M. (1998). Conceptualizing and measuring a power/interaction model of interpersonal influence. *Journal of Applied Social Psychology, 28* (4), 297–332.

Raven, B. H., & Rubin, J. Z. (1976). *Social psychology: People in groups.* New York: John Wiley and Sons.

Richardson, R. C. (1977). *Collective bargaining by objectives.* Englewood Cliffs, NJ: Prentice Hall.

Ritov, I. (1996). Anchoring in simulated competitive market negotiation. *Organizational Behavior and Human Decision Processes, 67,* 16–25.

Robinson, R., Lewicki, R. J., & Donahue, E. (2000). Extending and testing a five factor model of ethical and unethical bargaining tactics: The SINS scale. *Journal of Organizational Behavior, 21,* 649–64.

Rogers, C. R. (1957). *Active listening.* Chicago, IL: University of Chicago Press.

Rogers, C. R. (1961). *On becoming a person: A therapist's view of psychotherapy.* Boston, MA: Houghton Mifflin.

Ross, L., Green, D., & House, P. (1977). The false consensus phenomenon: An attributional bias in self-perception and social-perception processes. *Journal of Experimental Social Psychology, 13,* 279–301.

Ross, M. H. (2000). "Good-enough" isn't so bad: Thinking about success and failure in ethnic conflict management. *Peace and Conflict: Journal of Peace Psychology, 6,* 21–27.

Roth, A., & Malouf, M. (1979). Game-theoretic models and the role of information in bargaining. *Psychological Review, 86,* 574–94.

Roth, A. E., Murnighan, J. K., & Schoumaker, F. (1988). The deadline effect in bargaining: Some empirical evidence. *American Economic Review, 78,* 806–23.

Roth, J., & Sheppard, B. H. (1995). Opening the black box of framing research: The relationship between frames, communication, and outcomes. *Academy of Management Proceedings.*

Rubin, J., Pruitt, D., & Kim, S. H. (1994). *Social conflict: Escalation, stalemate and settlement* (2nd ed.). New York: McGraw-Hill.

Rubin, J. Z., & Brown, B. R. (1975). *The social psychology of bargaining and negotiation.* New York: Academic Press.

Rubin, J. Z., & Sander, F. E. A. (1991). Culture, negotiation, and the eye of the beholder. *Negotiation Journal, 7* (3), 249–54.

Rubinstein, R. A. (2003). Cross cultural considerations in complex peace operations. *Negotiation Journal, 19* (1), 29–49.

Russo, J. E., & Schoemaker, P. J. H. (1989). *Decision traps: The ten barriers to brilliant decision making and how to overcome them.* New York: Simon & Schuster.

Salacuse, J. (1998). So, what's the deal anyway? Contracts and relationships as negotiating goals. *Negotiation Journal, 14* (1), pp. 5–12.

Salacuse, J. W. (1988). Making deals in strange places: A Seginner's guide to international business negotiations. *Negotiation Journal 4,* 5–13.

Salancik, G. R., & Pfeffer, J. (1977). Who gets power and how they hold on to it: A strategic-contingency model of power. *Organizational Dynamics, 5,* 3–21.

Saorin-Iborra, M. C. (2006). A review of negotiation outcome: A proposal on delimitation and subsequent assessment in joint venture negotiation. *Canadian Journal of Administrative Sciences, 23* (3), 237–52.

Savage, G. T., Blair, J. D., & Sorenson, R. L. (1989). Consider both relationships and substance when negotiating strategically. *Academy of Management Executive, 3* (1), 37–48.

Schatzski, M. (1981). *Negotiation: The art of getting what you want.* New York: Signet Books.

Schein, E. (1988). *Organisational Culture and Leadership.* San Francisco: Jossey-Bass.

Schelling, T. C. (1960). *The strategy of conflict.* Cambridge, MA: Harvard University Press.

Schlenker, B. R., Helm, B., & Tedeschi, J. T. (1973). The effects of personality and situational variables on behavioral trust. *Journal of Personality and Social Psychology, 25* (3), 419–27.

Schneider, A. K. (2002). Shattering negotiation myths: Empirical evidence on the effectiveness of negotiation style. *Harvard Law Review, 7,* 143–233.

Schreisheim, C., & Hinkin, T. R. (1990). Influence strategies used by subordinates: A theoretical and empirical analysis and refinement of the Kipnis, Schmidt, and Wilkinson subscales. *Journal of Applied Psychology, 75,* 246–57.

Schroth, H. A., Bain-Chekal, J., Caldwell, D. F. (2005). Sticks and stones may break bones and words can hurt me: Words and phrases that trigger emotions in negotiations and their effects. *International Journal of Conflict Management, 16,* 102–127.

Schurr, P. H. (1987). Effects of gain and loss decision frames on risky purchase negotiations. *Journal of Applied Psychology, 72* (3), 351–58.

Schwartz, S. H. (1992). Universals in the content and structure of values: Theoretical advances and empirical tests in 20 countries. In M. Zanna (Ed.), *Advances in experimental social psychology* (Vol. 25, pp. 1–65). Orlando, FL: Academic Press.

Schwartz, S. H. (1994). Beyond individualism and collectivism: New cultural dimensions of values. In U. Kim, H. C. Triandis, C. Kagitcibasi, S-C. Choi, & G. Yoom (eds.), *Individualism and collectivism: Theory, method and application* (pp. 85–122). Thousand Oaks, CA: Sage Publications.

Schwartz, S. H., & Bilsky, W. (1990). Toward a theory of universal content and structure of values: Extensions and cross-cultural replications. *Journal of Personality and Social Psychology, 58,* 878–91.

Schweitzer, M. E. (1997). Omission, friendship and fraud: Lies about material facts in negotiation. Unpublished manuscript.

Schweitzer, M. E., & Croson, R. (1999). Curtailing deception: The impact of direct questions on lies and omissions. *International Journal of Conflict Management, 10* (3), 225–48.

Schweitzer, M. E., Brodt, S. E., & Croson , R. T. A. (2002). Seeing and believing: Visual access and the strategic use of deception. *International Journal of Conflict Management, 13,* 258–75.

Schweitzer, M. E., Hershey, J. C. & Bradlow, E. T. (2006). Promises and lies: Restoring violated trust. *Organizational Behavior and Human Decision Processes, 101,* 1–19.

Schweitzer, M. E., & Kerr, J. L. (2000). Bargaining under the influence: The role of alcohol in negotiations. *Academy of Management Executive, 14,* 47–57.

Sebenius, J. K. (1983). Negotiation arithmetic: Adding and subtracting issues and parties. *International Organization, 37,* 1–34.

Sebenius, J. K. (1992). Negotiation analysis: A characterization and review. *Management Science, 38,* 18–38.

Sebenius, J. K. (2002a, March). The hidden challenge of cross-border negotiations. *Harvard Business Review, 80,* 76–85.

Sebenius, J. K. (2002b). Caveats for cross-border negotiations. *Negotiation Journal, 18* (2), 121–33.

Selekman, B. M., Fuller, S. H., Kennedy, T., & Baitsel, J. M. (1964). *Problems in labor relations.* New York: McGraw-Hill.

Sen, A. K. (1970). *Collective choice and individual values.* San Francisco: Holden-Day.

Senge, P. (1990). *The fifth discipline: The art and practice of the learning organization.* New York: Doubleday Currency.

Shah, P. P., & Jehn, K. A. (1993). Do friends perform better than acquaintances? The interaction of friendship, conflict and task. *Group Decision and Negotiation, 2,* 149–65.

Shapiro, D. L. (1991). The effects of explanations on negative reactions to deceit. *Administrative Science Quarterly, 36,* 614–30.

Shapiro, D. L., & Bies, R. J. (1994). Threats, bluffs and disclaimers in negotiation. *Organizational Behavior and Human Decision Processes, 60,* 14–35.

Shea, G. F. (1983). *Creative negotiating.* Boston, MA: CBI Publishing Co.

Sheppard, B. H., Lewicki, R. J., & Minton, J. W. (1992). *Organizational justice: The search for fairness in the workplace.* New York: Lexington Books.

Sheppard, B. H., & Tuchinsky, M. (1996a). Micro-OB and the network organization. In R. Kramer & T. Tyler (Eds.), *Trust in organizations* (pp. 140–65). Thousand Oaks, CA: Sage.

Sheppard, B. H., & Tuchinsky, M. (1996b). Interfirm relations: A grammar of pairs. In B. M. Staw & L. L. Cummings (Eds.), *Research on organizational behavior* (Vol. 18, pp. 331–73). Greenwich, CT: JAI Press.

Sherif, M., Harvey, L., White, B., Hood, W., & Sherif, C. (1988). *The Robbers' Cave experiment: Intergroup conflict and cooperation.* Middletown, CT: Wesleyan University Press. (Original work published 1961.)

Short, J., Williams, E., & Christie, B. (1976). *The social psychology of telecommunications.* London: John Wiley and Sons.

Siegel, S. R., & Fouraker, L. E. (1960). *Bargaining and group decision making: Experiments in bilateral monopoly.* New York: McGraw-Hill.

Sims, R. L. (2002). Support for the use of deception within the work environment: A comparison of Israeli and United States employee attitudes. *Journal of Business Ethics, 35,* 27–34.

Simons, T. (1993). Speech patterns and the concept of utility in cognitive maps: The case of integrative bargaining. *Academy of Management Journal, 36,* 139–56.

Simons, T., & Tripp, T. M. (1997). "The Negotiation Checklist." *The Cornell Hotel & Restaurant Administrative Quarterly, 38,* 14–23. In R. J. Lewicki, David M. Saunders, & Bruce Barry, *Negotiation* (5th ed.), Burr Ridge, IL: McGraw-Hill/Irwin.

Sinaceur, M., & Tiedens, L. Z. (2006). Get mad and get more than even: When and why anger expression is effective in negotiations. *Journal of Experimental Social Psychology, 42,* 314–22.

Sitkin, S. B., & Bies, R. J. (1993). Social accounts in conflict situations: Using explanations to manage conflict. *Human Relations, 46,* 349–70.

Skarlicki, D. P., & Folger, R. (1997). Retaliation in the workplace: The roles of distributive, procedural and interactive justice. *Journal of Applied Psychology, 82* (3), 434–43.

Smith, P., & Schwartz, S. H. (1997). Values. In J. W. Berry, M. H. Segall., and C. Kagitcibashi (Eds.), *Handbook of cross-cultural psychology* (Vol. 3, pp. 77–118). Needham Heights, MA: Allyn & Bacon.

Smith, T. H. (2005). Metaphors for navigating negotiations. *Negotiation Journal, 21,* 343–64.

Solomon, R. H. (1987). China: Friendship and obligation in Chinese negotiating style. In H. Binnendijk (Ed.), *National negotiating styles* (pp. 1–16). Washington, DC: Foreign Service Institute.

Sondak, H., Neale, M. A., & Pinkley, R. (1995). The negotiated allocation of benefits and burdens: The impact of outcome valence, contribution and relationship. *Organizational Behavior and Human Decision Processes, 64* (3), 249–60.

Song, F. (2004). Trust and reciprocity: The differing norms of individuals and group representatives. Unpublished paper.

Spitzberg, B. H., & Cupach, W. R. (1984). *Interpersonal communication competence.* Beverly Hills, CA: Sage.

Sproull, L., & Kiesler, S. (1986). Reducing social context cues: Electronic mail in organizational communication. *Management Science, 32,* 1492–512.

Stacks, D. W., & Burgoon, J. K. (1981). The role of non-verbal behaviors as distractors in resistance to persuasion in interpersonal contexts. *Central States Speech Journal, 32,* 61–80.

Stark, A., Fam, K. S., Waller, D. S., & Tian, Z. (2005). Chinese negotiation practice: A perspective from New Zealand exporters. *Cross Cultural Management, 12* (3), 85–102.

Staw, B. M. (1981). The escalation of commitment to a course of action. *Academy of Management Review, 6,* 577–87.

Stein, J. (1996). The art of real estate negotiations. *Real Estate Review, 25,* 48–53.

Stein, J. G. (1999). Problem solving as metaphor: Negotiation and identity conflict. *Peace and Conflict: Journal of Peace Psychology, 5,* 225–35.

Stillenger, C., Epelbaum, M., Keltner, D., & Ross, L. (1990). The "reactive devaluation" barrier to conflict resolution. Working paper, Stanford University, Palo Alto, CA.

Swaab, R. I., Phillips, K. W., Diermeier, D. & Medvec, V. H. (2008). The pros and cons of dyadic side conversations in small groups. *Small Group Research.* In press.

Tajima, M., & Fraser, N. M. (2001). Logrolling procedure for multi-issue negotiation. *Group Decision and Negotiation, 10,* 217–35.

Taylor, P. J., & Donald, I. (2003). Foundations and evidence for an interaction based approach to conflict negotiation. *International Journal of Conflict Management, 14,* 213–32.

Taylor, S. E., & Brown, J. D. (1988). Illusion and well-being: A social-psychological perspective on mental health. *Psychological Bulletin, 103,* 193–210.

Tedeschi, J. T., Heister, D. S., & Gahagan, J. P. (1969). Trust and the prisoner's dilemma game. *Journal of Social Psychology, 79,* 43–50.

Tenbrunsel, A. E. (1998). Misrepresentation and expectations of misrepresentation in an ethical dilemma: The role of incentives and temptation. *Academy of Management Journal, 4* (3), 330–39.

Tenbrunsel, A. E. (1999). Trust as an obstacle in environmental-economic disputes. *American Behavioral Scientist, 42,* 1350–67.

The American Heritage Dictionary of the English Language (3rd ed.), (1992). Houghton Mifflin.

Thomas, K. W. (1992). Conflict and negotiation processes in organizations. In M. D. Dunnette and L. H. Hough, *Handbook of industrial & organizational psychology* (2nd ed., Vol. 3, pp. 651–718). Palo Alto, CA: Consulting Psychologists Press.

Thomas, K. W., & Kilmann, R. H. (1974). *Thomas-Kilmann conflict mode survey.* Tuxedo, NY: Xicom.

Thompson, L. (1990a). Negotiation behavior and outcomes: Empirical evidence and theoretical issues. *Psychological Bulletin, 108,* 515–32.

Thompson, L. (1990b). An examination of naïve and experienced negotiators. *Journal of Personality and Social Psychology, 59,* 82–90.

Thompson, L. (1991). Information exchange in negotiation. *Journal of Experimental Social Psychology, 27,* 161–79.

Thompson, L. (1995). They saw a negotiation: Partnership and involvement. *Journal of Personality and Social Psychology, 68,* 839–53.

Thompson, L. (1998). *The mind and heart of the negotiator.* Upper Saddle River, NJ: Prentice Hall.

Thompson, L., & DeHarpport, T. (1994). Social judgment, feedback, and interpersonal learning in negotiation. *Organizational Behavior and Human Decision Processes, 58,* 327–45.

Thompson, L., Gentner, J. & Loewenstein, J. (2000). Avoiding missed opportunities in managerial life: Analogical training more powerful than individual case training. *Organizational Behavior and Human Decision Processes, 82,* 60–75.

Thompson, L., & Hastie, R. (1990a). Social perception in negotiation. *Organizational Behavior and Human Decision Processes, 47,* 98–123.

Thompson, L., & Hastie, R. (1990b). Judgment tasks and biases in negotiation. In B. H. Sheppard, M. H. Bazerman, & R. J. Lewicki (Eds.), *Research on negotiation in organizations* (Vol. 2, pp. 31–54). Greenwich, CT: JAI Press.

Thompson, L., & Hrebec, D. (1996). Lose-lose agreements in interdependent decision making. *Psychological Bulletin, 120,* 396–409.

Thompson, L., Peterson, E., & Brodt, S. E. (1996). Team negotiations: An examination of integrative and distributive bargaining. *Journal of Personality and Social Psychology, 70,* 66–78.

Thompson, L., Valley, K. L., & Kramer, R. M. (1995). The bittersweet feeling of success: An examination of social perception in negotiation. *Journal of Experimental Social Psychology, 31,* 467–92.

Thompson, L. L., Nadler, J., & Kim, P. H. (1999). Some like it hot: The case for the emotional negotiator. In L. L. Thompson, J. M. Levine, & D. M. Messick (Eds.), *Shared cognition in organizations: The management of knowledge* (pp. 139–61). Mahwah, NJ: Erlbaum.

Ting-Toomey, S., & Kurogi, A. (1998). Facework competence in intercultural conflict: An updated face-negotiation theory. *International Journal of Intercultural Relations, 22,* 187–225.

Tinsley, C. H. (1997). Understanding conflict in a Chinese cultural context. In R. J. Bies, R. J. Lewicki, & B. H. Sheppard (Eds.), *Research on negotiation in organizations* (Vol. 6: 209–25). Greenwich, CT: JAI Press.

Tinsley, C. H. (1998). Models of conflict resolution in Japanese, German, and American cultures. *Journal of Applied Psychology, 83,* 316–23.

Tinsley, C. H. (2001). How negotiators get to yes: Predicting the constellation of strategies used across cultures to negotiate conflict. *Journal of Applied Psychology, 86,* 583–93.

Tinsley, C. H., Brett, J. M., Shapiro, S. L., & Okumura, T. (2004). When do cultural values explain cross-cultural phenomena? An introduction and test of cultural complexity theory. Unpublished paper, Dispute Resolution Research Center, Northwestern University, Evanston, IL.

Tjosvold, D. (1997). The leadership relationship in Hong Kong: Power, interdependence and controversy. In K. Leung, U. Kim, S. Yamaguchi, & Y. Kashima (Eds.), *Progress in Asian social psychology* (Vol. 1). New York: John Wiley.

Tomlinson, E., Dineen, B., & Lewicki, R. (2004). The road to reconciliation: Antecedents of victim willingness to reconcile following a broken promise. *Journal of Management, 30,* 165–187.

Tompkins, P. K. (1993). *Organizational communication imperatives: Lessons of the space program.* Los Angeles: Roxbury Publishing Company.

Touval, S. (1988). Multilateral negotiation: An analytical approach. *Negotiation Journal, 5* (2), 159–73.

Triandis, H. C. (1982). Review of culture's consequences: International differences in work values. *Human Organization, 41,* 86–90.

Tripp, T. M., Sondak, H., & Bies, R. J. (1995). Justice as rationality: A relational perspective on fairness in negotiations. In R. J. Lewicki, B. H. Sheppard, & R. J. Bies (Ed.), *Research on negotiation in organizations* (Vol. 5, pp. 45–64). Greenwich, CT: JAI Press.

Tuchinsky, M. (1998). Negotiation approaches in close relationships. Duke University. Unpublished doctoral dissertation.

Tuchinsky, M. B., Edson Escalas, J., Moore, M. C., & Sheppard, B. H. (1994). Beyond name, rank and function: Construals of relationships in business. In D. P. Moore, *Proceedings of the Academy of Management,* 79–83.

Tung, R. L. (1991). Handshakes across the sea: Cross-cultural negotiating for business success. *Organizational Dynamics, 19,* Winter. 30–40.

Tutzauer, F. (1991). Bargaining outcome, bargaining process, and the role of communication. *Progress in Communication Science, 10,* 257–300.

Tutzauer, F. (1992). The communication of offers in dyadic bargaining. In L. Putnam & M. Roloff (Eds.), *Communication and negotiation* (pp. 67–82). Newbury Park, CA: Sage.

Tversky, A., & Kahneman, D. (1982). Judgment under uncertainty: Heuristics and biases. In D. Kahneman, P. Slovic, and A. Tversky (Eds.), *Judgment under uncertainty: Heuristics and biases* (pp. 3–22). Cambridge: Cambridge University Press.

Tyler, T., & Blader, S. R. (2004). *Justice and negotiation.* In M. Gelfand & J. Brett, *The handbook of negotiation and culture* (pp. 295–312). Stanford, CA: Stanford University Press.

Tyler, T., & Hastie, R. (1991). The social consequences of cognitive illusions. In M. H. Bazerman, R. J. Lewicki, and B. H. Sheppard (Eds.), *Research on negotiation in organizations* (Vol. 3, pp. 69–98). Greenwich, CT: JAI Press.

Ury, W. (1991). *Getting past no: Negotiating with difficult people.* New York: Bantam Books.

Ury, W. L., Brett, J. M., & Goldberg, S. B. (1988). *Getting disputes resolved.* San Francisco: Jossey-Bass.

Valley, K. L., Moag, J., & Bazerman, M. H. (1998). A matter of trust: Effects of communication on the efficiency and distribution of outcomes. *Journal of Economic Behavior and Organization, 34,* 211–38.

Van Boven, L., Gilovich, T., & Medvec, V. H. (2003). The illusion of transparency in negotiations. *Negotiation Journal, 19,* 117–131.

van de Vliert, E. (1985). Escalative intervention in small group conflicts. *Journal of Applied Behavioral Science, 21,* 19–36.

van Dijk, E., Van Kleef, G., Steinel, W., & van Beest, I. (2008). A social functional approach to emotions in bargaining: When communicating anger pays and when it backfires. *Journal of Personality and Social Psychology, 94,* 600–614.

Van Kleef, G. A., de Dreu, C. K. W., & Manstead, A. S. R. (2004). The interpersonal effects of anger and happiness in negotiations. *Journal of Personality and Social Psychology, 86,* 57–76.

Van Kleef, G. A., de Dreu, C. K. W., & Manstead, A. S. R. (2006). Supplication and appeasement in conflict and negotiation: The interpersonal effects of disappointment, worry, guilt, and regret. *Journal of Personality and Social Psychology, 91,* 124–42.

Van Poucke, D., & Buelens, M. (2002). Predicting the outcome of a two-party price negotiation: Contribution of reservation price, aspiration price, and opening offer. *Journal of Economic Psychology, 23,* 67–76.

Veitch, R., & Griffith, W. (1976). Good news–bad news: Affective and interpersonal affects. *Journal of Applied Social Psychology, 6,* 69–75.

Volkema, R. J., & Fleury, M. T. L. (2002). Alternative negotiating conditions and the choice of negotiation tactics: A cross-cultural comparison. *Journal of Business Ethics, 36,* 381–98.

Walcott, C., Hopmann, P. T., & King, T. D. (1977). The role of debate in negotiation. In D. Druckman (Ed.), *Negotiations: Social-psychological perspectives* (pp. 193–211). Beverly Hills, CA: Sage.

Walton, R. E., & McKersie, R. B. (1965). *A behavioral theory of labor negotiations: An analysis of a social interaction system.* New York: McGraw-Hill.

Wanis-St. John, A. (2006). Back-channel negotiation: International bargaining in the shadows. *Negotiation Journal, 22* (2), 119–44.

Watkins, M. (2002). *Breakthrough business negotiations.* San Francisco: Jossey-Bass.

Weeks, H. (2001). Taking the stress out of stressful conversations. *Harvard Business Review,* July–August, 112–19.

Weingart, L. R., Bennett, R. J., & Brett, J. M. (1993). The impact of consideration of issues and motivational orientation group negotiation process and outcome. *Journal of Applied Psychology, 78* (3), 504–17.

Weingart, L. R., Hyder, E. B., & Prietula, M. J. (1996). Knowledge matters: The effect of tactical descriptions on negotiation behavior and outcome. *Journal of Personality and Social Psychology, 70,* 1205–17.

Weingart, L. R., Prietula, M. J., Hyder, E. B., & Genovese, C. R. (1999). Knowledge and the sequential processes of negotiation: A Markov Chain analysis of response-in-kind. *Journal of Experimental Social Psychology, 35,* 366–93.

Weingart, L. R., Thompson, L. L., Bazerman, M. H., & Carroll, J. S. (1990). Tactical behaviors and negotiation outcomes. *International Journal of Conflict Management, 1,* 7–31.

Weiss, J. (2003). Trajectories toward peace: Mediator sequencing strategies in intractable communal disputes. *Negotiation Journal,* 109–15.

Weiss, S. E. (1994). Negotiating with "Romans": A range of culturally-responsive strategies. *Sloan Management Review, 35* (1), 51–61; (2), 1–16.

Weiss, S. E. (1997). Explaining outcomes of negotiation: Toward a grounded model for negotiations between organizations. In R. J. Lewicki, R. J. Bies, & B. H. Sheppard (Eds.), *Research on negotiation in organizations* (Vol. 6, pp. 247–333). Greenwich, CT: JAI Press.

Weiss, S. E. (2006). International business negotiation in a globalizing world: Reflections on the contributions and future of a (sub) field. *International Negotiation, 11,* 287–316.

Weiss, S. E., & Stripp, W. (1985). Negotiating with foreign business persons: An introduction for Americans with propositions on six cultures. New York: New York University Graduate School of Business Administration, Working Paper 85–6.

Weldon, E., & Jehn, K. A. (1995). Examining cross-cultural differences in conflict management behavior: A strategy for future research. *The International Journal of Conflict Management, 6,* 387–403.

Wheeler, M. (2004). Anxious moments: Openings in negotiation. *Negotiation Journal, 20,* 153–169.

Xing, F. (1995). The Chinese cultural system: Implications for cross-cultural management. *SAM Advanced Management Journal, 60,* 14–20.

Yama, E. (2004). Buying hardball, playing price. *Business Horizons, 47* (5), 62–66.

Yan, A., & Gray, B. (1994). Bargaining power, management control, and performance in United States-China joint ventures: A comparative case study. *Academy of Management Journal, 37,* 1478–517.

Yankelovich, D. (1982, August). Lying well is the best revenge. *Psychology Today, 71,* 5–6, 71.

Yook, E. L., & Albert, R. D. (1998). Perceptions of the appropriateness of negotiation in educational settings: A cross-cultural comparison among Koreans and Americans. *Communication Education, 47,* 18–29.

Yukl, G. (1974). Effects of the opponent's initial offer, concession magnitude, and concession frequency on bargaining behavior. *Journal of Personality and Social Psychology, 30,* 323–35.

Yukl, G., & Tracey, J. A. B. (1992). Consequences of influence tactics used with subordinates, peers and the boss. *Journal of Applied Psychology, 77,* 525–35.

Zand, D. (1972). Trust and managerial problem solving. *Administrative Science Quarterly, 17,* 229–39.

Zand, D. (1997). *The leadership triad: Knowledge, trust and power.* New York: Oxford University Press.

Zartman, I. W. (1977). Negotiation as a joint decision making process. In I. Zartman (Ed.), *The negotiation process: Theories and applications* (pp. 67–86). Beverly Hills, CA: Sage.

Zartman, I. W. (1997). Conflict and order: Justice in negotiation. *International Political Science Review, 18,* 121–38.

Zartman, I. W., & Berman, M. (1982). *The practical negotiator.* New Haven: Yale University Press.

Zhu, Y., McKenna, B., & Sun, Z. (2007). Negotiating with Chinese: Success of initial meetings is the key. *Cross Cultural Management: An International Journal, 14* (4), 354–64.

Index